JUXTAPOSING LEGAL SYSTEMS AND THE PRINCIPLES OF EUROPEAN FAMILY LAW ON PARENTAL RESPONSIBILITIES

European Family Law Series

Published by the Organising Committee of the Commission on European Family Law

JUXTAPOSING LEGAL SYSTEMS AND THE PRINCIPLES OF EUROPEAN FAMILY LAW ON PARENTAL RESPONSIBILITIES

Edited by

Esin Örücü and Jane Mair

intersentia

Antwerp – Oxford – Portland

Distribution for the UK:
Hart Publishing Ltd.
16C Worcester Place
Oxford OX1 2JW
UK
Tel.: +44 1865 51 75 30
Fax: +44 1865 51 07 10

Distribution for Switzerland and Germany:
Stämpfli Verlag AG
Wölflistrasse 1
CH-3001 Bern
Switzerland
Tel.: +41 (0)31 300 63 18
Fax: +41 (0)31 300 66 88

Distribution for the USA and Canada:
International Specialized Book Services
920 NE 58th Ave Suite 300
Portland, OR 97213
Holmes Beach
USA
Tel.: +1 800 944 6190 (toll free)
Tel.: +1 503 287 3093
Fax: +1 503 280 8832
Email: info@isbs.com

Distribution for other countries:
Intersentia Publishers
Groenstraat 31
BE-2640 Mortsel
Belgium
Tel.: +32 3 680 15 50
Fax: +32 3 658 71 21

Juxtaposing Legal Systems and the Principles of European Family Law on Parental Responsibilities
Esin Örücü and Jane Mair (eds.)

ISBN 978-90-5095-979-7
D/2010/7849/11
NUR 822

PREFACE

We considered it worthwhile to produce once again an edited volume with the aim to assess the reality of legal systems in view of the Principles, and the Principles in view of the reality of these legal systems, following the publication of "Principles of European Family Law Regarding Parental Responsibilities" by the Commission on European Family Law (CEFL).

In the hope of creating a source of inspiration for legislators in the process of modernising their national family laws, the CEFL seeks. "functional equivalence" and adopts both the "common core" and "better law" approaches. As a rule, the drafters choose "the best", "the more functional" and the "most efficient" rules. Their touchstone is the modernisation of the law. Therefore, these CEFL Principles are not merely restatements of family laws in Europe, but contributions towards the establishment of a European Family Law.

Believing that only by empirical testing of the Principles in a number of legal systems can one demonstrate whether they are acceptable and/or are regarded as an improvement on existing national laws, we launched into our project. For our purposes, it was deemed appropriate first to test the Principles in the untested: Scotland, a mixed jurisdiction that has gained popularity within the European Union; Malta, a more recent EU member with a conservative background, Estonia, another more recent EU member with a socialist background; Romania, a new comer into the EU with a socialist background but a socio-culture different to Estonia; and finally Turkey, a country bridging eastern and western values and aspiring to membership of the EU. Next, the Principles were re-tested in two legal systems already considered by the CEFL: Denmark, a variation on the civilian theme, where changes have occurred in 2007 after the national report was prepared and the Principles formulated; and England, the mother of the common law tradition, where there are also some new developments.

The volume starts with an introductory overview and closes with a comparative assessment of our findings. Though this part considers the Principles as harmonious ideals, it is also critical of the shortfalls in the ideals as presented, and views the obstacles to harmonisation.

Our colleague Joelle Godard who had undertaken to contribute to our volume by juxtaposing the Principles to French law, as she had done in the previous volume on Divorce and Maintenance Between Former Spouses, recently suddenly passed away and we would like to dedicate this volume to her.

Jane Mair and Esin Örücü
1 April 2009

LIST OF AUTHORS

Canan Arın
Member of the Istanbul Bar Association, specialising in family law and criminal law (women's rights and violence against women and minors)

Marieta Avram
Associate Professor, Vice-Dean, Law Faculty, University of Bucharest

Dr. Flavius A. Baias
Associate Professor, Dean, Law Faculty, University of Bucharest

Dr. Christina G. Jeppesen de Boer
Lecturer in family and comparative law, University of Utrecht

Dr. Ruth Farrugia
Advocate and Senior Lecturer in Civil Law, University of Malta

Stephen Gilmore
Senior Lecturer in Family Law at King's College London

Triin Göttig
LL.M. (Kiel); Research Fellow of Civil Law, University of Tartu, Estonia

Liis Hallik
mag. iur.; Adjunct Instructor, Institute of Law, University of Tartu; Counsellor of the Civil Chamber, Supreme Court of the Republic of Estonia

Jonathan Herring
Fellow and Tutor in Law at Exeter College, University of Oxford.

Dr. Annette Kronborg
Associate Professor in family and inheritance law, University of Copenhagen

Dr. Jane Mair
Senior Lecturer in Law, University of Glasgow, Scotland

Cristina Nicolescu
Assistant, Law Faculty, University of Bucharest

Prof. Dr. Esin Örücü
Professor Emerita of Comparative Law and Honorary Senior Research Fellow, University of Glasgow, Professor Emerita of Comparative law, Erasmus University Rotterdam

Dr. Rebecca Probert
Senior Lecturer in Private Law at the University of Warwick, England.

Ian Sharpe
B.A., LL.M., Advocate, Scotland

Dr. Triin Uusen-Nacke
Adjunct Instructor, Institute of Law, University of Tartu; Counsellor of the Civil Chamber, Supreme Court of the Republic of Estonia

TABLE OF CONTENTS

PART TWO – RE-TESTING THE TESTED: THE SAME AND THE DIFFERENT

PART THREE – AN ASPIRANT CANDIDATE: DO VALUES CLASH?

HOW DOES TURKISH FAMILY LAW FARE COMPARED TO THE PRINCIPLES OF EUROPEAN FAMILY LAW REGARDING PARENTAL RESPONSIBILITIES?

PART FOUR – COMPARATIVE ASSESSMENT

HARMONISED NORMS OF PARENTAL RESPONSIBILITIES FACING REALITY

INTRODUCTORY OVERVIEW

CATERING FOR DIVERSE CULTURES THROUGH HARMONISED NORMS

Esin Örücü and Jane Mair

1. INTRODUCING THE TOPIC

Family law has moved to the foreground for comparatists, although until fairly recently, regarded as culturally defined and therefore living under the so-called "cultural constraints",[1] it was not seen to be appropriate for much meaningful comparison, let alone harmonisation. However, in Europe today, shared values are seen to form the basis of developments, the belief in universalism has gained strength, and the view that family law does not lend itself to comparison or harmonisation, has been superseded. These concerns have been largely replaced by a pragmatic and cosmopolitan approach to family law, and what this means is that family law can be now approached comparatively and most aspects of it can be harmonised.[2] "Comparative family law's days as an unlikely pioneer are over".[3] Changing social, religious and economic conditions of our day transcend the so-called "common law - civil law divide", "local context" and "cultural identity", and facilitate the application of similar principles to divergent societies.[4] The fact

---

1 For a thorough analysis of the "cultural constraints argument" in relation to family law see ANTOKOLSKAIA, M.V., *Harmonisation of Family Law in Europe: A Historical Perspective - A Tale of Two Millennia*, European Family Law Series No. 13 (Antwerp: Intersentia, 2006), pp. 3–47.

2 See for such work, BOELE-WOELKI, K., "The Road Towards a European Family Law", (1997) 1:1 *EJCL* http://law.kub.nl/ejcl/11/art11-1.html, and also BOELE-WOELKI, K., "Comparative Research-Based Drafting of Principles of European Family Law" in FAURE, M., SMITS, J., SCHNEIDER, H., (eds) *Towards a European Ius Commune in Legal Education and Research* (Antwerp: Intersentia, 2002) pp.171–190. Also see, MARTINY, D., "The Harmonization of Family Law in the European Community; Pro and Contra", in *ibid.*, pp. 191–201. For a thorough discussion of various aspects of harmonisation of family law in Europe, see the contributions in BOELE-WOELKI, K., (ed) *Perspectives for the Unification and Harmonisation of Family Law in Europe*, European Family Law Series No. 4 (Antwerp: Intersentia, 2003).

3 KRAUSE, H.D., "Comparative Family Law: Past Traditions Battle Future Trends - And Vice Versa" in REIMANN, M. and ZIMMERMANN, R., (eds) *The Oxford Handbook of Comparative Law* (Oxford: Oxford University Press, 2006), pp. 1099–1129 at 1101.

4 See DE CRUZ, P., "Legal Transplants: Principles and Pragmatism in Comparative Family Law", Chapter 6 in HARDING, A. and ÖRÜCÜ, E., (eds), *Comparative Law in the 21st Century* (London: Kluwer Law International, 2002,) pp. 101–121. Also see, ANTOKOLSKAIA, M., "Comparative Family Law: Moving with the Times?" in ÖRÜCÜ, E. and NELKEN, D., (eds), *Comparative Law: A Handbook* (Oxford: Hart Publishing, 2007), pp. 241–262.

that we live in an era of "equality" and "freedom" seems to override traditional values today, and comparative family lawyers are called on to help create a suitable receptive environment for a modern family law. Since many principles have universality, the hope is that there is transferability. Thus, cosmopolitan pragmatism may win over localism and culturalism, at least by suggesting a standardised legal framework.

Although there is no uniform family law in Europe, there are efforts to create standardisation in some aspects of family law through European Law and Conventions, such as those related to respect for family life, the equal treatment of men and women, the equal treatment of legitimate and illegitimate children, rights of the child, and the recognition of divorce, maintenance and custody judgments. European norms enunciated through the European Convention on Human Rights in relation to Article 8 on the right to family life have also had a substantial impact on the legislation of several countries.

1.1. THE EUROPEAN SCENE AND THE WORK OF THE COMMISSION ON EUROPEAN FAMILY LAW

1.1.1. The European Scene

Attitudes in the field of family law depend to a large extent on political agendas, and one such agenda is further integration in Europe.[5] Though European integration focuses on economics, there are some important social implications of economic change, such as changes in labour market regulations and social welfare systems, which in turn have an impact on the family. However, there has been considerable variation in the ways these changes have been implemented across Europe.[6] In addition, the European Court of Justice feels constrained by its lack of jurisdiction to intervene in family matters,[7] and although it treats aspects of family law under "freedom of movement", it cannot make specific rules for the family. The EU's lack of competence or reluctance to engage with family law

---

5 For a brief overview of other stances see ÖRÜCÜ, E. and MAIR, J., "Common Cultures and Diverse Laws – Common Laws and Diverse Cultures" in ÖRÜCÜ, E. and MAIR, J. (eds), *Juxtaposing Legal Systems and the Principles of European Family Law on Divorce and Maintenance*, European Family Law Series No.17 (Antwerp: Intersentia, 2007), p. 4, and for an analysis see, ÖRÜCÜ, E., "A Family Law for Europe: Necessary, Feasible, Desirable?" in BOELE-WOELKI, K., (ed), *Perspectives for the Unification and Harmonisation of Family Law in Europe*, European Family Law Series No.4 (Antwerp: Intersentia, 2003), pp. 551–572.

6 See LLOYD, C., "The Transformation of Family Life and Sexual Politics" in GUIBERNAU, M., (ed) *Governing European Diversity* (London: Sage Publications, 2001), p. 150.

7 See eg *Hofmann v Barmer Ersatzkasse* [1984] ECR 3047, where the ECJ, at para 24, refused to intervene in the "organisation of the family".

may even be leading to a European concept of the family which, far from being forward looking and modern, in fact lags behind that of many member states.[8]

Nevertheless, it has been argued that it is possible to find even in the Amsterdam Treaty, Article 65a, a legal basis for the development of a specific European Family Law, at least for cross-border situations, as this Article refers to measures in the area of judicial co-operation in civil matters that "have cross-border implications".[9] Therefore, though it may seem like a broad interpretation, it is feasible to envisage the EU being competent to take measures to harmonise or even unify the substantive family law in Europe. Indeed, the EU has unified for instance, the rules related to jurisdiction and the recognition and enforcement of judgments on parental responsibilities; since March 2005, these matters are governed by Council Regulation (EC) No. 2201/2003 concerning jurisdiction and the recognition and enforcement of judgments in matrimonial matters and the matters of parental responsibilities (Brussels II*bis*).[10]

If it is desirable to move towards a European civil society and to forge a European identity encompassing common values, the best way to achieve these aims could be via a harmonised family law.[11] There will always be diversity of culture and moral views that use arguments such as "harmonisation destroys national identity", but these do not seem to hinder the search for Europe-wide solutions, because European citizens need European answers. Though European norms, the European Convention on Human Rights and the European Courts already have considerable impact on national family laws, this is not enough. What may be needed is the creation of Europe-wide Principles to run at the start parallel with, if not to replace, national legislation. Incremental harmonisation seems to be a workable beginning with the hope that in the long term pragmatism and cosmopolitanism will prevail. Obviously, at this stage work can only be academic and is bound to remain at the level of finding, analysing and comparing the rules and then formulating and presenting General Principles.

---

8 See *Grant v South West Trains Ltd* [1991] ECR 1–621; *D v Council* [2001] ECR 1–4319.

9 See BOELE-WOELKI, K., "De competentie van de Europese Unie in familiezaken", *FJR* 2004, p. 289.

10 Brussels II*bis* Regulation replaced the Brussels II Regulation (EC) No. 1347/2000. See Official Journal 2003 L 338/1, 23.12.2003.

11 For a strong opposition to the need for such a project, however, see MCGLYNN, C., *Families and the European Union: Law, Politics and Pluralism* (Cambridge: Cambridge University Press, 2006).

1.1.2. The work of the Commission on European Family Law (CEFL)

With the above aim, the Commission on European Family Law (CEFL) was set up in September 2001 as a team of specialists from 22 jurisdictions[12] carrying out research in the field of comparative family law, dedicated to creating a set of Principles of European Family Law in areas thought to be most suitable for harmonisation. It may be possible that in time the Principles will function as a source of inspiration and a frame of reference for national, European and international legislators.[13] The view is that Europeanisation of family law could be achieved through a didactic elaboration of common principles, these principles serving as a basis.

The CEFL decided to concentrate first on divorce and maintenance as in those areas there was already growing convergence and the time for harmonising substantive divorce law and maintenance seemed ripe. The Commission drafted and published three years after its establishment,[14] the Principles of European Family Law regarding Divorce and Maintenance between Former Spouses.[15]

Common principles were distilled through "common core research" accompanied by functional equivalence. In addition, the "better law" approach, that is the one that provides the most choice, was opted for, and, inspired by the American Restatements, the "comparative research-based drafting of principles" became the process.

The six steps method that was used started with selecting family law fields most suitable for harmonisation, then drafting a questionnaire employing the functional approach, drawing up national reports reflecting both the law in the books and law in action, collecting, integrating and disseminating the material,[16]

12 Austria, Belgium, Bulgaria, Czech Republic, Denmark, England and Wales, Finland, France, Germany, Greece, Hungary, Republic of Ireland, Italy, The Netherlands, Norway, Poland, Portugal, Russia, Scotland, Spain, Sweden, and Switzerland.

13 The new Portuguese family law which entered into force on 1 December 2008 was to a large extent inspired by the CEFL Principles: see DE OLIVEIRA, G., "Changes going on in Portuguese Family Law" *FamRZ* 2008 vol. 18, p.1712.

14 See BOELE-WOELKI, K., FERRAND, F., BEILFUSS, C.G., JÄNTERA-JAREBORG, M., LOWE, N., MARTINY, D. and PINTENS, W., *Principles of European Family Law Regarding Divorce and Maintenance between Former Spouses*, European Family Law Series No. 7 (Antwerp: Intersentia, 2004).

15 For the working method of the CEFL see BOELE-WOELKI, K., "The Working Method of the Commission on European Family Law", in BOELE-WOELKI, K., (ed) *Common Core and Better Law in European Family Law*, European Family Law Series No. 10 (Antwerp: Intersentia, 2005), pp. 15–41.

16 See the two volumes: BOELE-WOELKI, K., BRAAT, B. and SUMNER, I., (eds), *European Family Law in Action Volume I: Grounds for Divorce, Volume II: Maintenance between Former Spouses*, European Family Law Series, No: 2 and 3 (Antwerp: Intersentia, 2003).The integral reports can also be found on the CEFL website: www.law.uu.nl/priv.cefl

drafting the Principles having chosen between the "common core" and "better law" approaches, and finally publishing the Principles. Such an approach provided the Principles with a basis built on in-depth and comprehensive comparative research. If there was a common core, this was selected as the best solution; sometimes, though there was a common core, a better solution was selected; at times, though there was a common core, the selection was left to national law. If there was no common core, either "a best solution" was selected, or the solution was left to national law.[17]

The drafters could have chosen to formulate new rules themselves instead of the "common core". Yet, comparatists know that "common core" is the better and safer method to use since it makes justification simpler by restating what represents the majority. This is the method predominantly used by the CEFL in all its work.

The crucial justification for the choices made appears in the comparative overviews referring to national reports and the comments, which elucidate the provisions: both published together with the Principles. As they are the product of academic and scientific work, the Principles are not meant to be binding. Neither are they presented as "model law". Though directed towards the legislators as recommendations, they are meant only to provide a "frame of reference" and inspiration for reform, a source of encouragement and an intellectual stimulation for change.

We juxtaposed the results of this first project.[18]

We are now undertaking quite a similar approach to the second project, the European Principles regarding Parental Responsibilities, conceived in the same manner by the CEFL,[19] which saw significant and natural links between the question of parental responsibilities and the financial consequences of divorce, encouraged in their choice of subject by the widened scope of the Brussels II*bis* Regulation. The Principles were published in 2007.[20]

---

17 See BOELE-WOELKI ET AL *supra* note 14. Also see, BOELE-WOELKI, K., "Building on Convergence and Coping with Divergence in the CEFL Principles of European Family Law" in ANTOKOLSKAIA, M., (ed) *Convergence and Divergence of Family Law in Europe*, European Family Law Series No: 18 (Antwerp: Intersentia, 2007), pp. 253–269 at 262.

18 ÖRÜCÜ, E. and MAIR, J., (eds), *Juxtaposing Legal Systems and the Principles of European Family Law on Divorce and Maintenance*, European Family Law Series, No: 17 (Antwerp: Intersentia, 2007).

19 See, BOELE-WOELKI, K., BRAAT, B. and CURRY-SUMNER, I., (eds) *European Family Law in Action Volume III: Parental Responsibilities*, European Family Law Series No. 9 (Antwerp: Intersentia, 2005). See the www.law.uu.nl/priv.cefl for national reports.

20 BOELE-WOELKI, K., FERRAND, F., BEILFUSS, C. G., JÄNTERA-JAREBORG, M., LOWE, N., MARTINY, D. and PINTENS, W., *Principles of European Family Law Regarding Parental Responsibilities*, European Family Law Series, No. 16 (Antwerp: Intersentia, 2007).

2. THE GENERAL OUTLINE OF THE PRINCIPLES

The Principles regarding Parental Responsibilities were distilled by the CEFL from the analysis of the 62 questions drafted in January 2004 and posed to the 22 national reporters from 19 EU Member States at the beginning of April 2004, following the methods discussed above. The national reports reflect the laws as they stood in 2004.[21] Not all the national systems played a role in the drawing up of the Principles, but neither was any one legal system the dominant model. In fact, these Principles reflect overall, the values enshrined in a number of international conventions. In the last 50 years or so, international organisations such as the United Nations,[22] the Hague Conference on Private International Law[23] and the Council of Europe[24] engaged with the field of family law and more specifically in the field of parental responsibilities. A number of international conventions, most dealing with cross-border relationships, have been drafted, binding many European countries. In the formulation of the Principles regarding Parental Responsibilities, the CEFL tried to adhere to a truly European perspective. The Principles have been drafted to follow the framework built by the international obligations. An integrated version of all the reports was published in 2005.[25]

On the basis of the above, the CEFL formulated 39 Principles classified into eight chapters. It must be noted here that, as the numbering of the Principles indicates (from 3.1 to 3.39), these Principles are regarded by the CEFL as a continuation of the Principles on Divorce and Maintenance. The next project on matrimonial property will add more Principles, and other fields will follow suit, until a more complete Family Law for Europe emerges.

The working language is English and the publication is in English. However the Principles themselves are in three languages: English, French and German. The complete list of Principles appears also in Dutch, Spanish and Swedish. All five versions are annexed to the publication. The Principles and the Questionnaire,

---

21 National reports and relevant provisions are available on CEFL website: www.law.uu.nl/priv/cefl.

22 Convention of 4 November 1950 for the Protection of Human Rights and Fundamental Freedoms; Convention of 20 November 1989 on the Rights of the Child, see http://www.untreaty.un.org.

23 Convention of 5 October 1961 Concerning the Powers of Authorities and the Law Applicable in Respect of the Protection of Minors; Convention of 25 October 1980 on the Civil Aspects of International Child Abduction; Convention of 19 October 1996 on Jurisdiction, Applicable Law, Recognition, Enforcement and Co-operation in Respect of Parental Responsibility and Measures for the Protection of Children, see http://www.hcch.net.

24 Convention of 20 May 1980 on Recognition and Enforcement of Decisions Concerning Custody of Children and on Restoration of Custody of Children; Convention of 25 January 1996 on the Exercise of Children's Rights; Convention of 15 May 2003 on Contact Concerning Children, see http://www.coe.int.

25 Accessible at CEFL's website, see http://www2.law.uu.nl/priv/cefl, under Working field 2.

originally sent to all the national reporters, are also annexed to the present volume to give a better understanding of the individual national contributions.

The concept of parental responsibilities – used in the plural rather than in the singular, as commonly used – is based on the concept established in Principle 18 of the White Paper on Principles concerning the Establishment and Legal Consequences of Parentage 2002 of the Council of Europe, and the Council of Europe definition has been chosen as the working definition.[26] The White Paper talks of a "collection of duties and powers which aim at ensuring the moral and material welfare of children". This encompasses in particular, care and protection, maintenance of parental relationships, provision of education, legal representation, determination of residence and administration of property.

There is a Preamble, which includes the general considerations and the perceived common desires of the European Union citizens, with its main guideline being the child's rights and welfare and the free movement of persons, the core principle of the EU. The Preamble indicates the vision underlying the Principles:

> Recognising that, notwithstanding the existing diversities of national family law systems, there is nevertheless a growing convergence of laws; Recognising that the free movement of persons within Europe is hindered by the remaining differences; Desiring to contribute to common European values regarding the child's rights and welfare; Desiring to contribute to the harmonisation of family law in Europe and to further facilitate the free movement of persons within Europe, The Commission on European Family Law recommends the following Principles.

An overview of the provisions of the relevant international and/or European instrument regarding the issue addressed in each Principle, and a comparative overview and comments, which refer both to the national reports and the relevant international and/or European instruments, follow the text of each Principle.

Chapter I of the Principles deals with definitions and consists of two Principles. Cited as 3:1 to 3:2, these Principles cover what are parental responsibilities and who are the holders of these responsibilities. The CEFL seems to have opted for a broad concept of parental responsibilities. Other concepts such as guardianship and custody have been abandoned and "parental responsibilities" has been preferred offering, as claimed, a more flexible approach, particularly when attributing rights and duties to persons other than the parents. This concept consists of a collection of rights and duties that concerns the taking care of the child's person and property and applies to children from birth until they reach maturity. The Principles make it possible to have even more than two holders – that is the

26 See http:/www.oeu.int.

parents – of parental responsibilities, so that third persons who have no legal ties with the child, can be attributed with and exercise parental responsibilities.[27] This Chapter constitutes one ingredient of the main general part of the Principles.

Chapter II deals with rights of the child in five Principles laid out as 3:3 to 3:7. They cover the best interests of the child; autonomy of the child; non-discrimination of the child; child's right to be heard; and conflict of interests. Each of these headings forms one Principle. Here we see the profound impact of the relevant international and European human rights instruments. First, the primary or paramount consideration is the best interests of the child, the assessment of which should always be made from the child's perspective, taking into consideration the present and the future interests and needs. Second, the Principles emphasise the link between the child's "developing ability" and his/her "increasing need to act independently" rather than regarding "age" as the decisive factor. Third, the Principle of non-discrimination of the child is to be understood widely, that is, irrespective of whether the grounds for discrimination refer to the child or the holders of parental responsibilities, and irrespective of the status, that is legality or illegality, of the child's residence. Fourth, the right of the child to be heard is taken as an obligatory point of departure, for which no special age or degree of maturity is determined: the views expressed by the child should be given more weight as the child grows older and becomes more mature. Finally, in case of a risk of conflict between the interests of the child and of the holders of parental responsibilities, the child's interests should be protected. This Chapter is another ingredient of the main general part of the CEFL Principles.

Chapter III deals with parental responsibilities of the parents and third persons in Principles 3:8 to 3:10, covering parents; third persons; and the effect of dissolution and separation. Regarding parental responsibilities as a consequence of parenthood, joint responsibility becomes the essence of the Principles regardless of the marital status of the parents. Thus, parents' relationship is of no consequence. In addition, parents are equally treated, irrespective of their gender. Third persons with no legal ties with the child can also be attributed with and exercise parental responsibilities, however, in view of the possibility of different factual situations, how and on what conditions such attribution can take place is left open by the Principles.

Chapter IV, dealing with the exercise of parental responsibilities, has two sections. Section "A" on parents covers Principles 3.11 to 3.16 on joint exercise; daily matters,

27 Persons other than the parents holding parental responsibilities instead of and in addition to parents in whole or in part is uncommon in most European jurisdictions and therefore, it must be said here that the CEFL has opted for the "better law" approach, rather than the "common core".

important and urgent decisions; agreement on exercise; disagreement on exercise; sole exercise upon agreement or decision; and sole exercise by one parent. Though the preferred option is joint exercise, one parent can be empowered to act alone in some situations for practical purposes. Section "B" is related to third persons and its two Principles deal with exercise in addition to or instead of the parents; and decisions in daily matters. All conflicts are to be resolved in the best interests of the child.

Chapter V on the content of parental responsibilities also has two sections. Section "A" looks at the child's person and property in six Principles. Care, protection and education; residence; relocation; administration of the child's property; restrictions; and legal representation each form one Principle with sub-sections. The child's distinctive character and developmental needs are the main considerations here. There is also an absolute ban on corporal punishment or any other humiliating treatment. Section "B" is on maintenance of personal relationships and in five Principles it covers contact with parents and other persons; content of contact; agreement; restrictions; and information to parents. Special attention has been paid to the relocation of the child, especially outwith the jurisdiction, as a response to the increasing mobility in European society. The competent authority has to strike a balance between the right of the child to maintain personal relationships – which the Principles prefer to call "contact" – with the non-resident parent and close relatives and persons with whom the child has a close relationship on the one hand, and the right of the residential parent to move in pursuit of a valid purpose on the other. The child's opinion in all this remains crucial.

Chapter VI on termination of parental responsibilities has two Principles, 3:30 and 3:31, covering termination and the death of the parents. The natural causes of termination are: the child reaching majority, death of the child, the child entering into a marriage or registered partnership and the child being adopted. The Principles do not deal with stepchild adoption. On the death of both parents, the competent authority should take protective measures.

The penultimate Chapter VII on discharge and restoration of parental responsibilities, covers discharge of parental responsibilities; request for discharge of parental responsibilities; and restoration of parental responsibilities between Principles 3:32 and 3:34. A "child in danger", arising from behaviour or neglect that poses a serious risk to the person or the property of the child, is the consideration here: the competent authority is empowered to take decisions. Having regards to the best interests of the child, parental responsibilities can be restored.

The final Chapter VIII is on procedure. Between Principles 3:35 and 3:39, the Chapter deals with competent authority; alternative dispute resolution; hearing of the child; appointment of a special representative for the child; and enforcement. It is to be noted that though the competent authority can either be a judicial or an administrative body, the importance of alternative dispute resolution is very much recognised. It is also paramount that the child should be heard in all proceedings concerning parental responsibilities. This is reiterated also in this Chapter. The Principles prefer a direct hearing, though accepting divergent national rules on the manner of this hearing. What is not negotiable is that the Principles set no age limit for this right of the child, the only criterion being "in a manner appropriate to age and maturity".

Many Principles are interconnected with others, and many show that they are based on common cores. The aim is to express the "modern common core" of the international and European instruments and the legal systems considered. Respect for the rights of the child, non-discrimination and self-determination of the holders of parental responsibilities are the bases on which the Principles are built. The provisions introduced by the Principles try to offer solutions that are workable and that avoid hardship and disputes. There is also an effort to strike a balance between civil and common law concepts. However, the provisions are futuristic, and reflect a particular vision of family life and therefore, family law. Some Principles may be seen as reflecting the values of an ideal world. In the end, the choice has to remain a subjective one, based on what the authors of the Principles consider to be the most appropriate or the "better" approach. Therefore, empirical testing of the Principles becomes worthwhile.

3. THE AIM OF THE PRESENT RESEARCH

3.1. INCEPTION

We asked ourselves the question: Is there a European consensus on European standards in family law? If there is such consensus, should these standards be in place before the further enlargement of Europe, or should not experiences emanating from Southern, Central and Eastern Europe become part of the European vision? Can the so-called "progressive North" and the "conservative South" benefit from the emerging value statements of Central and Eastern Europe? What about Romania and Malta, which are already members of the EU, and Turkey, a country aspiring to membership? Though for issues concerning principles such as "equality", "freedom", "best interests of the child", "free movement of persons" and property rights, global European solutions may seem more appropriate, and the European nations seem to live within the boundaries set by a number of Conventions, should not the principle of subsidiarity and value pluralism be respected? How far can the national legal systems have a leeway to balance this recommended European framework with national peculiarities?

Following the publication of the *Principles of European Family Law Regarding Parental Responsibilities* by the CEFL, we considered it to be worthwhile to produce an edited volume, *Juxtaposing Legal Systems and The Principles of European Family Law: Parental Responsibilities*, as we did with *The Principles of European Family Law: Divorce and Maintenance between Former Spouses.*[28] The aim is again to assess the reality of some legal systems in view of the Principles, and the Principles in view of the reality of these legal systems. We believe that only by empirical testing in a number of legal systems could we demonstrate whether the Principles are acceptable and/or an improvement on existing laws. Furthermore, we wanted to see whether the Principles are serving as a "frame of reference and an inspiration" to national legislators – which they are intended to do – in view of the ongoing law reform activities in the field of family law in many of the jurisdictions in Europe.

This time we also wanted to look, as far as possible, into practice, since the Principles are the product of an academic endeavour and there is no real discussion of law in action in the Comments and the Comparative Overviews. Thus, we asked our academic contributors to pair up, where possible, with a practitioner, or if they were also in private practice, to reflect any developments there.

3.2. CHOICE OF SYSTEMS

As in our previous project, we decided to follow a certain, though different, logic: to carry out a meaningful comparative law research and to include some legal systems not part of the original exercise. We thought it was important first to test the Principles in the untested: Scotland, a mixed jurisdiction that has gained popularity within the EU; Malta, a more recent EU member with a conservative background, Estonia, another more recent EU member with a socialist background; Romania, a new comer into the EU with a socialist background but a socio-culture different to Estonia; and finally Turkey, with a mix of eastern and western values and aspiring to membership of the EU. Then, the Principles are re-tested in two legal systems already considered by the CEFL: Denmark, a variation

28 See *supra* note 18. In a similar vein ANTOKOLSKAIA undertook a juxtaposition exercise in her inaugural speech, where she juxtaposed divorce laws in the Netherlands and the CEFL Principles. As an advocate of the "better law" approach, she was critical of the Principles which did not dare to go so far as to accept "divorce on demand", which Antokolskaia regards as the most modern and advanced option of our day, as seen in Sweden, Finland, Spain and indirectly in Russia. See ANTOKOLSKAIA, M.V., "Nederlands echtscheidingsrecht en the CEFL Principles on Divorce", November 2006 *Tijdschrift voor Familie en Jeugdrecht*, pp. 262–269.

on the civilian theme, where changes have occurred in 2007 after the national report was prepared and the Principles formulated; and England, the mother of the common law tradition, where case law brought in new developments.

Although two of these systems, Denmark and England, were among the 22 jurisdictions covered by the questionnaire leading to the drafting of the Principles,[29] our chosen authors were not part of the team of experts responsible for drawing up the Principles. This, we thought, would give a healthy slant to our research. On the other hand, Scotland, Estonia, Romania, Malta and Turkey were not considered in the original exercise and are not among the jurisdictions covered by the CEFL.

The reader will also immediately notice that some contributions such as those on Estonia, Romania, Malta and Turkey are much longer than others and contain additional information on family law in those jurisdictions beyond the Principles, having also taken into consideration the Questionnaire. There are legitimate reasons for these discrepancies. As these jurisdictions were not considered before the Principles were drafted, we thought it appropriate to give readers a brief history and information on relevant aspects of family laws of these jurisdictions. Further information on Denmark and England can be found in the CEFL publication: *European Family Law in Action Volume III: Parental Responsibilities*,[30] and the CEFL website.[31]

The overall aim of each contribution is to set the situation in parental responsibilities in that legal system at present and see whether the Principles could be introduced with ease into the existing framework of national family law. This might involve not only structural and substantive, but also sociological and political analysis.

3.3. ASSESSMENT OF LEGAL SYSTEMS AND CEFL PRINCIPLES

The purpose of this study is not to question whether family law in Europe should be going through a harmonisation process or whether European family laws are converging or not. In fact, through the efforts of the United Nations, the Hague Conference on Private International Law, and Council of Europe, harmonisation has been taking place for the last four decades, and as Katharina Boele-Woelki

29 This time Austria, Belgium, Bulgaria, Czech Republic, Denmark, England and Wales, Finland, France, Germany, Greece, Hungary, Republic of Ireland, Italy, Lithuania, The Netherlands, Norway, Poland, Portugal, Russia, Spain, Sweden, and Switzerland.

30 BOELE-WOELKI ET AL, *supra* note 19.

31 The integral national reports can be found on the CEFL website: www.law.uu.nl/priv.cefl.

says, "the train has left the station".[32] The question is: Are the Principles, as drafted, appropriate and sufficient to achieve this harmonisation?

The final part of this research has two aims. The first is to juxtapose the legal systems we have selected against the Principles. The national systems are assessed in order to identify whether they could accommodate the Principles and what the shortfalls in these legal systems are. Here there can be a chance to suggest improvements in those national laws. The second aim is to assess the Principles in view of the reality of these legal systems, accepting the provisions of the selected legal systems as suitable for those societies in relation to their social, economic and moral contexts. Here there would be a chance to be critical of the Principles and make suggestions for improvements, where possible.

4. CONCLUDING REMARKS

It must always be remembered that there is a strong interdependency of rules in the field of family law, all aspects of which add together and make up a whole. What may be needed, in the not too distant future, is standardisation of the whole of family law for Europe. The future work of the CEFL remains indispensable for the achievement of this. Indeed the CEFL does have other ongoing projects.

The project, the results of which we are testing, is the distillation, creation and publication of Principles regarding Parental Responsibilities. This field of work is linked to the first project on divorce and maintenance, as both fields have been modernised in national systems in recent years. In addition, EU instruments and Conventions have played a significant role in these matters regarding cross-border relationships. In family law, the principle of the "rights of the child" is increasing in importance and reform is needed to clarify and reinforce the legal status of the child in the member states.

Consideration of these issues by the CEFL is most timely when solutions to Europe's pressing problems are urgently sought, and in an atmosphere of increasing Europeanisation. The creation of an "area of freedom, security and justice" in matters with cross-border implications – a goal of the European Union – can best be served by work such as this. If nothing more, these Principles are most "useful for academic debate" and add "another dimension to the discussion."[33]

---

32 BOELE-WOELKI, "Comparative Research-Based Drafting of Principles of European Family Law" *supra* note 2, p.183.

33 See a Book review by SCHERPE, J. M., in (2008) 20 *Child and Family Quarterly*, pp. 556–558.

There are however, quite a number of questions to be addressed, some of which are dealt with in the final part of this study.[34] For instance, to what extent is there a common value system and further, a common legal culture in the European Union? Is freedom of movement to be regarded as the main vehicle for protecting family life rather than EU citizenship and human rights? Should family law not be treated as part of economic law? Is it the researchers and academics, legislators, or judges who have the remit of and the competence for harmonisation? How should harmonisation and unification be achieved: through general principles, restatement, competition of rules, directives, regulations, a code, through top-down or through bottom-up approaches? Should any such development be applicable to cross-border family ties only? Should there be respect for diverse family forms in the present family laws even when these clash with cultural values? How do we cope with "context" and "fit"?

In contrast to the focus of the Principles on convergence, the alternative arguments should also be kept in mind. While the argument may be made that, by harmonising the regulation of parent/child relations, greater consistency throughout Europe shall be achieved with consequent benefits for children and parents, it might also be argued that this focus pursues consistency at the expense of diversity and pluralism. As McGlynn has argued, "[i]f ever there was a field of law which required a jurisprudence of pluralism and of dignity and compassion it is the regulation of families and family law."[35] These are questions which form the basis for considerable debate in respect of harmonisation of European family law, and they underpin some of the analysis in this volume, but to a great extent the discussion is directed towards what has emerged from this Commission for European Family Law project.

34 See MAIR, J. and ÖRÜCÜ, E., "Harmonised Norms of Parental Responsibilities Facing Reality", *infra*.

35 MCGLYNN, *supra* note 11 at p.22. For a general critical analysis of the CEFL's work, also see BRADLEY, D. "Family Law", in SMITS, J.M. (ed.), *Elgar Encyclopedia of Comparative Law* (Cheltenham: Edward Elgar, 2006) pp.262–264 and 269–270.

PART ONE
TESTING THE UNTESTED: CAN THERE BE ONE WAY FORWARD?

PRINCIPLES OF EUROPEAN FAMILY LAW REGARDING PARENTAL RESPONSIBILITIES AND THEIR IMPLICATIONS FOR ESTONIA

Liis Hallik, Triin Göttig and Dr. Triin Uusen-Nacke

1. GENERAL

The laws applicable in the Republic of Estonia do not recognise a concept of parental responsibilities defined under the aegis of the Council of Europe.[1] The rights and duties of a parent are listed, in general terms, in section 50 of the Republic of Estonia Family Law Act (FLA).[2] They[3] are further defined in specific provisions in the FLA and in other statutes: the right and the duty to raise a child and care for the child and to protect the child's rights and interests, the statutory right to represent the child, the right to determine the child's residence, and the right to maintain contact with the child (sections 50-52 FLA). Parents have equal rights and duties with respect to their children (section 49 FLA). A parent must not exercise parental rights in a manner contrary to the interests of the child (section 50(4) FLA). The FLA, as amended to date, does not specifically include educating

---

1 See Principle 18 of the White Paper of the Council of Europe of 15 January 2002 on principles concerning the establishment and legal consequences of parentage (available on the Internet site of the Council of Europe: http://www.legal.coe.int/family (viewed on 1 November 2008)).

2 The official Estonian title of the statute is *Perekonnaseadus*. It was passed on 12 October 1994 and published in the *Riigi Teataja* (The State Gazette, below: RT), publication reference: RT I 1994, 75, 1326. All references to statutes cited in this article are to statute versions amended to 3 November 2008. References will be given below according to the following scheme: Estonian official title, date of adoption, first State Gazette publication reference (in parentheses). The Estonian text of the statutes can be accessed via the Estonian State Gazette website (www.riigiteataja.ee). Information-purpose English-language translations of selected statutes and other legislation of the Republic of Estonia may be accessed via the website of the Estonian Ministry of Justice (www.just.ee). Unfortunately, the translations are not always up to date and there is no direct English-language path to the query page.

3 The fact that Estonian law literally speaks about the "rights and duties" of a parent may to a large extent be due to the fact that there is no good equivalent in Estonian for the English (or French) notion of "responsibilities". For ease of comprehension, where this is permitted by the context, the translator has used "responsibilities" as an English equivalent of Estonian "rights and duties"—transl.

the child among the responsibilities of a parent, although it is undoubtedly part of the parental duty of raising the child and caring for him or her.

Experts at the Estonian Ministry of Justice have relatively recently completed work on a draft Act to reform Estonian family law (the DFLA),[4] which proposes to enact a concept of parental responsibilities that is essentially similar to the one defined by experts of the Council of Europe.

The law as it stands provides for (presumably) equal rights and duties for the man and the woman listed as a child's parents in the child's birth record. A person's parental responsibilities arise at the time that the person is entered as a parent in the record made of a child's birth. Under the terms of the DFLA, the parents entered in a child's birth record will only have joint custody of the child if they are married. If the parents are not married, they must bring an application for joint custody, in addition to being identified as the child's parents in the birth record. Should one of the parents refuse to sign the application, joint custody will not be granted. In such a case, custody of the child will vest in the mother, and only a limited set of responsibilities will be attributed to the father.

The introduction of an institution of custody of the child does not affect the scope of parental responsibilities significantly. A parent having custody of the child must care for the child and raise him or her, and act as the child's statutory representative, much like the duty of parents under Estonian family legislation currently in force.

Under applicable Estonian legislation, the parents in principle have equal responsibilities vis-à-vis the child, regardless of whether they live together and regardless of which of the parents is actually raising the child. On the grounds specified in relevant statutes, a child can be removed from the family, or the parents' parental responsibilities suspended. The DFLA allows a parent's parental rights to be circumscribed so as to reflect the share assumed by that parent in the raising of the child, or the risk that the parent poses to the child. This means that it would be possible to limit or to suspend the parent's custody of the child's person or property. Not all of a parent's parental responsibilities would have to be suspended at the same time. In respect of the responsibilities suspended, the child could be appointed a special representative, who would be authorised to protect the corresponding interests of the child instead of the parent.

---

4 The official title of the draft Act is *Perekonnaseaduse eelnõu*. The draft Act and its explanatory letter (both in Estonian) are accessible at: www.riigikogu.ee (last viewed on 3 November 2008). The first reading of the DFLA took place in the Riigikogu on 28 May 2007. The sweeping changes proposed in the draft Act regarding property relationships between spouses have resulted in a wave of contrary public opinion that has halted further progress of the DFLA.

When one compares the Principles of European Family Law regarding parental responsibilities, elaborated by the Commission on European Family Law (Principles of the CEFL),[5] Estonian law essentially meets the requirements of the definition of parental responsibilities stated in Principle 3:1 of the CEFL. The set of rights and duties that are attributed to a parent in order that he or she may ensure and protect the well-being of his or her child in essence corresponds to the notion of "parental responsibilities".

2. CONTENTS OF PARENTAL RESPONSIBILITIES

As has already been pointed out, Estonian family legislation in force does not recognise the concept of "parental responsibility". The rights and duties of a parent are listed, in general terms, in section 50 FLA. They are further defined in specific provisions in the FLA and in other statutes.

2.1. CARE

The right and the duty of a parent to raise the child and to care for the child is provided in section 50(1) FLA. Actually, the parent's responsibility for raising his/her children and caring for them is already enshrined in Article 27 of the Constitution of the Republic of Estonia (the Constitution).[6]

Certain rights of the child are also provided in the Republic of Estonia Child Protection Act (CPA).[7] For instance, by virtue of sections 9(1) and 10 CPA, children have the right to receive assistance and care.

The right to raise a child naturally includes living with the child, having contact with the child, taking physical care of the child, assisting the child, supporting the child's mental and physical development, teaching the child, ensuring the child's education, and treating the child with dignity.

At the same time, the courts[8] have tended to interpret the parents' duty of raising and caring for the child, for instance, in the light of their duty to maintain the

---

5 *Principles of European Family Law Regarding Parental Responsibilities* (available on the Internet site of the CEFL: http://www2.law.uu.nl/priv/cefl/ (last viewed on 1 November 2008)).

6 *Eesti Vabariigi põhiseadus*. adopted on 28 June 1992 (RT 1992, 26, 349).

7 *Lastekaitseseadus*, adopted on 8 June 1992 (RT I 1992, 28, 370).

8 See judgment of 23 April 2004 by the Civil Law Chamber of the Supreme Court in case 3-2-1-57-04 and judgment of 9 March 2005 by the same chamber in case 3-2-1-7-05. The Estonian text (and in the case of selected judgments, an English translation) of the Supreme Court's judgments cited here and *infra* is accessible at www.riigikohus.ee (last viewed on 3 November 2008).

child.[9] Thus, parents are obligated to ensure that the child receives the maintenance required for growing up and developing. In the case that the other parent fails to make sufficient provision toward the child's maintenance, the parent with whom the child resides is obligated to require the other parent to fulfil his/her duty of maintenance in respect of the child.

The first sentence of clause 116(1) DFLA defines the parent's right of custody of the child as the responsibility of the parent to care for his/her child.[10] The parent's custody comprises the right to care for the child's person (custody of the person) and the right to administer the child's property (custody of property), and to make decisions in matters related to the child (second sentence of clause 116(1) DFLA). Custody of the person of the child means the duty and the right of the guardian to raise the child, to supervise the child, to determine where the child stays and to take other steps necessary for ensuring the welfare of the child in all respects (clause 124(1) DFLA).

For the most part, the family legislation in force in Estonia (section 50 FLA), similar to Principle 3:19, is based on the premise that the holder of parental responsibilities should provide the child with care and protection in accordance with the child's interests. However, unlike Principle 3:19(1), Estonian legislation does not recognise the child's distinctive character and developmental needs as specific criteria to be taken into account when giving effect to the principle.

2.2. DETERMINATION OF RESIDENCE

By virtue of section 15 of the Republic of Estonia General Part of the Civil Code Act (GPCCA),[11] the residence of a minor is determined in the first place with regard to the place of residence of the parent or guardian. If a minor who is of limited legal capacity does not live together with his or her parents or guardian, the place where the minor permanently or primarily resides may, with the consent of a parent or guardian, be deemed to be his or her residence. Under the terms of the first sentence of section 51(1) FLA, if a child's parents live apart, they must reach an agreement as to which parent the child will reside with. If the parents fail to agree, the dispute will be determined by the courts if one of the parents so requests (second sentence of section 51(2) FLA). Any decision to be

9 Most of the judgments handed down by the Supreme Court in matters concerning children deal with maintenance issues.

10 For the most part, this represents a shift to the German concept of custody.

11 *Tsiviilseadustiku üldosa seadus*, adopted 27 March 2002 (RT I 2002, 35, 216).

rendered by a court or a guardianship authority[12] in a dispute concerning a child should give priority to the interests of the child. The court or authority should consider the wishes of the child if he or she is at least 10 years of age. The wishes of a child younger than 10 years of age should also be considered if the level of development of the child allows it (section 58 FLA). Such a legislative scheme by and large corresponds to Principle 3:20, although, unlike paragraphs (b) and (c) of that Principle, it does not specify what additional facts should be taken into account by the courts in determining a dispute concerning a child. This lack of specification, however, does not mean that those facts would not be taken into account in practice.

In the judgment handed down in case 3-2-1-7-05[13] the Supreme Court of Estonia has stressed that the responsibilities of a parent, provided in subsections 1-4 of section 50 FLA, remain applicable to both parents even in the case where the parents are separated and the child is residing with one parent.

In civil cases 3-2-1-123-06[14] and 3-2-1-142-06,[15] the Supreme Court has also had occasion to consider certain aspects of the Hague Convention of 25 October 1980 on the Civil Aspects of International Child Abduction related to returning a child and thus determining the child's residence.

2.3. EDUCATION

Unlike the rules established in the family legislation in force, the DFLA gives specific consideration to matters related to schooling of the child as part of the custody of the child's person. In schooling of the child, the parents must above all have regard to the child's abilities and inclinations. If necessary, the parents should seek the advice of the child's teacher or another competent person (DFLA).

With respect to schooling, it should also be pointed out that Article 37 of the Constitution provides everyone's right to an education and establishes the principle that parents should play a decisive role in the educational choices of their children.

---

12 As a rule, it is local councils that are required by law to act as a guardianship authority. Pursuant to s. 24 (1) (4) of the Republic of Estonia Social Welfare Act (*Sotsiaalhoolekande seadus*, adopted 8 February 1995 (RT I 1995, 21, 323)) executive boards of local councils must make arrangements for the guardianship of children residing in their jurisdiction in order to arrange for the care of those children and the creation of an environment conducive to their development. By virtue of s. 63 (1) of CPA, social service departments of local councils are authorised to perform the duties of a guardianship authority.

13 See judgment of the Civil Chamber of the Supreme Court (CCSC) of 9 March 2005 in case 3-2-1-7-05.

14 See judgment of the CCSC of 6 December 2006 in case 3-2-1-123-06.

15 See judgment of the CCSC of 22 February 2007 in case 3-2-1-142-06.

After Estonia ratified the United Nations Convention on the Rights of the Child[16] (UNCRC) in 1992, the CPA was adopted.[17] Among other things, the CPA provides the right of every child to an education that develops the child's mental and physical abilities and allows the child to form a healthy personality (see section 39 CPA).

Under the terms of the CPA, the teaching of a child may not be linked to physical or psychological abuse. By virtue of section 41 CPA, all teaching must have regard to the child's distinctive character, take into consideration the differences between the sexes and be based on recognising the progress of the child.

The duty of children to attend school emanates from section 8 of the Republic of Estonia Education Act,[18] subsection 2 of which provides that a child must attend school starting on 1 October of the year in which he or she will have attained seven years of age. The child must continue to attend school until he or she has acquired a basic education or attained 17 years of age.

Under the terms of paragraph 1 of Principle 3:19, the holders of parental responsibilities should provide the child with education in accordance with the child's distinctive character and developmental needs. Overall, Estonian legislation is currently compatible with Principle 3:19(1). As for the future, the DFLA proposes to enact a direct reflection of the Principle in its clause 125.

2.4. RELIGIOUS UPBRINGING

Social rights of the child, including the freedom of religion, are listed in section 11 of the CPA.

By virtue of section 10(1) of the Republic of Estonia Churches and Congregations Act,[19] every person of at least 15 years of age may independently become a member of a congregation or leave a congregation pursuant to such procedure as may be established in relevant statutes. A child who is younger than 15 years of age may become a member of a congregation if his or her parents or guardian consent to it (section 10(2) CCA). Section 3(4) of the Basic Schools and Upper Secondary

16 *ÜRO Lapse õiguste konventsiooni ratifitseerimise otsus*, adopted 26 September 1991 by the Supreme Soviet of Estonian Soviet Socialist Republic (RT 1991, 35, 428)

17 The CPA – as, indeed, the FLA – has been often criticised for its declaratory style and weak regulatory content. For this reason, there exists broad agreement regarding the need to draft a new CPA that would be a better guide to practitioners working in the field in implementing child protection principles.

18 *Haridusseadus*, adopted 23 March 1992 (RT I 1992, 12, 192).

19 *Kirikute ja koguduste seadus*, adopted 12 February 2002 (RT I, 2002, 24, 135).

Schools Act[20] requires religious education to be non-confessional. A school is required to teach religious studies if at least 15 students in a stage of study request it. Religious education is voluntary.

2.5. DISCIPLINARY MEASURES AND CORPORAL PUNISHMENT

As a general principle, corporal punishment of children in schools, children's care homes and juvenile detention centres is not permitted. Yet there is no express prohibition in Estonian legislation of corporal punishment in relation to children. Neither are there any provisions on the books that would make it expressly unlawful for parents, step-parents, guardians or carers to resort to corporal punishment vis-a-vis their wards in the home.

Section 31(1) CPA provides a prohibition against humiliating, frightening or punishing the child in any way that abuses the child, causes bodily harm to the child, or otherwise endangers his or her mental or physical health.

Yet, Anu Uritam, advisor to Estonia's Chancellor of Justice, has expressed the view that corporal punishments that do not specifically fulfil the criteria listed above, would appear to be in line with the CPA as amended to date. Practitioners have been reluctant to take corporal punishment cases of children needing help to the courts for fear of complicated proceedings and the difficulty of justifying an interference in the family's life and providing corresponding evidence.[21] A further problem lies in the attitude of the Estonian public regarding corporal punishment – it is still considered an acceptable part of raising a child. For this reason, Anu Uritam has also expressed doubts as to whether the amendments proposed to reform the CPA would meet with the agreement of the general public.[22] The authors of this article share this view.

According to clause 124(2) DFLA, any form of physical or psychological mistreatment, as well as any child-rearing methods that humiliate the child, would be prohibited.

In conclusion, one may say that public opinion in Estonia is shifting towards prohibiting any humiliating treatment of the child. The rules proposed in the

---

20 *Põhikooli- ja gümnaasiumiseadus*, adopted 15 September 1993 (RT I 1993, 63, 892).

21 URITAM, A. "Lapsed ja nende karistamine: kas lüüa või mitte?" [Children and punishment: to strike or not to strike?], in *Juridica* (2007), 8, p. 550 (in Estonian).

22 *Ibid.*, p. 537.

DFLA and the proposals made to reform the CPA appear compatible with Principle 3:19(2) of the CEFL.

2.6. MEDICAL TREATMENT

Pursuant to section 766(4) of the Republic of Estonia Law of Obligations Act (LOA),[23] as a rule, if a patient himself or herself is unable to consider the pros and cons of a healthcare service responsibly, the consent of the patient's statutory representative is required for the provision of those services to the patient. Still, there are certain cases in which the consent of the patient or his or her statutory representative is not required, or is required only to a limited extent (section 766(6) LOA).

By virtue of section 5(2) of the Republic of Estonia Act to Govern Terminations of Pregnancies and Sterilisation,[24] pregnancies of women of limited legal capacity (i.e., also pregnancies of children) may be terminated pursuant to a written application from the guardian.

2.7. STATUTORY REPRESENTATION

A parent is the child's statutory representative in all legal relationships in which the limited legal capacity of the child prevents him or her from acting as an independent party,[25] provided the law allows the parent to represent the child in those relationships. The rules of guardianship established in the FLA include a reference to general provisions laying down restrictions and bars on certain transactions, which are declared applicable in the relationships between parent and child (sections 99(3) and 100(4) FLA). In the cases where the parent may not represent the child (barred transactions), the DFLA proposes the appointment of a special guardian. Under the FLA, this is not possible. In the cases listed in section 99 FLA, parents are required to obtain the prior consent of a guardianship authority in order to perform a transaction validly.

Both the FLA and the DFLA (cf. second and third sentence of section 50(2) FLA and clauses 120 and 127 DFLA) recognise the parent as a statutory representative of the child – which allows a parent to act for his or her child in matters concerning the child's person and property. In this regard, the family legislation currently in

---

23 *Võlaõigusseadus*, adopted 26 September 2001 (RT I 2001, 81, 487).

24 *Raseduse katkestamise ja steriliseerimise seadus*, adopted 25 November 1998 (RT I 1998, 107, 1766).

25 For a discussion of cases in which a child may perform a transaction independently, see VARUL, P., AVI, A. and KIVISILD, T., "Restrictions on Active Legal Capacity", *Juridica International* (2004), *1*, pp. 99–107.

force in Estonia complies with the principles proposed by the CEFL (cf. Principle 3:24). The prohibition of statutory representation in the case of a conflict of interests between the child and the person exercising parental responsibility by virtue of statutory provisions is provided in section 100 FLA, in certain respects even in more detail than in the Principles of the CEFL. This prohibition is retained in the DFLA.

2.8. THE CHILD'S RIGHT TO BE HEARD

The DFLA tends to be more specific than current legislation regarding the substance of parental rights and the principles governing the exercise of those rights. In caring for a child and raising him or her, parents must take into account the fact that the child's ability and need for independent and responsible action is bound to grow. If the level of development of the child allows it, parents should discuss matters regarding care for the child and the raising of the child with the child (clause 116(2) DFLA).

The FLA does not impose any obligation on parents to consider a child's wishes in deciding matters regarding the child. In principle, such an obligation could be derived from the first sentence of section 31(1) CPA, which provides that every child must at all times be treated as an individual, and that due consideration should be given to his or her character, age and sex.

In disputes concerning children, Estonian courts have, in addition to the interests of the child, started to have regard to the child's wishes.[26]

By virtue of section 58 FLA, when hearing a dispute concerning a child, a guardianship authority or court is required to give priority to the interests of the child, considering the wishes of the child if he or she is at least 10 years of age. The wishes of a child younger than 10 years of age should be considered if the level of development of the child allows it.

The Code of Civil Procedure (CCP)[27] that entered into force on 1 January 2006 also makes provision for hearing the child in non-contentious family matters such as determination of a parent's rights with respect to the child, determination of arrangements concerning contact with the child and giving consent to perform a transaction in the name of the child or other ward (see section 550 CCP).[28]

26 LIIV, E., "Lapse ärakuulamine tsiviilkohtumenetluses" [Hearing a child in civil proceedings], in *Juridica* (2006), 4, p. 257 (in Estonian).

27 *Tsiviilkohtumenetluse seadustik*, adopted 20 April 2005 (RT I 2005, 26, 197).

28 For a discussion of hearing a child in civil proceedings, see Procedural issues, *infra*.

According to Judge Ele Liiv of Harju County Court (Tallinn, Estonia), hearing the child should not be regarded as a mere formality, and should be dispensed with only in exceptional cases that involve a serious risk to the child's health or psychological well-being.[29] Judge Liiv sees a problem in the fact that, to date, no special training events have been organised to teach judges to take into account the child's level of development when hearing the child in relation to a court case.[30] It should be pointed out that Judge Liiv's article, published in 2006, is the first theoretical piece written on the subject in Estonia.

2.9. THE RIGHT TO ADMINISTER THE CHILD'S PROPERTY

By virtue of the FLA, a parent is a statutory representative of his or her child. As the child's representative, the parent has the authority of a guardian (second and third sentence of section 50(2) FLA). This means that the parent has a responsibility to administer the child's property. When administering the child's property, the parent's decisions must be informed by the interests of the child. Section 50(4) FLA provides a prohibition against exercising parental rights in a manner contrary to the interests of the child.

The legislation in force does not contain any other rules regarding the administration of the child's property by the parents. More specific provisions are only laid down with respect to guardians. The DFLA, on the other hand, lists a parent's responsibility for administering the child's property as an integral part of the concept of custody of the child's property.

In accordance with Principle 3:22(1), the DFLA proposes to enact rules that would obligate parents to manage the child's property with due care, to ensure that it does not lose in value, and to increase its value when possible. The FLA does not impose such an obligation on parents.

Pursuant to the FLA, a guardian is prohibited from giving away any movable that belongs to his or her ward without prior approval of a guardianship authority, except in the case of a customary gift (section 99(1)(3) FLA). This principle is retained in the DFLA. In this respect, both are compatible with the prohibition of using the child's property to make gifts, recommended in Principle 3:22(2).

Paragraph 3 of Principle 3:22 recommends that it should be possible to use income derived from the child's property for the needs of the family, if it is not needed for the proper management of the property or for the maintenance and education of

29 LIIV, *supra*, note 26, p. 261.
30 *Ibid.*

the child, and if it is necessary to use it for the family's needs. A corresponding provision is included in the rules proposed in the DFLA. Although absent from the FLA, similar arrangements appear well established in practice. Still, no supervisory or oversight mechanism exists to ensure their appropriate use.

The DFLA (clauses 128(1)(1) and 128(1)(2)) proposes a limitation of the custody of the child's property similar to the one suggested in Principle 3:23(1).

Under the terms of the relevant clauses of the DFLA, custody of the child's property would not apply to any property that vests in the child by virtue of succession or gift (clause 128 DFLA). Any property that a child has acquired by way of succession or gift should normally be administered by the parents in accordance with the instructions provided by the donor.

The FLA, as amended to date, only provides that a guardian should not transfer a movable of his or her ward without prior approval of a guardianship authority if the movable is of special value to the ward (section 99(1)(2) FLA).

The recommendation in Principle 3:23(2), that the earnings of the child should not be administered by the holders of parental responsibilities unless the child is not of sufficient age and maturity to decide their use himself or herself, is not fully reflected in the legislation in force in Estonia. As for the FLA, it does not deal with the matter at all. Section 11 CCP – a provision that governs multi-party transactions by persons of limited legal capacity – may be interpreted narrowly, such that any transactions on account of the proceeds of the person's labour also require the consent of the person's statutory representative. The rule for transactions performed from the proceeds of one's labour is contained in section 11(3)(2) GPCCA, which provides that a transaction entered into by a person of limited legal capacity without prior consent or subsequent ratification of his or her statutory representative is valid only if the person performed the transaction from the means that were granted to him or her for this purpose or for free use by the statutory representative or, with the consent of the statutory representative, by a third party. The view expressed by the drafters in the DFLA is that a parent's right to administer the child's property does not rule out the child's right to make independent dispositions of his or her property in the cases provided by law (clause 127 DFLA). This, however, begs the question of the meaning of the provision of the GPCCA discussed above. Yet, if one were to take into account the principle expressed in the DFLA, that in caring for and raising a child the parents should consider the fact that the child's ability and need to act independently and responsibly gradually increases, one may also be able to resolve the matter of interpreting the relevant provisions of DFLA and the GPCCA in a way that agrees with the recommendation in Principle 3:23(2).

Similar to the recommendation in Principle 3:23(3),[31] the restrictions listed in section 99(1) FLA[32] require previous consent of a guardianship authority in order for the corresponding transactions to be valid.

Under the terms of the DFLA, the parents' right of administration of the child's property will normally extend to all of the child's property. However, in the cases specified in clauses 131, 187 and 188 DFLA, the authorisation of a court would be made mandatory in order to perform the transaction. A parent, however, would not be required to obtain authorisation in all of the cases in which this should be done by a guardian. For transactions that a parent is not authorised to perform in the child's name, a special guardian would have to be appointed.

3. ATTRIBUTION OF PARENTAL RESPONSIBILITIES

3.1. MARRIED AND UNMARRIED PARENTS

The mutual rights and obligations of parent and child arise from the filiation of the child, established pursuant to a procedure provided by law. A child descends from the mother who gave birth to the child, and from the father by whom the mother conceived the child (section 38 FLA). If the parents are married, a child who is born or conceived during the marriage of the parents, also a child who is born within 10 months following the death of the husband or after the divorce or annulment of the marriage, is deemed to be descended from the husband (section 39 FLA). If the parents are not married, the filiation of a child is established on the basis of a joint written application of the father and mother, which they must submit to a vital statistics office.

This means that parental responsibilities may only be regarded to have been attributed to a parent if, pursuant to the procedure provided by law, his or her name has been entered as that of a parent in the record made of the child's birth.[33] The attribution to a parent of parental responsibilities does not depend on the

---

31 To the effect that, where transactions can have significant financial consequences for the child, the authorisation of the competent authority should be necessary for those transactions to be performed.

32 These restrictions are that a guardian may not, without prior approval of a guardianship authority, transfer an immovable of a ward or encumber it with any real rights; a guardian may not transfer a movable of a ward that is of special value to the ward, or give away such a movable, except in the case of a customary gift; a guardian may not pledge a movable of a ward, take a loan in the name of a ward or waive the collection of a debt owed to a ward, or decline in the name of a ward to accept an estate in succession.

33 The courts have taken a similar view. See judgment of 21 March 2007 by the Civil Chamber of the Supreme Court in case 3-2-2-2-07.

parents being married or not. It only depends on the parent being recognised as such in law.

The law does not limit the scope of parental responsibilities of parents who are not married to each other. The rule is simply that parents have equal rights and duties with respect to their children (section 49 FLA). It has also been stressed that a child who descends from parents who are not married to each other has the same rights and duties with respect to his or her parents and their relatives as a child who descends from parents who are married to each other (section 45 FLA). Similarly, children born of an annulled marriage are deemed to have the same rights and duties as children born in a marriage (section 37 FLA).

Since the law does not provide for any change in the rights and duties of a parent in the event of separation, divorce or annulment of marriage, the attribution of parental responsibilities does not depend on any of these events. It only depends on whether the parent is recognised as such in law. The fact that the parents are married does not alter the scope of either parent's responsibilities, which is in harmony with Principles 3:8 and 3:10. The FLA does not contain any rules that would expressly alter the scope of responsibilities of either parent in a situation where the parents live separately and the child resides with one of them.[34] Nevertheless, an important proportion of Estonian public appears to have a considerable tolerance for the opposite and does not express disapproval regarding an eventual limitation of responsibilities of one of the parents upon separation.[35] As a rule, raising children is considered the task of the wife or mother.[36]

The Supreme Court of Estonia has stated that living apart from the child unavoidably reduces the opportunities that parent and child have to be together, and thus places a limitation on the parent's right to raise his or her child and to care for him or her.[37] Hence, in principle, although the responsibilities of both parents are formally regarded as equal, their exercise in practice considerably depends on which parent the child resides with and which parent is only entitled to have contact with the child.

---

34 See also KULLERKUPP, K., "Family Law in Estonia", *The International Survey of Family Law* 2001, pp. 105–106.

35 Ministry of Social Affairs, "Lapsed ja Eesti ühiskond. Väärtushinnangute uuring RISC" [Children and society in Estonia. A RISC study of social values], January-April 2006 (in Estonian).

36 Statistical information for 2006 shows that there were 22,400 single mothers versus 1650 single fathers in Estonia. The figures were derived from a study of households' budgets (source: Information and publications unit of the Estonian Statistics Board, in response (dated 7 October 2007) to a public information request).

37 See judgment of 21 March 2007 of the Civil Chamber of the Supreme Court in case 3-2-1-13-07.

If the parents live apart, they should by mutual agreement determine which parent the child is to reside with and how the parent living apart from the child may have contact with the child (sections 51–52 FLA).

Yet, the law does not provide any specific requirements for such mutual agreement. This means that parents are free to determine the child's residence and contact arrangements by mutual agreement. In practice, parents who are about to go their separate ways often reach an agreement (explicit or implicit). The law does not require that the parents' agreement to determine the residence of the child and arrangements for contact with the child be reviewed and approved by a competent authority. If one parent subsequently fails to abide by the agreement, the other parent is entitled to bring an action to determine the child's residence or arrangements for contact with the child. The parent bringing the action may seek an order whose terms are different from those of the original agreement.

Up to the end of 2005, there were cases in Estonia in which the parents of a child born out of marriage would conclude a notarially authenticated agreement, when their co-habitation ended, to deal with the maintenance of children, and in addition, in certain cases also with the division of responsibilities related to raising the child. Often, those agreements contained clauses allowing immediate compulsory enforcement. After the amendments to the Code of Enforcement Procedure (CEP)[38] took effect (as of 1 January 2006), notarised agreements that constitute an executory title may only be enforced in respect of obligations the due date of which has expired – a category that normally excludes periodically payable maintenance claims.[39]

Estonian laws in effect to date do not expressly allow parents to agree on the division of parental responsibilities in the event of separation, i.e. during the time that the parents are still living together. No clear position regarding the validity of such agreements has emerged in judicial practice either. There have been cases in which spouses have concluded a marital property agreement and, in that agreement, also established a division of parental responsibilities in the event of a

38 *Täitemenetluse seadustik*, adopted 20 April 2005 (RT I 2005, 27, 198).

39 Pursuant to s. 2(18) CEP as amended to date, a notarially authenticated agreement giving rise to a claim for the payment of a sum of money, and containing a clause by which the debtor consents to immediate compulsory enforcement when the due date of the claim has passed, also constitutes an executory title. Under the terms of s. 11(4) Act to Implement the Code of Civil Procedure and the Code of Enforcement Procedure (as amended to date), enforcement proceedings in respect of notarially authenticated agreements dealing with the maintenance of a child and executed until 31 December 2005, may continue to be brought after 1 January 2006, provided they contain a clause by which the debtor consents to immediate compulsory enforcement.

divorce.[40] In the case of a dispute, nevertheless, the matter of the child's residence and of arrangements for contact with the child would ultimately be determined by a competent court. If the dispute only concerns contact arrangements, the determination may also be made by a guardianship authority (sections 51–52 FLA).[41]

According to the DFLA, custody would, in general, be exercised by the parents jointly. Custody may be attributed to a parent solely only to the extent that that parent actually takes part in raising the child.

Parents who are married to each other would enjoy joint custody by virtue of the operation of relevant provisions of the DFLA. Parents who are not married to each other at the time their child is born, would not automatically be attributed joint custody under the DFLA. Joint custody would only arise if the parents subsequently entered into a marriage, or if they applied for joint custody of the child. Failing that, the mother would have sole custody.

The introduction of custody in the provisions of the DFLA serves the purpose of clarifying the law with respect to relationships between parent and child under civil law. This has special relevance in cases where the parents are not raising their child jointly – in those cases, it would be impractical to regard both parents as representatives of the child. In situations where the parents are permanently separated, or no longer wish to exercise joint custody of the child, the DFLA proposes to allow the attribution of custody to one of the parents. The attribution must be ordered by a court.

According to the terms of the DFLA, the right to contact with the child does not mean that the parent has custody of the child's person. Custody of the child's person is a right that derives from the close blood relationship that parent and child enjoy and that is also part and parcel of constitutionally guaranteed parental rights (Article 27 of the Constitution). Thus, as a rule, a parent who does not have custody of his or her child still would enjoy the right to contact with the child.

As a novelty, the DFLA proposes to extend the concept of parental decision-making authority to cases in which parents, although separated, have retained joint custody. This means that the responsibilities of the parent raising the child would, regardless of the fact of joint custody, be somewhat broader in scope than those of the parent who also has custody but lives separately from the child. In

---

40 See Explanatory Letter to the DFLA, p. 20. It is understandable for marital property agreements to include provisions dealing with the payment of maintenance to children upon a divorce of the parents. Explicitly or implicitly, this often also reflects a determination as to with which parent the child will reside.

41 See also section 5: Contact, *infra*.

essence, the parent raising the child would be entitled to decide everyday matters concerning the child without consulting the other parent. Another novelty proposed in the DFLA consists in obligating the courts to undertake regular reviews of long-term orders affecting the rights of a parent, with a view to lifting any limitations imposed if this should be deemed possible. Under the terms of the DFLA, the courts would be authorised to undertake these reviews of their own motion.

3.2. OTHER PERSONS

The mutual rights and obligations of parent and child arise from the filiation of the child. This means that parental responsibilities are exercised predominantly by the parents, who are entitled to require any person who has obtained control of their child without a valid foundation in law, to return the child immediately. Nevertheless, a parent may not require the return of his or her child if this is clearly contrary to the interests of the child (section 50(3) FLA).

The law provides very few rules to govern legal relationships between a child and a person not recognised in law as the child's parent. In certain cases, the FLA provides a duty for a child who has come of age to maintain his or her step-parent or foster parent (i.e. a person married to the child's parent or a person who actually raised the child but is not a parent of the child (section 68 FLA)). It does not, however, impose a duty on a step-parent or foster parent to maintain the child. Neither does it create any immediate parental responsibilities for persons who actually raise the child, be they married to a parent of the child, or simply living together in a common-law arrangement, be they of the same sex or not.

The existence and opinion of a person who acts as a child's parent is nevertheless taken into account in the case of a dispute concerning the child. If a child has lived, for an extended period of time, with one parent, or with a person entitled to have contact with the child, or with a foster family, the courts will hear such persons or family members in a matter concerning the child, except for cases where it is clear that this has no relevance to determining the matter or clarifying the facts (section 560 CCP).

Under the terms of the DFLA, the right to make decisions for a child would also extend to a parent who does not have custody of the child, and to a foster parent, provided the parent is in fact caring for the child. This statutory right to make decisions for the child should facilitate representing the child and help clarify the legal relationships between the parents themselves and between the parents and third parties.

Third parties may only hold parental responsibilities vis-à-vis a child if they have been appointed guardian of the child. A guardian is appointed for the purpose of raising the child and protecting the child's personal and property rights and interests. Guardians are appointed to children whose parents are deceased or missing, or have limited legal capacity, or whose parents' parental rights have been suspended. A guardian may also be appointed to a child who is deprived of parental care for other reasons (sections 92(1) – (3) FLA). The practice of the courts suggests that in addition to situations where the child is left without parents recognised as such in law, a guardian can also be appointed in a situation where the child has a parent or both parents,[42] which is in accordance with the recommendation expressed in Principle 3:17. By virtue of section 97(1) FLA, the guardian is a statutory representative of the child. This means that in certain cases, the right to represent a child may be exercised on an equal legal footing by the child's parents and a third party.

Guardianship relationships are established in Estonia by the courts, acting on an application brought by a guardianship authority, or by a person who requires the assistance of a guardian. The information required to make an order appointing a guardian must be collected and prepared by the guardianship authority.

In certain cases, a guardian-ward relationship may be created by operation of statute – for instance, this is so in a situation where parents have given their consent to a guardianship authority for their child to be put up for adoption and the identity of the adopter is not known.

By virtue of section 95(5) FLA, it is the duty of a guardianship authority to perform the guardian's duties until a guardian is appointed. The Supreme Court of Estonia has found that a guardianship authority derives its powers from the operation of the relevant statutory provision and should act as a child's guardian if no guardian has been appointed to the child, without the need for specific appointment.[43] A guardian is a statutory representative of the ward (section 98(1) FLA). The guardian's responsibilities include raising the child and protecting his or her personal and property interests and rights (section 92(1) FLA).

It is a peculiarity of Estonian family legislation that according to the tenor of section 95(3) FLA, only a natural person may be appointed a guardian. A guardianship authority is regarded as unable to participate in raising a child and supervising him or her in a manner that a natural person can. Still, pursuant to section 95(5) FLA, the benefits of guardianship must extend to a child who

---

42 See judgment of 5 June 1996 of the Civil Chamber of the Supreme Court (CCSC) in case 3-2-1-79-96.

43 See judgment of 28 October 2005 of the CCSC in case 3-2-1-101-05.

does not have any parents and to whom a guardian has not been appointed. Since it is the duty of a guardianship authority to obtain an order establishing a guardianship (section 93(1) FLA) and appointing a guardian (section 93(2) FLA), the appointment of a guardian to a child to a significant extent depends on the actions of the guardianship authority.

A guardian is under a duty to ensure that the child is raised and maintained properly. A person may only be appointed guardian if he or she consents to the appointment in writing. A guardian is required to report to a relevant guardianship authority regarding the performance of his or her duties. A guardian must submit an annual written report to a relevant guardianship authority concerning administration of a ward's property.

In the case that a guardian fails to fulfil his or her duties, or does not fulfil them properly, the court, acting on an application of the relevant guardianship authority, must revoke the guardian's authority. Regrettably, in practice there are many cases in which, for one reason or another, no natural person guardian has been appointed, and the duties of the guardian are performed by the relevant guardianship authority. In this situation there is no oversight whatsoever of the actions of the agency performing the duties of the guardian. Such a state of affairs should not be regarded as acceptable.

In selecting a guardian, the candidate's character and ability to perform the duties of a guardian, and the candidate's relationship to his or her prospective ward should be taken into account, as should the views of a child at least 10 years of age, or those of other wards of limited legal capacity. The wishes of a child below 10 years of age should also be taken into account, if the level of development of the child allows it.

The following persons may not be appointed guardians: minors, persons of limited legal capacity; persons whose parental rights have been suspended or from whom a child has been removed without suspension of parental responsibilities, persons who have been relieved of the performance of the duties of a guardian or carer, persons who for some other reason are not capable of performing the duties of a guardian (section 96 FLA).

The Republic of Estonia Social Welfare Act (SWA) also provides for the possibility of ordering a child's care in another family, without that family being attributed the responsibilities emanating from the rules of guardianship.

The SWA provides a list of criteria in cases where a child may be removed from the home and the family in order to provide him or her with a social service or other assistance. Siblings should be kept together upon removal from their home and family unless this is contrary to their interests (section 25(3) SWA).

If a child is admitted to foster care and a case plan is prepared for him or her, the wishes of the child should be taken into account if he or she is at least 10 years of age. The wishes of a child younger than 10 years of age should also be considered if the level of development of the child allows it. Before consent, the child is entitled to get acquainted with the person who wishes to become a carer, the members of that person's family and the family home, and to be provided information on them. The child has the right to bring his or her personal effects when he or she moves to live with the family of the carer (section 25(1) SWA).

A person who wishes to become a carer must submit a corresponding application to the local council of his or her residence or to the local council of the residence of the child if the residence of the child and the residence of the person who wishes to become a carer are not in the jurisdiction of the same council.

A competent guardianship authority will determine the suitability of the person who wishes to become a carer providing foster care to the child. The determination of suitability will be made on the basis of the following criteria: compliance with statutory requirements by the person who wishes to become a carer and by the adult members of his or her family, the results of social counselling and of a visit to the home of the person, and the results of a relevant training course, if the person who wishes to become a carer has taken the course. In the case of a positive determination, a foster care agreement will be concluded with the person, incorporating the terms of the case plan prepared for the child (section 25(3) SWA).

The main problem with a child's care in a foster family lies in the lack of clarity as to the legal status of the foster family. The foster carers are not entitled to represent the child, and since current legislation does not provide any other legal schemes for adults to protect the interests of an underage care receiver (such as custody, or the special guardianship proposed in the DFLA), the foster family is left without a legal basis to represent the child in his or her relationships with third parties.

Under the terms of the DFLA, in the case that parents should give a child into foster care for an extended period of time, courts conducting the care proceedings would be authorised to attribute decision-making authority to the carer if the parents or the carer so request. In the case that the request is made by the carer (step-parent), the DFLA proposes, by way of additional requirement, that the parents should consent to the attribution. To the extent of the responsibilities attributed to the carer, he or she will hold the authority of a special guardian.

The DFLA proposes to vest oversight of guardians in the courts. It suggests that a court should, once it has learned of a relevant situation, open proceedings to establish a guardianship relationship of its own motion. Executive boards of local councils and other interested parties (for instance, relatives of a person requiring appointment of a guardian) will have the right of initiating appointment proceedings.

According to the FLA as amended to date, and to judicial rulings on issues related to it, a guardian may be appointed to a child even if the child already has a parent as a statutory representative. The DFLA proposes to enact a rule that provides for the appointment of a guardian only in cases in which the child does not have any parents qualifying for the status of a statutory representative. In the cases in which it is necessary to appoint a guardian to protect the interests of the child, but there are no grounds for suspending the parent's parental rights (for instance, where a parent is unable to provide financially for the child because of health problems, or for the simple reason of being abroad), the DFLA suggests an order of special guardianship to the extent of the duties that the parent is or the parents are unable to fulfil. In such a case the parents retain their parental rights, whereas custody of the child's property and to that extent, also the right to represent the child, is attributed to the special guardian. The DFLA has retained the preference for natural persons as guardians, yet still provides for the possibility of appointing legal persons as guardians. The legal person in question would have to search for natural person candidates for guardianships on a permanent basis, to advise and to train them. The way the provision is worded suggests that, above all, the drafters were thinking of charitable organisations active in the field of child protection. The DFLA proposes to vest the Minister of Social Affairs with authority to make orders to establish a list of such organisations.

The DFLA also makes provision for the appointment of multiple guardians to the same person, if this is deemed reasonable given the facts of the case and considering the needs of the ward. The DFLA retains the requirement of consent for appointment as a guardian. If no suitable natural or legal person guardian can be found to a child, the DFLA proposes to attribute the duty to act as the child's guardian to the council in whose jurisdiction the child habitually stays. The council would continue to act as the guardian until a proper guardian is appointed.

Unlike the current legislation, a guardian's status would not entail a responsibility to maintain the child. This responsibility would be attributed to the guardian only in the case that he or she is a person who is under a duty to maintain the child by virtue of other provisions in family legislation. Nevertheless, the guardian as a statutory representative of the child, would be entitled, and obligated to require, from persons who have a legal duty to do so, the payment of maintenance to the child.

The FLA contains no rules to govern performance of parental responsibilities in the case of the death of one of the parents. Should both parents die, the child will be appointed a guardian (cf. *supra*).

The FLA in force does not make provision for delegation of parental responsibilities to third parties by agreement. Parents' agreements or expressions of intent, that purport to designate the person of the guardian for the event of the death of one or both parents, are seldom seen in Estonian practice and are not regulated in current legislation. The DFLA stresses the parents' right to make determinations regarding the child's living arrangements also after their death. According to clause 182 DFLA, a parent's testamentary disposition regarding the identity of the guardian should be taken into account, except for the case where it is contrary to the interests of the child.

Since parental responsibilities in Estonia may, as a rule, also be attributed to a person other than a parent, Principle 3:9 has been recognised in Estonia.

4. EXERCISE OF PARENTAL RESPONSIBILITIES

4.1. INTERESTS OF THE CHILD

Child protection is based on the principle that the best interests of the child should have priority at all times and in all cases (section 3 CPA). Therefore a parent may not exercise parental rights in a manner contrary to the interests of the child (section 50(4) FLA) and in hearing a dispute concerning a child, a court or guardianship authority should give priority to the interests of the child (section 58 FLA). This means that all decisions concerning a child should be informed by the best interests of the child.

Unfortunately, there is no legal definition of those interests, and they are not specified in any way in relevant statutes.

The DFLA deals with giving priority to the interests of the child in clause 123(1), which proposes that a court hearing a case concerning a child must dispose of the case in a manner that gives priority to the interests of the child, giving due consideration to all facts of the case and the legitimate interests of the parties concerned. According to the DFLA, the courts should also regularly review long-term measures affecting the rights of a parent, with a view to lifting any limitations that have been ordered if this is deemed possible (clause 135(3) DFLA). The court may proceed to review a measure of its own motion – the right to review is not limited to cases in which review is sought by an interested party (the parent whose parental rights have been circumscribed). The court should vary the previous order if this appears justified by facts that affect the welfare of the child on a permanent basis. Measures limiting a parent's custody of the child should be lifted when the interests of the child are no longer in jeopardy (clause 123(2) DFLA).

4.2. JOINT AND SOLE PARENTAL RESPONSIBILITIES

The legislation in force in Estonia does not recognise the notions of joint and sole parental responsibility. By law, the responsibilities of the parents are equal, regardless of whether they are living together or not. Where possible, parental responsibilities should be exercised jointly – as recommended by Principle 3:11. Yet, the law does not specify whether and when a parent is entitled to determine a matter concerning the child without regard to the views of the other parent, and on what basis to resolve disputes that may arise when parents fail to agree on a matter concerning their child. No clear position has emerged in judicial practice either. Thus, the application of Principles 3:12 – 3:15 in Estonia is currently not guaranteed.

A parent is only entitled to exercise parental rights without regard to the other parent's views in the case that the record made of the child's birth only lists one parent, or if the parental responsibilities of the other parent have been suspended.[44] In other cases, the rule is that parents should exercise parental responsibilities jointly. In essence, this agrees with Principle 3:16.

Under the terms of the DFLA, in a situation where the parents live together, a parent's custody of a child may also be limited in part, by the suspension of that parent's authority to decide matters for the child (including the parent's right to represent the child). Parents who live apart may continue to exercise joint custody, but the parent living with the child will enjoy a statutory prerogative to decide day-to-day matters without consulting the other parent. If parents live apart, sole custody may be attributed to one parent, while the other parent is entitled to maintain contact with the child (including a limited right of decision-making during the time of contact). The other parent's right to contact with the child, and that parent's decision-making authority, may be subject to limitations if this is deemed to be in the interests of the child.[45]

In addition to the above, Estonian legislation in force does not regulate the relationship between the parents in the event that the parent with whom the child resides should wish to change his or her place of residence. The law does not

44 See section 8: Discharge of parental responsibilities.
45 See DFLA and its explanatory letter (*supra* note 4).

currently require a parent whose residence is also the principal residence of the child to obtain the consent of the other parent if the first parent wishes to move to another location in Estonia, or abroad. Although the CPA guarantees a child whose parents reside in different countries the right to have personal contacts and a relationship with both parents, as well as a right (for the child or the child's parents) to travel in and out of Estonian territory at will, subject to applicable regulations, there are no specific provisions in statutes regarding the exercise of either of those rights. Neither are there any specific rules regarding a situation in which the child has an alternating residence. The opinions expressed by the courts suggest that this could be accepted in principle,[46] but do not provide any details as to particular situations in which this might be so.

On the basis of what has been said above, the rules governing determination of the child's residence should be reconsidered in whole. This means that Estonian law in this matter is not yet compatible with Principles 3:20 and 3:21. It should be pointed out further that the DFLA does not propose to introduce any significant details in the rules governing determination of the child's residence in cases where the parents live separately but continue to exercise joint custody.

5. CONTACT

5.1. CONTACT WITH PARENTS AND OTHER PERSONS

Pursuant to Article 26 of the Constitution, everyone is entitled to respect of his or her private and family life. The protection of family life extends to various relationships between members of the family, primarily to the reciprocal rights of parent and child to enjoy each other's company, which more specifically means the right to live together and to have contact with each other.[47] The right to have contact is not premised on the parent having custody of the child's person, since that right is a natural part of any close blood relationship and is part and parcel of the rights that a birth parent enjoys by virtue of Article 27(3) of the Constitution.[48]

The right to contact acquires a special significance in situations where parent and child live apart. A child's right to contact with the parents is provided in the CPA:

---

46 In a judgment handed down on 2 October 2008 in case 3-2-1-66-08, the Civil Chamber of the Supreme Court has found that in granting a claim for the payment of maintenance, it is important to take into account which parent the child resides with and to what extent the child has contact with the parent who lives separately, and whether the child's residence alternates from one parent to the other.

47 "Eesti Vabariigi põhiseadus: kommenteeritud väljaanne" [Constitution of the Republic of Estonia with commentaries], Tallinn, 2002, pp. 226–246 (in Estonian).

48 DFLA and its explanatory letter, *supra* note 4.

"A child who is separated from one or both parents has the right to maintain a personal relationship and contact with both of the parents as well as with other close relatives, except if the relationship is likely to harm the child"[49] (section 28 CPA). Even if the parents reside in different countries the child has the right to direct contacts and a personal relationship with both parents (section 30 CPA). The child is also entitled to retain contact with a parent if he or she is separated from the parent or if the parent's parental responsibilities have been suspended. If guardianship has been ordered for the child or the child is living with a "support family" or "support person" or in a social welfare institution, the child has the right to contact with his or her parents and close relatives, except where such contact endangers the health and development of the child or the security of carers or staff members or other children in the social welfare institution. The social service departments and care institutions are under a duty to take all measures to promote the initiation and continuation of contacts between a child and his or her parents and close blood relatives. Still those departments and institutions are also entitled to limit such contacts on the grounds mentioned above. On the same grounds, a social service department may refuse to disclose the whereabouts of a child to his or her parents or close blood relatives (section 64 CPA). Above all, it is the child who should be guaranteed the right to contact with parents and close relatives.[50]

The right of parents to contact with their child derives from the FLA. The responsibilities of parents with respect to their children are equal (section 49 FLA). This means that, in principle, either parent is entitled to raise the child and care for him or her, which in turn presumes being with the child. A parent living apart from the child has the right to contact with the child (section 52(1) FLA). The law does not specify the scope of the right to contact either from the perspective of the parent or the child. In fact, no obligation to have contact with the child is imposed on parents by law, nor has any such obligation been recognised by the courts.[51] According to the DFLA, in addition to the right to personal contact, the parents would also have a duty to engage in such contact with the child (clause 143(1) DFLA).

A parent's right to contact with the child is not extinguished when the child is removed from the parent, since removal of the child does not automatically entail a suspension of parental rights. Even if a parent's parental rights have been suspended, a guardianship authority may permit the parent to visit with his or her child if this does not have a negative influence on the child (section 55(2) FLA). No specification is provided in the law of the scope of the right to contact in such a case either.

49 Unofficial translation, revised for the purposes of this work—transl.
50 See judgment of 21 March 2007 of the Civil Chamber of the Supreme Court in case 3-2-1-13-07.
51 See judgment of 1 March 2007 of the Civil Chamber of the Supreme Court in case 3-2-1-4-07.

Although the CPA provides for the right of a child to contact with close relatives, relevant statutes do not provide a similar right to those relatives. There is currently no basis in the law for persons other than parents to demand an opportunity to exercise their right to contact with the child. Although the persons in question may in fact have that right (for instance, if they have been appointed the child's guardian), there is no express basis in the law for them to demand a possibility to exercise their right.

In conclusion, in accordance with Principle 3:25(1), children in Estonia have the right to contact with their parents, except for cases in which such contact is harmful to the child, and parents have the right to contact with their child, provided that the parent's parental rights have not been suspended. A child is also guaranteed the right to have contact with close relatives, if this does not have a harmful influence on the child, whereas close relatives are not attributed a corresponding right by law. While this may ensure the application in Estonian of the recommendation of Principle 3:25(2), it need not be entirely compatible with it. Since the law does not expressly provide for the right of the child to have contact with other persons, or the right of other persons having a close relationship with the child to have contact with the child, Principle 3:25(3) does not appear to be recognised in Estonian legislation.

In Estonian practice, the right to have contact means, similar to the recommendation in Principle 3:26, that a child stays for a limited period of time with or meets a person holding parental responsibilities, and includes any other form of communication. However, no specific provisions have to date been enacted to define or regulate contact or communication.

5.2. CONTACT ARRANGEMENTS

By virtue of Article 26 of the Constitution, government agencies, local authorities and their officials are prohibited from interfering with the private or family life of a person, unless interference is authorised by statute and takes place in a manner provided in statute with the aim of protecting public health, public morals, public policy or the rights and freedoms of other people, or serves the purpose of preventing a crime, or apprehending a criminal. This means that a competent authority may only intervene in arrangements concerning contacts between parent and child in the cases provided by law.

Parents are free to make contact arrangements on their own, taking into account the needs of the child and those of their own. Nevertheless, a parent should have regard to the interests of the child and refrain from exercising parental rights in a way contrary to those interests (section 50(4) FLA). An eventual dispute concerning the parents' difference of opinion regarding the manner in which the parent living apart should participate in the raising of the child and have contact with the child, may be settled by a guardianship authority or, at the request of a parent, by a court (section 52(2) FLA). In determining the dispute, the authority or court must give priority to the interests of the child (section 58 FLA). With regard to determinations of contact arrangements, the law does not provide any criteria other than the interests of the child. The Supreme Court of Estonia has found that contact arrangements must guarantee the right of the child and of the parent living separately from the child to have contact with each other to the extent that corresponds to the interests of the child and allows the child living separately from one of the parents to maintain a personal relationship and contact with both parents.[52] A variety of facts have been accepted as relevant in current judicial practice. These include the parents' character, their previous performance of parental duties, the relationships in the parents' new families, the living conditions and amenities in their homes, and also the age and the wishes of the child.

If the child's contacts with the parents appear to be contrary to the child's interests and are likely to harm the child, the competent authority may refuse to permit a parent to have contact with the child, or impose significant restrictions on such contact. The law does not provide specific grounds for resorting to these measures. The Supreme Court has found that if a child and a parent lack the desire to have contact with each other, this may constitute grounds for limiting the right to contact. However, a desire of the parent living with the child to prevent the other parent from having contact with the child does not constitute such grounds. In addition, grounds for limiting the right to contact may also lie in the fact that a parent's previous behaviour (for instance, the fact that the parent has threatened the child with violence) has given rise to a reasonable doubt that justifies an assumption that it would be against the best interests of the child to have direct contact with that parent.[53]

Since the holders of parental responsibilities can determine the matter of contact with the child by mutual agreement, Principle 3:27(1) appears to be applied in Estonia. At the same time, in principle, in determining contact arrangements in Estonia, an evaluation must be made as to the potential harm that this may cause to the child (Principle 3:28). Yet, there is currently no efficient oversight mechanism in regard to the parents' agreements regarding contact with the child (Principle 3:27(2)).

---

52 See judgment of 21 March 2007 of the Civil Chamber of the Supreme Court in case 3-2-1-13-07.
53 *Ibid.*

5.3. BREACH OF THE RIGHT TO CONTACT

A parent with whom a child resides should not obstruct the other parent's contact with the child (section 52(1) FLA). If one of the parents is obstructing the other parent's exercise of his or her right to contact with the child, the parent whose interests are being prejudiced may seek a determination of contact arrangements by a competent authority. In principle, it would appear to be possible to request an order to change the child's residence. This, of course, should be in the child's interests.[54]

Persons other than the parents have not been expressly granted any right by law to request an order of contact arrangements allowing them to have contact with the child.

6. DELEGATION OF PARENTAL RESPONSIBILITIES

The legislation in force in Estonia does not expressly allow specific parental rights and duties to be attributed to third parties. In certain cases, however, it is possible for a court to appoint a guardian to a child, as an additional statutory representative of the child beside the child's parents. As for the DFLA, its drafters propose to create an institution of special guardianship (for details, see section 3.3. above).

7. TERMINATION OF PARENTAL RESPONSIBILITIES

The responsibilities of a parent vis-à-vis a child cease when the child attains majority,[55] is adopted (section 86(3) FLA)[56] or dies (section 6(1) GPCCA). These grounds of termination of parental rights and duties are also listed in Principle 3:30. The difference between Principle 3:30 and the current legal situation in Estonia, as well as the situation intended to result from a reform of the relevant statutes proposed in the DFLA, consists in the fact that parents' responsibilities in respect of a child will no longer automatically cease upon the child contracting marriage.[57] In the case of a minor who is at least 15 years of age, section 9 GPCCA permits a court to extend the limited legal capacity of the minor to an extent that may substantively signify recognition of full legal capacity. An extension like this may be ordered in the case of the minor contracting marriage. However, starting

---

54 See section 9, *infra*: Procedural issues.

55 By virtue of s. 8 (2) GPCCA, full legal capacity is enjoyed by persons who have attained majority (18 years of age).

56 The recommendation of Principle 3:30(2) finds expression in ss. 86 (3)-(4) FLA.

57 In addition to marriage, Principle 3:30(1)(b) also mentions registered partnerships, a concept not recognised in current Estonian law.

on 1 July 2002, when a new version of the GPCCA entered into force, full legal capacity can no longer be acquired automatically upon marriage.[58]

8. DISCHARGE OF PARENTAL RESPONSIBILITIES

Suspension of parental rights is governed by section 54 FLA.

At the request of a parent or guardian, or of a guardianship authority, a court may suspend a parent's parental rights if the parent:

1) does not fulfil his or her duties in raising or caring for a child due to an addiction to alcoholic beverages, narcotics or psychotropic substances, or due to other reasons that the court does not regard as valid; or
2) abuses parental rights; or
3) is cruel to the child; or
4) exerts a negative influence on a child in another manner; or
5) without good reason, has for at least a year failed to participate in the raising of a child who has been placed in a child care institution.

The list of grounds provided in section 54(1) FLA is not exhaustive. In the case of a dispute, the courts should give priority to the interests of the child.

By virtue of currently applicable legislation, a court may suspend a parent's responsibilities vis-à-vis a child if the parent has abused parental rights, or has unlawfully and intentionally or negligently failed to fulfil parental duties in respect of the child. For instance, a parent's failure to fulfil his or her duties in raising the child may take the form of leaving the child without care and supervision, i.e. an intentional omission to comply with his or her duties as a parent.

Parental responsibilities will not be suspended in cases in which the parent was unable to discharge his or her duties in respect of the child as a matter of fact, that is,the parent's failure to discharge those duties was neither intentional nor negligent. For instance, this may be the case in situations where failure to take proper care of the child is caused by the parent's health problems.

Yet, the FLA does not provide for limiting a parent's right to represent the child in a situation where the parent acts in a way detrimental to the property interests of

[58] See pp. 3–4 of the explanatory letter to the DFLA (detailed reference *supra* note 4). As a matter of fact, the expected birth of a child does not constitute such grounds, since in that case it is not the interests of an underage parent that have priority. For an argument in support of this position, see VARUL ET AL. (*supra* note 25), p. 102.

the child (dissipates the child's property), but does not pose any risk to the child or to the child's health or well-being.

In applying section 54(1)(4) FLA, the courts have noted that, for the most part, parents exert negative influence on their children through the example of their own behaviour and habits. A parent's wandering and morally loose lifestyle is bound to affect the child, who is likely to pick up the habits of the parents and thus end up in conflict with generally accepted standards of social behaviour. This is, for instance, the case where, due to insufficient parental care and supervision, a child has taken to wandering and stealing.[59]

The courts have also found that the fact that a person is missing, or serving a prison sentence, does not consitute valid grounds excusing failure to fulfil parental responsibilities. A parent who has been the subject of a criminal sanction still remains responsible for raising his or her child and caring for the child. The mere possibility that the parent serving a criminal sentence might exert a harmful influence on the child should not be regarded as grounds for suspending parental responsibilities.

In a judgment delivered in case 3-2-1-4-07,[60] the Civil Chamber of the Supreme Court has noted that:

> [...] suspending a parent's responsibilities vis-à-vis a child constitutes an extreme remedy whose purpose is to protect the interests of the child. A consequence of the suspension of parental responsibilities is that the person in whose respect this is ordered loses all rights vis-à-vis the child (section 55(1) FLA). The intended meaning of the law is not to punish the parent by a suspension of his or her parental rights, but to protect the child against a parent who, without valid grounds, has failed to fulfil parental duties properly, or whose actions prejudiced the child's interests. By virtue of section 50(2) FLA, a parent is a statutory representative of the child and as such enjoys the authority of a guardian. Being a statutory representative of the child, the parent is authorised to act in the name of the child. Thus, one of the aims served by suspending a parent's parental responsibilities is to prevent the parent from acting for the child.

Under section 54(1)(1), the mere fact that a parent has failed to fulfil the duty to maintain a child does not constitute grounds for suspension of parental responsibilities. For the purposes of the provision in question, failure to fulfil parental duties in caring for the child primarily denotes a parent's total lack of interest in the life of the child, and an absence of contact with the child.

---

59 See judgment of 18 October 2001 by Ida-Viru County Court in case 2-767/2001 (in Estonian), accessible via the database of court judgments at http//:kola.just.ee.

60 Judgment of 1 March 2007 by the Civil Chamber of the Supreme Court in case 3-2-1-4-07.

The negative influence referred to in section 54(1)(4) FLA does not have to take the form of a parent's violent or threatening behaviour with respect to the child himself or herself. The criteria established in the provision will also be fulfilled by the parent acting in a violent or threatening manner, in respect of persons with whom the child has a close relationship, understandable to the child.[61]

The FLA, as amended to date, does not provide for partial suspension of parental responsibilities which is recommended in Principle 3:32. Section 53 FLA only provides the possibility of imposing specific limitations on particular aspects of a parent's rights.

By virtue of section 53 FLA, at the request of a parent or guardian, or of a guardianship authority, a court may decide to remove a child from one or both parents without suspension of parental rights, provided leaving the child with the parents would risk the child's life or limb.

The possibility of partial, as well as of full suspension of a parent's right of custody is proposed in clauses 134(3) and 135(2) DFLA. Compared to currently applicable rules, the DFLA provides a more flexible regime, allowing amongst other things, the suspension of only custody of property, leaving the parent with custody of the child's person.

A court may suspend a parent's parental responsibilities at the request of the other parent or guardian, or of a guardianship authority (section 54(1) FLA). Unlike the legislation currently applicable in Estonia, Principle 3:33(1)(a) recommends that it should also be possible for the child, and any institution protecting the interests of the child to request the suspension of parental responsibilities of a parent. The wording of Principle 3:33(1)(a) –"any institution" – is broader than that of section 54(1) FLA "a guardianship authority". According to the DFLA, public servants, officials employed by a local council, police officers, judges, prosecutors, notaries public, bailiffs, teachers or other persons who have information regarding a child at risk should notify a court, or the executive board of the local council in whose jurisdiction the child resides, of any risks to a child's well-being.

Under the FLA currently in force, courts are not authorised to suspend a parent's parental responsibilities of their own motion, as recommended by Principle 3:3(2). The authority of the courts in this respect will increase when the DFLA is enacted.

By virtue of section 55(2) FLA, a guardianship authority may permit a parent whose parental rights have been suspended, to visit with his or her child if this does not have a negative influence on the child.

---

61 Unofficial translation prepared for the purposes of the present chapter —transl.

At the request of a person whose parental responsibilities have been suspended, a court may reinstate those responsibilities with respect to a child if the person in question has improved his or her conduct, desires to exercise parental responsibilities properly and is capable of doing so. In hearing an application for reinstatement of parental responsibilities, the court should invite a relevant guardianship authority to provide its opinion in the matter. Parental rights should not be reinstated if the child has been adopted in the meantime (sections 56(1), (2) and (3) FLA).

The above-mentioned rules of the FLA do not give priority to the best interests of the child, as has been done in Principle 3:34. According to clause 123(2) DFLA, measures restricting a parent's right of custody should be lifted as soon as the child's interests are no longer in jeopardy.

9. PROCEDURAL ISSUES

9.1. COMPETENT AUTHORITIES

As a rule, disputes concerning the responsibilities of a child's parents, the child's residence and contact with the child are dealt with by the courts. A child's residence and arrangements for contact with the child are determined by court order, as is suspension of parental responsibilities. In addition to courts, certain responsibilities in this respect have been attributed to guardianship authorities. Matters of contact with a child (section 52 FLA) may be determined by a guardianship authority, which is also empowered to decide whether to allow a parent whose parental responsibilities have been suspended, to have contact with his or her child (section 55(2) FLA). Similarly, a guardianship authority is entitled to remove a child from his or her parent before obtaining a corresponding judicial order (section 53(2) FLA). The authority is also under a duty to take responsibility for the living arrangements of a child deprived of parental care (sections 53(3), 54(4) and 91(4) FLA and section 25(2) SWA).

In judicial proceedings concerning a child, courts must work hand in hand with the relevant guardianship authority. A relevant guardianship authority is often requested to provide its opinion. The relevant authority is required to provide an opinion in matters concerning suspension or reinstatement of a parent's parental rights (sections 54–56 FLA), and in relation to applications for interim relief brought in proceedings concerning a child (sections 384(4) and 551(2) CCP). In other matters concerning children, it is left to the court's discretion whether to invite the relevant authority to participate or not. In hearing a dispute concerning a child, a court should, if it appears necessary, invite a relevant guardianship authority to provide its opinion in the matter (section 59 FLA). In proceedings concerning a minor, or a guardianship relationship, a court must invite the relevant guardianship authority to provide its opinion (section 552(2) CCP).

If a guardianship authority has been invited to participate in the proceedings, it must establish the circumstances of the child and parents concerned. Often, the authority will provide a proposal for how the dispute should be dealt with.

Since all decisions on parental responsibilities are taken by a judicial or administrative body and there is a possibility for the courts to appoint a competent authority to investigate the circumstances of the child and his or her parents, Principle 3:35 appears to be fully recognised in Estonian law.

As regards the review of orders or agreements regarding parental responsibilities, the law does not provide any specific grounds the presence of which would require a review of a legally effective decision. Determinations entered in disputes concerning children are made for an unspecified period of time. This means that neither the court nor the guardianship authority concerned are obligated to review those determinations after the passing of any given period of time. Furthermore, there is no express provision in the law to force a review of a determination the underlying facts of which have changed. Still in practice a change in the facts may constitute grounds for a reconsideration of the issue and for varying the terms of any orders previously made, with a view to ensuring that the interests of the child are not prejudiced. Should parents have reached an agreement in matters concerning their child, the court, acting on an application of one of the parents, may nevertheless at any time reconsider its terms and enter a new ruling in the matter, regardless of the time that has elapsed since the agreement was concluded, or regardless of whether the facts have changed in the meantime or not.

9.2. ALTERNATIVE DISPUTE RESOLUTION MECHANISMS

In family disputes, an ADR tradition is only starting to develop in Estonia.[62] As a rule, disputes concerning children for the most part end up in the courts. It should be pointed out, however, that amongst other things, Estonian civil courts are under a duty to steer the parties – also the parties to a dispute concerning a child – towards settlement. During proceedings, a civil court must take all possible measures to settle the case or a part of it by compromise or other agreement of the parties if this is reasonable in the view of the court. For such purpose, the court may, amongst other things, present a draft contract of compromise to the parties or request that the parties appear before the judge in person, or propose

---

62 KOVE, V., "Tsiviilvaidluste kohtuväline lahendamine Eestis" [Extrajudicial resolution of disputes pertaining to civil law in Estonia], *Juridica* 2005, 3, pp. 152–166.

that the parties settle the dispute out of court or call upon the assistance of a conciliator (section 4(4) CCP). In proceedings that concern a child, the court must try, as early as possible and at each stage of the proceedings, to steer the parties towards settling their dispute by mutual agreement. The court should hear the parties as early as possible and draw their attention to the possibility of seeking the assistance of a family counsellor with a view to, above all, reaching an understanding with respect to taking care of and assuming responsibility for the child. The court may suspend proceedings concerning a child if this does not result in a delay that might prejudice the interests of the child and if the parties agree to take part in extra-judicial counselling or if, in the court's view, there are prospects to settle the dispute by way of mutual agreement of the parties due to another reason (section 561 CCP).

Conciliation proceedings are only required under Estonian law in cases of breach of arrangements regarding contact with the child. If the parent living with the child exercises his or her rights in a manner contrary to the interests of the child, and obstructs contacts between the child and the parent living separately from the child, that is, breaches the contact arrangements ordered by a court, or creates obstacles to the observation of those arrangements, the other parent is entitled to initiate a conciliation proceeding to resolve the dispute concerning the child by mutual agreement. During this proceeding, the court will take up with the parents the effects of an absence of contact with the child on the child's well-being, and will draw the parents' attention to enforcement measures that may be imposed to ensure compliance with the court's order, including a limitation or suspension of the right to have contact with the child, and to the possibility of having recourse to the assistance of a family counsellor. If this proceeding fails to bring about an agreement between the parents regarding contact arrangements, or regarding recourse to family counselling, or if one or both parents fail to appear at the hearing, the court will declare the conciliation proceeding failed and make an order regarding the measures to be imposed to compel compliance with the previous order. In the order, the court may also vary the terms of any previous order regarding contact arrangements, and make any adjustment that it sees fit in the responsibilities of the parent vis-à-vis the child. If conciliation fails the court is entitled to warn the parties of the possibility of a fine, or order one. The court may also vary the arrangements for contact with the child, or change the details of the legal relationship between the child and the parent (section 563 CCP).[63] Obligatory conciliation proceedings are not prescribed by law in any other matters.

On the basis of the above, it can be said that Principle 3:36 is recognised in Estonia, although stable ADR mechanisms have yet to emerge.

63 See judgment of 21 March 2007 of the Civil Chamber of the Supreme Court in case 3-2-1-13-07.

9.3. THE POSITION OF A CHILD IN PROCEEDINGS

In hearing a dispute concerning a child, a court or a guardianship authority must give priority to the interests of the child, and consider the wishes of the child if he or she is at least 10 years of age. The wishes of a child younger than 10 years of age should also be considered if the level of development of the child allows it (section 58 FLA).

In a matter pertaining to the rights of a parent vis-à-vis a child, the court should hear the child if he or she is at least seven years of age and of sufficient capacity to exercise discretion and volition, provided the child's wishes, relationships or choices are relevant to the adjudication of the matter, or if this is clearly necessary for a clarification of the facts. When a child is to be heard, he or she must be informed of the object and potential outcome of the proceedings unless this would clearly entail harmful consequences to the development or upbringing of the child. The child should be given an opportunity to state his or her views. The court may only refuse to hear the child if cogent reasons speak against it (section 559 CCP).[64]

The law does not impose any limitations as to the place or manner of hearing a child. The hearing may take place in the courthouse or outside it, i.e. in an environment that the child is accustomed to and in a manner that corresponds to the level of maturity of the child.[65]

Since the court or guardianship authority must hear the child directly in all proceedings concerning parental responsibilities, provided the maturity of the child permits it and unless there is a cogent reason to refrain from hearing the child, Estonian law appears to be in harmony with Principle 3:37.

In addition to being heard, the child should also be recognised as a party in any proceedings that concern him or her. Since under the rules of civil procedure applicable in Estonia, a child is not deemed to have the legal capacity required to represent himself or herself in judicial proceedings, he or she must act through

64 The Estonian Parliament has recently concluded the first reading of a draft Act that proposes to reintroduce the 10-years age limit for mandatory hearing of children in judicial proceedings. One of the reasons given for the proposal is that the level of development of children of similar age may vary widely. See the draft Act to Amend the Code of Civil Procedure and Other Related Statutes (parliamentary reference: 194 SE I), and its explanatory letter (both in Estonian), accessible at www.riigikogu.ee (last viewed on 3 November 2008).

65 See LIIV, *supra* note 26, pp. 257–261. According to a proposed reform of the CCP, the court should hear a child in an environment to which the child is accustomed. If necessary, the child should be heard in the presence of a psychiatrist, psychologist or social worker. The court may allow other persons to be present as well, provided the child or his or her representative does not object to it. See also previous footnote.

a representative. A minor of at least 15 years of age may participate in judicial proceedings together with his or her legal representative (section 202(3) CCP) and a child of up to 14 years of age and of sufficient capacity to exercise discretion and volition may, in relation to a petition pertaining to his or her person in a family matter, file an appeal against a ruling on that petition without the assistance of his or her legal representative (section 553(1) CCP).

As a rule, children are represented in judicial proceedings by the parents, who are their statutory representatives. In disputes concerning parental responsibilities, the court should appoint a representative to the child concerned, since the interests of the child may be different from those of at least one of his or her statutory representatives, i.e. the parents. A court-appointed representative is also required in proceedings as a result of which an order of measures to ensure the well-being of a child may be made that involves removing the child from his or her family (or from a foster family or from any other person entitled to contact with the child), or suspending a parent's parental rights (sections 219(2)(1), 219 (2)(3) and 219(2)(4) CCP). In this question, Principle 3:38 appears to be duly recognised in Estonian law.

9.4. ENFORCEMENT OF AGREEMENTS AND ORDERS

Naturally, it would be best if parents would voluntarily comply with the terms of an agreement they have reached or an order made by a competent authority. If a parent fails to do that, it is possible to bring enforcement proceedings against him or her. Nevertheless, compulsory enforcement is only available in cases of judgments that have become final, or judgments that contain an order of immediate execution. An agreement between the parents does not qualify for compulsory enforcement. There are also doubts regarding the enforceability of contact arrangements approved by a guardianship authority (section 2(1) CEP).

By law, the courts are not obliged, of their own motion, to include an order of immediate execution in a judgment concerning a child. However, they may do this if a party to the case so requests.[66] In such a case it is possible to execute the judgment before it has become final (section 467 CCP). A still more expeditious means of obtaining execution of a ruling concerning a child is to request an interim relief order during proceedings or even before the opening of those proceedings.[67] In a family matter, the court may, for the time of the proceedings, make an order dealing with the following: the rights of the parents vis-à-vis

66 Amendments are currently being considered that would bar the inclusion of orders of immediate execution in judgments concerning children.

67 As for the rules of interim relief, no amendments have been proposed so far.

their child, the contact of parent and child, the surrender of a child to the other parent, or other matters, related to marriage and the family, that need to be settled expeditiously due to the circumstances (section 378(3) CCP). Interim relief orders are normally made on a request from a party. If circumstances are revealed in a case that suggest a risk to the well-being of a child, the court may make an order dealing with the disputed legal relationship on the basis of an application by a relevant guardianship authority, regardless of whether or not a petition for interim relief has been filed (section 384(5) CCP). This means that the law allows immediate execution of a ruling entered in respect of a child – which shows recognition of Principle 3:39(1).

Enforcement proceedings may be brought on the basis of a judgment that has become final, or contains an order of immediate execution. In a matter concerning the return of a child and the right to contact with a child, a bailiff must perform any act of compulsory enforcement in the presence of a representative of the local authority in whose jurisdiction the child resides or, as an exception, in the presence of the person who is the subject of enforcement proceedings. The representative of the local authority must have received special training in how to communicate with a child. Where an enforcement debtor obstructs enforcement, the bailiff should, if this is requested by the enforcement creditor, ask that the competent court impose a fine on the debtor. If necessary, a bailiff may raise, with a representative of the local authority in whose jurisdiction the child resides or, as an exception, with a representative of the local authority in whose jurisdiction the enforcement debtor resides, the matter of placing a child, on a temporary basis, in a children's social welfare institution. A bailiff should not use force in respect of a child or a debtor obligated to return the child or to allow contact with the child (section 179 CEP). The law does not provide any grounds the presence of which would entitle a bailiff to refuse enforcement of a ruling entered in respect of a child. This suggests that in Estonia, Principle 3:39(2) is not recognised, since the bailiff may not refuse enforcement even if it appears manifestly contrary to the best interests of the child.

Although the law allows the use of enforcement proceedings to obtain compliance with arrangements regarding contact with the child, the Supreme Court of Estonia has noted that, as a rule, court-ordered contact arrangements cannot be executed by way of enforcement proceedings, because in such cases the law provides for a mandatory conciliation proceeding,[68] the failure of which may, amongst other things, expose the parents to a fine. Therefore, compulsory enforcement should be primarily employed to obtain compliance with an order imposing a fine, and

68 See section 9(2): Alternative dispute resolution mechanisms.

should not be used to compel a meeting between parent and child in accordance with the contact arrangements ordered by a court.[69]

10. SUMMARY

The draft Act to reform Estonian family law proposes to enact a concept of parental responsibilities that is essentially similar to the one defined by experts of the Council of Europe and the regulation is more detailed than the Estonian law in force, and meets the requirements of the definition of parental responsibilities stated in Principle 3:1 CEFL.

The attribution of parental responsibilities does not depend on separation of the parents, divorce or annulment of marriage. It only depends on whether the parent is recognised as a parent in law. The fact that the parents are, or are not, married does not alter the scope of either parent's responsibilities, which is in harmony with Principles 3:8 and 3:10 CEFL. The FLA does not contain any rules that would expressly alter the scope of responsibilities of either parent in a situation where the parents live separately and the child resides with one of them. According to the DFLA, custody would be exercised in general by the parents jointly. Custody may be attributed to a parent solely only to the extent that that parent actually takes part in raising the child. The DFLA proposes to extend the concept of parental decision-making authority to cases in which parents, although separated, have retained joint custody. This means that the responsibilities of the parent raising the child would, regardless of the fact of joint custody, be somewhat broader in scope than those of the parent who also has custody but lives separately from the child. In essence, the parent raising the child would be entitled to decide everyday matters concerning the child without consulting the other parent.

The legislation in force in Estonia does not recognise the notions of joint and sole parental responsibility. By law, the responsibilities of the parents are equal, regardless of whether they are living together or not. Where possible, parental responsibilities should be exercised jointly – as recommended by Principle 3:11 CEFL. Yet, the law does not specify whether and when a parent is entitled to

---

69 See judgment of the Civil Chamber of the Supreme Court of 21 March 2007 in case 3-2-1-13-07. Since the law is not clear as to whether and how bailiffs should enforce orders concerning children, amendments have been tabled that will clarify the law and guarantee due consideration of the interests of the child in enforcement proceedings. It does not appear right to vest (sole) authority for enforcing the orders in question in the bailiffs. It is clear that force may not, as a rule, be used in respect of children and that any problems concerning them should be dealt with by working with their parents. If conciliation proceedings fail, enforcement of orders concerning children should be supervised by a competent child protection worker, acting beside or instead of a bailiff. See Explanatory Letter to the draft Act to Amend the Code of Civil Procedure and Other Related Statutes, p. 38 (in Estonian).

determine a matter concerning the child without regard to the views of the other parent, and on what basis to resolve disputes that may arise when parents fail to agree on a matter concerning their child. No clear position has emerged in judicial practice either. Thus, the application of Principles 3:12—3:15 CEFL in Estonia is currently not guaranteed. The DFLA proposals are here more detailed.

The legislation in force in Estonia does not expressly allow specific parental rights and duties to be attributed to third parties. The practice of the courts suggests that in addition to situations where the child is left without parents recognised as such in law, a guardian can also be appointed in a situation where the child has a parent or both parents. This is in accordance with the recommendation expressed in Principle 3:17 of the CEFL, but according to Estonian law in certain cases, the right to represent a child may be exercised on an equal legal footing by the child's parents and a third party.

Unlike Principle 3:19(1), Estonian legislation compared to the draft law (see eg. cl. 125 DFLA on education) does not recognise the child's distinctive character and developmental needs as specific criteria to be taken into account when giving effect to the principle.

Additionally, there is no express prohibition in Estonian legislation of corporal punishment in relation to children. The rules proposed in the DFLA and the proposals made to reform the CPA appear compatible with Principle 3:19(2) CEFL.

For the most part, the family legislation in force in Estonia (section 50 FLA) is similar to Principle 3:19 CEFL.

Regarding the rules governing determination of the child's residence, the Estonian law is not yet compatible with Principles 3:20 and 3:21 CEFL. It should be pointed out further that the DFLA does not propose to introduce any significant details in the rules governing determination of the child's residence in cases where the parents live separately but continue to exercise joint custody.

Both the FLA and the DFLA recognise the parent as a statutory representative of the child – which allows a parent to act for his or her child in matters concerning the child's person and property. In this regard, the family legislation currently in force in Estonia complies with the principles proposed by the CEFL (cf. Principle 3:24). The prohibition of statutory representation in the case of a conflict of interests between the child and the person exercising parental responsibility by virtue of statutory provisions is provided in section 100 FLA, in certain respects even in more detail than in the Principles of the CEFL. This prohibition is retained in the DFLA.

On the other hand the FLA does not impose an obligation on parents to manage the child's property with due care, to ensure that it does not lose in value, and to increase its value when possible. In accordance with Principle 3:22(1) CEFL, the DFLA proposes such rules.

Also the DFLA includes a corresponding provision to Principle 3:22(3) CEFL, which recommends that it should be possible to use income derived from the child's property for the needs of the family, if it is not needed for the proper management of the property or for the maintenance and education of the child, and if it is necessary to use it for the family's needs.

The recommendation in Principle 3:23(2) CEFL, that the child's earnings should not be administered by the holders of parental responsibilities unless the child is not of sufficient age and maturity to decide their use himself or herself, is not fully reflected in the legislation in force in Estonia. As for the FLA, it does not deal with the matter at all.

Similar to the recommendation in Principle 3:23(3) CEFL (where transactions can have significant financial consequences for the child, and the authorisation of the competent authority should be necessary for those transactions to be performed), the restrictions listed in section 99(1) FLA, require previous consent of a guardianship authority in order for the corresponding transactions to be valid. Under the terms of the DFLA, the authorisation of a court would be made mandatory in order to perform the transaction. A parent, however, would not be required to obtain authorisation in all of the cases in which this should be done by a guardian. For transactions that a parent is not authorised to perform in the child's name, a special guardian would have to be appointed.

In accordance with Principle 3:25(1) CEFL, children in Estonia have the right to contact with their parents, except for cases in which such contact is harmful to the child, and parents have the right to contact with their child, provided that the parent's parental rights have not been suspended. A child is also guaranteed the right to have contact with close relatives, if this does not have a harmful influence on the child, whereas close relatives are not attributed a corresponding right by law. While this may ensure the application in Estonia of the recommendation of Principle 3:25(2) CEFL, it need not be entirely compatible with it. Since the law does not expressly provide for the right of the child to have contact with other persons, or the right of other persons having a close relationship with the child to have contact with the child, Principle 3:25(3) CEFL does not appear to be recognised in Estonian legislation.

In Estonian practice, the right to have contact means, similar to the recommendation in Principle 3:26 CEFL, that a child stays for a limited period of time with or meets a person holding parental responsibilities, and includes any other form of communication. However, no specific provisions have to date been enacted to define or regulate contact or communication.

Since the holders of parental responsibilities can determine the matter of contact with the child by mutual agreement, Principle 3:27(1) CEFL appears to be applied in Estonia. At the same time, in principle, in determining contact arrangements in Estonia, an evaluation must be made as to the potential harm that this may cause to the child (Principle 3:28 CEFL). Yet, there is currently no efficient oversight mechanism in regard to the parents' agreements regarding contact with the child (Principle 3:27(2)).

The responsibilities of a parent vis-à-vis a child cease when the child attains majority or dies. These grounds of termination of parental rights and duties are also listed in Principle 3:30 CEFL. The difference between Principle 3:30 and the current legal situation in Estonia, as well as the situation intended to result from a reform of the relevant statutes proposed in the DFLA, consists in the fact that parents' responsibilities in respect of a child will no longer automatically cease upon the child contracting marriage.

The FLA, as amended to date, does not provide for partial suspension of parental responsibilities which is recommended in Principle 3:32 CEFL. The FLA only provides the possibility of imposing specific limitations on particular aspects of a parent's rights. The possibility of partial, as well as of full suspension of a parent's right of custody is proposed in the DFLA. Compared to currently applicable rules, the DFLA provides a more flexible regime, allowing amongst other things, for instance, to suspend only custody of property, leaving the parent with custody of the child's person.

As all decisions on parental responsibilities are taken by a judicial or administrative body and there is a possibility for the court to appoint a competent authority to investigate the child´s and parents circumstances, the CEFL Principle 3:35 is fully recognised.

The Principle 3:36 CEFL is also recognised in Estonia, although stable ADR mechanisms have yet to emerge.

Since the court or guardianship authority must hear directly from the child in all proceedings concerning parental responsibilities, provided the maturity of the child permits it and unless there is a cogent reason to refrain from hearing the child, Estonian law appears to be in harmony with Principle 3:37 CEFL.

Estonian law allows immediate execution of a ruling entered in respect of a child – which shows recognition of Principle 3:39(1) CEFL.

The law does not provide any grounds the presence of which would entitle a bailiff to refuse enforcement of a ruling entered in respect of a child. This suggests that in Estonia, Principle 3:39(2) CEFL is not recognised, since the bailiff may not refuse enforcement even if it appears manifestly contrary to the best interests of the child.

PRINCIPLES RELATING TO PARENTAL RESPONSIBILITY AND AUTHORITY IN MALTA

Ruth Farrugia

1. INTRODUCTION

The Maltese law on parental authority is based on Roman Law although the law has been revised through the Code de Rohan, the Code Napoleon and a series of amendments throughout the 19th and 20th centuries.

Malta has also ratified a number of international conventions, including the United Nations Convention on the Rights of the Child, the International Covenants on Civil and Political Rights and Economic, Social and Cultural Rights, and the Hague Convention on Jurisdiction, Applicable Law, Recognition, Enforcement and Co-operation in respect of Parental Responsibility and Measures for the Protection of Children. Malta joined the EU in 2004 and is bound by EU Regulations, such as Brussels II Bis.

Parental Responsibilities is not a term used under Maltese law in the context of the relationship between parents and children. The Civil Code[1] when dealing with issues relating to the responsibilities between parents and children still uses the Roman law concept of parental authority.[2] However, although the terminology may differ, the component responsibilities salient to the concept are very much the same as those applied in other jurisdictions using the term "parental responsibility."

The law has evolved to permit the sharing of responsibility between both parents while retaining the Roman law concept of parental authority. Until 1993 parental authority was termed paternal authority and was exercised solely by the father (*patria potestas*). Malta ratified the United Nations Convention on

1 Laws of Malta, Chapter 16.

2 Laws of Malta, Chapter 16 Article 131 (1) *"A child shall be subject to the authority of his parents for all effects as by law established"*.

the Elimination of All Forms of Discrimination against Women (CEDAW) in 1991 and a commission was set up to review all legislation which discriminated against women. The articles of law dealing with paternal authority were revised and amended to reflect the notion of equality between mother and father, coming into force on the 1 December 1993.

Meanwhile, the courts have continued to help in the development of the law by interpreting articles within the changing constraints of society's demands. For instance, although the notion of joint custody was debated in Parliament prior to the enactment of Act XXI, the legislators decided that it would not be workable and opted to exclude it from the law. In practice, applications for its inclusion as a resolution of custody demands have increasingly appeared before the courts which have acceded to these requests notwithstanding the silence in the law. The courts were also instrumental in bringing about the amendment of provisions relating to discrimination between children born in and out of wedlock culminating in changes to the law through Act XIIII.2004. The influence of judgements of the European Court of Human Rights is also worth mentioning, particularly as Malta has had the right of individual petition since 1989.[3]

The Office of the Child Commissioner has spearheaded a number of initiatives including the request for a revision of child capacity to be viewed in terms of maturity and understanding rather than age. This has led to a debate relating to parental authority in terms of consent and representation on behalf of young people/children who have not attained the age of majority at 18.[4] The Opposition has also called for 16 year olds to be given the right to vote in local council elections with similar repercussions on the diminishing power of parental authority.

2. DEFINITIONS

Principle 3:1 Concept of parental responsibilities

Parental authority entails being responsible for the provision of maintenance (which under Maltese law includes food, clothing, health, habitation, education),[5]

---

3 Although only a few cases brought by Maltese nationals have referred to issues relating to parental authority. The most recent was the case of Mizzi versus Malta [Application no. 26111/02 delivered by the European Court of Human Rights on 12.01.2006] relating to the right of a man to repudiate a child beyond a peremptory prescriptive period when genetic testing otherwise proved conclusive.

4 The author is legal consultant to the Commissioner for Children.

5 Laws of Malta, Chapter 16, Article 19.

succession rights, giving the child a name (and status) through acknowledgment, and incorporates a duty of care.[6]

Apart from the more practical concepts of provision of maintenance and succession rights, the law assigns to parents the obligation to "take into account the abilities, natural inclinations and aspirations of the children" and failure to comply may result in the termination of parental authority. However in practice, this relatively recent amendment[7] is difficult to prove and the child has no *locus standi* to bring an action against the parent where there is lack of compliance.

All the components listed in the Council of Europe definition, *viz* care and protection, maintenance of personal relationships, provision of education, legal representation, determination of residence and administration of property form part of the concept of parental authority under Maltese law.

Parental authority imputes an obligation of care, protection and education to the child. Failure to provide care and protection may result in the State intervening to place the child under a Care Order in terms of the Children and Young Persons (Care Orders) Act[8] and/or in the termination of parental authority. The definition of maintenance includes education as one of the essential elements owed to children by parents.[9] Where a parent is found to "neglect the education" of the child or "if the conduct of the parent is such as to endanger the education of the child", the Court may proceed to deprive the parent of parental authority over the child.[10]

The maintenance of personal relationships forms a part of parental authority but is not one of the elements which is easily enforceable. Although as a general rule, parents are anxious to spend as much time as they can with their children, there

---

6 Laws of Malta, Chapter 16, Article 3B.

7 The notion was introduced through Act XXI.1993.

8 Laws of Malta, Chapter 285.

9 Laws of Malta, Chapter 16, Article 19:
(1) *Maintenance shall include food, clothing, health and habitation.*
(2) In regard to children and other descendants, it shall also include the expenses necessary for health and education.

10 Laws of Malta, Chapter 16, Article 154(1):
Saving any other punishment to which he may be liable according to law, a parent may be deprived, by the said court, wholly or in part, of the rights of parental authority, in any of the cases following:
(a) if the parent, exceeding the bounds of reasonable chastisement, ill-treats the child, or neglects his education;
(b) if the conduct of the parent is such as to endanger the education of the child;
(c) if the parent is interdicted [articles 520 to 527 inclusive of the COCP and articles 189,190 CC];
(d) if the parent mismanages the property of the child;
(e) if the parent fails to perform any of the obligations set out in article 3B in favour of the child.

are cases where parents, particularly following marriage breakdown, become estranged from their children or choose not to pursue a personal relationship with them for a variety of factors.[11] The courts only intervene when an order is made determining contact which is not honoured as this may have penal repercussions.[12]

Parents in virtue of their parental authority decide where the child is to reside. According to Article 131(2):[13]

> Saving any other provision of law respecting enlistment in any disciplined force, it shall not be lawful for a child, without the consent of the parents, to leave the parental house, or such house as his parents may have appointed for him. (3) Where the child leaves the house without such consent, the parents shall have the right to recall him, and, if necessary, demand the assistance of the Police.

It is however possible for the court to authorise the child to leave the parental home[14] and to respond to an application by parents for the child to be removed to alternative accommodation.[15] In the case of children born out of wedlock the law retains an outdated discrimination in permitting the parent "to deny maintenance to the child, if such child refuses to live in the house which the parent for just cause ... has appointed for his habitation".[16]

---

11 In court proceedings these are cited as including, the formation of an alternative family, the lack of support or reluctance to include the child by the new partner, the attitude of the custodial/primary parent, alienation, etc.

12 Laws of Malta, Chapter 9, Article 338.

13 Laws of Malta, Chapter 16.

14 Laws of Malta, Chapter 16, Article 132(1): *Nevertheless, it shall be lawful for the competent court as may be prescribed by or under any law in force from time to time, for just cause, and without disclosing the same, to authorize the child to leave the parental house.*

15 Laws of Malta, Chapter 16, Article 133 (1) *It shall be lawful for the parents, if they are unable to control the child, to remove him from the family, assigning to him, according to the means of the parents, such maintenance as is strictly necessary.*
(2) *In any such case, the parents may also, where necessary and upon obtaining the authority of such court ...place the child, for such time as is stated in the decree, in some alternative form of care, which the court will according to circumstances consider suitable, to be, at the expense of the parents, cared for and treated in such manner as the court may deem conducive to the discipline and education of the child.*

16 Laws of Malta, Chapter 16, Article 97: *It shall also be lawful for the parent, whether he or she has acknowledged the child or not, to deny maintenance to the child, if such child refuses to live in the house which the parent for just cause and with the approval of the court has appointed for his habitation, as also in any other case in which according to law it is competent to a parent to refuse maintenance to a child conceived or born in wedlock.*

According to Article 136(1), "parents jointly administer the property of their children."[17,18] The thrust of this article is to empower both parents to take steps independently although *in solidum* for day to day administration, but when it comes to issues deemed to be of extraordinary nature the consent of both parents is then a requisite at law.

A recent amendment has been introduced relating to the administration of insurance policies clarifying at which point parents may enter into such contracts and when children may exercise their rights independently.[19]

Legal representation of children is vested in the parents. Article 135[20] states clearly: "The parents jointly represent their children, whether born or to be born, in all civil matters."

According to the Code of Organisation and Civil Procedure, "The following persons may not sue or be sued: (a) a minor, except in the person of the parent exercising paternal authority, or, in the absence of such parent, of a tutor or a curator."[21]

---

17 Laws of Malta, Chapter 16, Article 136:
While according to subarticle (2*) Acts of ordinary administration may however be performed by either of the parents without the intervention of the other.*
and subarticle (3) *Acts of extraordinary administration which must be performed by the parents jointly include -*
(a) the alienation of movables by nature, including motor vehicles for the object of profitably investing the proceeds thereof;
(b) the collection of capitals that may become due;
(c) the granting of personal rights of enjoyment over immovable property;
(d) the acceptance of an inheritance, legacy or donation in the name of the child;
(e) the partition of movables by nature.

18 Unless the property has devolved on the child under the condition that it shall be administered solely by one of the parents or by third parties.

19 Laws of Malta, Chapter 16: Civil Code, Article 1712L: (1) *It shall be lawful for parents of a child to enter into a contract of life insurance, for the child as policyholder, in the administration of the child's property.*
(2) Any such contract may be entered into by either parent and the name of the child as policyholder shall be recorded in the policy.
(3) Payments of any proceeds under the policy, at maturity, during the term by way of withdrawals or on earlier surrender, may only be made to the parents jointly or to a bank account designated as property of the child. The provisions of article 136 shall apply to any relevant acts in relation to the life insurance policy.
(4) It shall not be lawful for the parents to designate a third party as a beneficiary of a contract of life insurance entered into for a child as policyholder.
(5) On reaching maturity the child shall be entitled to exercise all rights in relation to the policy without the need to any formality other than giving notice to the insurer and providing him with evidence of his identity and age.

20 Laws of Malta, Chapter 16.

21 10 Laws of Malta, Chapter 12, Article 781,
Vide also Article 782 *The provisions of article 781 shall not apply to -*
(a) any minor, if such child carries on trade with the consent of the parent exercising paternal

Principle 3:2 Holder of parental responsibilities

A person may have complete or partial rights and duties as defined under Principle 3:1 without being the holder of parental authority over the child. A person may be entrusted with the care of a child and be responsible for the care, protection and education of the child and for maintenance of personal relationships listed in (a) and (b) of the Principle, as in the case of foster care, without parental authority being vested in him/her.[22] For such transmission of authority to occur, the courts would have to divest the parent of parental authority in terms of the articles of the Civil Code and entrust it to an alternative person.[23] This occurs in the instance of adoption, tutorship (known as guardianship in common law jurisdictions), and in the case of the issue of a Care Order where the Minister takes on the parental authority for the child, limited to the person of the child (not the property) on the proven grounds of the child being in need of care, protection or control.[24]

Parental authority entails the provision of maintenance which includes food, clothing, health, habitation and education. It also requires the giving of a family name to the child although where there is a male parent the child must take his name and may add the family name of the mother. Recent amendments have enabled the child to retain an established name (different to that of the father) where this may prove less prejudicial to the child's well being[25].

authority even though the action touches matters not relating to trade, or if the said parent has expressly given his assent for the child to sue or be sued without his assistance;
(b) any minor in any action against the said parent provided the child is represented by a curator ad litem.
and Article 783 (1) In the cases referred to in this sub-title, the curator ad litem may be appointed by the same court before which the action has been brought, or is about to be brought, upon the application of any person interested.
(2) The application for the appointment of a curator to represent a minor who desires to sue, may be made by any person.

22 Laws of Malta, Chapter 491 Article 24: (2) *Any rights and duties pertaining to the foster carer in accordance with the foster care agreement shall not be perceived to be seen as a permanent right or duty.*
(3) The foster care agreement in terms of subarticle (1) shall be in the best interest of the child and shall provide for detailed information related to the rights and duties of the foster carer and it shall specifically include:
(a) the extent to which the foster carer may make decisions with regard to the child in his care;
(b) the frequency of contact of the child with the natural parent or parents;
(c) the child's care plan;
(d) matters of education, health and maintenance of the child; and
(e) any other matter pertinent to the child in foster care.
Article 25: *A foster carer shall ensure that the child placed in his care shall be cared for, maintained, instructed and educated according to the child's abilities, aspirations and natural inclinations. The child shall also have access to the social worker who is taking care of the placement.*

23 Laws of Malta, Chapter 16, Articles 150–156.

24 Laws of Malta, Chapter 285, Children and Young Persons (Care Orders) Act.

25 Laws of Malta Chapter 16, Article 92A: *The person giving notice of the birth shall also deliver a declaration by the parents of the child indicating the surname to be used*

Parents are responsible for their children even after attaining majority if the child never becomes able to take care of him/herself independently.[26] Any child also has the right to expect a portion of the parent's inheritance (*legitimo portio*) determined according to a number of criteria including how many children there are in the family.[27]

In order to exercise such authority parents are given the right to expect the child to obey them and to live where they decide to appoint the family home. A child may be commercially emancipated at age 16 in which case s/he is free to trade without constraints of parental involvement and without parental responsibility for the child's actions.[28] A child may marry or set up a separate domestic establishment at age 16 which also removes the obligation of the parent to continue to provide for maintenance should the parent disagree with this step and formally take proceedings to divest him/herself of the obligation.[29]

Post separation, the child may be entrusted to the care of one parent and arrangements made for contact with the other. This does not affect the rights and obligations set out under parental authority.[30] This means that both parents

---

(1) Where no such declaration is made in the case of a child conceived and born in wedlock the father's surname shall be presumed to have been so declared

(2) In the case of a child conceived and born out of wedlock the maiden surname of the mother shall be presumed to be the surname so declared in subarticle (6) so that a person whose surname is to change in virtue of the procedure of filiation, notification or application relating to the presumption may request the competent Court by means of an application against the Director of Public Registry to be permitted to use another surname.

-omissis-

(6)Where the Court decides that such use would not prejudice the rights of third parties and in the case of minor, where it is shown that this would be in the best interests of the minor, the application shall be acceded to and the Director shall be ordered to annotate the decision on the relative Act of Birth.

26 Under Maltese law, where a child has a disability which renders him/her dependent beyond the age of eighteen, parents remain liable for support and care, otherwise liability ceases on the child attaining the age of eighteen years. [Judgement of the Civil Court, First Hall, 05/11/1991: George MALLIA v Teresa MUSCAT nomine]

27 Laws of Malta, Chapter 16, Articles 615–630.

28 Laws of Malta, Chapter 13, Article 9 and Laws of Malta, Chapter 16:
Article 156(1) *Where a minor, who has attained the age of sixteen years, has been authorized under article 9 of the Commercial Code, to trade, or, not being a trader, to perform certain acts of trade, such minor shall, in regard to all matters relating to his trade, or in regard to such acts, be considered as being of age.*

29 Laws of Malta, Chapter 16, Articles 27–29.

30 Judgement of the Civil Court, First Hall, 02/10/2003, Tabone Lea proprio et nomine versus Tabone Jesmond " ... il-ġenituri ghandhom l-istess obbligi verso l-ulied taghhom, u ghalhekk it-tnejn li huma ghandhom jikkontribwixxu ghat-trobbija ta' l-istess, aktar u aktar meta llum il-mizzewgin huma f'pozizzjoni ta' ugwaljanza u ghandhom l-istess drittijiet u allura, anke skond l-artikolu 2 tal-Kap 16 "jerfghu r-responsabilitajiet indaqs matul iz-zwieg taghhom." [my informal translation : Parents have the same obligations towards their children, and therefore both are bound to contribute to their upbringing. This is even more so now today that the

remain jointly responsible for maintenance,[31] choosing the child's school, paying for school fees where applicable and attending parents' evenings, etc. Both parents are responsible for decisions taken relating to the health of the child and to any consent requirements in a medical intervention on behalf of the child. Similarly both parents are required to request and consent to the travel documents which enable a child to be removed from the jurisdiction of the Island.

On a day to day basis the custodial parent may be the sole arbiter of decisions relating to ordinary administration but they are notionally taken on behalf of both parents and any decisions relating to acts of extraordinary administration would require joint consent.

Throughout any deliberation made relating to parental authority, particularly but not exclusively, within the context of allocation of custody the court always looks to the best interests of the child as a criterion for determining its judgement. A long standing blanket section in the law supports the notion that the courts may always turn to this premise in any decision they may make where children are involved.[32]

The more usual holders of parental authority are indeed the child's parents. Persons other than the child's parents do not usually hold authority over the child, except in the cases highlighted above, i.e. following transmission in adoption (where the adopters become the parents), or following the issue of a care order where the Minister takes on the role of parental authority insofar as this affects the person of the child (but not the administration of property or legal representation in patrimonial issues). Tutors only replace parents in the exercise of parental authority where the parents are unable to do so as in the instance of their

---

spouses are in a position of equality and have the same rights and they must according to Article 2 of Chapter 16 " assume equal responsibilities during marriage"].

31 Failure to provide maintenance in terms of a court judgement which as ordered such imputes criminal sanctions under Article 338(z) of Laws of Malta Chapter 9: *when so ordered by a court or so bound by contract fails to give to his or her spouse the sum fixed by that court or laid down in the contract as maintenance for the spouse and, or, the children, within fifteen days from the day on which, according to such order or contract, such sum should be paid:*
Provided that, notwithstanding any other provision of this Code, the criminal action for an offence under this paragraph is barred by the lapse of six months.

32 Laws of Malta, Chapter 16, Article 149: *Notwithstanding any other provision of this Code, the court may, upon good cause being shown, give such directions as regards the person or the property of a minor as it may deem appropriate in the best interests of the child.*
In a judgement of the 29/05/2003 the Civil Court, First Hall, decided that in the case of Azzopardi Anthony versus Azzopardi Rita "il-kaz il-gid tat-tfal jista' jirrikjedi revizjoni tal-ftehim bejn il-partijiet, anke ghaliex l-interess suprem tat-tfal u ulied hija l-iktar haga li l-ligi u l-Qorti huma tenuti li jissalvagwardjaw u jipprovdu ghalih." [my informal translation: "the issue of the best interests of the child may necessitate a revision of the agreement between the spouses, especially because the supreme interests of the child are the most important thing in the law and the courts are bound to safeguard them and provide for them"].

death, interdiction or following the termination of parental authority for a reason contemplated at law.[33] The allocation of parental responsibility is determined by a *de jure* presumption on marriage or following an acknowledgement effected *ex parte* or following a court judgement.

Once conferred, parental authority is the same, irrespective of the status of the holder. The relationship between parent and child is governed by rules which do not consider the status of the parent other than in the forfeiture of legal usufruct over the property of the child for parents who have children outside wedlock.[34]

In practice, the exercise of parental authority among parents who do not cohabit may lead to the apportionment of the day to day obligations and rights in a way which is different to that of cohabiting parents. Therefore, for example, times and modalities of contact may have to be adjusted, decisions relating to daily events may be taken by just one parent but the legal relationship between the parent and child and the rights and obligations emanating from the institute of parental authority remain the same until they are changed by law.

Parental authority cannot be determined by the parents. It is a matter of public interest determined by law and subject to the adjudication of the courts. The allocation of responsibilities within the purview of parental authority may be distributed subject to the agreement of the parents but this must also be sanctioned by the court. If the matters relate to ordinary administration the distribution of tasks may be carried out on the agreement of the parents but if there are issues of an extraordinary nature then these require both parents to agree or to seek court intervention where consent is withheld.

Agreements relating to the exercise of parental authority are subject to court scrutiny. In fact where such agreements are concluded, failure to comply with the contents of the agreement would lead to contempt of court with the possibility of criminal detention as a penalty.

---

33 Laws of Malta, Chapter 16, Articles 150–156.

34 Laws of Malta Chapter 16, Article 90(1): *The parent who has acknowledged a child conceived and born out of wedlock shall have in regard to him all the rights of parental authority other than the legal usufruct.*

3. RIGHTS OF THE CHILD

Principle 3:3 Best interests of the child

There is no clearly identifiable definition or reference of the term "best interests" in Maltese law although numerous articles make reference to the welfare of the child, the interest or best interests of the child and on occasion they also mention that the interests of the child are of paramount consideration. Pre-1993, Section 47 spoke about the "*greater benefit*" of the child as being the "paramount consideration" substituted by the 1993 amendments to those of "the paramount consideration being the welfare of the child". "Welfare" incorporates every type of welfare ranging from physical, social, intellectual to moral welfare.

The Civil Code includes the best interests of the child principle in:

> Section 47 dealing with the custody of the children pending the action;
> Section 56(4) empowering the court to revoke or vary such directions respecting the children, where the interests of the children so require;
> Section 57(3) dealing with access or forbidding access if it is detrimental to the welfare of the children;
> Section 58(1) directs the court to suspend an action of separation in the interests of the spouses and children;
> Section 61(1) stating that agreements between the spouses respecting the custody of the children may at any time, on the demand of either of the spouses, be annulled by the competent court, in the interests of the child.

The concept of interests of the child has consistently been adjudged as a matter of great relevance in the courts. Their placement varies from their being alluded to as "paramount" or "supreme" to "important in deciding on matters which affect the family".

Within the context of separation and custody allocation, best interest is central to the decision taken by the court in allocating primary care and deciding matters relating to contact or access. Article 149 of the Civil Code empowers the court to make any provision it may deem fit in the best interests of the child: "Notwithstanding any other provision of this Code, the court may, upon good cause being shown, give such directions as regards the person or property of a minor as it may deem appropriate in the best interests of the child."

Principle 3:4 Autonomy of the child

The issue of children's rights determined in terms of maturity and understanding as opposed to age is a matter for lively debate at present. The Commissioner for

Children has raised awareness relating to this issue and drawn attention to the artificiality of imposing a set age which is often very high before a child may exercise a fundamental right to be heard.

Within the context of care and care proceedings, the opinion of the child is included at all ages so that there is no lower threshold for inclusion of the child at case conferences held by social workers or by the Children and Young Persons Advisory Board.

In relation to care by persons exercising parental authority this is regulated by the Civil Code and the authority of parents over their child lasts until the child reaches the age of 18 or until the child marries (at age 16) or is authorised to leave home.[35]

Children are invited to participate in decisions relating to their education insofar as parents invite them to do so. Parents have an obligation to send their children to school until the age of 16 which is the compulsory upper limit. In practice children are frequently encouraged to receive formal education beyond this age and are supported by a State stipend which is often supplemented by parents.[36] Student councils give children the right to be heard in matters relating to the running of their school but it has been questioned how much effective voice children are actually given in such matters. A recent launch of a new curriculum for the entire educational sector has included an invitation for feedback from children. Although children have the right to receive an education which helps them to realise their "natural inclinations and aspirations", in practice it is not possible for the child to enforce this right at law unless represented by an adult.

Religious upbringing is taken very seriously. Malta claims to be predominantly Roman Catholic and the Constitution of Malta in Article 2 sets out:

> (1) The religion of Malta is the Roman Catholic Apostolic Religion.
> (2) The authorities of the Roman Catholic Apostolic Church have the duty and the right to teach which principles are right and which are wrong.[37]

---

35 The latter two scenarios are included in the law but rarely put into practice.

36 Over 2000 persons graduated from the University of Malta in 2008 but that does not take into account higher diplomas from technical colleges and students studying with foreign universities either by distance learning or by enrolment on that campus. The population is estimated at just over 400,000 persons so this is said to make a good proportion which is ever on the increase [statistics released by University of Malta 2009 and National Office of Statistics (NSO)].

37 The Constitution of Malta, http://docs.justice.gov.mt/lom/legislation/english/leg/vol_1/chapt0.pdf.

Malta remains the only country in the EU which has not introduced divorce and where abortion is a criminal offence. However freedom of conscience is also a right enshrined in the Constitution and protected under Criminal Law.[38] Children are expected to wait until they reach the age of 18 to make any decisions about religious commitment in view of the fact that they remain subject to parental authority until they are 18 but in practice parents are more flexible in giving their children the space to make choices.

In relation to disciplinary measures and corporal punishment, children may use resources such as a State helpline to make a report or school facilities which respond to any such allegations. The Church also has its own Response Team to deal with matters of sexual abuse and has set up investigations into allegations of physical abuse against children by persons who were acting under its mandate. These persons rarely exercise parental authority but are entrusted with a duty of care for children removed from their parents. Children have the right to be heard in all such procedures. Medical and legal procedures pose some of the strongest problems when it comes to child participation and the child's right to be heard.

Principle 3:5 Non-discrimination of the child

The Principle of non-discrimination is echoed in the Constitution and reflected in legislation relating to equal opportunities and equality.[39] There are criminal sanctions against any person who commits an offence which is racially or religiously aggravated.[40]

Principle 3:6 Child's right to be heard

In the Maltese experience, a Child Advocate may be appointed within the context of marital breakdown or family proceedings.

> The job of this lawyer is to multitask: s/he must represent the child through the Court process and in any negotiations between the parents or other parties to the case; find out the child's views and make the Judge aware of them; make sure the child's best interests and all issues affecting welfare are put before the Court for its consideration;

---

38 Laws of Malta Chapter 9, Articles 163–165 relate to crimes against the religious sentiment (referring to the Roman Catholic faith) and Article 222A outlaws any offence which is "racially or religiously aggravated" where religious group means "reference to religious belief or lack of religious belief" (subarticle (6)).

39 Laws of Malta, Chapter 413, Equal Opportunities Act; Laws of Malta, Chapter 456, Gender Equality Act.

40 Laws of Malta, Chapter 9, Article 222A.

explain the Court process to the child and, at the end of the process, explain the Judge's decision.[41]

Whether this adequately serves the child's rights within a client-lawyer relationship is another matter altogether.

The Child Commissioner has started a series of consultation meetings to encourage people of all ages to become aware of the rights of children in the legal scenario. Although children have the right to be heard at age 14 in legal proceedings the courts may be reluctant to include them, citing the best interests of the child as their reason for doing so.[42]

Health issues and consent to request and refuse treatment remain a problem particularly with rising child pregnancies and a continued debate as to the right of the child to request contraception without parental consent.[43]

Where children are opposed to access or custody arrangements made on their behalf there is no possibility for them to access the court to request the changes. It has already been shown that the courts penalise parents who refuse to obey court mandated access arrangements, notwithstanding the opposition of the child(ren).

When children are heard they may be heard directly by the court, informally in the judge's chambers, by a social worker or psychologist appointed by the court, through the services of the Child Advocate who may be appointed at the request of the parents or the mediator or by the judge.

Issues relating to the confidentiality which protects children's views are currently a matter for debate. Once information is shared with the court, principles of justice demand that such information be shared with the alleged perpetrator so that s/he may answer to them. This stance has precluded a number of children from sharing information. The report made by the Child Advocate is similarly deemed to be part of the court proceedings file and any information disclosed by

41 FARRUGIA, R., "Children's Rights in Family Court Proceedings" in *The UN Children's Rights Convention: theory meets practice*, ALEN, A. ET AL (eds), (Antwerp: Intersentia, 2007), pp. 401–418.

42 FARRUGIA, R., "Achievements in taking children's rights further in civil justice: Towards European guidelines on child-friendly justice: Identifying good principles and sharing examples of good practices" as part of Council of Europe, Stockholm 2008: *Building a Europe for and with Children – Towards a Strategy for 2009–2011*, www.coe.int/T/TransversalProjects/Children/pdf/StockholmProgramme.pdf *or* http://www.crin.org/docs/Farrugia_en.doc.

43 Reminiscent of the UK decision in *Gillick v West Norfolk and Wisbech Area Health Authority* [1986] AC 112; [1985] 3 WLR 830; [1985] 3 All ER 402.

the child belongs to the domain of the court case. In these circumstances Child Advocates have started to advise children of this eventuality.

Principle 3:7 Conflict of interests

The child is represented by the parent. A Child Advocate may be appointed (as explained *supra*). Where there is a clear conflict of interest the court may decide to appoint a special curator to represent the interests of the child. For instance, this is standard practice in cases referring to contested filiation proceedings.

4. PARENTAL RESPONSIBILITIES OF PARENTS AND THIRD PERSONS

Principle 3:8 Parents

Where the parents are married to one another at the time of the child's birth both are deemed to have equal parental responsibility. The law states that they both have parental authority over the child which equates with a number of responsibilities and the right to legal usufruct over the property of the child, if applicable.

Where parents marry after the birth of their child(ren), their marriage imputes the status to a child born in wedlock although after the amendments of Act XVIII.2004 there is said to be no remaining distinction between children born in wedlock and those born out of wedlock.[44]

> Article 103. Children deemed to have been conceived or born in wedlock by subsequent marriage of their parents shall be vested with the rights of children conceived or born in wedlock as from the day of the celebration of the marriage, if they shall have been acknowledged on that day or previously, or if their filiation shall have been declared before the marriage by a judgment of the court.

---

[44] With respect, in my opinion the continued existence of Article 815 has maintained a lasting discrimination in apportionment of inheritance under intestate succession. The provision sets out an inferior right to children conceived and born out of wedlock and will probably become the ground for further litigation.
Article 815: *Where a person conceived and born out of wedlock succeeds ab intestato with adoptive children of the deceased or other children of the deceased who are not so conceived or born or descendants of such children, or with the surviving spouse of the deceased, the person conceived and born out of wedlock shall receive only three quarters of the share to which he would have been entitled if all the heirs of the deceased, including such person, had been conceived or born in wedlock, and the remaining quarter of the share to which he would have been so entitled shall devolve on the other heirs of the deceased to the exclusion of any of such heirs who is conceived and born out of wedlock as if it were a separate estate.*

Article 104. Where the acknowledgment or judicial declarator take place after the marriage, the children shall only acquire the rights of children conceived or born in wedlock as from the day of such acknowledgment or declarator.

Principle 3:9 Third persons

Parental responsibilities emanating from parental authority may be attributed to a person other than a parent in the cases set out in Principle 3:2 (2). Where parents are unable or unwilling to assume parental authority the child is accorded an alternative. A tutor may be appointed in substitution of the dead, missing or incapable parent where both parents are not in a position to exercise parental authority.[45] The tutor may be a relative of the child and the law states that it would prefer to foster such bond where possible, however, any other suitable person may be appointed by the court in the best interests of the child. [46]

The Minister for Social Policy may also undertake to exercise limited parental authority over the person (not the property) of the child through the issue of a Care Order in terms of Chapter 285 of the Laws of Malta. [47]

Under the Children and Young Persons Care Orders Act, a child may be placed under the care of the Minister for Social Policy after having been removed from the care of the parents. This impacts on the exercise of the parental authority of the parents but does not remove it completely. For example, the Minister is not empowered to place the child for adoption unless additional requirements are adhered to bringing about the termination of their parental authority according to law.

Principle 3:10 Effect of dissolution and separation

Once conferred, parental authority is the same, irrespective of the status of the holder. The relationship between parent and child is governed by rules which do not consider the status of the parent other than in the forfeiture of legal usufruct over the property of the child for parents who have children outside wedlock. [48]

---

45 Laws of Malta, Chapter 16, Article 158: *Any minor, whose parents have died or have forfeited parental authority and who has not married, is subject to be placed under tutorship until he becomes of age or until he marries.*

46 Laws of Malta, Chapter 16, Article 160: *Where among the relatives of the minor there are competent persons, the court shall appoint one of such persons, preference being given, subject always to the best interests of the child, to the nearest relative by consanguinity.*

47 Laws Of Malta, Chapter 285,Article 8: General Duties: *The Minister has the duty to provide care and custody.*

48 Laws of Malta Chapter 16, Article 90 (1): *The parent who has acknowledged a child conceived and born out of wedlock shall have in regard to him all the rights of parental authority other than the legal usufruct.*

In practice, the exercise of parental authority between parents who do not cohabit may lead to the apportionment of the day to day obligations and rights in a way which is different to that of cohabiting parents. Therefore times and modalities of contact may have to be adjusted, decisions relating to daily events may be taken by just one parent but the legal relationship between the parent and child and the rights and obligations emanating from the institute of parental authority remain the same until they are changed by law.

Malta does not have a law on divorce. However divorce judgments of a competent court abroad are recognised so any dispositions relating to parental responsibility would be applied locally. Following legal separation the courts usually allocate care and custody to a primary carer and access or contact to the other parent. Although joint custody is not listed as an option in the law, in practice the courts agree to this option when it is put forward by the spouses in a separation agreement.

The courts do not usually enter into the issue of parental authority assuming that it will continue to be shared between the parents. The focus is instead on finding a *modus vivendi* for the parents and children which causes the least possible disruption to the child. However according to Article 56(5) cited below the court may "where circumstances so require" remove parental authority from a parent or from both. In practice this is an exceptional intervention and there are few cases where a court has taken this step.[49]

---

49 Laws of Malta, Chapter 16, Article 56 (1): *On separation being pronounced the court shall also direct to which of the spouses custody of the children shall be entrusted, the paramount consideration being the welfare of the children.*
(2) It shall be lawful for the court, if it considers such measures to be strictly necessary, having regard to all relevant circumstances, to direct that the children be placed in the custody of third parties or in alternative forms of care.
(3) It shall be lawful for the court to give any such directions in the judgment of separation, although in the action relating thereto no demand has been made respecting the custody of the children.
(4) The court may, at any time, revoke or vary such directions respecting the children, where the interests of the children so require.
(5) The court may moreover where circumstances so require, determine that one or both of the parents shall be deprived wholly or in part of the rights of parental authority.
Article 57 (1): *Whosoever may be the person to whom the children are entrusted, the father and mother shall maintain their right to watch over their maintenance and education, and shall still be bound to contribute thereto, according to law.*
(2) It shall be in the discretion of the court, according to circumstances, to fix the time, place, and manner in which the father or mother shall have access to the children.
(3) It shall be lawful for the court entirely to forbid such access if it may be detrimental to the welfare of the children.
Article 60 (1): *The court, on authorizing the separation, shall in the decree give its directions as to the person in whose custody the children are to be placed.*
(2) It shall be lawful for the court at any time to revoke or vary such directions, for the better welfare of the children.

The provisions for annulment do not enter into the merits of parental authority. The relationship between parents and children of an annulled marriage is deemed to be the same as that between parents and children of a putative marriage. In tandem with the annulment proceedings, it is necessary to conclude a separate arrangement for the care and custody of children similar to that identified under separation.

Factual separation or *de facto* separation does not affect parental authority in any legal way, although again, the practical implications may, and often do, impact on the practical application of such responsibility. The law provides a very general article on the interim period between the *de facto* separation and the conclusion of proceedings: "Article 47: During the pendency of the action the court shall give such directions concerning the custody of the children as it may deem appropriate, and in so doing the paramount consideration shall be the welfare of the children."

5. EXERCISE OF PARENTAL RESPONSIBILITIES

5.1. PARENTS

Principle 3:11 Joint exercise

It is contrary to public policy to enter into an agreement whereby parental authority may only be exercised by one parent. [50]

While parental authority itself is always joint, the exercise of the authority in circumstances where the parents no longer cohabit leads to the allocation of primary care and custody to one parent and access to the other. In practice, parents frequently propose joint custody arrangements and the Family Court has been amenable to sanctioning this as long as it can be proved to be in the best interests of the child.

Article 61: *(1) Any agreement between the spouses respecting the custody of the children may at any time, on the demand of either of the spouses, or of any relative of either of the spouses, be annulled by the competent court, where the interests of the children so require.*
(2) In any such case, the court shall give the necessary directions as to the person in whose custody the children are to be placed, and as to the mode of their maintenance and education.

50 Laws of Malta, Chapter 16, Article 1238: (1) *It shall not be lawful for the future spouses to enter into any agreement whereby either of them is established as head of the family, or into any agreement in derogation of any of the rights deriving from parental authority...*

Principle 3:12 Daily matters, important and urgent decisions

In matters of so called ordinary administration which encompass decisions of a daily nature, either parent may act unilaterally. Where the issue relates to matters of extraordinary nature, the two parents must give their consent. [51]

Where one spouse withholds consent and the other still wishes to pursue the action it is possible to go to the court and ask for assistance resolving the matter.

> Article 131(3): In case of disagreement between the parents on matters of particular importance, either parent may apply to such court as may be prescribed by or under any law in force from time to time indicating those directions which he or she considers appropriate in the circumstances.
> (4) The court, after hearing the parents and the child if the latter has reached the age of fourteen years, shall make those suggestions which it deems best in the interest of the child and the unity of the family. If the disagreement between the parents persists, the court shall authorise the parent whom it considers more suitable to protect the interests of the child in the particular case, to decide upon the issue.

Where a decision must be taken in an emergency the law provides that a sole parent may act independently: "Article 131(5) In the case of an imminent danger of serious prejudice to the child, either parent may take such measures which are urgent and cannot be postponed."

This notion is also reflected in the law sanctioning any such emergency decisions taken by third parties in good faith in the absence of parental consent by both

---

51 Laws of Malta, Chapter 16, Article 136: (1) *The parents jointly administer the property of their children, whether born or to be born, except such as has devolved on such children on condition that it shall be administered solely by one of the parents or by third parties.*
(2) Acts of ordinary administration may however be performed by either of the parents without the intervention of the other.
(3) Acts of extraordinary administration which must be performed by the parents jointly include -
(a) the alienation of movables by nature, including motor vehicles for the object of profitably investing the proceeds thereof;
(b) the collection of capitals that may become due;
(c) the granting of personal rights of enjoyment over immovable property;
(d) the acceptance of an inheritance, legacy or donation in the name of the child;
(e) the partition of movables by nature;
(f) acts which require the authorisation of the court in terms of sub-article (4) of this article.
(4) The parents may not alienate immovables or movables by operation of law belonging to the child nor may they contract loans or other debt, on his behalf hypothecate or pledge his property, enter into a suretyship, enter into any compromise, or submit a dispute to arbitration except in case of necessity, or manifest utility and with the authority of the court and in any such case the court may, at the request of the parents, authorise one only of the parents to represent the child on the relative deed.
(5) In case of disagreement between the parents the provisions of article 131 shall apply.

parents where it would otherwise be required by law. Where the child is living with only one parent all matters of a daily nature would be decided on by that custodial parent but all other extraordinary issues would still require the consent of both parents, whether living together or not.

Principle 3:13 Agreement on exercise

All agreements between parents relating to the exercise of parental authority are subject to the scrutiny of the court which has the final say in determining what constitutes the "best interests" of the child.

Principle 3:14 Disagreement on exercise

The only criterion for court intervention is that the matter be one of importance.[52] Over the past years, courts have expressed their reluctance to impose a decision in relation to issues which they deem fundamental to parenting (such as choice of school) and have counselled parents to reach an amicable settlement where possible.

Principle 3:15 Sole exercise upon agreement or decision

A parent may act independently only in the cases listed at law under Article 136, cited *supra.*

Principle 3:16 Sole exercise by one parent

Where a parent has sole parental authority this is either because of the death of the other spouse, his/her declared absence (as an absentee under the provisions of the law) or because the other parent has had his/her parental authority terminated for a reason under Article 154 of the Civil Code or Article 275A of the Criminal Code. In such cases the parent with sole custody can act alone with no other authorisation.

It is possible that the court may impose a condition on the parent exercising sole parental authority to seek court authorisation for specific decisions in the child's life, for instance in relation to administration of property, but this would be unusual.

The law also provides that, "In the case of an imminent danger of serious prejudice to the child either parent may take such measures which are urgent and cannot

52 See under Principle 3:12, *supra.*

be postponed", which empowers either parent to exercise parental authority independently where the interests of the child so require.[53]

5.2. THIRD PERSONS

Principle 3:17 Exercise in addition to or instead of the parents

Persons other than parents may only exercise parental authority where so authorised by the court.

Principle 3:18 Decisions in daily matters

The partner of the parent exercising parental authority has no right to make any decisions relating to parental authority although in practice the partner of a parent exercising parental authority may share in such authority in relation to day to day administration by also exercising it. This means that unless that partner applies for parental authority over the child, s/he would not be in a position to legally have any authority over the child.

In practical terms the spouse of a parent of a child may apply to adopt that child thereby assuming parental authority. If the other parent opposes such procedure and the court feels this is justified the spouse would not be able to take on parental authority.

However, the partner is expected to morally support the parent of a child in fulfilling duties towards that child: Civil Code, Article 9 "A spouse shall not withhold his or her moral support to the other in any obligation such other spouse may have towards his or her descendants or ascendants."

6. CONTENT OF PARENTAL RESPONSIBILITIES

6.1. THE CHILD'S PERSON AND PROPERTY

Principle 3:19 Care, protection and education

(1) Article 3B of the Civil Code states that: "Marriage imposes on both spouses the obligation to look after, maintain, instruct and educate the children of the marriage taking into account the abilities, natural inclinations and aspirations of the children."

---

53 Laws of Malta, Chapter 16, Article 131(5).

The care of the child is usually entrusted to the parent(s) exercising parental authority. The Civil Code gives no definition and makes no mention of the duty of care or standard of care expected from a parent towards the child within the articles devoted to the issue of parental authority. It makes reference to notions of care within the context of custody in separation proceedings, in the placement required preceding and post adoption and in the context of foster care.

Under the Children and Young Persons (Care Orders) Act[54] a child is deemed to be in need of care (protection or control) when

(a) he is beyond the control of his parents or guardian; or
(b) he is not receiving such care, protection and guidance as a good parent may reasonably be expected to give and -
(i) the child or young person is falling into bad associations or is seriously exposed to moral danger; or
(ii) such lack of care, protection or guidance is likely to cause the child or young person unnecessary suffering or seriously affect his health or proper development.[55]

If the Minister does proceed to take a child into his/her care then, according to Article 8 of the same Act, "the Minister would have the same powers and duties with regard to [the child's] care and custody as the parents or guardian of such child or young person".

The obligation that emanates from taking the child into care in this context is, "the duty (of the Minister) to exercise his powers with respect to the care and custody of such child or young person so as to further his best interests and to afford him opportunity for the proper development of his character and abilities".[56]

However the Minister is not expected to provide such care personally and the law provides that in order to discharge the duty imposed through the legislation, the child may be cared for:

(a) by accommodating and maintaining him in a residential home, hostel or similar institution provided by the Minister for the reception of children or young persons in his care; or
(b) by boarding him out with a fit person, whether a relative or not, or with a private institution willing to undertake the care of him on such terms as to payment by the Minister and otherwise as the Minister may, subject to any regulations made under

54 Laws of Malta, Chapter 285.
55 *Ibid*, Article 7.
56 *Ibid*, Article 9.

this Act, determine in agreement with such person or the management of such institution.[57]

Parents have an obligation to provide an education for their children. The term is not restricted to formal education through schooling but also to the communication of moral and social ideals and standards. The law states that parents have a responsibility to educate their children.[58] When the marriage breaks down, the law reaffirms the responsibility of parents to continue to be responsible for the education of the children and remain bound not only to contribute towards it but also to keep watch over it. Article 57(1) "Whosoever may be the person to whom the children are entrusted, the father and mother shall maintain their right to watch over their maintenance and education, and shall still be bound to contribute thereto, according to law."[59] Where a parent "neglects the education" of the child or exhibits such "conduct as to endanger the education of the child", the court may remove wholly or in part the rights of parental authority. [60]

Where a tutor assumes the parental authority over a child (for instance, in cases where the child's parents are dead or incompetent to exercise such authority) "the court shall, as appropriate, prescribe the place in which the minor is to be brought up, the education which it is proper to give him, and the expense to be incurred for his maintenance and education."[61]

In listing the items which spouses are jointly responsible for, irrespective of the terms of their matrimonial regime, the law includes "the expenses and obligations, even if incurred separately, for the needs of the family including those for the education and upbringing of the children".[62] In terms of the Children and Young Persons (Care Orders) Act the Minister may remove a child on the grounds that "it is expedient in the interest of the education" of the child.[63]

(2) Parents are empowered to exercise "reasonable chastisement" over their children, however the law does not explain what this entails. The consequence of "exceeding the bounds of [such] reasonable chastisement" is the termination of parental authority.[64]

57 *Ibid*, Article 10(1).
58 Laws of Malta Chapter 16, Article 3B and 7.
59 Laws of Malta Chapter 16.
60 Laws of Malta Chapter 16, Article 154(1) (a) and (b).
61 Laws of Malta Chapter 16, Article 173.
62 Laws of Malta Chapter 16, Article 1327(c) and 1342 (c).
63 Laws of Malta Chapter 285, Article 6(1).
64 Laws of Malta Chapter 16, Article 155(1)(a).

The law considers discipline an essential element of the exercise of parental authority so that where a request is made for the child to be placed in alternative care, the placement is chosen subject to where the court "may deem conducive to the discipline and education of the child."[65]

However where a spouse uses "excesses, cruelty, threats or grievous injury against a child of the other spouse (who may not be his/her own child) this is deemed to be" a ground for personal separation between spouses.[66]

The Criminal Code sanctions ill-treatment of a child particularly under the age of 12, although this is not restricted to persons exercising parental authority:

> Article 247A (1) Whosoever, having the responsibility of any child under twelve years of age, by means of persistent acts of commission or omission ill-treats the child or causes or allows the ill-treatment by similar means of the child shall, unless the fact constitutes a more serious offence under any other provision of this Code, be liable on conviction to imprisonment for a term not exceeding two years.

The law also defines the concept of ill-treatment which "includes neglecting the child's need for adequate nutrition, clothing, shelter, and protection from harm, persistently offending the child's dignity and self-esteem in a serious manner and persistently imposing upon the child age-inappropriate tasks or hard physical labour."[67]

Principle 3:20 Residence

The court is expected to take into consideration the best interests of the child in reaching its decision. Case law shows that the courts have repeatedly stated that their primary consideration in determining custody/residence for a child is motivated solely by the child's best interests so that alternate residence would only be possible if it is shown to be advantageous to the child.[68] Similarly the choice of

---

65 Laws of Malta Chapter 16, Article 134(2). It is worth noting that in terms of the Education Act, Laws of Malta Chapter 327, Article 30: *A person shall not be qualified to obtain or shall not retain a warrant [to teach] in terms of this Act if such person has been convicted by any court of criminal jurisdiction b) Of having abused the students' trust or having used violence in their regard.*

66 Laws of Malta Chapter 16, Article 40.

67 Laws of Malta, Chapter 9, Article 247A(1) and (2).

68 Laws of Malta, Chapter 16, Article 56(1): *On separation being pronounced the court shall also direct to which of the spouses custody of the children shall be entrusted, the paramount consideration being the welfare of the children.*
27/06/2002 Civil Court, First Hall, RCP Micallef Melissa pro et noe versus Scotto Konrad
It-tfal, f'kawzi bhal dawn, mhumiex oggett in kontraversja u l-interess tal-udituri fil-kwistjoni dwar il-kustodja taghhom huwa nservjenti ghall-interess tat-tfal. [Informal translation : Children, in cases such as these, are not the object of controversy and the interest of the parents in the matter of custody is subservient to the interests of the children.]

the appropriate primary custodial parent is also determined by the needs of the child.[69]

Children have the right to be heard when they reach the age of 14 years. Before this time their inclusion is a matter left to the discretion of the court. The Commissioner for Children has been lobbying for a change in this attitude by considering the maturity and understanding rather than age as the criteria for child participation.

The child is represented by the parent. A Child Advocate may be appointed at the request of either parent, the mediator or at the Court's instigation. Where there is a clear conflict of interests the court may decide to appoint a special curator to represent the interests of the child, however, this is more usual in cases referring to contested filiation proceedings. Where children are opposed to access or custody arrangements made on their behalf there is no possibility for them to access the court to request changes. The courts penalise parents who refuse to obey court mandated access arrangements, notwithstanding the opposition of the child(ren).[70]

Principle 3:21 Relocation

Although parental authority is exercised jointly, where one of the holders of parental responsibilities wishes to change the child's residence within or outside the jurisdiction, this would require court intervention as this would involve an amendment to an existing court order.

Anthony Azzopardi vs. Rita Azzopardi and in Lourdes Magro pro et noe vs. Carmelo Bonnett (both Civil Court, First Hall, "…f'Malta jidher li din il-Qorti ghandha dejjem thares lejn l-interess suprem tal-istess minuri, liema interess huwa dejjem superjuri ghal dak ukoll sekondarju tal-partijiet fil-kawza u cioe` il-genituri tal-istess tant li tali principju gie indikat bhala il-paramountcy principle. [Informal translation : In Malta it would appear that the Court must always look to the supreme interest of the child, which interest is always superior to the secondary element of the case, namely the parties who are the parents, so that this principle may be termed the paramountcy principle.]

69 Civil Court (Family Division) NC 14.11.2006 Citazzjoni Numru/ Writ of Summons Number 168/2004, A v B Il-principji regolaturi fil-materja, huma li l-kura u kustodja tat-tfal ghandha tigi affidata lil dak il-genitur li jkun l-aktar idoneju sabiex jedukahom u jikkurahom, tenut kont ta' l-eta' ta' l-istess tfal u c-cirkostanzi tal-kaz. Illi apparti l-hsieb ta' ordni morali u dak ta' ordni legali, li ghandhom setgha f' din il-materja, il-principju dominanti huwa dak ta' l-aktar utilita' u dak ta' l-aqwa vantagg u interess ta' l-istess minuri fl-isfond tac-cirkostanzi personali u de facto li jkunu jirrizultaw mill-provi.
[Informal translation: The regulatory principle in this matter is that the care and custody of children must be entrusted to the parent who is more suited to educate and care for them, taking into account the age of the same child and circumstances of the case. Apart from considerations of moral order and legal order which are authoritative in this context the dominant principle is that of best utility and best advantage to the same child, taking into account the personal and de facto circumstances which may be educed from the proof.]

70 See Laws of Malta, Chapter 16, Article 131(3) and (4), under Principle 3:12, *supra*.

Where the parents are separated, any arrangements concluded relating to contact are scrutinised by the court and sanctioned by it. Where the parents agree to any amendment in the modality of contact without referring to court, the spouses risk criminal sanctions should one party decide to unilaterally withdraw from the agreement.

Any order of the court is enforceable so that an order relating to contact or custody issues is enforceable, even under criminal law where failure to respect the judgment is deemed contempt of court. Failure to abide by an order given by the court may be taken up at the police station where the alleged offender is brought before the criminal court to answer to the charge. [71]

The courts have repeatedly applied criminal sanctions where a parent fails to permit the other parent to visit with the child or to return the child following an access visit. In a Criminal Appeal (Inferior Jurisdiction) case decided on the 14th February 2001, the court held that the fact that minor children did not wish to visit their father or mother because they were afraid of them could not be deemed to be reasonable cause for the custodial parent to withhold access.[72]

Refusal to enforce must be backed by "reasonable cause". In another judgement of the Court of Criminal Appeal, diversely presided, of 19 December 1996, the court held that in cases where access to children was stopped the grounds of "reasonable cause" required that the circumstances showed that the parent so doing had acted reasonably. Obvious cases of reasonable cause are when the child is ill and cannot leave the house because to do so would be detrimental to his health.[73]

---

71 Laws of Malta Chapter 9, Article 338(ll): ... *when ordered by a court or bound by contract to allow access to a child in his or her custody, refuses without just cause to give such access.*

72 14/02/2001 Appell Kriminali (Inferjuri) Il-Pulizija versus Micallef Oliver [Criminal Appeal (Inferior) Police versus Micallef Oliver]" Il-fatt li t-tfal minuri ma jkunux iridu jmorru ma missierhom jew ommhom ghaliex jibzghu minnhom ma titqiesx bhala raguni xierqa ghaliex min ikollu l-kustodja taghhom jikser l-ordni tal-access." [Informal translation : The fact that minor children do not wish to go to their father or mother because they are afraid of them is not considered reasonable cause for the person who has custody to break an access order.]

73 19/12/1996 Appell Kriminali (Inferjuri) Il-Pulizija versus Ebejer Joseph [Criminal Appeal (Inferior) Police versus Ebejer Joseph] "F'kazijiet li wiehed iwaqqaf l-access ghat-tfal, biex ikun jista jinvola r-"raguni xierqa" li tezenta lil dak li jkun jirrizulta li hu jkun, fic-cirkostanzi, agixxa ragonevolment. L-espressjoni "raguni xierqa" hi sinonima f'dan il-kuntest ghal "raguni tajba", li tista' tigi tradotta bhala "reasonable cause". Kazijiet ovvji ta' "raguni xierqa " jew "raguni tajba" huma meta t-tifel jew tifla jkun marid jew marida b'mod li l-hrug barra mid-dar jista jkun ta' detriment ghalih jew ghaliha. [Informal translation: "For a person to stop access to children invoking "reasonable cause" it should result that in the circumstances that person acted reasonably. The expression "reasonable cause" is synonymous with "good cause". Obvious cases of reasonable cause or good cause include instances where a child is unwell and where leaving the home may be detrimental to his/her health".]

In determining the effect of the change on the child, the court would enter into the merits listed in the Principle and make its decison on the basis of the feedback of the child, depending on the child's age, the impact such a move would have on continued access rights of the child to parents, siblings, extended family and significant persons in the child's life. The criteria adopted by the court include the fitness of the parent vis a vis the child. In practice the courts have looked to the best interests of the child although recently the courts have added another dimension in the "moral best interests" of the child.[74]

Principle 3:22 Administration of the child's property

The law states that "The parents jointly administer the property of their children, whether born or to be born, except such as has devolved on such children on condition that it shall be administered solely by one of the parents or by third parties."[75]

At the termination of the administration the parents are expected to render accounts:

> The parents are bound to render to the child, on the latter attaining majority, an account of the property and the fruits of those things of which they have not the usufruct; and of the property only and of the administration thereof in regard to things of which they have the legal usufruct.[76]

Parents are given the enjoyment of such legal usufruct to help offset "the expenses for the maintenance and education of the child."[77] The right signifies that parents are empowered to care for a series of items jointly on behalf of the child and to enjoy the usufruct on those items in recompense for their administration. Such legal usufruct does not apply where the child was born out of wedlock.

The items include:

> (a) the alienation of movables by nature, including motor vehicles for the object of profitably investing the proceeds thereof;
> (b) the collection of capitals that may become due;
> (c) the granting of personal rights of enjoyment over immovable property;
> (d) the acceptance of an inheritance, legacy or donation in the name of the child;

---

74 Civil Court (Family Division) judgement of 14 November 2006, Writ of Summons Number 168/2004 [A versus B, Qorti Civili (Sezzjoni tal-Familja) 14.11.2006 Citazzjoni Numru. 168/2004].

75 Laws of Malta Chapter 16, Article 136(1).

76 Laws of Malta Chapter 16, Article 140(1).

77 Laws of Malta Chapter 16, Article 143(d).

(e) the partition of movables by nature;
(f) acts which require the authorisation of the court in terms of sub-article (4) of this article.
(4) The parents may not alienate immovables or movables by operation of law belonging to the child nor may they contract loans or other debt, on his behalf hypothecate or pledge his property, enter into a suretyship, enter into any compromise, or submit a dispute to arbitration except in case of necessity, or manifest utility and with the authority of the court and in any such case the court may, at the request of the parents, authorise one only of the parents to represent the child on the relative deed.[78]

Such administration also extends to the acceptance or refusal of an inheritance on behalf of the child. [79]

Parents are bound to render accounts of the administration of the property of the child and cannot burden the child's property without court authorisation. At the termination of the administration the court must be satisfied that due care and diligence has been paid and will only release the property of the parents which has been hypothecated in favour of the child when such approval is concluded. In the case of unjustified enrichment, the usual procedures available at law would be applicable to the child who has attained majority and feels action is forthcoming.

Article 140(1): The parents are bound to render to the child, on the latter attaining majority, an account of the property and the fruits of those things of which they have not the usufruct; and of the property only and of the administration thereof in regard to things of which they have the legal usufruct.
(2) If parental authority ceases before the child attains majority the parents shall render the account on the date of such cessation.
(3) Without prejudice to any liability of the parent, either parent may render such account on behalf also of the other parent.[80]

Principle 3:23 Restrictions

The authorisation of the court may be required by the parents before they may administer the child's property. Also with regard to inheritances, the refusal of the inheritance may lead the court to appoint an alternative curator to represent the child or the child who has reached the age of 14 may be authorised to accept the inheritance him/herself.[81]

---

78 Laws of Malta, Chapter 16, Article 136(3) *et seq.*
79 Laws of Malta, Chapter 16, Article 137.
80 Laws of Malta, Chapter 16, Article 140.
81 Laws of Malta, Chapter 16, Article 137(2): *If one of the parents is unable or unwilling to accept such inheritance, the inheritance may be accepted by the other parent with the authority of the court. If both parents are unable or unwilling to accept such inheritance the court may, upon*

The parents have no right to deduct any legal usufruct from the salary of the child:

> Article 142: The following property shall not be subject to the legal usufruct:
> (a) property bequeathed or given to the child on condition that the parents or either of them shall not have the usufruct thereof:
> *-omissis*
> (b) property given to the child to undertake a career, an art or a profession;
> (c) property devolved on the child by inheritance, legacy or donation where such inheritance, legacy or donation has been accepted in the interest
> *-omissis-*
> (d) property which the child may have acquired by his own work or his own separate industry.[82]

Principle 3:24 Legal representation

Parents are responsible for the legal representation of their children. The Civil Code, Article 135:[83] "The parents jointly represent their children, whether born or to be born, in all civil matters." According to the Code of Organisation and Civil Procedure, "The following persons may not sue or be sued: (a) a minor, except in the person of the parent exercising paternal authority, or, in the absence of such parent, of a tutor or a curator".[84]

Where parents are in a conflict of interests with their child, a curator may be appointed to represent the interests of the child in that particular case. Children only have *locus standi* before the court when they attain majority, ie reach the age of 18 years in general terms, however they may share their wishes with the court which is bound to hear them, from the age of 14.

---

the demand of the child or of any of his relatives, authorise the acceptance thereof either by the child himself, if he has attained the age of fourteen years, or otherwise by a special curator to be appointed by the court.

82 Laws of Malta, Chapter 16, Article 142.

83 Laws of Malta, Chapter 16.

84 Laws of Malta, Chapter 12, Article 781,
Vide also Article 782: *The provisions of article 781 shall not apply to -*
(a) any minor, if such child carries on trade with the consent of the parent exercising parental authority even though the action touches matters not relating to trade, or if the said parent has expressly given his assent for the child to sue or be sued without his assistance;
(b) any minor in any action against the said parent provided the child is represented by a curator ad litem.
and Article 783 (1) *In the cases referred to in this sub-title, the curator ad litem may be appointed by the same court before which the action has been brought, or is about to be brought, upon the application of any person interested.*
(2) *The application for the appointment of a curator to represent a minor who desires to sue, may be made by any person.*

The Civil Code Article 139 states:

> In case of conflicting interests between the children, or between the children and either parent, the competent court shall, according to circumstances, appoint one or more special curators:
> Provided that it shall be lawful for either parent to decline to represent any of the children against another or against the other parent.

6.2. MAINTENANCE OF PERSONAL RELATIONSHIPS

Principle 3:25 Contact with parents and other persons

The concept of contact is mentioned within the context of separation and also in those cases where a child is placed under the care of the Minister and it may be deemed in the interest of the child to maintain or resume or start a relationship with a parent or family member or significant person in the child's life.

In the context of parental responsibility, it is more usually the parent who demands contact with the child rather than the child who may exercise a right to have contact with the parent. This is mainly owing to the notion that children are not capable at law (*incapax*) and may not initiate proceedings of their own accord. The introduction of the Child Advocate in 2004 has started to address this issue, however the child remains unable to initiate proceedings and remains reliant on the court, the parents or the mediator to make any request even for the appointment of the Child Advocate. The Office of the Child Commissioner, among others, is lobbying for a change in this law.

In terms of Article 57 (2):

> It shall be in the discretion of the court, according to circumstances, to fix the time, place, and manner in which the father or mother shall have access to the children.
> (3) It shall be lawful for the court entirely to forbid such access if it may be detrimental to the welfare of the children.

Within the context of care proceedings where case conferences and reviews are held with the participation of the child, such demands are easier to bring to the attention of the decision makers. However care proceedings under the Children and Young Persons Care Orders Act (Chapter 285) are quasi judicial in nature and do not go to court. At court level, it is only children aged 14 and over who have the right to be heard while those who are younger may be heard at the discretion of the court. Again this is an issue which is the subject of a lobby for change.

Where contact is awarded to a parent by a court and a child is unhappy with the arrangement and refuses to observe the court decree this may result in penal sanctions taken against the custodial parent. A recent case of a mother with two teenage children who refused to visit with their father resulted in her being accused of failure to honour a court decree and incurred criminal liability[85] leading to five days imprisonment. The judgment is under appeal.

Principle 3:26 Content of contact

There is no definition of the term contact although it has been interpreted by the courts to signify a means whereby the child may spend time with a person who has significance to his or her life. As previously stated, all decisions which may impact on the child are motivated by the best interests principle.

Principle 3:27 Agreement

Agreement relating to contact and custody of the child is always dependent on the authorisation of the court so that, rather than "[t]he competent authority may scrutinize the agreement", in the Maltese experience it would be more appropriate to say that, "[t]he competent authority SHALL scrutinize the agreement."

In terms of the Civil Code, Article 47: "During the pendency of the action the court shall give such directions concerning the custody of the children as it may deem appropriate, and in so doing the paramount consideration shall be the welfare of the children".[86]

---

85 Civil Court, First Hall, Dr. Stephen Thake Vassallo noe vs. Joseph Portelli:
After abduction by the defendant, plaintiff instituted an action demanding care and custody "...il-gudikant ghandu jara x'inhuma l-veri interessi tal-minuri qabel ma jindaga fuq il-legalita` ta` xi azzjoni tal-genituri" (informal translation: "the judge must look to the the real interests of the minor before attempting to establish the legality of the action by a parent").
However on appeal, custody was given to the father notwithstanding the previous abduction since "...l-ottika principali taghha hija wahda – fuq kollox, l-interess tal-minuri" (informal translation: the principle point of view is one – above all, the interests of the child")
Civil Court (Family Division)) NC 14.11.2006 Citazzjoni Numru. (Writ of Summons Number) 168/2004 A v B – the Court rejected a request for a change in access arrangements on the grounds that this would be detrimental to the children : Fic-cirkostanzi l-Qorti tifhem li ma jkunx fl-interess tal-minuri li dawna jergghu jghaddu minn bidla radikali ohra fl-ambjent tat-trobbija taghhom. Ghalhekk il-kura u kustodja ta' l-ulied ghandha tibqa' dik ezistenti llum (informal translation: In the circumstances the Court understands that it is not in the best intersts of the children that they undergo another radical change in the environment in which they are brought up. Therefore the care and custody of the children should remain unchanged.")

86 See further Laws of Malta, Chapter 16, Article 56 discussed under Principle 3:10, *supra*.

Principle 3:28 Restrictions

The court always retains the right to intervene in the best interests of the child and to review any decision made by the parents even if they had reached an agreement independently. In practice, the court tries to help the parties reach an amicable settlement in the child's best interests so any agreement they have reached is not overturned frivolously. [87]

Principle 3:29 Information to parents

This Principle is clearly affirmed in the law: Civil Code, Article 57:

> (1) Whosoever may be the person to whom the children are entrusted, the father and mother shall maintain their right to watch over their maintenance and education, and shall still be bound to contribute thereto, according to law.
> (2) It shall be in the discretion of the court, according to circumstances, to fix the time, place, and manner in which the father or mother shall have access to the children.
> (3) It shall be lawful for the court entirely to forbid such access if it may be detrimental to the welfare of the children.

7. TERMINATION OF PARENTAL RESPONSIBILITIES

Principle 3:30 Termination

In terms of the Civil Code, Article 150, parental authority ceases *ipso jure* in each of the cases following:

> - omissis -
> (b) when the child attains the age of eighteen years;
> (c) on the marriage of the child;
> (d) if the child, with the consent of the parents, has left the parental home and set up a separate domestic establishment;

On adoption, the parental authority between the birth parent or parent exercising parental authority and the child is terminated and substituted with the new

87 One unreported case [in which I was involved as Court Registrar in 1984] where the court intervened was where the parents had decided to split the children equally by apportioning the two boys to the custody of the father and the two girls to the custody of the mother. The court requested a professional social work evalulation and felt that splitting the children in this way and curtailing their access to siblings would be detrimental to the children and convinced the parents to keep the children together and pursue arrangements for liberal access.

adoptive parental authority. This is equally applicable to any adopter, including the partner of the parent who adopts the child. [88]

Principle 3:31 Death of the parents

According to the Civil Code, Article 146:

> (1) In the event of the death of one of the parents, parental authority shall vest solely in the surviving parent in respect of his or her children and their property, including property devolving on the children from the property of the deceased parent and from any other cause after the death of the predeceased parent.

In fact, in terms of Article 150, parental authority ceases *ipso jure* : "(a) on the death of both parents or of the child". On the death of the last person exercising parental authority, a tutor may be appointed to continue the care of the child. In such procedure the court is not bound by the person nominated to succeed to the parental authority but takes this recommendation into account and where satisfied that such appointment would be in the child's best interests proceeds to confirm the nomination

Civil Code, Article 159:

> (1) A tutor is appointed by the court on the demand of any person.
> (2) In appointing a tutor the court shall take into account any disposition contained in the will of either of the parents of the child relating to the appointment of a tutor.

Although in practice, where the child is left with no person to exercise parental authority, the extended family steps in to care for the child or a care order is issued to place the child in the care and protection of the Minister, there is no automatic mechanism in place as in some other jurisdictions. Fortunately the small size of the country and the continued social conscience corroborate to ensure that the child who is left with no parent invariably finds alternative persons to provide protection. The courts then ensure that administration of any property is carried out according to law. However this remains a lacuna.

88 Laws of Malta, Chapter 16, Articles 113- 130A.

8. DISCHARGE AND RESTORATION OF PARENTAL RESPONSIBILITIES

Principle 3:32 Discharge of parental responsibilities

Parental authority may be terminated where, in terms of Civil Code, Article 154(1):

> Saving any other punishment to which he may be liable according to law, a parent may be deprived, by the said court, wholly or in part, of the rights of parental authority, in any of the cases following:
> (a) if the parent, exceeding the bounds of reasonable chastisement, ill-treats the child, or neglects his education;
> (b) if the conduct of the parent is such as to endanger the education of the child;
> (c) if the parent is interdicted, or under a disability as to certain acts, as provided in articles 520 to 527 inclusive of the Code of Organization and Civil Procedure, and articles 189 and 190 of this Code;
> (d) if the parent mismanages the property of the child;
> (e) if the parent fails to perform any of the obligations set out in article 3B in favour of the child.[89]

A parent may also have parental authority terminated in terms of Article 247A of the Criminal Code:

> (1) Whosoever, having the responsibility of any child under twelve years of age, by means of persistent acts of commission or omission ill-treats the child or causes or allows the ill-treatment by similar means of the child shall, unless the fact constitutes a more serious offence under any other provision of this Code, be liable on conviction to imprisonment for a term not exceeding two years.
> (2) For the purposes of subarticle (1), ill-treatment includes neglecting the child's need for adequate nutrition, clothing, shelter, and protection from harm, persistently offending the child's dignity and self-esteem in a serious manner and persistently imposing upon the child age-inappropriate tasks or hard physical labour.

In the case of a parent committing an act of violence as defined under the Domestic Violence Act against the other parent of the child, this would be taken into account in determining allocation of custody and modalities of access/or contact if deemed applicable at all in the circumstances. It is also worth pointing out that an act of violence within the terms of the Domestic Violence Act is defined as

---

[89] Laws of Malta, Chapter 16, Article 3B. *Marriage imposes on both spouses the obligation to look after, maintain, instruct and educate the children of the marriage taking into account the abilities, natural inclinations and aspirations of the children.*

"any act of violence, even if only verbal, perpetrated by a household member upon another household member and includes any omission which causes physical or moral harm to the other".[90]

The law states that for such deprivation to have effect it must be ordered by the competent court but it does not specify who may bring the action. This may happen in different circumstances. The court may take cognisance of circumstances which arise in the course of adjacent court proceedings which lead it to terminate parental authority: for instance within the proceedings for a separation where evidence comes to light showing that the parent or parents should not be permitted to exercise parental authority over the child or children.

The court may also be informed of events which warrant such termination by the Social Welfare Agency after investigations through the Child Protection Unit or by the Office of the Attorney General following information from the said department in response to a complaint by any citizen on behalf of the child. The court may also be responding to criminal prosecution for acts which the parent carried out against the child and which warrant such termination of parental authority.

Within the context of adoption the court may terminate parental authority when it dispenses with the consent of the parent who should normally be expected to consent to the adoption. This may take place additionally when the child is not in the care of the parent and the Adoption Board deems that there is "no reasonable hope that the child will be reunited with his mother or father" or "where the parent or parents unjustifiably have not had contact with the child to be adopted for a period of eighteen months".[91]

Principle 3:33 Request for discharge of parental responsibilities

A parent may request to have the child removed from direct care in the case where "they are unable to control the child". However this does not remove parental authority but only the exercise of care of the child.

Civil Code, Article 134:

> (1) It shall be lawful for the parents, if they are unable to control the child, to remove him from the family, assigning to him, according to the means of the parents, such maintenance as is strictly necessary.

---

90 Laws of Malta Chapter 481, Article 2.

91 Laws of Malta, Chapter 16, Article 117(1)(a)(v) and (vi).

> (2) In any such case, the parents may also, where necessary and upon obtaining the authority of such court as may be prescribed by or under any law in force from time to time, place the child, for such time as is stated in the decree, in some alternative form of care, which the court will according to circumstances consider suitable, to be, at the expense of the parents, cared for and treated in such manner as the court may deem conducive to the discipline and education of the child.
> (3) The demand for such authority may be made even verbally; and the court shall make the necessary order thereon without any formal proceedings, and without giving its reasons therefor.

Children may report the failings of their parents to provide care, protection and control through school or social work networks although this is not a common occurrence and children may not be sufficiently empowered to do so. There is a helpline (179) which children may access but this provides support rather than direct intervention and has a waiting list. Children may not be parties to a suit and may therefore not petition the court directly for such removal of parental authority.

In the case of tutorship there is an exception to this rule whereby a child under tutorship may request the court to intervene if the tutor is not carrying out the responsibilities expected of the office. In practice children do not know of this option and the article is not put into practice.[92]

It is possible for the Ministry for Social Policy to issue a care order over a child whereby parental authority relating to care for the child is terminated and the child is placed under the care and protection of the Minister. [93]

The Children and Young Persons Care Orders Act impacts on the exercise of the parental authority of the parents but does not remove it completely. For example, the Minister is not empowered to place the child for adoption unless additional requirements are adhered to bringing about the termination of their parental authority according to law.

Principle 3:34 Restoration of parental responsibilities

Parental authority may always be reinstated where the court is convinced that the reasons for which parental authority was terminated have changed.

---

92 Laws of Malta, Chapter 16, Article 175 (2): *Where the tutor abuses his authority, or neglects his duties, the minor himself or any other person on his behalf, may make a complaint to the competent court; and the court shall caution the tutor or give any other expedient direction.*

93 Laws of Malta, Chapter 285.

> Civil Code, Article 151; – *omissis* – it shall be lawful for the court, if it deems it expedient in the interests of the child, to reinstate the parent in the parental authority wholly or in part upon his performing that by reason of the omission of which he had forfeited such authority.

The court may always review the situation in the best interest of the child.[94] The court may always reinstate a parent with parental authority where the reasons for deprivation "cease to exist". Within the case of adoption this would only be possible where the parties have agreed to an open adoption.[95]

9. PROCEDURE

Principle 3:35 Competent authority

The Family Court is entrusted with decisions relating to parental responsibilities, questions of residence of the child or access/contact arrangements. Parents may opt to refer a dispute to the Family Court in terms of the law.[96] In relation to issues of child abduction the Central Authority is housed at the Department of Social Welfare Standards but recourse is also made to the courts.

Parents may reach agreement relating to apportionment of duties within the context of parental authority following a mediated settlement sanctioned by the Family Court or be directed to apply provisions as determined in a judgement handed down by the same court.

It is the duty of the court to "direct to which of the spouses custody of the children shall be entrusted, the paramount consideration being the welfare of the children" although the court may decide that it is in the best interests of the child to be placed in alternative care to the exclusion of one or both parents. [97] Such order may be amended or revoked "at any time" depending on the interests of the child.[98,99]

---

94 Laws of Malta, Chapter 16, Article 154(2).

95 Laws of Malta, Chapter 495, Adoption Administration Act, Article 22(4).

96 See Laws of Malta, Chapter 16, Art.131(3) and (4) under Principle 3:12, *supra*.

97 Laws of Malta Chapter 16, Article 56(1) and (2).

98 Laws of Malta, Chapter 16, Article 56(4): *The court may, at any time, revoke or vary such directions respecting the children, where the interests of the children so require.*

99 Cases on this topic include [all First Hall Civil Court]: Edwin Schembri pro et noe vs Dr. Tonio Azzopardi et; Anthony Azzopardi vs. Rita Azzopardi; Lourdes Magro pro et noe vs. Carmelo Bonnett.

Principle 3:36 Alternative dispute resolution

Mediation is available and is mandatory within the family court system. The only reason for mediation not being pursued is proof of domestic violence which when demonstrated at the first conciliation session would bring to an end any possibility of mediation. Otherwise, mediation is a standard requirement of all court proceedings before the family court and is utilised in determining parental authority issues. The fact that it is mandatory has been the subject of criticism from various quarters but recent statistics seem to show some effectiveness in facilitating resolution of disputes. At the enforcement stage no such mechanism is applied.

Principle 3:37 Hearing of the child

Children have the right to be heard when they reach the age of 14 years. Before this time their inclusion is a matter left to the discretion of the court. The Commissioner for Children has been lobbying for a change in this attitude by considering the maturity and understanding rather than age as the criteria for child participation.

Where children are opposed to access or custody arrangements made on their behalf there is no possibility for them to access to court to request the changes. It has already been shown that the courts penalise parents who refuse to obey court mandated access arrangements, notwithstanding the opposition of the child(ren).

When children are heard they may be heard directly by the court, informally in the judge's chambers, by a social worker or psychologist appointed by the court, through the services of the Child Advocate who may be appointed at the request of the parents or the mediator or by the judge.

Issues relating to the confidentiality which protects children's views are currently a matter for debate. Once information is shared with the court, principles of justice demand that such information be shared with the alleged perpetrator so that s/he may answer to them. This stance has precluded a number of children from sharing information. The report made by the Child Advocate is similarly deemed to be part of the court proceedings file and any information disclosed by the child becomes in the domain of the court case. In these circumstances Child Advocates have started to advise children of this eventuality.

It is interesting to note that in many cases the reluctance of judges to interview children is invariably based on the principle of best interests of the child, as a number of courts view interviewing children as detrimental to the child's psychological well being. The introduction of the office of the Child Advocate was a step towards addressing this issue but where the child has no power to engage the advocate *proprio motu* much remains to be done.[100]

Principle 3:38 Appointment of a special representative for the child

Where there is a clear conflict of interest between the child and the holders of parental responsibilities, the court may decide to appoint a special curator to represent the interests of the child, however this is more usual in cases referring to contested filiation proceedings.

It has been explained that the issue of age set at 14 years is a matter which is debatable. The standard of maturity and understanding is gaining momentum in the feedback of numerous children who refer to the Office of the Commissioner for Children for assistance in making their voices heard in court.

Within procedures relating to children taken into alternative care, recent amendments have included the child in the process at a much earlier age and taken the stance that all children have the right to have their wishes heard and considered.

Principle 3:39 Enforcement

Any executive order of the court is enforceable so that an order relating to contact or custody issues is enforceable, even under criminal law where failure to respect the judgement is deemed contempt of court. Failure to abide by an order given by the court may be taken up at the police station where the alleged offender is brought before the criminal court to answer to the charge. [101]

The courts have repeatedly applied criminal sanctions where a parent fails to permit the other parent to visit with the child or to return the child following an access visit. In a Criminal Appeal (Inferior Jurisdiction) case decided on the 14th February 2001, the court held that the fact that minor children did not wish to visit their father or mother because they were afraid of them could not be deemed to be reasonable cause for the custodial parent to withhold access.[102]

100 Legal Notice 397 of 2003 introduced the office of the Child Advocate who may be appointed by the Court *ex proprio*, at the request of at least one of the parents or at the request of the mediator to the separation proceedings.

101 Laws of Malta Chapter 9, Article 338(ll): … *when ordered by a court or bound by contract to allow access to a child in his or her custody, refuses without just cause to give such access.*

102 14/02/2001 Appell Kriminali (Inferjuri) Il-Pulizija versus Micallef Oliver "Il-fatt li t-tfal minuri ma jkunux iridu jmorru ma missierhom jew ommhom ghaliex jibzghu minnhom ma titqiesx bhala raguni xierqa ghaliex min ikollu l-kustodja taghhom jikser l-ordni tal-access."

Refusal to enforce must be backed by "reasonable cause". In another judgement of the Court of Criminal Appeal, diversely presided, of 19 December 1996, the court held that in cases where access to children was stopped the grounds of "reasonable cause" required that the circumstances showed that the parent so doing had acted reasonably. Obvious cases of reasonable cause are when the child is ill and cannot leave the house because to do so would be detrimental to his health.[103]

In relation to cases involving child abduction, recent rules now allow for the courts of the Member State where the child last had residence to decide where the child is to stay. The regulation also strengthens and complements the Hague Convention on Child Abduction of 1980 by imposing stricter obligations to ensure prompt return where a child is abducted to a Member State. The Central Authority as designated under the Hague Convention for cases of child abduction has been identified as responsible to carry out the duties incorporated into the Brussels II Regulation. As Malta had already ratified the Hague Convention on child abduction,[104] it is expected that the present structure will assume the functions listed in Chapter IV of the Regulation.

It remains to be seen how the Central Authority will help to bridge the gap between the decision taken to authorise access to a child and the practical arrangements for enabling the exercise of such right. To date, the Central Authority is wholly dependent on the services of the state welfare support agency which is entrusted with supervised access where necessary and which is seriously overstretched by local constraints and funding limitations.[105] Enforcement in such cases therefore may pivot on procedural principles rather than best interests.

10. CONCLUSION

The motivation of the Commission on European Family Law leading to the recommendation of these Principles is underpinned by the aspiration to contribute to the harmonisation of family law while reinforcing standards relating to children's rights. In view of Malta's often isolated stance on certain

103 19/12/1996 Appell Kriminali (Inferjuri) Il-Pulizija versus EBEJER Joseph "F'kazijiet li wiehed iwaqqaf l-access ghat-tfal, biex ikun jista jinvola r-"raguni xierqa" li tezenta lil dak li jkun jirrizulta li hu jkun, fic-cirkostanzi, agixxa ragonevolment. L-espressjoni "raguni xierqa" hi sinonima f'dan il-kuntest ghal "raguni tajba", li tista' tigi tradotta bhala "reasonable cause". Kazijiet ovvji ta' "raguni xierqa" jew "raguni tajba" huma meta t-tifel jew tifla jkun marid jew marida b'mod li l-hrug barra mid-dar jista jkun ta' detriment ghalih jew ghaliha."

104 Hague Convention of 1980 on the Civil Aspects of International Child Abduction.

105 FARRUGIA, R., "Brussels II BIS: The position in Malta" in BOELE-WOELKI, K. and GONZALEZ BEILFUSS, C. (eds), *Brussels II BIS – Its Impact and Application in EU Member States* (Antwerp: Intersentia, 2007).

issues within family law, this may at first appear unfeasible but in reality there are numerous commonalities in approach and application.

Notions of parental responsibility in the Maltese context tally effortlessly with those proposed under the Principles, although the notion of responsibility is still to replace authority vis-à-vis children. Although parental authority remains a vestige of the Roman law tradition common to numerous civil law jurisdictions in Europe, the impact of its interpretation continues to attribute responsibility to parents entrusted with the care of their children. Similarly, the best interests principle has long been a mainstay of the law reflecting the core values of the theory and practice of law relating to children.

A number of issues remain items for deliberation, particularly in relation to the child's right to be heard and the ongoing debate of age versus maturity and understanding. For instance, the Principles set out that the "child's autonomy should be respected in accordance with the developing ability and need of the child to act independently". The legal position in Malta does not reflect this principle and maintains that children must have reached a set age (of 14) before imposing an obligation on the court to hear them. In practice, it has been shown that the trend is to respect this child's right using developing ability as a criterion, even though the legislator remains reluctant to do so.

Malta has a system in place whereby a Child Advocate may be appointed to represent the child, however this may not be done at the instance of the child but where either parent, the mediator or the judge so request. Furthermore, there are currently a small number of part time child advocates who carry out this role and the judicial reaction has been to increase opportunities for the child they deem needful of such response to be heard in the judge's chambers. Whether such practice benefits the child remains a moot point but it is certainly a measure born out of necessity rather than design. The result has been for the authorities to assume that the situation is adequate and that the child's right to be heard is being respected. In practice, unless each child is automatically accorded a child advocate in every case and given the right to accept or refuse representation, children will continue to go unheard. This is echoed in the Principle that "the competent authority should hear the child in all proceedings concerning parental responsibilities but if it decides not to hear the child it should give specific reasons."

Another issue which may bear discussion relates to the exclusion of corporal punishment. Malta, along with a number of European countries, still permits "reasonable chastisement" and although there are legal provisions in place to define what is unacceptable the topic still remains a matter for interpretation and manages to provoke fiery reaction.

Finally the intervention of the court in deciding issues relating to children is frequently offered as an option under the Principles while it is mandatory in Malta. The balance between parental responsibility and child rights is tempered with court intervention only on occasion according to the Principles. In a jurisdiction such as Malta where parental authority determines all outcomes for children, the best interests of the child are constantly served by judicial input whenever the child's stability and present and future well being are put into doubt. State responsibility for children, whether subject to parental responsibility or not, would possibly indicate that such intervention is another means of ensuring the best interests of the child.

PARENTAL PROTECTION IN ROMANIAN LAW JUXTAPOSED TO THE CEFL PRINCIPLES

Flavius A. Baias, Marieta Avram and Cristina Nicolescu

1. GENERAL ISSUES[1]

1. The Romanian concept in this field is *parental protection*, the rights and duties of the parents towards their minor children being enshrined *de lege lata* by the provisions of Articles 97-112 Family Code of 1954, which are completed by Law no. 272/2004 regarding the protection and promotion of children. As a legal institution, parental protection represents the "ensemble of legal norms which intend to ensure, as regards the most complete protection of the minor by his father and mother, the person as well as regards the goods."[2] As far as its content is concerned, the notion of parental protection designates all the rights and obligations recognised to parents for the purpose of ensuring the conditions needed for the raising, education and formation for life of the child,[3] specifying that parental rights are recognised only for the fulfilment of the duties, as a means of fulfilling parental protection.[4]

The responsibility to protect the minor is, firstly, the parents' charge,[5] the responsibility of the community being subsidiary, and the state's intervention – complementary. Where the protection of the child through his parents is not possible or desirable, the law offers alternative solutions of fulfilment of the

---

1 The numbering in this chapter adheres to the numbering on the Questionnaire (see Annex).

2 BARASCH, E., NESTOR, I., ZILBERSTEIN, S., *Ocrotirea părintească (Drepturile şi îndatoririle părinţilor faţă de copiii minori) [Parental protection (Rights and duties of the parents to their minor children)]*, (Bucharest: Editura Ştiinţifică, 1960), pp. 14–15.

3 FLORIAN, E., *Protecţia drepturilor copilului [Protection of the children's rights]*, second edition, (Bucharest: C.H. Beck Publishers, 2007), p. 69.

4 BARASCH ET AL, *supra* note 2 pp. 16–17; FLORIAN, *supra* note 3, p. 69; FILIPESCU, I.P., FILIPESCU, A.I., *Tratat de dreptul familiei [Family Law Treaty]*, 8th edition reviewed and completed, (Bucharest: Universul Juridic Publishers, 2006), p. 617.

5 In the Romanian legal system the term of "parents" designates the parents in the marriage, those outside the marriage, if the parenthood was established by the manners provided by the law, as well as the adoptive parents.

minor's protection, respectively the institution of tutorship, the measures of special protection provided by Law no. 272/2004 (placement, emergency placement, specialised supervision) and adoption.[6]

The dominant principle which assures compliance with and guarantee of children's rights at each stage of development is the "superior interests of the child", a principle imposed inclusively in relation to the rights and obligations of the child's parents, to his other legal representatives, as well as any other persons with whom the child was legally placed in custody – Article 2(2) Law no. 272/2004. Also, according to Article 2(3) of the same Act, "the principle of the superior interests of the child will prevail in all actions and decisions regarding children taken by public authorities and by authorised private bodies, as well as in cases settled by the courts". The idea is the same as the content of the CEFL Principle 3:3 which provides for the "best interests of the child".

2. According to the provisions of Article 48(1) of the Constitution,[7] "The family is based on (...) the right and duty of the parents to ensure the raising, education and instruction of the children". Also, according to Article 29(6) of the fundamental law, "The parents or tutors have the rights to ensure, according to their own principles, the education of minor children for whom they have responsibility."

(a) These constitutional provisions are completed with the fundamental principles contained in Article 101 Family Code, according to which parents have the duty to *care for* the child and have the obligation to *raise* the child, taking care of his health and physical development, his education, studies and professional training. The essence of parental protection is given by the fundamental duty of the parents to raise the child, the other components, concerning the personal side, or the patrimonial side, representing only instruments subordinated to the same purpose, respectively the insurance of the material and spiritual wellbeing of the child – Article 31(2) Law no. 272/2004.

(b) The parent's right to have *personal relations* with the child is considered in Romanian law for those situations in which, due to various reasons, the minor is not in the effective care of the respective parent such as, in the case of divorce of the parents – Article 43(3) Family Code, or the situation of the child separated from both parents or from one of them by a measure ordered under the provisions of the law – Article 16 Law no. 272/2004.

---

6 Art. 39 of Law no. 272/2004.

7 The Romanian Constitution was adopted in 1991 and was reviewed in 2003; provisions related to the family were not modified on review.

(c) An aspect of parental protection is also the parents' right to choose the type of *education* to be offered to the child, together with the obligation to register the child at school and to ensure regular school attendance by the child – Article 47(2) Law no. 272/2004.

(d) Among the rights regarding the child is also the parents' right to establish the child's home. According to Article 100(1) Family Code the minor child lives with his parents, and if they do not live together they will decide, on mutual agreement, with which of them the child will be living.[8] In case of disagreement the court of law will decide, considering the child's interests – Article 100(2) and (3) Family Code. The child with limited capacity to act[9] can personally ask for an agreement to have the house needed for the completion of studies or professional preparation – Article 102 Family Code – the authority competent to decide on the request of the child being the court of justice.[10]

(e) Parental rights and duties are recognised not only as regards the child, but also as regards his patrimony. For the protection and promotion of the child's interests of patrimonial nature, Article 105 Family Code and Article 31(2) Law no. 272/2004 provide expressly the parents' right and obligation to ensure legal representation and administration of the child's patrimony.

Even if the concept is different, one may note that the content of *parental protection* in the Romanian Law is very similar to *parental responsibilities*, provided by the CEFL Principle 3:1.

3. With general character, parental rights and obligations terminate on the date when the child becomes of age (reaching the age of 18, according to the provisions of Article 8(2) Decree no. 31/1954 regarding individuals and legal entities) or on the date of the marriage of the minor,[11] when, according to Article 8(3) of the same decree, he acquires full capacity to act.

---

8 The provisions of Art. 26(2) Government Emergency Ordinance no. 97/2005 regarding evidence, domicile, residence and identity documents of Romanian citizens, approved with modifications and completions by Law no 290/2005, with the subsequent modifications and completions being similar: "*The domicile of the minor is with his parents or with the parent with whom he is living or with his legal representative or the individual or legal entity where he is given in custody*".

9 In the Romanian legal system, the minor of 14 years acquires limited capacity to act – Art. 9(1) Decree no. 31/1954.

10 Although Art. 102 Family Code makes reference *in terminis* to the competence of the tutelary authority, the text must be considered implicitly modified by the provisions of Art. 47(3) Law no. 272/2004. In this regard, see FLORIAN, *supra* note 3, p. 78.

11 According to Art. 4 Family Code, as modified by the Law no. 288/2007, the capacity to marry is acquired at 18 years of age, the text providing, as an exception, the possibility of conclusion of the marriage by the minor (both man and women) of 16 years: for grounded reasons, with the agreement of the legal guardians, based on a medical certificate and authorisation from the General Direction of Social Assistance and Child Protection.

There is also a series of situations regulated in Romanian legislation when parental protection terminates, although the child is still a minor. Thus, in the case of institution of tutorship,[12] parental rights and duties are exercised by the tutor, and if the adoption of the minor is granted, the natural kinship between the adopted child and his descendants, on one side, and his natural parents and their relatives, on the other side, terminates (Article 50(3) Law no. 273/2004 regarding the legal regime of the adoption). Also, if the child benefits from an alternative protection measure provided by Law no. 272/2004, the exercise of parental rights and obligations is transferred temporarily to other individuals or legal entities through which the guardianship of the minor is performed.

4. The main legal source in the domain of parental rights and duties is the Family Code[13] which is completed by the provisions of Law no. 272/2004 regarding the protection and promotion of the child's rights and with those of Law no. 273/2004 regarding the legal regime of adoption – all these laws constituting the general legal framework regarding compliance with, promotion and guarantee of children's rights.

But there are also numerous specific provisions which regulate particular aspects of parental protection. As an example, the following Acts are relevant in this area:

- Decree no. 31/1954 regarding individuals and legal entities: Articles 8–14;
- The Civil Code: Article 1000(2) (the parents' responsibility for the illicit acts committed by their minor children);
- The Criminal Code: Articles 64 and 71 (prohibition of the exercise of parental rights as a complementary or accessory punishment); Article 214 (fraudulent administration – which can be applicable in the case of guardianship); Article 305 (family neglect), Article 306 (bad treatment of the minor), Article 307 (non-compliance with measures regarding custody of the minor); Article 314 (endangering of a person without capacity of self care);
- The Education Law no. 84/1995, republished, with subsequent modifications and completion: Articles 9(1) and (2), 180 and 182;
- Law no. 95/2006 regarding reform in the area of health: Article 145 (taking of cells from minor living donors); Article 152 (consent of parents or other persons who are legal representatives/guardians in case of transplant);
- Law no. 192/2006 regarding the mediation and exercise of the profession of mediator: Articles 64–66 (special provisions regarding family conflicts).

---

12 According to Art. 40(1) Law no. 272/2004, "*The guardianship is instituted if both parents are dead, unknown, no longer have parental rights or are punished by the interdict of the parental rights, under restraining order, declared by a court decision dead or missing, as well as if, at the termination of the adoption, the court decides that it is in the interest of the child to institute a guardianship*".

13 The Family Code – Law no. 4/1953 entered in force on 1 February 1954, according to Art. 161 of this Code.

5. At the normative level, the evolution can be seen of regulation in the field of parental responsibility, from *parental power* – regulated by the Civil Code of 1864[14] – which was characterised by the tendency to subordinate the child to the parents (mainly to the father), to the exercise of parental protection in the interests of the child; a principle first introduced by the Family Code of 1954, and further amended and developed by the coming into force, on 1 January 2005, of Law no. 272/2004 regarding the protection and promotion of children's rights (becoming the *superior interests of the child*).

Title IX of the Civil Code (former Articles 325–341) was named "On parental power", the concept being defined by the literature as "the totality of the rights offered by the law to parents over the person and assets of the child, as long as he is minor and not-emancipated".[15] In the Civil Code system, a clear difference was made between the child born within marriage, named "legitimate", over whom parental power was exercised, and the child born outside marriage, the "illegitimate" or "natural" child, to whom the establishment of any legal relation with the father was refused, (even when the latter acknowledged paternity), as regards natural children, "legally recognised", only the mother having the "right to correction" – former Article 337 of the Civil Code.

A significant change in the legal status of the child outside marriage occurred with the coming into force of the Family Code on 1 February 1954, which proclaimed the principle of the full legal assimilation of the child outside marriage to the one in marriage – Article 63.[16] In the Romanian legal system this principle acquired constitutional status, being provided in Article 48(3) of the Constitution; it is reiterated also by the provisions of Article 7 Law no. 272/2004 which enshrines the equality of children regardless of their status on birth or as acquired. Taking into consideration the general constitutional principle of non-discrimination, provided by Article 16(1) of the Romanian Constitution – which obviously applies to the children as well – we can say that the non-discrimination of the child (provided by the CEFL Principle 3:3) is also characteristic of the Romanian legal system.

---

14 By Art. 49 Decree no. 32/1954 for the appliance of the Family Code and the Decree regarding the individuals and legal entities the provisions of the Civil Code regarding the persons and family (Book I) were expressly abrogated on 1 February 1954.

15 HAMANGIU, C., ROSETTI-BĂLĂNESCU, I., BĂICOIANU, A.L., *Tratat de drept civil roman [Romanian civil law Treaty]*, vol. I, (Bucharest: All Publishers, 1996), p. 364. Under the provisions of the Civil Code majority is at the age of 21 years (Art. 342). The possibility of the minor's emancipation at the age of 18 years by the sole declaration of the father or the mother in the court is also regulated (Art. 422).

16 It is important to highlight in this context that under the aegis of the Council of Europe the European Convention on the legal status of the children born outside the marriage was adopted in Strasbourg only in 1975. The declared objective of this Convention is the improvement of the legal condition of this category of children by establishing common rules, and harmonising the legislation in this domain at the level of the member states. Romania adhered to this convention by Law no. 101/1992.

While the provisions of the former Article 327 Civil Code provided that during marriage the father alone exercised parental authority, as head of the family and of the marital association, the provisions of the Family Code enshrined the principle of the equality of the spouses as regards the exercise of their rights towards the children – Articles 1(4), 97 and 98 (similar to the CEFL Principle 3:11).

Also, under the former provisions of the Civil Code, the right of use of the child's assets was granted to the father or, in case of termination of the marriage by death, to the surviving wife; Article 106 Family Code introduced the principle of patrimonial independence between the parents and their children, meaning that the parent does not have any right to the child's assets, nor the child to the parent's assets, beyond the rights to inheritance and to care.

A series of important regulations in the domain of parental protection were adopted after 1990;[17] one of the objectives being the alignment of Romanian laws to the requirements of international legal instruments in the field of the protection of children's rights.

In the context of adoption, by means of the Emergency Government Ordinance, no. 25/1997[18] the provisions of the Family Code regarding adoption were repealed. The possibility was removed of adoption with limited effects, which was characterised by the maintenance of the relation of natural kinship between the adopted child and his biological family (mainly his natural parents), the adopted child and his descendants establishing, by the effect of the adoption, civil kinship relations only with the adopting person, not with his relatives.

The legislative package in the domain of children's protection which was adopted in 2004[19] represented the basis of a modern, European system of protection of rights of all the children, completely harmonised with the international treaties to which Romania has adhered. The focus changed from the child in need to the child in the context of all his rights but mainly in the context of his family.

Romania has also ratified a series of significant international legal instruments in this domain. For example, the UN Convention on the Rights of the Child, ratified by Romania by Law no. 18/1990; the Hague Child Abduction Convention,

---

17 For example, Law no. 47/1993 regarding the judicial pronouncement of abandonment of children (expressly repealed by Law no. 273/2004 regarding the legal regime of the adoption) regulated the conditions and procedure of declaration of the abandonment of the child by court decision in cases where the parents were not interested in the child for a period longer then six months.

18 Expressly repealed by Law no. 273/2004 – Art. 75 (3)(a).

19 Contains mainly Law no. 272/2004 regarding the protection and promotion of the children's rights and Law no. 273/2004 regarding the legal regime of adoption, regulations entered into force on 1 January 2005.

to which Romania adhered by Law no. 100/1992; the European Convention on the Legal Status of Children Born out of Wedlock, to which Romania adhered by Law no. 101/1992; the European Convention on the Adoption of Children, to which Romania adhered by Law no. 15/1993, the Hague Conventions on child protection, and cooperation in international adoption, ratified by Romania by Law no. 84/1994; the European Convention on Recognition and Enforcement of Decisions Concerning Custody; the Convention on Contact Concerning Children, adopted in Strasbourg on 15 May 2003 – ratified by Law no. 87/2007 and the Hague Convention on the competence, applicable law, recognition, enforcement and cooperation regarding parental responsibility and measures of children's protection – ratified by Law no. 361/2007.

6. The Draft of the new Romanian Civil Code, already adopted by the Senate[20] on 13 September 2004, is under debate in the Chamber of Deputies. Among other substantial modifications, this project proposed the repeal of the Family Code and the regulation of the domain regarding persons and family within the Civil Code, on the model of other European codes, thus returning to the normative architecture of the Romanian Civil Code of 1864. At the level of the Ministry of Justice, a commission of specialists was established, which formulated certain significant amendments to the project adopted by the Senate, which will be discussed on the occasion of the debate in the Chamber of Deputies.

Thus, in the domain of parental rights and duties it is proposed to use the concept of *parental authority*; a notion similar to that of the French Civil Code which is defined as an ensemble of rights and duties, held equally by both parents and concerning both the person and the assets of the child (Article 367(1) Draft).

An innovatory solution to the legal regulation in force is proposed for the situation of divorce; a situation in which, according to Article 317(1) Draft, as a rule, parental authority should belong jointly to both divorced parents (the same solution set out in the CEFL Principle 3:11, which makes no distinction between married, unmarried or divorced parents), and only if there are good reasons, the child is given to the care of one of the parents; the court will establish the child's residence as being that of the parent with whom he lives constantly. The consequence will be that parents will exercise parental protection together and equally, without the occurrence of a separation of it, as is currently provided under the conditions of Articles 42 and 43 Family Code.

[20] The version adopted by the Senate can be found at: *http://www.cdep.ro/proiecte/2004/500/30/7/se537.pdf.*

2. THE CONTENT OF PARENTAL PROTECTION

7. Parental rights and duties are recognised in relation to the child's person, as well as to the child's patrimony (Articles 98(1), 101 and 105 Family Code).

In essence, the following parental rights and duties are recognised as regards the person of the minor:

- the right and duty to *raise* the child, enshrined by Article 101(2) Family Code and by Article 31(1) Law no. 272/2004, with a complex content which includes the right and duty to care for the health and physical development of the child, the education, studies and professional preparation, as well as the guarding and supervision of the child;
- the right to take *certain measures* towards the child (this right concerns the measures of discipline, which we shall develop below – no. 8(d));
- the right to *request the return of the child* from any person holding him without a right – Article 103(1) Family Code;[21]
- the right to *consent to the adoption* of the child (Article 12(1) Law no. 273/2004);
- the right to *permit the marriage* of the minor between 16 and 18 years (Article 4 Family Code, as modified by Law no. 288/2007);
- the right to have *personal relations* with the child (Article 43(3) Family Code, Articles 14–17 Law no. 272/2004);
- the right to *supervise the raising, education, studies and professional preparation* of the child (Article 43(3) Family Code);
- the right to *establish the home of* the child (Article 100 Family Code).[22]

For the promotion and protection of the patrimonial interests of the child the right and the duty of the parent to administer the child's assets were set up, as well as the one of representing the minor in civil acts or to consent to these acts (Article 105 Family Code).[23]

The exercise of parental rights and the compliance with their duties concerning the child's person and property must take into consideration the superior interests

[21] It is important to note that in two cases (Ignaccolo-Zenide v. Romania – Official Gazette of Romania no. 6 of 8 January 2001 and Monory v. Romania – Official Gazette of Romania no. 1055 of 26 November 2005), the European Court of Human Rights condemned Romania for the infringement of Art. 8 of the Convention, considering that the Romanian authorities did not make adequate and efficient efforts to support the plaintiffs in the attempt to obtain the returning of the child for the exercise of the parental rights.

[22] For this list, see FILIPESCU ET AL, *supra* note 4, p. 635 and following. For different formulations, but similar as regards the content, see BARASCH ET AL, *supra* note 2, p. 88 and following; BACACI, A.L., DUMITRACHE, V.-C., HAGEANU, C., *Family Law*, 4th edition, (Bucharest: All Beck Publishers, 2005), p. 315 and following; FLORIAN, *supra* note 3, p. 77 and following.

[23] For further information, see FILIPESCU ET AL, *supra* note 4, pp. 647–649; FLORIAN, *supra* note 3, pp. 86–92; BARASCH ET AL, *supra* note 2, p. 228 and following.

of the child, the purpose being to ensure the material and spiritual welfare of the minor (Article 31(2) Law no. 272/2004). According to the provisions of Law no. 272/2004, the court of justice is the sole competent authority to decide in the domain of parental protection[24] and the jurisprudence has developed significant guidelines concerning the content of parental rights and duties.

Thus, as a principle, it became statutory that the regulations of the Family Code "impose imperatively a legal conduit of protection and help and protection of the parents towards the minor".[25] As regards the exercise of relations between parents and minor children it was established that "the parent who does not have in his care the child, as a consequence of *de facto* separation, keeps the same rights and obligations concerning the child, among which are the right to visit him and have personal relations with the latter".[26]

8. According to the provisions of Article 101 Family Code, the parents have the duty to take care of the child and the obligation to raise the child, taking care of his health and physical development, education, training and professional preparation of the child. In the same sense are the provisions of Articles 31 and 32 Law no. 272/2004. These provisions are fully compliant with the CEFL Principle 3:1(1): "The holders of parental responsibilities should provide the child with care, protection and education in accordance with the child's distinctive character and developmental needs".

(a) Without any doubt, the obligation to raise the child has a complex content, partially shaped by the legal provisions mentioned above, which do not exhaust the substance of this primordial duty of the parents, analysed in the doctrine in a series of manifestations regarding different sides of the relations between the parent and the minor child.[27] Correlative to this obligation, Article 32 Law no. 272/2004 enshrines the child's right to be raised in conditions which allow his physical, mental, spiritual, moral and social development. The text enumerates a series of obligations which are within the parents' duty for this purpose,[28] the enumeration only having a character of enunciation, establishing only certain

---

24 For example, in the case of disagreement between the parents regarding the exercising of parental rights and obligations, the court decides considering the superior interests of the child – Art. 31(3), and regarding the manner in which the parental rights are exercised and the parental obligations are fulfilled – Art. 38; consent to the child adoption, and so on.

25 The High Court of Justice – administrative department, decision no. 663 of 18 February 2003, available at www.scj.ro.

26 Bacau Court of Appeal, civil decision no. 82 of 9 January 1996 – taken over of the legislative soft "Lege 4".

27 BARASCH ET AL, *supra* note 2, p. 89.

28 For example, the obligation to supervise the child, to take all measures needed for the fulfillment of the child's rights, to cooperate with the individuals and legal entities exercising attributions in the domain of raising, education and professional formation of the child.

important guidelines for the conduct of the parents in the relations with the minor.

One of the important aspects of the duty to raise the child is the legal obligation of support, provided by Articles 86(1) and 107(1) Family Code: the child – as the recipient of the support – benefiting from privileged legal treatment in comparison to other persons who have the same right.[29] The parents, who have the main responsibility for raising the children, have the obligation to provide, within the limits of their possibilities, the best conditions of life needed for the raising and development of the children; respectively a house and the full material support needed for the raising, education, studies and professional preparation (Article 44(2) Law no. 272/2004).[30] The complex character of the support obligation towards a child consists of a "multitude of obligations related to the support – including food, clothing, corporal care, school pen-and-ink etc. – and not only the fulfilment of support in terms of the provision of food and accommodation".[31] If the parent does not fulfil this obligation due to imputable reasons, he can be criminally punished for family neglect, by means of Article 305 Criminal Code.

Other aspects of the parents' duty to raise the child are the obligation to take care of the physical development of the minor, education, studies and professional preparation, to ensure the protection and supervision of the child, all having a sole purpose, that is the material and spiritual welfare of the minor.

The non-fulfilment or the inadequate fulfilment of the obligation to raise, generates the possibility of the minor committing prejudicial deeds, a situation in which the parents' liability is involved, as provided by Article 1000(2) Civil Code.[32]

---

29 Thus, according to Art. 86(3) Family Code, the descendant, as long as he is a minor, has the right to support regardless of the cause of the need he is in – an important derogation from the common law rule according to which the person has the right to support if the need is caused by the incapacity to work.

30 For further information regarding the content of the parents' duty to provide for the child, see FLORIAN, *supra* note 3, p. 79 and following; BARASCH ET AL, *supra* note 2, p. 100 and following.

31 See, for example, Timiş County Tribunal, civil department, decision no. 202 of 11 February 1971, in the Romanian Law Revue no. 8/1971, p. 159 – in TIŢIAN, D., CONSTANTIN, A., CÎRSTEA, M., *Codul Familiei Adnotat [Annotated Family Code]*, (Bucharest: Hamangiu Publishers, 2007), p. 261.

32 For further information regarding the parents' responsibility for the illicit deeds of the minor children, see STĂTESCU, C., BÎRSAN, C. , *Drept civil. Teoria generală a obligaţiilor [Civil Law. General Theory of Obligations]*, (Bucharest: All Publishers, 1995), p. 192 and following;, BARASCH ET AL, *supra* note 2, p. 154 and following; ELISEI, C., *Implicaţiile informatizării societăţii asupra răspunderii părinţilor pentru prejudiciile cauzate de copiii lor minori [Implications of the state-of-the-art technology of the current society upon the parents' responsibility for their minor children]*, in *Law Review* no. 2/2002, pp. 70–85. Regarding the fact that the lack of an adequate education can be deduced from the illicit, prejudicial deeds,

(b) The right of the parents or, where relevant, of the tutors to ensure, according to their own principles, the education of their minor children is a fundamental right, enshrined by the provisions of Article 29(6) of the Constitution, being reiterated in the provisions of Article 180(1) Education Law no. 84/1995, as amended.

According to the child's right to receive an education which allows him to develop his aptitudes, the parents have the right to choose the manner of education which is going to be received by the child, having the obligation to register the child with a school and to make sure that the child attends school regularly – Article 47(2) Law no. 272/2004.[33] According to Article 47(3) of the same Act, "the child who is of 14 years of age can request a court of law to change the type of studies and professional preparation".

The complex content of the right of the child to education has been revealed also by the jurisprudence which has considered that "the purpose of education is not only the assimilation of the fundamental elements in learning (learning to read and write, expression, arithmetic etc.), but also one of overall development of the entire potential of the child."[34]

(c) Article 25(1) Law no. 272/2004 proclaims the child's right to freedom of thought, conscience and religion.[35] But as the child does not have the necessary maturity, his discernment being in formation, the parents are the ones who have to provide the education of the child according to their own principles (Article 29(6) of the Constitution) and to guide him in choosing a religion, under the provisions of the law, considering the opinion, age and stage of maturity of the child, without having the right to compel him to adhere to a certain religion or religious cult (Article 25(2) Law no. 272/2004). It is important to note that the right to guide is granted exclusively to the parents, not to other legal representatives. Thus, according to Article 5(4) Law no. 272/2004, "When the child benefits from special protection, the persons who are his guardians are prohibited from taking any actions having the purpose of influencing the child's religious convictions." The 14 year old child's religion cannot be changed without his consent; the child of 16 years of age has the right to choose his own religion (Article 25(3) Law no. 272/2004).

committed by the minor, see Galaţi Court of Appeal, decision no. 160 of 23 March 1995, in the legislative programme Lege 4.

33 The internal provisions regarding children's education comply with the exigencies of Art. 2 "Right to education" of Protocol no. 1 to the European Convention on Human Rights which enshrines the parents' rights to decide regarding the education of the children, in accordance with their philosophical and religious conceptions.

34 Craiova Court of Appeal, minors and family department, decision no. 114 of 16 March 2006 in TITIAN ET AL, *supra* note 31, p. 334.

35 This wide formula was taken over from Art. 14(1) of the UN Convention on the Rights of the Child, ratified by Romania by Law no. 18/1990.

(d) Respect for the dignity of the child is a fundamental principle within the range of children's rights (Article 6(g) Law no. 272/2004), and the child's dignity is indissolubly related to respecting his individuality and personality; the consequence being the one that, according to Article 28(1) of the same law, the minor cannot be subjected to physical punishment or other humiliating or degrading treatment. According to paragraph (2) of the same Article, "The measures of discipline taken towards the child can only be established in accordance with the dignity of the child, physical punishment or those in relation to the physical, psychological development, or which affect the emotional state of the child not being permitted." This legislative solution is reiterated in the content of Article 90 of the same law, in the context of the protection of the child against abuse or negligence.[36] These Romanian legal provisions are clearly in line with the CEFL Principle 3:11(2): "(2) The child should not be subjected to corporal punishment or any other humiliating treatment."

When the values protected by the above legal provisions are endangered by the abusive conduct of the parent, the sanction of total or partial removal from the parent of the exercise of his rights can be ordered, as provided by Articles 109–112 Family Code and Article 36 Law no. 272/2004.[37] This kind of measure can be also found in the CEFL Principle 3:32 ("Discharge of parental responsibilities").

In such situations, according to Article 39(2) Law no. 272/2004, the child will benefit from an alternative protection measure, respectively custody, another special measure provided by Law no. 272/2004,[38] or adoption. Also, if the constitutive elements of the offence of abuse of the minor are met, the parent can be criminally sanctioned, as provided by Article 306 Criminal Code.

(e) The right to health is a fundamental right, guaranteed to all citizens by the provisions of Article 34 of the Constitution, republished. Applying this principle, Article 43(1) Law no. 272/2004 proclaims the child's right "to enjoy the best state of health which he can reach and to benefit from the medical services and the recuperation services needed to ensure the effective execution of this right".[39]

---

36 According to Art. 90 Law no. 272/2004, "*The application of physical punishment in any form is forbidden, as well as deprivation of the child of his rights so as to endanger his life, his physical, mental, spiritual, moral or social development, the corporal integrity, the physical or psychological integrity of the child, in the family and in any institution ensuring the protection, attendance and education of the children.*" For further information regarding the child's right to respect for his personality and individuality, see FLORIAN, *supra* note 3, pp. 50–51.

37 For further information, see, FLORIAN, *supra* note 3, p. 106 and following; AVRAM, M., BÂRSAN, C., *Unele considerații cu referire la sancțiunile care au ca efect pierderea drepturilor părintești [Certain considerations regarding the sanctions having as effect the losing of the parental rights]*, in *Dreptul* nr. 11/2002, p. 48 and following.

38 Placement and emergency placement, specialised supervision– Art. 55 of the law.

39 Certain positive obligations to ensure the effective guarantee of this right of the child, all the costs corresponding to the medical and recovery services, as well as the value of the medication

The parents are compelled to request medical assistance to provide for the child the best state of health and to prevent situations endangering the child's life, upbringing and development (Article 43(4) Law no. 272/2004). The medical acts regarding the child are taken with the agreement of the parent or of another representative of the child, and only in exceptional situations "when the life of the child is in imminent danger or there is the risk of serious consequences regarding the health or integrity of the child, the physician has the right to perform medical acts of strict necessity to save the child's life, even without having the parents' or another legal representative's agreement" (paragraph (5) of the same Article).[40]

(f) Given his lack of age, the child cannot exercise personally his rights and fulfil his obligations. The intervention of the parents is necessary or, where relevant, of the other persons to whom parental rights and duties have been transferred; intervention which is concretised in the legal mechanism of representation (in the case of the minor who lacks capacity to act – "capacity to act") and of approving acts concluded by the child (in the situation of the minor with limited capacity of exercise, respectively between 14 and 18 years), according to Articles 105 and 124 Family Code, Articles 8–11 Decree no. 31/1954 and Article 31(2) Law no. 272/2004. These provisions are similar to the CEFL Principle 3:24(1) ("Legal representation"): "The holders of parental responsibilities should legally represent the child in matters concerning the child's person or property".

Until the age of 14 a minor is represented in legal acts[41] by his parents or, where relevant, by his tutor, the representation having legal character (being provided by the law, which establishes the conditions as well as the limits of the representation) and general character (meaning that the empowerment is not limited to one or

being paid from the National Unique Fund for social and health assurances and by the state budget are provided –Art. 43(2) Law no. 272/2004, provisions which are completed with those of the frame law in the domain, respectively Law no. 95/2006 regarding the reform in the area of health.

40 These provisions with general character are concretised, for various particular situations, by a series of provisions of the Law no. 95/2006 regarding the reform in the area of health. As regards the taking of cells from a minor donor, Art. 145 of the law establishes that it is conditional, in the case of the minor under 14 years, on the existence of the agreement of the legal representative, and only if the minor is over 14 years old the taking of cells is made only with his consent and the written agreement of the legal guardian, respectively the parents, tutor or custodian. Also, in the case of transplant, if the receiver is a minor, the consent is given by the parents or by the other persons who may be the legal representative/protector of the minor – Art. 152 Law no. 95/2006.

41 The mechanism of legal representation functions not only in the case of legal acts of substantive law, but also for procedural acts, Art. 42 Civil Procedure Code providing that the persons who cannot exercise their rights can appear before the court only if they are represented, assisted or authorised according to the law. For further information, see CIOBANU, V. M., *Tratat teoretic şi practic de procedură civilă [Theoretical and practical treaty of civil procedure]*, tome I., *Teoria generală [General Theory]*, (Bucharest: Naţional Publishers, 1996), pp. 276–279.

more individual acts).[42] The parents or the tutor, themselves, can conclude acts of administration of the assets of the child and acts of administration of his patrimony, while for the valid conclusion of acts of disposition the prior agreement of the tutelary authority is needed[43] (Article 105(3) together with Article 129(2) Family Code). These provisions of Romanian legislation are consistent with the CEFL Principle 3.23(3): "Where transactions can have significant financial consequences for the child the authorisation of the competent authority should be necessary."

Non-compliance with the rules in the field of legal representation results in the nullity of the substantial legal act – Article 129(3) Family Code, respectively of the procedural law – Article 43(2) Civil Procedure Code.[44]

Where guardianship could not be instituted for the child and the court ordered the measure of placement,[45] parental rights and obligations regarding the person and assets of the child (including legal representation) are exercised respectively by the president of the county council or, where appropriate, by the mayor of the Bucharest city department, according to Article 62(2) Law no. 272/2004. During the emergency placement,[46] the exercise of parental rights is suspended. During the suspension, parental rights and obligations regarding the person of the child, are exercised, respectively by the person, family, maternal assistant or by the head of the residential service which received the child in placement in emergency regime, and, those regarding the assets of the child, by the president of the county council or, where relevant, by the mayor of the Bucharest city department (Article 64(3) Law no. 272/2004).

After the age of 14, (when the minor acquires limited capacity to act, according to Article 9(1) Decree no. 31/1954), he personally exercises his rights and also performs his obligations, but with the prior approval of the parents or, where relevant, of the tutor, in order to be protected against abuse from third parties (Articles 105(2) and 133(1) Family Code). The parental protection of the child with limited capacity to act is also manifested in relation to the exercise of his procedural rights, which means that the minor between 14 – 18 years can stand

42 FLORIAN, *supra* note 3, p. 89.

43 The tutelary authority exercises the attributions provided by the law regarding the parental protection and the minor's guardianship, according to Art. 159 Family Code; according to Law no. 215/2001, the function of tutelary authority is performed by the mayor of the local public administration.

44 For further information, see FLORIAN, *supra* note 3, p. 88 and following; FILIPESCU ET AL, *supra* note 4 pp. 648–649; BARASCH ET AL, *supra* note 2, p. 268 and following.

45 The placement is one of the special protection measures regulated by Law no. 272/2004.

46 The emergency placement of the child is a special measure of protection, with temporary character, which is established in the situation of the abused or neglected child, as well as in the situation of the child found or abandoned in health units – Art. 64(1) Law no. 272/2004.

personally in front of the court of justice, assisted by the legal guardian (Article 42 Civil Procedure Code), the assistance being needed during the whole trial.[47] As a special measure of protection for the protected child, in the case of procedural acts of disposition (such as renouncement to judgment, renouncement of the claimed right), the assistance of the legal guardian must be accompanied by the authorisation of the tutelary authority.

In the field of labour relationships, the Labour Code – Law no. 53/2003 – provides the rule according to which each person acquires capacity to work at the age of 16. By exception, the individual can conclude a labour contract as an employee on reaching the age of 15, if a series of conditions are cumulatively fulfilled, conditions among which is the approval of the parents or the legal guardians – Article 13(1) and (2) of the mentioned Code[48] (the conclusion of a labour contract by a minor under 15 years is prohibited by Article 49(4) of the Constitution).

A last remark regarding the representation or approval of the minor's acts: according to Article 29(1) Law no. 272/2004, as regards the infringement of his fundamental rights, the child has the right to file on his own claims, regardless of his age and, therefore, without being represented.

9. Article 24 Law no. 272/2004 provides the right of the child, capable of discernment, to freely express his opinion on any issue concerning him; the text being in agreement with the provisions of Article 12 of the UN Convention on the Rights of the Child (ratified by Romania by the Law no. 18/1990). The opinions of the child will be taken into consideration and they will enjoy adequate importance, with regard to the age and maturity of the child (Article 24(4) Law no. 272/2004).

In any judicial or administrative procedure regarding the child, he has the right to be heard,[49] with the following distinction: listening to the child over 10 years old is compulsory, while listening to the child under this age is permissible, being under the competent authority's decision (Article 24(2) of the same law). The child can also have an active attitude, requesting the judicial or administrative authority to listen to him, regardless of whether he is 10 years old or not, in which case any refusal of the competent authority must be justified (Article 24(5)).

---

47 The non-assistance of the minor with limited capacity to act party in the trial, leads to the nullity of the decision issued (see Supreme Court, civil department, decision no. 2546/1985 in the Romanian Law Review no. 9/1986, p. 65, in FLORIAN, *supra* note 3, p. 91).

48 For further information, see ATHANASIU, A.L., DIMA, L., *Dreptul muncii [Labor Law]*, (Bucharest: All Beck Publishers, 2005), pp. 33–34.

49 As regards the legal content of the legal right of the child to be heard and the legal value of his opinion, see also CERCEL, S., GHIȚĂ, D., *Comment* on the decision no. 284 of 11 July 2005 of Craiova Court of Appeal – family and minors department, in the Curierul Judiciar no. 6/2006, p. 10 and following.

It is important to note that the right to be heard offers the child the possibility to request and receive any pertinent information, to be consulted, to express his opinion and to be informed of the consequences of his opinion, if it is complied with, as well as on the consequences of any decision regarding him (Article 24(3)).

In respect of certain serious decisions concerning the child, including some which are irreversible, the law requires the personal consent of the child. Thus, in the field of adoption, the lack of consent of the child over 10 years of age, has the effect of preventing the finalising of the procedure of adoption– Articles 11(1)(b) and Article 17(2) Law no. 273/2004 – and according to Article 53(3)(I) Law no. 272/2004, "the measures of special protection of the child older then 14 years are established with consent of the latter". In this last instance, the request for the consent of the minor is more flexible, the above mentioned text allowing the court to ignore the refusal of the minor to express his opinion, in very well grounded situations.[50]

Regarding education, as already mentioned, according to Article 47(3) Law no. 272/2004, the child older then 14 years has the right to request the court to change the type of his studies and his professional preparation. Also, as regards the religion of the child, Article 25(3) of the same Act provides that it cannot be changed without the consent of the child older then 14 years, and from the age of 16 the child has the right to choose his religion.

In divorce cases, in order to decide which parent should have primary care of the child, the court will listen to the child (compulsory or permissible depending on whether the child is or is not 10 years old), his opinion being taken into consideration and granting it adequate importance, depending on the child's age and maturity.[51] In the case of *Ignaccolo-Zenide vs Romania*,[52] the European Court of Human Rights considered that where the parents' interests are in conflict, the opinion and preferences of the children must be heard and taken into consideration in the procedures and decisions regarding them.

All these provisions of Romanian legislation and their application in the jurisprudence can be seen to reflect in the domestic legal field the CEFL Principle 3:6 ("Child's right to be heard"), which states: "Having regard to the child's age and maturity, the child should have the right to be informed, consulted and to

---

50 See FLORIAN, *supra* note 3, p. 48.

51 In a case settled by the Craiova Court of Appeal (minors and family department, decision no. 284 of 11 July 2005, in Curierul Judiciar no. 6/2006), considering that the minor does not have the needed maturity to acknowledge the consequences of his opinion, the custody of the child was given to the mother, although he manifested the wish to be given to the custody of the father.

52 Published in the Official Gazette of Romania, Part I, no. 6 of 8 January 2001.

express his or her opinion in all matters concerning the child, with due weight given to the views expressed by him or her."

10. As has been shown, parental rights and duties are exercised not only in relation to the child's person, but also his property; the Family Code (Articles 43, 105 and 124) and Law no. 272/2004 (Article 31(2)) providing the right and the duty of the parents or, where appropriate, of the tutor, to administer the minor child's assets. The measures regarding the child's assets are taken by the parents in mutual agreement; if one of the parents is dead, no longer has parental rights, is subject to interdict or, for any reason, is not able to manifest his will, the other parent exercises parental rights alone (Article 98 Family Code).

If the court has ordered the placement or the emergency placement of the child, the parental rights and obligations regarding the assets of the child are exercised by the president of the county council or by the Mayor of the Bucharest city department, respectively, according to Articles 62(2) and 64(3) Law no. 272/2004.

11. As regards the content of the right to administer the minor's property, some clarification is needed. We reiterate a general principle applicable in the domain of parental protection, according to which patrimonial relationships between parents and children are governed by the rule of patrimonial independence, instituted by Article 106 Family Code.[53] Thus, the two patrimonies do not merge, but remain completely distinct and do not have elements of contiguity, with the exception of the right to inheritance and the right to support.[54]

The parent, as well as the tutor, is forbidden to conclude any acts that would supercede the right to administration of the child's patrimony without the prior consent of the tutelary authority (Article 105(3) together with Article 129(2) Family Code). In the absence of legal definition, the doctrine attributed a wider meaning to the notion of "administration of the child's assets", including not only the intrinsic administration acts, but also the disposition acts, if – by their finality – they constitute acts of administration of the patrimony (for example, the acts of sale of assets subject to destruction or deterioration and of those not useful for the minor, if the value of the latter is under RON 250, approximately EUR 60 – Article 129(4) Family Code).[55]

---

53 According to Art. 106 Family Code, "*The parent has no right on the child's assets, nor the child on the parent's assets, except for the right to inheritance and support.*"

54 As we have mentioned, under the provisions of the Civil Code of 1864 the parents had the right to usufruct and legal use of their child's assets.

55 For further information, see BARASCH ET AL, *supra* note 2, p. 228 and following; FLORIAN, *supra* note 3, pp. 87–88; FILIPESCU ET AL, *supra* note 4, p. 647.

In the situation of intrinsic disposition acts (for example the alienation or pledge of the child), prior agreement from the tutelary authority is needed, which is issued for each case and only if the act is the consequence of a need or present an undoubted use for the child (Article 130(1) and (2) Family Code). In the doctrine, acts which exceed the limits of the right to administration are also taken into consideration: acceptance of a bequest in the name of the child, the real estate lease agreement concluded on an excessive period and the contracting of a loan in the name of the child.[56]

As we have already underlined (*supra* 8(f)), these provisions contain "restrictions" regarding the exercise of parental responsibility in the field of the child's property, similar to those provided by the CEFL Principle 3:23.

12. For the protection of the patrimonial interests of the child, certain legal acts are forbidden to the legal representative: thus, according to Article 105(3) and Article 129(1) Family Code, the parent or the tutor, where there is one, cannot make donations in the name of the child or secure the other's obligation.

One may recognise here the idea which is also present in the CEFL Principle 3:22(2) ("Administration of the child's property"), forbidding the holders of the parental responsibility to make gifts, unless these gifts are deemed to be made under a moral obligation.

At the same time, according to Article 128 of the same code, "it is forbidden to conclude legal acts between the tutor, spouse, a direct relative or brothers or sisters of the tutor, on one side and the minor, on the other side".

Other protective measures introduced by the Family Code for the purpose of avoiding prejudice of the patrimonial interests of the child by faulty administration of the assets by his legal representatives are:

- appointment of a curator under the conditions of Article 132 Family Code, when the parents or the tutor – on the one side – and the minor – on the other – have a conflict of interest (the same idea can be found in the CEFL Principle 3:24(1): "Legal representation should not take place where there is a conflict of interest between the child and the holders of parental responsibilities");
- the preparation of an inventory regarding the minor's assets; the parents have this obligation only if the minor has assets other than those for personal use (Articles 105(3) and 126 Family Code);
- the obligation of the parent or the tutor to present to the tutelary authority a report on the manner of administration of the minor's assets, annually or

[56] FLORIAN, *supra* note 3, p. 88.

whenever requested, as well as a general report at the end of the guardianship (Articles 134 and 140 Family Code);

- to deposit, in the name of the minor, with a "state savings institution",[57] the amounts of money higher then the needs of the minor and of the administration of his assets, as well as the debentures, from where they can be withdrawn only with the agreement of the tutelary authority (Article 131(1) Family Code);
- the claims the tutor, spouse, direct relative or brothers or sisters of the tutor have towards the minor can only be paid with the approval of the tutelary authority (Article 126(2) Family Code, text applicable also to the parents, according to Article 105(3) of the same Code);
- the obligation of the tutelary authority to exercise effective and continuous control on the manner in which the parents/tutor fulfil their duties regarding the minor's assets (Article 136 Family Code).

13. As regards protection of children against the indebtedness caused by the holders of parental protection, reference can be made, on the one hand, to the general principle of patrimonial independence between parents and children (Article 106 Family Code) and the prohibition of donations and of granting security over the other's obligation in the name of the child (Article 129(1) Family Code).

On the other hand, the parents, as well as the tutors, are responsible for the damage caused to the minor by their fault in the administration of his assets, regardless of whether the respective acts are committed by acting against the provisions of the law or by not taking action as provided by the law – Articles 105(3) and 141(2) Family Code. If the constitutive elements of the crime of fraudulent administration are met, in terms of Article 214 Criminal Code,[58] the parents or, where relevant, the tutor, can be criminally charged.

In conclusion, we can say that some of the CEFL Principles concerning the content of parental responsibility regarding the child's property have their express correspondent in the Romanian Law (e.g., Principles 3:22(2), 3:23(3) or 3:24(1) and (2)), others are reflected in our domestic legislation by several different

---

57 We consider that in the present configuration of the banking system of Romania, the expression "state savings institution" of the Family Code (adopted in 1954) must be interpreted as regarding the credit institutions, as defined by Art. 7(1)(10) Emergency Governemet Ordinance no. 99/2006 regarding the credit institutions and the capital adequacy (Official Gazette of Romania no. 1027 of 27 December 2006), approved with modifications and completions by Law no. 227/2007 (Official Gazette of Romania no. 480 of 18 July 2007) – the Romanian regulation in this domain.

58 According to Art. 214 Criminal Code, fraudulent administration crime is constituted by the "causing of a damage to a person, in bad faith, on the occasion of the administration or conservation of the assets of the respective person, by the one who administers or protects or should administer or protect the respective assets."

provisions (e.g. Principle 3:22(1), whilst others have no correspondent in our laws (e.g., Principles 3:22(3), 3:23(1) and (2)).

14. The content of parental rights and duties is the same regardless of whether they are exercised by married parents – living together or separately, unmarried or adoptive parents (foster parents),[59] they being the only persons who have the right to exercise the full complement of rights and obligations covered by parental protection (for the stepparent, see *infra*, 27(a)).

But there are certain circumstances when the separation of parental protection can occur; the situation in which parents exercise the protection not-equally, (in case of divorce, the termination of marriage, as well as the custody of the child born outside marriage with the parenthood established towards both parents),[60] or where the protection of the child is divided between the parents and the person, family or institution with whom the minor has been placed.[61]

The measure of the placement of the child, ordered by the court according to Article 61(2) Law no. 272/2004, also determines the division of parental protection. Thus, in this situation, the parental rights and obligations are exercised respectively by the president of the county council or, where appropriate, by the Mayor of the Bucharest city department. In respect of a child who is the subject of a placement order, the parent retains the right to have personal relations, the right to consent to the adoption of the child (including the parent who no longer has rights or the parent who has been prohibited from exercising parental rights) and has the obligation to support him (Articles 62(3) and 63 Law no. 272/2004).

Certain "prerogatives" foreseen by parental protection can also benefit other persons (for example according to Article 14 Law no. 272/2004, the child has the right to maintain direct contact not only with the parents, but also with the relatives, as well as other persons with whom he has developed relations of attachment). These persons may also have certain specific duties regarding the minor (the support obligation of the grand-parents towards the grand-children – Art. 86 Family Code), but this does not imply the exercise of the parental authority.

All these situations provided by Romanian law are also covered by some of the CEFL Principles: Principle 3:15 ("Sole exercise upon agreement or decision"), Principle 3:16 ("Sole exercise by one parent") and Principle 3.17 ("Exercise in addition to or instead of the parents").

---

59 According to Art. 51(1) Law no. 273/2004, towards the adopted child the adopting person has the rights and duties of the natural parent towards his child.

60 For details, see *infra*, **16.**

61 BARASCH ET AL, *supra* note 2, p. 50; FLORIAN, *supra* note 3, p. 96.

3. THE ATTRIBUTION OF PARENTAL PROTECTION

3.1. THE SITUATION OF MARRIED PARENTS

15. The fundamental principle of the equality of the spouses, enshrined by the provisions of Article 48(1) of the Constitution, is also applicable to the relations between parents and their children, Article 97(1) Family Code providing that "both parents have the same rights and duties towards their minor children", while Article 98(1) of the same Code gives statutory force to the provision that "the measures regarding the person and assets of the child are taken by the parents, on mutual agreement". The provisions of Article 31(1) Law no. 272/2004, according to which "both parents are responsible to raise their children", are in a similar vein. Thus, the rule is that parental protection should be exercised at the same time and equally by both parents which is similar to the CEFL Principle 3:11 ("Joint exercise").

(a) If the parents are married at the time of the child's birth, they will exercise parental protection together and equally. But, if the husband of the mother – the supposed father of the child according to Article 53 Family Code – challenges the presumption of paternity, the court decision admitting his claim retroactively modifies the civil status of the child, who becomes born outside marriage, and consequently parental protection is exercised only by the mother. The subsequent establishment of paternity in respect of the unmarried father (by acknowledgement or court decision) will adequately complete the parental protection.

(b) In the Romanian legal system, the subsequent marriage of the child's parents does not produce effects regarding the civil status of the child, he remaining a child born outside the marriage. The institution of "legitimisation" by marriage is no longer provided by the current legal framework[62] due to the fact that, under the principle of the full assimilation of the legal status of the child outside marriage with the one from marriage,[63] this institution would no longer be of interest.

If parenthood of the child is established in respect of both parents, they have equal rights and duties regarding the person and property of the child.

---

62 Under the provisions of the Romanian Civil Code of 1864, according to Art. 304 the natural children could be legitimated by the subsequent marriage of the parents, but only if they recognised them by the birth certificate or by an authentic act prior to the marriage, or by the marriage certificate.

63 Enshrined in the provisions of Art. 48(3) of the Constitution, republished and reaffirmed by the provisions of Art. 63 Family Code and of Art. 7 Law no. 272/2004. The principle is proclaimed also by Art. 10 of the European Convention on the legal status of the children born outside the marriage, concluded in Strasbourg on 15 October 1975, to which Romania adhered by Law no. 101/1992.

16. There are some specific points concerning the exercise of parental protection in the case of divorce and annulment of marriage. Legal separation of the spouses is not regulated in Romania and, in principle, the factual separation does not affect the exercise of parental protection, as will be described below.

(a) In case of divorce, parental protection is exercised by the parent having custody of the child; the other parent keeping the right to have a personal relationship with the child,[64] as well as to supervise his raising, education, studies and professional preparation (Article 43(1) and (3) Family Code).[65]

The right to maintain a personal relationship with the child has the same content as that provided by the CEFL Principle 3:25(1) ("Contact with parents and other persons"): "The child and the parents should have the right to obtain and maintain regular contact with each other".

The divorced parent who did not receive custody of the child still has the obligation to support the minor (Articles 42(2), 86 and 107 Family Code), also keeping the right to consent to the child's adoption (Article 11(a) Law no. 273/2004).[66] It is important to specify the fact that the court decision giving the custody of the child has provisory *res judicata* power, meaning that the divorced parent who has not received child custody can request the court, in case of change of circumstances, to modify the measures regarding the personal or patrimonial rights and obligations between the divorced parents and the children (Article 44 Family Code).[67]

---

64 Where the children and the parents live in different states, provisions of the Strasbourg Convention become incidental on the personal relations regarding the children, ratified by Romania by Law no. 87/2007 (Official Gazette of Romania no. 257 of 17 April 2007).

65 By Decision no. 411/2006 (Official Gazette of Romania no. 530 of 20 June 2006), the Constitutional Court decided that the provisions of Art. 43(3) Family Code are not contrary to the principle of equality of rights enshrined in Art. 16 of the fundamental law. In the reasoning of the decision it was noted that "*The parent who did not receive custody of the child keeps the exercise of parental rights, even if it appears as being different to the exercise of parental rights during marriage and to the exercise of parental rights of the parent who received custody of the child. These differences are determined by the separation of the parents and the objective possibility of sustenance after the termination of the marriage of the same manner of exercise of parental rights and duties.*"

66 For further information regarding the rights recognised to the divorced parent who did not receive the custody of the child, see FLORIAN, *supra* note 3, p. 97 and following.

67 It was decided that a partial change of the conditions which all together determined that the giving of the custody of the child be made to one of the parents must not necessarily result in reconsideration of the measure as long as the basic elements of the decision still exist, which confirm the necessity that the measure taken in the minor child's interest be maintained. (The Supreme Court, civil decision no. 616 of 23 April 1981, in *Romanian Law Journal – Revista Română de Drept* – no. 1/1982, p. 59, in FILIPESCU ET AL, *supra* note 4, p. 298).

Also in case of divorce, if the court decides to give custody of the child to another person or protection institution, for good reasons concerning the superior interests of the child (according to Article 42(2) Family Code), the exercise of the parental rights and duties will be divided as follows: the parent appointed by the court will exercise all the rights regarding the assets of the child, while the person or institution of special protection will have the rights and obligations regarding the person of the child (Article 43(2) Family Code).

The above rules are similarly applicable in the situation of the annulment of marriage (Article 24(2) Family Code),[68] as well as in the case of giving custody of a child born outwith marriage whose parenthood was established towards both parents (Article 65 Family Code).[69]

(b) *De lege lata*, Romanian law does not regulate the separation of spouses as a legal institution, but Article 23 Law no. 105/1992 regarding private international law relationships contains conflicting norms to determine the substantial law applicable to the situation when both spouses have the right to request separation according to their national law or the law of their domicile.

In internal law, the fact that the spouses are actually separated *de facto* has no influence on the manner of exercise of parental protection; nevertheless, according to Article 100(2) and (3) Family Code, if the child will live with one parent, his home will be determined either by the parents' agreement, or, in case of disagreement, by the court of justice.[70] This gives rise to a number of consequences for the fulfilment and exercise of parental rights: for example, only the parent with whom the child is living has the right to request the return of the child from any person holding him without right; this parent will be responsible, according to Article 1000(2) Civil Code for the torts committed by the minor.[71]

17. According to Article 42(4) Family Code, in case of divorce the parents can reach an agreement regarding the custody of minor children, but this agreement

---

68 Although according to Art. 23(2) Family Code the declaration of the nullity of the marriage does not have any effect as regards the child resulting from the null or annulled marriage (who retains his legal status as a child born in marriage), still the termination of the parents' marriage affects the exercise of parental protection. See also FLORIAN, *supra* note 3, p. 101 and decision no. 58/1993 of the Supreme Court of Justice – civil department, in *Jurisprudence Bulletin, data base*, (C.H. Beck).

69 For further information, see FILIPESCU ET AL, *supra* note 4, pp 623–624; BARASCH ET AL, *supra* note 2, pp. 53–55.

70 See High Court of Justice – civil department, decision no. 2665 of 13 December 1991, in the *Jurisprudence Bulletin, data base*, (C.H. Beck) in which the court established the domicile of the minor with the mother, noting that in assessing the child's interests it was wrong to consider only the living conditions and material means of one or the other parent.

71 BARASCH ET AL, *supra* note 2, p. 173.

can only have effects if it is approved by the court of law,[72] by means of which it can be checked that it is in the superior interests of the child. This is a consequence of the impossibility of derogation by legal act from the legal regulation.[73] The provisions are applicable, in a similar way, in the case of granting custody of a child following the annulment of the parents' marriage (Article 24(2) Family Code) or in the case of unmarried parents (Article 65 Family Code).

18. In case of divorce, as well as in other similar cases, a division of parental protection occurs and, as a consequence, the exercise of parental rights and duties is not performed at the same time and equally by both parents; the court needing to decide to which of the parents custody of the child should be granted, due to the fact that the present legislation does not provide the solution of the joint exercise of the parental authority in such situations. In practice, the court is guided by a wide range of factors (among them, the violent attitude of one of the parents, which cannot be, obviously, ignored), all of which share the principal objective of complying with the higher interests of the child.[74]

19. No statistical information exists.

3.2. THE SITUATION OF UNMARRIED PARENTS

20. In our legal system, as we have already shown (*supra*, **5**), the principle of the full assimilation of the legal situation of the child outside marriage with one born in marriage (Article 48(3) Constitution and Article 63 Family Code) applies. If parenthood is legally established as regards both parents, they have, according to Article 97(1) Family Code, the same rights and the same obligations towards a minor child born outwith marriage. Thus, if they are in agreement, the unmarried parents of a child, regardless of whether or not they are cohabiting, jointly exercise parental protection.

21. *De lege lata*, the Romanian legal system does not have provisions regulating civil unions (partnerships) between persons of the same sex or of different sex,

---

72 Even if an express request from the parents regarding the custody of the minor children does not exist, the court of justice is not compelled to decide with the divorce decision also on this aspect, in order to avoid the subsequent filing of a new claim, which would not be in the best interests of the children. (Supreme Court, guiding decision no. 10 of 13 November 1969, **5(b)**, in FILIPESCU ET AL, *supra* note 4, p. 293).

73 In this regard, see BARASCH ET AL, *supra* note 2, p. 153.

74 See Timişoara Court of Appeal, civil department, commission specialised for minors and family, decision no. 254 31 January 2006, taken from *http://portal.just.ro* – portal of the courts of justice, through which the following was decided: the higher interests of the child "*is determined by the examination of all the criteria of appreciation, as are the age of the child, each parent's conduct, their material circumstances, their capacity to effectively take care of the child*".

which are recognised in some other legal systems on the model of the marriage. Thus, for unmarried parents there is no alternative legal manner of "formalisation" of their relationship, which has implications for parental protection.

22. If the parents of a child born outwith marriage do not reach an agreement regarding the exercise of parental protection, it can be divided[75] by the court, which – at the request of any parent – will decide to give the custody of the child to one or to the other. In this respect, according to Article 65 Family Code, "if the parenthood of the child outwith marriage is established as regards both parents, his custody, as well as the contribution of the parents to the expenses for raising, education, studies and professional preparation, will be decided according to the provisions of Articles 42 – 44 inclusively, which apply by analogy." Due to the fact that the texts to which reference is made are those in the domain of divorce, the solutions provided in this domain (see *supra*, **16** – **17**) will apply, according to the law, also in the case of the division of parental protection as a result of the fact that the minor is born outwith marriage.

23. The termination of the cohabitation of unmarried parents does not necessarily affect the exercise of parental protection, which can still be performed jointly, if neither of the parents requests the custody of the children born from that cohabitation relationship (see *supra*, **22**).

24. Due to the fact that Romanian legislation does not provide the possibility that the court attribute the joint exercise of the parental protection, but only gives custody of the child to one of the parents (Articles 42 – 44 and 65 Family Code), the non-agreement of the parents on this issue cannot arise. A diverse range of criteria is taken into consideration by the court in deciding to give custody of the child to one or other parent (applicable regardless of the marital status of the parents): age of the child, his attachment to either parent, the moral behaviour of the parents, their violent attitude etc.

25. As mentioned, due to the fact that in the case of unmarried parents the custody of the child is given according to the rules applicable in case of divorce (Articles 42–44 and 65 Family Code), the parents can reach an agreement regarding custody, but the agreement must be approved by the court (Article 42(4) Family Code).

26. There is no statistical information available.

---

[75] In this regard, see BARASCH ET AL, *supra* note 2, p. 200.

3.3. OTHER PERSONS

27. The Romanian law regulates the exercise of parental protection by persons other than the parents, as the CEFL Principles also do: the Principles 3:9 – "Third persons" ("Parental responsibilities may in whole or in part also be attributed to a person other than a parent") and 3:17 – "Exercise in addition to or instead of the parents" ("A person other than a parent may exercise some or all parental responsibilities in addition to or instead the parents"). But Romania has no legal provisions similar to the Principle 3:18 ("Decisions in daily matters"), which provides that "The parent's partner living with the child may take part in decisions with respect to daily matters, unless the other parent having parental responsibilities objects".

(a) The person who is married to the natural parent of the child (step parent) can become a holder of parental rights and obligations regarding the child only if he or she adopts the child.[76] Once the adoption is agreed, the exercise of parental protection is fulfilled by the adopting person and by the natural parent married to that person (Article 51(2) Law no. 273/2004), the parental rights and obligations being exercised according to the provisions of Article 97 *et seq* Family Code. The extinctive effects produced by the adoption regarding the relations of natural parenthood and kinship will be produced only partially, Article 50(3) Law no. 273/2004 providing that in the case of adoption concluded under these conditions the termination of the kinship relations are applied only regarding the natural parent and the relatives of the natural parent who is not married to the adopting person.

If the natural parent of the child and the step parent – the adoptive parent of the minor – divorce,[77] the rules of divorce apply as regards the custody of the child, with division of parental protection between the natural parent and the adoptive parent, under the conditions mentioned *supra* (**16** and **17**).

Even in the absence of a relation of civil parenthood derived from adoption, the spouse of the natural parent who has charge of the minor may be subject to an obligation of support under the conditions of Article 87 Family Code, according to which "The spouse who contributed to the child support of the other spouse is

---

76 Law no. 273/2004 provides a simplified procedure in the hypothetical case when the adopting person is the spouse of the natural parent of the child. Thus, in such a situation it is not necessary to obtain a "certificate of person able to adopt" (Art. 20(b) of the law) or pass through the first two steps of the adoption: the opening of the internal adoption procedure and the giving in custody in view of adoption (Art. 24 and Art. 29). The request for agreement of the adoption can be filed directly by the adopting person (Art. 35(1) of the law).

77 As we have shown, the sole legal manner through which the partner of the natural parent acquires parental rights and duties regarding the respective child is adoption.

compelled to carry on in sustaining the child, as long as he is a minor, but only if his natural parents are dead, missing or are in need".

(b) As already mentioned, Romanian law has no regulation of cohabitation, as some other legal systems do (registered partnership, civil union, *pacte civil de solidarité*).

(c) Concubinage of the natural parent of the child with another person who is not the parent, does not give rise to parental rights and obligations regarding that child.

28. In Romanian law, relationships between persons of the same sex are not regulated and, even less, the situation in which such couples raise a child; the doctrine does not analyse, and the jurisprudence has not been confronted with, such a hypothesis.

29. The lack of regulation of unmarried cohabitation, as well as the regulation according to which parental protection is exercised only by the parents, means that there is no issue relating to the exercise of parental protection, arising as a result of the separation of unmarried partners (where one is the parent of a child). Also, in such a hypothesis, there cannot exist the issue of the adoption of the child of the other partner, due to the fact that – according to Law no. 273/2004 regarding the legal regime of adoption – the adoption of the child of a person who wishes to keep parenthood relations with his child can only be made by the spouse of that person.

30. For the same reasons as above (**29**) unmarried partners (where only one is the parent of the child) cannot make an agreement regarding the parental protection of that child.

31. Any child who lacks, temporarily or permanently the protection of his parents or who, for the protection of his interests cannot be left in their care, has the right to alternative protection – Article 39(1) Law no. 272/2004 – the ways of substitution for parental protection being, according to paragraph (2) of the same Article, the institution of tutorship, measures of special protection and adoption.

The role played by the tutor is to substitute the parents, he being compelled to raise the child, to take care of his health and physical development, education, studies and professional preparation and, as regards the patrimonial side of protection, to administer the child's assets and ensure his legal representation – Articles 123 and 124 Family Code. Considering also the circumstances which determine the institution of tutorship,[78] the tutor must exercise on his own the rights and duties implied by the minor's protection, substituting the lack (physical or legal) of the parents. Certain "remnants" of parental rights and obligations can still be found in the parents' person, the legal solution in this sense being imposed by the need to comply with the principle of the superior interests of the child.[79]

According to Article 42(1) Law no. 272/2004, "the court appoints with priority as tutor, if there are no justifiable reasons against such action, a family member or relative or friend of the child's family, who is able to fulfil such charge", the person of the tutor being therefore selected from the group of persons most probably emotionally attached to the child and vice-versa.[80]

In the case of adoption, according to Article 51(1) Law no. 273/2004, the adopting person has towards the adopted the rights and obligations of the natural parent towards his child. From the moment adoption is established, the natural kinship between the adopted and his descendants, on one side, and the natural parents and their relatives, on the other side, is terminated.

There are also certain situations when, in order to comply with the superior interests of the child, a division of parental protection between the parents and a third party, either an individual or legal entity, occurs.

Thus, in case of divorce, "for justified reasons, the children can be given in custody to relatives or other persons with their consent, or to protection institutions" – Article 42(2) Family Code. The exercise of parental rights and obligations will be divided as follows: the parent appointed by the court will exercise the rights regarding the property of the child and the person or the social protection institution will exercise the rights and duties regarding the person of the child (Article 43(2) Family Code).

---

78 The parents of the child are deceased, unknown, no longer have the right to exercise parental rights or are punished by the removal of parental rights, under restraining order, declared by a court decision dead or missing – Art. 113 Family Code and Art. 40(1) Law no. 272/2004.

79 Thus, according to Art. 12(2) Law no. 273/2004, the parent or parents who no longer have parental rights keep the right to consent to the adoption of the child. In this case the consent of the tutor is also obligatory. According to Art. 110 Family Code, the loss of parental rights does not exempt a parent from his duty to support the child. Also, the right of the parents who no longer have parental rights or who have been forbidden to have personal relationships with the child is not automatically terminated by the effect of these sanctions, due to the fact that there is a fundamental right to protection of family life enshrined in Art. 26 of the Constitution and by the international legal instruments regarding the protection of the human rights. (in this regard, AVRAM ET AL, *supra* note 37, p. 57). Only exceptionally, the court – taking into consideration mainly the superior interests of the child – can limit the exercise of this right, if there are grounded reasons which can endanger the physical, mental, spiritual, moral or social development of the child – Art. 16(2) Law no. 272/2004.

80 FLORIAN, *supra* note 3, p. 121.

32. If a special protection measure has been made in respect of the child, according to Articles 55 *et seq.* Law no. 272/2004 (placement or emergency placement), parental rights are delegated to a public authority, under the conditions of Articles 62(2) and 64(3) of the same law: the parental rights and obligations will be exercised by the president of the county council or by the Bucharest department Mayor (see also *supra*, **8(f)** and **14**].

33. In case of the death of one of the parents, physically ascertained or declared by a court decision, according to Article 98(2) Family Code, parental protection devolves to the surviving parent. When both parents are dead, one of the alternative measures of protection provided by Law no. 272/2004 will be ordered regarding the child: either the institution of tutorship, a special measure of protection or adoption (Article 39 of the law).

34. The appointment of the person who will exercise the parental rights and duties if the parents are dead is within the exclusive competence of the court.[81] It is impossible in the Romanian legal system to transmit rights and obligations of parental protection through an *inter vivos* or *mortis causa* act. The legal provisions in this domain are mandatory in the Romanian legal system; therefore deviations from them are not possible.

4. THE EXERCISE OF PARENTAL RESPONSIBILITIES

4.1. INTERESTS OF THE CHILD

35. Parental rights and duties must be exercised only according to the superior interests of the child; a principle enshrined expressly by Articles 1(5) and 97(2) Family Code as well as by Articles 2(2) and 5(2) Law no. 272/2004, which corresponds to the CEFL Principle 3:3 ("Best interest of the child"), which provides that "In all matters concerning parental responsibilities the best interests of the child should be the primary consideration".

Thus, according to Article 1(5) Family Code, "The parental rights and obligations are exercised only in the superior interests of the child", and according to Article 97(2) Family Code, the parents "exercise their parental rights only in the children's interests."

81 According to Art. 38(a) Law no. 272/2004, the court of justice is the sole authority competent to decide, taking into consideration the higher interests of the child, who would be the person who exercises parental rights and fulfils parental obligations if the child lacks, temporarily or permanently, the protection provided by his parents.

Also, Article 2(2) Law no. 272/2004, "The principle of the superior interests of the child is imposed inclusively concerning the rights and obligations of the parents, of other legal representatives of the child, as well as any persons with whom the child was placed legally", and Article 5(2) provides that "The responsibility for raising and providing the development of the child is mainly the charge of the parents, they having the obligation to exercise their rights and fulfill their obligations concerning the child taking into consideration mainly his superior interests."

Legislative evolution marked the rephrasing of this principle: recent regulations mention expressly the "superior" interests of the child, in full compliance with international regulations in the domain, especially the UN Convention on the Rights of the Child, while the phrasing of the Family Code referred only to the "child's interests".

Outside these general texts which establish the principle of the superior interests of the child, there are numerous other legal provisions in the Family Code and in other special laws which, in various domains, concern the interests of the child.

The law does not define *expresis verbis* the expression of "superior interests" of the child, but, Article 31(2) Law no. 272/2004 provides that "The exercise of parental rights and the fulfilment of parental obligations must take into consideration the superior interests of the child and to provide the material and spiritual welfare of the child, especially by attending to him, maintaining personal relations with him, providing the raising, education and support, as well as by his legal representation and the administration of his patrimony."

For these reasons, as it was highlighted in the doctrine, the expression of *superior interests* of the child is a *complex* one, which combines the private side with the social side, as well as the aspects of personal nature with those of patrimonial nature, considering the concrete needs of the child and his stage of development.[82] The superior interests of the child are protected if, by the exercise of parental rights and fulfilment of parental obligations, the ultimate objective is – the welfare of the child. The expression "interests of the child" has also a *dynamic* content, in relation with the concrete facts.

As regards the jurisprudence relevant in this area, reference can be made to Decision no. 6 of 5 April 2005, the case *Monory vs. Romania and Hungary*, in which the European Court of Human Rights decided:

---

82 See FLORIAN, *supra* note 3, p. 372; BACACI ET AL, *supra* note 22, pp. 306–307.

> The Court recalls that the interests of the child are paramount in such cases. Thus it may well have been justified, eight months after the removal from Hungary of the applicant's daughter, for the courts to hold that the child had adapted to her new environment and that it was in her best interests to remain in Romania with her mother although, at that time, no final decision had established her residence there (…). However, where the Court accepts that a change in the relevant facts may exceptionally justify such a decision, it must be satisfied that the change was not brought about by the State's actions or inactions.

In Romania there is also a wide jurisprudence in the domain of the custody of the child after divorce, with the superior interests of the child being the fundamental criterion with reference to which decisions are made.

In this regard, the courts take into consideration the age of the child, the behaviour of the parents as regards the child before and after the divorce, the affective relations between the child and the parents, the work place of the parents and the state of health of the child. Any one of these elements must not be minimised or exaggerated or analysed as the sole criterion. Also, the reasoning of the judge cannot neglect the factual elements which can determine that one or another of these elements has a higher weight. For this reason, the preeminence of one or other criterion, even if it is not erroneous, must be demonstrated by the judge through the relevance of the evidence supporting the court decision.[83]

The interests of the individual minor must be considered, by examining all the prevailing criteria in making a decision granting custody of the child to one of the parents.[84] For this reason, besides the classical criterion of the child's interests, the courts must always take into consideration the ability in practice of each parent to take care of the child.[85]

83 See Bucharest Court of Appeal, third civil department, decision no. 1378 of 17 December 2007, in *Pandectele Române* no. 2/2005, pp. 81–85; Bucharest Court of Appeal, third civil department, department for minors and family, decision no. 1590 of 24 November 2005, in *Pandectele Române* no. 4/2006, p. 130.

84 See Bucharest Court of Appeal, third civil department for minors and family, decision no. 882 of 11 April 2006, in *Pandectele Române* no. 5/2006, p. 98.

85 In a case, the court of first instance and the court of appeal noted that both parents have equal circumstances for raising the child, but the child was not given in custody to the father, considering the young age of the child (2 years), justifying the presence of the child with the mother. But in the appeal, the settlement was changed, since in reality the mother was abroad, where she worked, and her allegation regarding the fact that she intended to effectively care for the child, to be near him, ensuring him an environment of stability could not be accepted in the existing situation. Bacau Court of Appeal, civil decision no. 1238/8.11.2006.

4.2. JOINT PARENTAL RESPONSIBILITIES

36. In principle, the protection of the child is performed by the parents jointly and equally, regardless of the fact that they are natural, adoptive, married or unmarried parents. In this regard, Article 97(1) Family Code provides that "Both parents have the same rights and duties towards their minor children, whether they are born from the marriage, outside the marriage or they are adopted", and, according to Article 98(1) Family Code, the measures regarding the person and assets of the child are taken by the parents jointly. Also, Article 31(1) Law no. 272/2004 provides that "Both parents are responsible for the raising of their child."

These provisions reflect the same ideas as some of the CEFL Principles: Principle 3:8 – "Parents" ("Parents, whose legal parentage has been established, should have parental responsibilities for the child") and Principle 3:11 – "Joint exercise" ("Parents having parental responsibilities should have an equal right and duty to exercise such responsibilities and whenever possible they should exercise them jointly").

Still, there are cases when parental protection is divided, meaning that the parents are not exercising it equally:

(a) Termination of the marriage by divorce
According to aricle 42(1) Family Code, the court judging the divorce must decide, at the same time as the divorce, which of the parents will be given custody of their minor children, irrespective of the fact that they were born before or during the marriage, or were adopted by both spouses. The court must decide on the custody, even if there is no express request from one of the parents in this regard.

Usually, the children are given in custody to one of the parents (Article 42(1) Family Code), to comply with the idea that siblings should not be separated. Still, when the specific conditions require, it is possible for one or more children to be given in custody to one parent, and the other, or the others, to the other parent.

The parent who receives custody of the child will exercise all the rights regarding the person and property of the child (Article 43(1) Family Code), and the other parent will have the right to have personal relations with the child and to supervise his raising, education and professional preparation (Article 43(3) Family Code).

As a consequence, the parent who receives custody of the child has obviously more possibilities to provide and influence the development of the child. The measures regarding the person and the property of the child are taken by the parent who has been granted custody of the child. There is no need for agreement to exist between the parents before action is taken, as happens in the case when the parents are not divorced. The measures are taken by one parent. If the other parent does not agree with the measures taken by the parent who has custody of the child, he can request the court to give the custody of the child to him, if this is in the superior interests of the child. Also, even if the law does not expressly provide so, there is nothing to stop the other parent from asking the court to annul the act or to compel the custodial parent to take certain measures towards the child.

Exceptionally and only for justified reasons, the child can be given in custody to certain relatives or other persons, with their consent, or to a protection institution (Article 42(2) Family Code). To take this extreme measure, the court must take into consideration also the provisions of Article 33 Law no. 242/2004, according to which "the child cannot be separated from his parents, or one of them, against their will, except for the cases expressly provided by the law under the reserve of judicial review and only if such action is required by the superior interests of the child" (*subl. ns.*).

The granting of custody of the child to a person other than his parents is an exceptional measure imposed only when the care of the child would suffer[86] and only with the prior consent of the third party. In this case the person who receives custody of the child exercises all the rights regarding the person of the child (Article 43(2)(II) Family Code). The parents have the right to have personal relations with the child and to supervise the manner in which he is raised (Article 43(3) Family Code); also, the court will decide which of the parents exercises all the rights regarding the property of the child (Article 43(2)(I) Family Code). As a consequence, in this case, parental protection is divided between the parents and the third party and, also, parental protection is divided between the parents,

86 See the Supreme Tribunal, civil department, decision no. 757/1965, in *Culegere de Decizii [Decisions Collection]* 1956, p. 188. See also Craiova First Instance Court, civil decision no. 10077 of 2.07.2007. The court considers that the higher interests of the child demand that custody be given to the mother, except in the case of a child who lacks the protection of his family, in which case the minor can be raised by a person of the extended family, respectively by the paternal grandmother. It cannot be alleged that giving the custody to the mother affects seriously the raising and education of the child, on the contrary, his separation from the mother and preventing her from having relations with him, constitutes a serious infringement of the child's rights. The attachment of the minor to the paternal grandmother, or the material and moral good conditions of the latter, are not challenged, but the mother can offer material and moral conditions for the raising and education of the child, thus, it is in the higher interests of the child to be given to the custody of his mother. The court has also taken into consideration the provisions of Art. 8 of the European Convention on Human Rights, regarding the protection of the private, intimate and family life, considering that only with his mother can the minor develop a real family life, or have a favourable physical and psychological development. As a consequence, the father's request for the child to be given to the custody of the paternal grandmother, grounded on the fact that the child was born and raised in their house, was rejected.

considering that only one of them has the right to exercise rights regarding the property of the child.

After the divorce, both parents have an obligation to support the children. According to Article 42(3) Family Code, along with the custody of the children in the divorce, the court will also establish the contribution of each parent to the expenses corresponding to the raising, education, studies and professional preparation of each child. As in the case of custody, the divorce court is compelled to decide on this aspect, even if neither of the parents files an express petition in this regard.

According to Article 44(1) Family Code, if the circumstances taken into consideration by the court when ordering the initial measures have changed, these measures regarding the custody of the children at the time of divorce can be modified by the request of either of the parents or of the child, if he has reached the age of 14, of the tutelary authority or the protection institution. This request can also be addressed to the court by the district attorney, according to Article 45 Civil Procedure Code.

These measures can be modified, according to Article 44(2) Family Code, only in compliance with the conditions provided by Article 42 Family Code, that is the same conditions provided by the law for taking the measures when the divorce is pronounced.

(b) Annulment of marriage

According to Article 23(2) Family Code, the annulment of marriage has no effect on the children, who keep their status as children born during marriage, regardless of the good or bad faith of one or both parents at the date of the marriage.

Due to the fact that, concerning children, nullity of marriage has only prospective effect, Article 24(2) Family Code provides that the personal and patrimonial relationships between the parents and the children will be regulated, according to the provisions applicable in the case of divorce. As a consequence, by applying the above mentioned rules, there is division of parental protection.

(c)The custody of a child born outside marriage

According to Article 65 Family Code, "if the parenthood of the child outside the marriage is established in relation to both parents, his custody, as well as the parents' contribution to the expenses for his raising, education, studies and professional preparation, will be decided according to the provisions of Articles 42–44."

Together with Article 97(1) Family Code, the mentioned text must be understood to mean that, from the moment when parenthood is established as regards both parents, in principle they will exercise parental protection jointly and equally until the moment when they eventually decide to cease their cohabitation. If unmarried parents no longer live together, the custody of the child will be decided by the court according to Article 65 Family Code (cited *supra*) and parental protection will be divided according to the rules applicable in the case of divorce.

(d) In the situation of placement as a measure of protection of the child ordered by court decision, according to Law no. 272/2004, parental protection is also divided. Parental rights will be exercised either by the president of the county council or the mayor of the Bucharest city if a child is not one for whom guardianship was not instituted, (Article 62(2) of the law), or according to the court's decision in all other cases (Article 62(3) of the law). The parents keep the right to have personal relations with the child, as well as the maintenance obligation.[87]

From this short presentation of the regulation of parental protection in case of divorce, it is clear that, in Romanian law, divorce always affects the manner of exercise of parental rights. The Constitutional Court when notified of unconstitutionality of Article 43(3) Family Code in relation with Article 16(1) of the Constitution, which enshrines the principle of the equality in rights, established by Decision no. 411 of 16 May 2006, that the text is constitutional, due to the fact that "these differences in the exercise of parental rights are determined by the parents' separation and the objective impossibility of maintaining, after the termination of the marriage, the same manner of exercising parental rights and obligations".

The basis of this decision of the Constitutional Court is questionable, as the Romanian lawmaker is still preoccupied with the need to attenuate, as much as possible, the effects of the divorce on the manner of exercise of parental rights.

Thus, the New Draft Civil Code proposes the rule according to which parental authority (the new concept proposed, see *supra*, **6**) is held jointly by both parents also after the termination of the marriage by divorce and, only if justifiable reasons exist, action is taken to divide parental authority, which means the exercise of the authority only by one of the parents. Also, with the decision of divorce, the court will establish the child's place of residence, considering mainly the agreement between the parents, if such agreement is in the interests of the child.

In addition the New Draft Civil Code contains certain clarifications for the case of the child outside marriage whose parenthood was established at the same time,

---

87 See FLORIAN, *supra* note 3, pp. 396 -397.

or, where relevant, successively, by both parents. The principle is that parental authority is exercised jointly and equally by the parents if they are living together. If the parents of the child outside marriage are not living together, the manner of exercise of parental authority is established by the court, the provisions regarding the divorce being applicable. The court, petitioned with a claim for the establishment of parenthood, is compelled to order on the manner of the exercise of parental responsibility, the provisions applicable to divorce being applicable.

One can conclude that all the situations described above (**a-d**) are consistent with the principles of the sole exercise of parental responsibility set out in the CEFL Principles 3:15 – "Sole exercise upon agreement or decision" and 3:16 – "Sole exercise by one parent". The competent authority, mentioned by the Principle 3:15(b) is the court which – as we have shown above – always decides taking into consideration the superior (best) interests of the child. The difference is that, in Romanian law, the sole exercise upon agreement between the parents (Principle 3:15(a) does not exist.

37. According to Article 98(2) Family Code, the measures regarding the person and property of the children are taken by the parents, *by mutual agreement*. This means that the parents should decide *together* and not that they could divide the parental protection or transfer it to one of them by their agreement.

De lege lata, in the field of parental protection there are no express provisions which allow, in case of disagreement, the exercise of parental rights only by one of the holders (similar to the CEFL Principles 3:13 and 3:15(a)). Also, there is no legal distinction between the serious, important measures regarding the child, and the daily acts (similar to the CEFL Principle 3:12 – "Daily matters, important and urgent decisions").

If the parents are married, the simple separation in fact does not change the conditions of the exercise of parental rights, even though, in fact, the child is living with only one of the parents. In other words, in this case, the exercise of parental rights pertains to both parents equally. If the parents are not married and the parenthood of the child is established in relation to both parents, the solution is the same, if the court did not issue a decision which gives the custody of the child to one of the parents. In case of disagreement between the holders of the parental authority, the court of justice will decide.

38. According to Article 31(3) Law no. 272/2004, "In case of existence of certain disagreement between the parents regarding the exercise of parental rights and the fulfilment of parental obligations, the court, after hearing both parties, decides according to the superior interests of the child."

Also, according to Article 38 of the same law, "The court is the sole authority competent to decide, considering with priority the superior interests of the child, on the:

(a) person who exercises the parental rights and fulfils the parental obligations if the child lacks, temporarily or permanently, the protection of his parents;
(b) the manner in which parental rights are exercised and parental obligations are fulfilled;
(c) total or partial loss of the exercise of parental rights;
(d) return of the exercise of parental rights."

We underline that the "competent authority", provided by the CEFL Principle 3:14(1), under Romanian law, is the court of justice; even if the family legislation does not have a specific provision concerning the obligation of the judge to promote agreement between the parents (similar to the CEFL Principle 3:14(2)), there is a general provision in the Civil Procedure Code imposing on the judge the obligation to promote agreement between the parties in any case (Article 131). Thus, the courts also have jurisdiction to settle disagreements between the parents regarding the exercise of parental rights and the fulfilment of parental obligations (Article 31(3) Law no. 272/2004), the giving of the custody of the child in case of termination of marriage by divorce (Articles 42 and 43 Family Code), and settlement of disagreements regarding the child's home (Article 100 Family Code).

In principle, the court's competence is not limited to certain domains, considering free access to justice (Article 21 of the Constitution and Article 6 of the ECHR). Special provisions exist only in the domain of the name. Thus, according to Article 7 Government Ordinance no. 41/2003 regarding the acquiring and change of the name of the individuals by administrative means, if the parents do not agree on the change of the name of the child, the tutelary authority will decide.

In case of disagreement between the parents regarding the exercise of parental rights, the establishment of the domicile of the children or their support, mediation is possible, according to Article 64 Law no. 192/2006 regarding mediation and the organisation of the profession of mediator.

39. *De lege lata*, there is no general provision which allows one of the parents to act solely in exercising parental rights in certain domains, as those of daily acts or those of lesser importance.

According to Article 98(2) Family Code, parental rights can be exercised by only one parent if the other parent is incapable of acting. The exercise of parental protection by both parents supposes that each has full capacity to act, together with the capacity to express their will. If one of the parents is dead, no longer has parental rights, is under interdict or, due to any circumstance, is unable to express his will, the other parent will take over the responsibility of parental protection. If this is not possible or according to the superior interests of the child, alternative protection measures may be taken, under the conditions of Law no. 272/2004.

Nevertheless, accompanied minors are permitted to travel abroad, even if only one parent agrees (Article 30(3) Law no. 248/2005 regarding the regime of free movement of Romanian citizens abroad) in certain situations, such as: (a) if the companion grounds the necessity of the travel abroad by the fact that the minor needs medical treatment not available in Romania and without which his life or his health would be seriously endangered, under the conditions that he presents documents, issued or authorised by the Romanian medical authorities, which prove the period and the state or states where the medical treatment will be applied; (b) if the companion proves that the minor is traveling abroad for studies or official contests, by presenting adequate documents, showing the period and the state or states where these studies or contests take place.

Also, parental rights regarding the property of the child can be exercised only by one parent, without the agreement of the other parent being required and even if the latter opposes, if the act concluded by the parent is an act of conservation (for example, registration in the land registry), taking into consideration that these acts always benefit the holder of the right (the child).

But the New Draft Civil Code provides that "Towards the third parties of good faith, any one of the parents, who fulfils alone a daily act for the exercise of parental rights and fulfilment of parental duties, is presumed to have the consent of the other parent". Thus, a "presumption of mutual tacit mandate" between the parents will apply in the fulfilment of daily acts of parental authority. The solution is natural, considering the fact that, anyhow, in practice, even in the absence of such express provision, the normal tendency is that these acts be fulfilled only by one parent, without the express consent of the other. If the New Draft Civil Code comes into force, this provision will be similar to the CEFL Principle 3:12(1): "Parents having joint parental responsibilities should have the right to act alone with respect to daily matters".

40. As regards the residence of the child, according to Article 100 Family Code, the minor child lives with his parents. If they do not live together, they shall decide by mutual agreement with which of them the child shall live. In case of disagreement, the court will decide, by listening the tutelary authority, as well as the child, if he is over 10 years, and considering the interests of the child. Also, Article 102 Family Code and Article 47(3) Law no. 272/2004 allow a child older then 14 years to obtain court approval – against the parents' will – to have a residence necessary for his studies or professional preparation.

These provisions are different to the CEFL Principle 3:20 ("Residence"), because the Romanian law system does not regulate the possibility of alternative residence of the child. Nevertheless, when the court is deciding on the residence of the child, it takes into consideration, among others, the same factors as the ones provided by the Principle 3:20(a) and (c): such as the age and the opinion of the child, the personal situation of the parents etc.

As regards children's travel abroad, according to Article 12(2) Law no. 262/2004, the travel of children abroad is made with the notification and agreement of both parents; any disagreement between the parents is settled by the court. The text makes no distinction based on the fact that the exercise of parental rights is made equally or unequally by the parents, which means that it would also be applicable when the child is in the custody of only one of the parents.

Article 30 Law no. 248/2005, regarding the regime of the free movement of Romanian citizens abroad, provides that the travel of a child abroad is permitted where accompanied by only one of the parents if the latter presents a declaration issued by the other parent showing his agreement regarding travel in the state or states of destination, as well as regarding the period of the travel. Still, the declaration of the other parent is not necessary if the accompanying parent proves that the minor was given in custody to him or her by a definitive and irrevocable court decision. Therefore, the text has a different content compared with the provisions of Article 12 Law no. 262/2004: it allows the travel of the child abroad based only on the consent of the parent who received the custody of the child. At the same time, the Constitutional Court, by the decision no. 947/2007 rejected the claim of unconstitutionality of this text and ascertained that the provisions of Article 30 Law no. 248/2005 are constitutional.[88] The Constitutional Court opined that the institution of a different legal treatment as regards the divorced parent who did not receive the custody of the child, opposed to the other parent, is objectively and reasonably justified by the fact that the two parents are in different legal situations. These differences are determined by the separation of the parents and by the objective possibility of maintaining, after the termination of the marriage, the manner of exercise of parental rights and obligations. Where the custody of the child was given to one parent, the other parent continues to have the right and obligation to raise the child, but not the right of guardianship and supervision. The fact that the child is living and cohabiting with the parent who received the custody means that these rights cannot be exercised by the parent who does not live with the child. Therefore, in the opinion of the Constitutional Court,

---

88 The Constitutional texts claimed to be infringed were: Art. 16(1) regarding the equality of rights, Art. 48 regarding the family and Art. 53 regarding the restraint of the exercise of certain rights or freedoms, Art. 8 regarding the right to respect of the private life and family life and Art. 14 regarding the prohibition of discrimination in the European Convention on Human Rights, as well as Art. 5 (regarding the equality of spouses) of Protocol no. 7 to this Convention.

the parent who received the custody of the child has the right to decide on his own the residence of the child, not only in the country, but also abroad. Consequently, he or she can decide alone regarding the travel of the child abroad. This solution is not beyond criticism, due to the fact that, by such a prerogative, the other parent is completely ignored as regards this very important aspect concerning the child and it is impossible for him or her to exercise parental rights, in particular the right to have personal relations with the child and to supervise the raising and education of the child.

For these reasons, "*de lege ferenda*" a review of the solutions in this field is needed. In any case the existence of a special norm regarding the establishment of residence and travel of a child in the country and abroad is required, in the hypothesis of the custody of the child given to one of the parents or to third parties.

In this respect, the New Draft Civil Code provides that, if it affects the exercise of the authority or certain parental rights, the change of the child's residence, together with the parent he is living with, can take place only with the prior agreement of the other parent. In case of disagreement between the parents, the court will decide according to the superior interests of the child, taking into consideration the conclusions of the psycho-social investigation report and listening to the parents. The views of the child must be taken into account, under the conditions provided by the law.

If the New Draft Civil Code comes into force, the above mentioned provisions of the Draft could be considered as similar to the CEFL Principle 3:21, which provides the right of the parent who is not living to the child to be informed about the intention of the other parent to change the residence of the child and the possibility of the competent authority to decide in case the parents cannot reach an agreement (Principle 3:21(2) and (3)).

41. In Romanian law there are no provisions allowing the minor to live alternately with both parents. For the situation of the divorced parents, see *supra* **36**.

4.3. SOLE PARENTAL RESPONSIBILITIES

42. **(a)** If parental protection is exercised by a sole parent, in the hypothesis provided by Article 98(2) Family Code, this parent does not need agreement from the other parent.

If parental protection is divided (see *supra*, **36(a)**-**(d)**), the parent who has custody of the child exercises on his own the parental rights. He does not need the agreement or consent of the other parent, whom he is not compelled to consult in advance, but he has the obligation to subsequently inform that parent regarding the measures taken as regards the child, considering the right of that parent to supervise the manner in which the child is raised and educated.

Still, exceptionally, in the case of the adoption, when both parents' consent is requested, and not only that of the parent who has the child (Law no. 273/2004 regarding the legal regime of the adoption); the consent of the divorced parent who did not receive custody of the child is required.

Also, in the case of the parent who lost parental rights (see *supra*, 7), Article 12(2) Law no. 273/2004 requires the consent of the parent who lost parental rights as a condition of adoption. In other words, the parent or the parents who lost parental rights keep the right to consent to the adoption of the child. The consent of the legal representative is also compulsory.

As regards the administrative change of the name of the child, the Government Ordinance no. 41/2003 provides that, when the request to change the name of the child is made by one of the parents, the other parent must accept the change, in the presence of a notary. Agreement is not needed when the other parent is under interdict or declared missing by a court of justice or without parental rights. The cases when the agreement of the other parent is not needed are exhaustively provided by law, therefore, both parents must consent to a child's change of name and not only the parent who has custody of the child.

There is special discussion in Romanian legal doctrine regarding the consent of parents to the marriage of their minor child. According to Article 4 Family Code, as modified by Law no. 288/2007, a minor older then 16 years may marry for justified reasons, with a medical certificate and with the consent of his parents or, where relevant, the tutor, and with the authorisation of the General Director of Social Assistance and Child Protection with territorial jurisdiction. Article 4 Family Code, as amended, does not provide for when the parents are divorced, with one of them having custody of the minor, according to Article 42(1) Family Code. As a result, the question arises as to whether the consent of the parent not having custody is necessary for the marriage of the child or if, in such a case, the agreement of the other parent suffices. In a strict interpretation of the text, it would mean that in this situation also the rules provided by Article 4(2) Family Code, should apply; the minor should receive consent from both parents.

On one side, in this regard the fact that Article 4(2) Family Code does not distinguish *as regards* the situation of the parents, specifically if they are married or divorced at the time when consent is needed, can be invoked; on the other side, it can be said that in paragraph 3 of the same Article the lawmaker expressly and exhaustively provided for the situations when the consent of only one parent suffices, and this provision – providing an exceptional rule – cannot be extended by way of interpretation.

Starting from the premise that the right to consent to marriage is part of parental protection and – as a consequence of the custody given by court decision according to Article 42(1) Family Code – only the parent who has custody of the child exercises parental rights both as regards the person and the property of the minor, another interpretation is also possible: the marriage can be concluded with the sole acceptance of the parent who has custody of the child, due to the fact that only he or she exercises parental rights.

The same solution should be given in the hypothesis of the annulment of marriage, related to the child born outside the marriage, Articles 24(2) and 65 Family Code providing that, in these situations, the provisions of Articles 42 – 44 of the same Code, regarding divorce, apply, by analogy.[89]

(b) The parent who alone exercises parental rights does not have a duty to obtain consent from other persons, bodies or authorities. A clarification is needed concerning acts regarding the child's property; thus, according to Article 129(2) Family Code, for acts overriding the right to administration, such as the sale or pledge of the minor's assets and the renunciation of his patrimonial rights, prior approval of the tutelary authority is required (see *supra*, **8(f)** and **10 – 13**). But this is a provision applicable regardless of the fact that the rights are exercised by both parents or only by one of the parents.

5. CONTACT

43. According to Article 16(1) Law no. 272/2004, the child who is separated from both parents or only one of them has the right to maintain personal relations and direct contact with both parents, except when this is not in the superior interests of the child. Also, Article 15 of the same law lists the main ways in which the right to maintain personal relations is exercised, namely:

> a) meetings of the child with the parent or another person who has, according to this law, the right to personal relationships with the child;
> b) visiting the child at his domicile;
> c) accommodation of the child for a set period by the parent or other person with whom he is not usually living;

[89] See, BAIAS, FL.A., AVRAM, M., NICOLESCU, C., *Modificările aduse Codului familiei prin Legea nr. 288/2007 [Modifications brought to the Family Code by Law no. 288/2007]*, in *Dreptul* no. 3/2008, p. 20.

> d) correspondence or another form of communication with the child;
> e) transmission of information to the child regarding the parent or the persons who have, according to this law, the right to have personal relationships with the child;
> f) transmission of information regarding the child, including recent photographs, medical or school evaluations, to the parent or other persons who have the right to have personal relations with the child.

The transmission of information provided in (e) and (f) will be made in compliance with the superior interests of the child, as well as with the special provisions regarding confidentiality and passing of information of a personal character. Also, concerning private international law, Article 17 Law no. 272/2004 contains a special provision according to which,

> the child whose parents live in different states have the right to maintain personal relations and direct contacts with them, except in the situation where this is contrary to the superior interests of the child. The exercise of this right will be facilitated by the National Authority for Children's Rights Protection, in cooperation with the Ministry of Foreign Affairs, based on a procedure approved by common order.

These provisions are similar to the CEFL Principle 3:25 ("Contact with parents and other persons"), particularly paragraph 1 ("The child and the parents should have the right to obtain and maintain regular contact with each other"), and also with the Principle 3:26 ("Content of contact") and 3:29 ("Information to parents"), the last ones having the same content – though more briefly – as Article 15 Law no. 272/2004.

44. (a) If the exercise of parental rights is divided, the parent who has custody of the child following divorce has the right to have personal relations with the child. The same is true of a child given in custody to a third party (Article 43 Family Code). See also *supra* **36**.

Also, in the situation when the parents are separated in fact and one of them obstructs the exercise of the other parent's right to have personal relations with the child, the latter could ask the court to decide the residence of the child, as well as the concrete manner of exercise of the right to have personal relations with the child. [90]

If we compare this situation with the CEFL Principle 3:27 ("Agreement"), we can say that the agreement (Principle 3:27(1)) on contact is obviously possible in our

[90] The parent, who does not have custody of the child following the separation in fact, has the right to visit the child and have personal relations with the child, see Bacau Court of Appeal, civil decision no. 82 of 29 January 1994, in Lege 4).

legal system, but it is not necessary for it to be scrutinised (Principle 3:27(2)) by the competent authority (the court), except in the situation when this agreement is part of a more comprehensive one concerning custody after divorce, which must be scrutinised by the court.

(b) According to Article 98(2) Family Code, parental rights are exercised by one parent if the other parent is dead, no longer has parental rights (being discharged of these), is under interdict or, is not able to manifest his will.

A parent who has been discharged of his parental rights is in a special situation. Indeed, the parent who no longer has parental rights can maintain personal relations with the child, if it is not against the superior interests of the child, the court being able to limit the exercise of this right. In this case, the right of the parent who no longer has the right to have personal relations with the child is not an intrinsic component of parental rights, but is a fundamental part of the parent's right and the child's right to the protection of family life, enshrined in Article 26 of the Constitution and Article 22(1) Law no. 272/2004.[91]

The restriction of contact between the child and a parent discharged of his parental rights, provided by Romanian law, has a correspondent in the CEFL Principle 3:28 ("Restrictions"), which states: "Contact may be restricted, terminated or made subject to conditions by the competent authority if the best interests of the child so require."

(c) According to Article 14 Law no. 272/2004, the child has the right to maintain personal relations and direct contact with the parents and relatives, as well as other persons with whom the child has developed close relationships. Also, the child has the right to know his relatives and to have personal relations with them, as well as with other persons with whom he has a family life, if this is not contrary to his superior interests. The parents or other legal representative of the child cannot stop or impede his personal relations with the grandparents, brothers and sisters or other persons with whom the child has a family life, except in the case where the court decides so, considering that there are good reasons likely to endanger the child's physical, psychological, intellectual or moral development.[92]

---

91 See AVRAM ET AL, *supra* note 37, p. 53.

92 Although the Family Code does not expressly provide the grandparents' right to have personal relations with the minor, even before the Law no. 272/2004, the jurisprudence decided that grandparents can have such a right. In this regard, see the Supreme Tribunal, civil department, civil decision no. 182/1982, in R.R.D. no. 10/1982, pp. 50–60; The Supreme Court of Justice, civil department, civil decision no. 28 of 9 January 1992, in *Jurisprudence Bulletin, data base*, (All Beck Publishers); Bucharest Court of Appeal, fourth civil department, civil decision no. 3584 of 6 December 2001, in *Practică judiciră în materie civilă [Judicial practice in civil domain]* 2001–2002, p. 576. See also the Alba Iulia Court of Appeal, department for minors and family, decision no. 26 of 28 February 2006, in TIȚIAN, D., *Cauzele pentru minori în materie civilă*

This child's right – recognised by Romanian law – is the same as the one provided by the CEFL Principle 3:25(2) ("Contact should be established between the child and his or her close relatives") and (3) ("Contact may be established between the child and persons with whom the child has close personal relations").

45. The right to have personal relations with the child is not only a right of the child, but also a right of the parents. Thus, in the situation of divorced parents, Article 43(3) Family Code expressly provides that the parent who did not receive the custody of the child keeps the right to have personal relations with him. The text is also applicable in the case of the annulment of marriage (Article 24(2) Family Code), in the case of the child born outside of marriage (Article 65 Family Code), as well as in the case of placement (Article 60(3) Law no. 272/2004).

The Constitutional Court decided that the regulation protecting the right of the divorced parent who did not receive custody of the child to have personal relations with the minor provides a way by which the public authorities can fulfil their obligations to comply with and protect personal, familial and private life. This also constitutes a component of the special regime of protection and assistance of children and young people in the fulfilment of their rights. Correspondingly, the parent who received custody of the child is the debtor of the obligation to allow the former spouse, to effectively perform the right to have personal relations with the child.[93] In addition, even in the absence of an express legal provision, the jurisprudence decided that grandparents also have the right to have personal relations with the child.[94]

According to Article 71 Law no. 272/2004, a child who is subject to a special protection measure has the right to maintain relations with other persons, if they do not have a bad influence on his physical, mental, spiritual or social development.

46. In the domain of divorce, Article 42(4) Family Code provides that "The convention of the parents regarding the custody of the children and the

și penală. Practică judiciară [Cases regarding minors in civil and criminal domain. Judicial practice], (Bucharest, 2006), p. 55. In this case, the maternal grandmother requested, against the father of the minor, the agreement of the court to have personal relations with the minor, after the death of the minor's mother.

93 The provisions of Art. 43(3) Family Code which provide the parent's right to have personal relations with the minor were found to be in accordance with Art. 26(1) of the Constitution, see the Decision of the Constitutional Court no. 82 of 25 February 2003, published in the *Official Gazette of Romania* no. 189 of 26 March 2003. Also, see the Decision of the Constitutional Court no. 141 of 8 April 2003, published in the *Official Gazette of Romania* no. 307 of 7 May 2003, as well as the Decision of the Constitutional Court no. 411 of 16 May 2006, published in the *Official Gazette of Romania* no. 530 of 20 June 2006.

94 See *supra* **44**.

contribution of each parent to the expenses for their raising, education, studies and professional preparation will have effects only if it was aproved by the court."

The parents can agree on the custody of minor children, as well as on the ways of exercising the right to have personal relations with the child. But, in all cases the superior interests of the child must be respected. As a consequence, the court of justice has the obligation to verify that the agreement of the parents complies with this condition.

47. The right to maintain personal relations with the child is not an absolute right; however it can be limited only by the court of justice. Thus, according to Article 16(2) Law no. 272/2004, the court, with priority being given to the superior interests of the child, can limit the exercise of this right, if there are good reasons to believe that contact would endanger the physical, mental, spiritual, moral or social development of the child. The right to have personal relations with the child is, therefore, recognised exclusively in the interests of the child.

A parent has the right to have personal relations with his child, even in the case of opposition by the other parent. But when the opposition is justified and in accordance with the child's interests, personal relations with the minor can be restricted or suspended, depending on the circumstances. For example, considering the young age of the minor, as well as a bad state of health, it was decided that if the minor needs special care and permanent assistance, it is not in his interests to be separated from the mother, even during the visitation programme at the father's domicile.[95]

Also, the abusive exercise of the parent's rights regarding the person of the child, which disturbs or endangers the process of raising, education, instruction and formation of the child, gives the court – following a claim filed by the other parent – the right to order the suspension and even the suppression of the exercise of this right, considering the nature and seriousness of the ascertained abuse.[96] Thus, if inadequate and violent manifestations of the parent who did not receive the custody of the child was proved, and based on a fragile psychological equilibrium of the child, the claim to set up a visitation programme can be rejected until the underlying circumstances have changed.[97]

But it must be pointed out that, in establishing the practical means of exercising the right to have personal relations with the minor, the courts must not establish

95 See Târgu-Mureş Court of Appeal, civil department, decision no. 297 of 5 April 2001, in TITIAN, *supra* note 31, p. 43.
96 See FLORIAN, *supra* note 3, pp. 203–204.
97 See Bucharest Court of Appeal, decision no. 124 of 28 February 1997, in *Jurisprudence Bulletin, Data base*, (All Beck Publishers).

conditions which can void this subjective right of its content and transform its exercise into a formal one, unless there are special circumstances. [98]

48. **(a)** If the holder of parental protection infringes the parent's right to have personal relations with the minor, the parent can file a claim with the court, which will ascertain the right and establish the manner of exercise of this right, considering the superior interests of the child. This has no direct consequences by itself on the parental authority exercised by this parent. If the court decision which established the right and the manner of its exercise is not complied with, this behaviour represents an offence of non-compliance with the decisions regarding the custody of the minor incriminated by Article 307 Criminal Code, which provides:

> The keeping by one parent of his minor child, without the consent of the other parent or of the person who received the custody of the child according to the law, is punished with imprisonment from one month to 3 months or with a fine.
>
> The same sanction is applied for the deeds of the person who received the custody of the child by court decision, for raising and education, to impede repeatedly any of the parents to have personal relations with the minor, under the conditions established by the parties or by the competent organ.
> The criminal action is started on the complaint of the damaged party.
> The reconciliation of the parties removes the criminal liability.

(b) Also, when the child's right to have personal relations with other persons is infringed, it is possible for the interested person to file a claim with the court, which shall issue a decision to recognise this right and establish the concrete manner of its exercise.

6. DELEGATION OF PARENTAL RESPONSIBILITIES

49. Romanian law does not regulate the possibility of parents to delegate the exercise of parental rights to other persons.

50. This is not applicable in view of **49**, *supra*.

---

[98] Thus, it was decided that the imposition of the mother's monthly visits to the father's domicile to be carried out under the supervision of the father, is a limitation on the mother's right to contact. Such a limitation of the exercise of the right is contrary to the finality of the measure to agree to the personal relations of the parent with the child. See Bucharest Court of Appeal, third civil department, civil decision no. 1443 of 22 June 2004, in *Pandectele Române* no. 6/2004, p. 151.

7. DISCHARGE OF PARENTAL RESPONSIBILITIES

51. According to Article 109 Family Code, the discharge of parental rights, as a civil sanction,[99] can be applied only if the health or physical development of the child is endangered in the family by the manner of exercise of the parental rights or by abusive behavior or neglect in the fulfilment of the parental duties. In essence, the discharge of parental rights can be requested if the physical, mental, spiritual, moral or social development of the child is endangered by abuse or by neglect.

According to Article 89(1) Law no. 272/2004, "abuse of the child" is understood as meaning any voluntary action of a person who is in a relation of responsibility, trust or authority to the child, through which the life, the physical, mental, spiritual, moral or social development, the corporal integrity, the physical or psychological health of the child are endangered. Article 90 of the same law forbids the application of physical correction in any form, as well as the depriving of the child of any of his rights, having the nature to endanger his life, the physical, mental, spiritual, moral or social evolution, the corporal integrity, the physical or psychological health, in the family and in any institution ensuring the protection, care and education of children.

Article 89(2) of the same law, defines the "neglect of the child" as being the omission, voluntary or involuntary, of a person who has the responsibility to raise, care for or educate the child to take any measure subordinated to this responsibility, which endangers the life, the physical, mental, spiritual, moral or social development, the corporal integrity, the physical or psychological health of the child.

The reasons for the loss of parental rights are exhaustively provided by law, the text being interpreted strictly. Thus, the abandonment of the child, the failure to provide support,[100] the lack of supervision, immoral behaviour of the mother or aggressive behaviour of the parent[101] constitute grounds for the discharge of the parental rights.

---

99 See the European Court for Human Rights, Decision of 28 September 2004, *Sabou and Pîrcălab v Romania*, where it was decided that the automatic withdrawal of parental rights as accessory penalty of the imprisonment penalty constitutes an infringement of the exercise of the plaintiff's right to family life.

100 The existence of a behaviour characterised as serious negligence does not suppose only aggression, violence or abandonment of the family, but also the lack of the maintenance of the minor, which can endanger his health and physical development. See the Supreme Court of Justice, civil department, decision no. 2396 of 10 June 1997, in *Jurisprudence Bulletin* 1997, p. 65.

101 Aggressive behavior which endangers the health and physical development of the minor results in the loss of parental rights. See Iasi Court of Appeal, decision no. 178 of 24 February 2004.

The sanction is applied only to the guilty parent, with the extension of the sanction to the other parent not being justified, and if it is proved that the facts were committed in the absence of this parent who, afterwards, took care of the child.[102]

In this field, the Romanian legal provisions have the same content – more comprehensive – as the CEFL Principle 3:32 ("Discharge of parental responsiblities") which states: "The competent authority should discharge the holder of parental responsibilities, wholly or in part, where his or her behaviour or neglect causes a serious risk to the person or the property of the child".

52. In the context of Law no. 272/2004, the General Department of Social Assistance and Child Protection – which is an administrative body, at the county level, having authority in the field of child protection – has the competence to file with the court a claim for discharge of parental rights.

According to Article 36(1) Law no. 272/1997, if there are justified reasons to suspect that the life and security of the children are endangered in the family, the representatives of the public service of social assistance or, where relevant, the general department for child protection at the level of the department of Bucharest city have the right to visit the children at their home and be informed of the manner in which they are taken care of, of their health and physical development, their education, studies and professional preparation, granting, if needed the necessary directions. If, following the visits, it is found that the physical, mental, spiritual, moral or social development of the children is endangered, the public service of social protection has the obligation to notify immediately the General Department for Social Assistance and Child Protection to take the measures provided by the law.

The General Department for Social Assistance and Child Protection is obliged to file a claim with the court in the situation when it considers that the legal conditions are established for the total or partial discharge of the right to exercise the parental rights of one or both of the parents.

Article 91 provides that any person who, by the nature of profession or occupation, works directly with a child and has suspicions regarding the existence of a situation of abuse or neglect of that child, has the obligation to notify the public service of social protection or the General Department of Social Protection and Child Protection in whose territorial jurisdiction the respective case was identified. Of course, by "any person" is understood also the child in question.

---

102 See the Supreme Court of Justice, civil department, decision no. 1817 of 10 May 2002, in *Dreptul* no. 12/2003, p. 230.

The request for discharge of parental rights can be made also by the district attorney (Article 45 Civil Procedure Code).

Comparing the Romanian legal provisions concerning the request for discharge of parental rights with the corresponding CEFL Principle (3:33), we observe that, in our system, only the institution protecting the interest of the child (Principle 3:33(1)(a)) and the district attorney have the right to file the claim with the competent court, which cannot order the discharge on its own motion (as provided in Principle 3:33(2)).

53. According to Article 111 Family Code, the tutelary authority will allow the parent who lost his parental rights to keep personal relations with the child, except where, by such relations, the raising, education, studies or professional preparation of the child would be endangered. The provisions of Article 16 Law no. 272/2004 are also applicable: the child separated from one or both parents has the right to have personal relations and direct contacts with both parents if this is not against the superior interest of the child. The court, taking into consideration, with priority for the superior interests of the child, can limit the exercise of this right if there are justified reasons which can endanger the child's development.[103]

54. If the circumstances that led to the discharge of the parental rights ceased and there is no further danger for the minor, the court can restore the exercise of parental rights to the interested parent (Article 112 Family Code and Article 38(d) Law no. 272/2004).

According to Article 37 Law no. 272/2004, the General Department of Social Assistance and Child Protection will take all necessary measures in order to ensure that the parents who were discharges of their rights, as well as those whose exercise of certain rights was limited, benefit from specialised assistance to increase their capacity to take care of their children, in order to recover their parental rights. The parents who request recovery of the exercise of parental rights benefit from free assistance, as provided by the law.

All these provisions correspond to the CEFL Principle 3:34 ("Restoration of parental responsibilities"): "Having regard to the best interests of the child, the competent authority may restore parental responsibilities if the circumstances that led to the discharge no longer exist."

---

[103] See FLORIAN, *supra* note 3, pp. 402–403; the Supreme Court of Justice, civil department, decision no. 3876/1996, in *Jurisprudence Bulletin* 1996, pp. 84–87.

8. PROCEDURAL ISSUES

55. The authority competent to decide in relation to the parental rights is the court of justice. The Law regarding judicial organisation no. 304/2004 provided the setting up of courts, courts' departments or tribunals specialised in minors and family matters, who had double competence: *in the civil field* – for cases regarding family relations, but also those regarding child protection by certain civil law methods (tutorship, guardianship etc.) – and *in the criminal field* – judging crimes committed by minors or against minors. Until now only one separate tribunal was set up in this field, that is the Tribunal for minors and family in the county of Braşov. At the level of the other courts (first instance courts, tribunals and courts of appeal) there are separate sections (departments) for civil matters, which are also competent for minors and family matters.

In the civil field, the competence regarding judgment in first instance of cases regarding child protection is divided between the first instance courts and the tribunals. Thus, according to Article 124 Law no. 272/2004, the cases provided by this law regarding the establishment of measures of special protection have to be judged by the tribunal with jurisdiction for the area of the child's domicile. If the child's domicile is unknown, the competence is of the tribunal in whose jurisdiction the child was found. This provision takes into consideration only the special measures provided by Article 55 of this law, respectively "placement", "emergency placement" and "specialised supervision".

By decision no. III of 15 January 2007, The Plenary of the High Court of Cassation and Justice established that, concerning the institution of the tutorship, the competent court is the first instance court.

In the domain of adoption, according to Article 61 Law no. 273/2004 and Article 2(1)(g), the competent court is the tribunal in whose jurisdiction is the domicile of the adopted child.

The competent court for measures of child protection on the termination of marriage by divorce is the first instance court, because these measures are accessory to the divorce, which falls in the competence of this court. All other cases concerning minors fall within the competence of the first instance court, where the law does not institute the special competence of the tribunal.

The competent authority to perform investigations and draft the social investigation report is the tutelary authority; an administrative body. According to Article 158 Family Code, together with Articles 63 and 64 Law no. 215/2001 regarding local public administration, the attributions of tutelary authority belong to the local public administration authorities, which are the mayors of the cities, villages or sectors of Bucharest, who may delegate the authority to the public officers of specialised administrative bodies with competencies in this field. According to the law, the tutelary authority should be listened to by the court in the following situations:

– in respect of divorce and termination of marriage, when the issue is the granting of custody of the children to one of the parents (Articles 42(1) and 24(2) Family Code), as well as when the issue is the modification of measures taken by the court regarding custody of minor children after the divorce (Article 44(2) Family Code);
– when, following the establishment of parenthood outside marriage by court decision, custody has to be awarded (Article 65 Family Code);
– when the establishment of the child's residence by the court is requested, if the parents do not live together and do not agree on this issue (Article 100(3) Family Code);
– when the court is called upon to decide regarding the exercise of the right to personal relations with the minor.

These provisions are in accordance with the CEFL Principle 3:35 ("Competent authority"), which proposes as a competent authority in the field of parental responsibilities either a judicial or an administrative body.

56. In general, the decisions in this domain have provisory *res judicata* authority, in that they can be subsequently reviewed if the circumstances initially taken into consideration by the court have changed.

Article 44(1) Family Code provides that, where circumstances have changed, the parents, the child, if he is older then 14 years, the tutelary authority or a protection institution, may ask the court to modify the measures regarding the personal or patrimonial rights and obligations between the divorced parents and the children.

In this regard, it has been decided that the measure of transferring the custody of the minor child from one parent to another is justified and can be taken if the parent who has custody can no longer provide the conditions needed for the adequate development of the child. The partial modification of the conditions which, as a whole, determined the custody of the child need not necessarily result in review of the measure, as long as the fundamental and decisive elements which justified it still exist.

The review of a measure – changing the custody of the child – must be well grounded, based on powerful reasons, which demonstrate that keeping the initial measure has consequences damaging to the development of the child, his raising and education; a child's way of life should not otherwise be forcibly changed.[104]

57. Taking into consideration the recommendation of the Committee of Ministers of the European Council no. 1/1998, which highlights the need for member states to reach settlement of family conflicts by mediation as the most adequate manner of settlement of this type of conflict ensuring also the compliance with the interests of the children, the Law no. 192/2006, regarding the mediation and organisation of the profession of mediator, dedicates certain provisions specific to mediation in family conflicts.

According to Article 2, if it is not otherwise provided by the law, the parties, individuals or legal entities, can follow the mediation procedure voluntarily, even after starting a law suit in front of the competent courts. They can agree to settle in this way any conflict in civil, commercial, *family*, criminal fields, as well as in other fields, under the conditions provided by this law. Article 64 of the same law provides that the disagreements between spouses regarding the continuation of the marriage, the exercise of parental rights, the establishment of the home of the children, the parents' contribution to the raising of the children, as well as any disagreements in the relations between spouses regarding rights of which they can dispose as provided by the law, can be settled by mediation. Combining these two texts, the outcome is that mediation has wide application in the domain of parental protection and can extend to the enforcement of judicial decisions, including those regarding residence of the child and the right to contact with the child.

In addition, according to Article 65, the mediator will take care that the result of the mediation is not contrary to the superior interests of the child: he will encourage the parents to concentrate firstly on the needs of the child, and the requirement that factual separation or divorce do not affect the raising and development of the child.

If the case is settled by mediation, an agreement is drafted, which will contain all the clauses agreed on by the parties and which has the status of a document issued under private signature. The parties' agreement can be subject to the verification of the public notary in view of its authentication, or, where appropriate, agreement

[104] See the Supreme Court of Justice, civil department, decision no. 2448 of 2 November 1993, in *Jurisprudence Bulletin, data base*, (Publishers All Beck); Timişoara Court of Appeal, civil department, court specialised for minors and family, decision no. 254 of 31 January 2006, in TIŢIAN ET AL, *supra* note 31, p. 124.

of the court of justice. Presentation of the document to the court is needed if the agreement of the spouses regarding the termination of the marriage and settlement of the aspects accessory to the divorce is filed by the parents with the court competent to order the divorce, as well as if the mediation of a conflict took place in front of the court (Articles 63 and 64 of the law).

The practical effects of these legal provisions are not yet visible, considering the fact that it is a recent regulation, which required the prior establishment of an institutional framework in respect of the performance of the profession of mediator.[105]

Thus, Romanian legislation corresponds to the European requirements and to the CEFL Principle 3:36 ("Alternative dispute resolution"): "In all disputes regarding parental responsibilities alternative dispute resolution mechanisms should be available."

58. In principle, the simple agreement regarding the exercise of parental rights, the residence of the child or the rights to have personal relations with the child does not have the value of enforceable title, therefore it cannot be forcibly enforced. If the agreement results from a court decision, it constitutes a writ of execution and could be enforced.

The enforcement is performed according to the Civil Procedure Code by the enforcement officers (bailiffs). "*De lege lata*" there are no express provisions in the Civil Procedure Code regarding the enforcement of court decisions in this field. Nevertheless, there are general provisions in the Civil Procedure Code, which are applicable. Thus, according to Article 583(2) of this Code, if the debtor refuses to fulfil an obligation to act (to perform a certain activity), required by a writ of execution, within 10 days of receipt of the summons, the creditor can be authorised by the court, through an irrevocable decision, issued with the summoning of the parties, to fulfil the obligation himself or by other persons, on the debtor's expense.

In addition, Article 580(3) provides that if the obligation to act cannot be fulfilled by a person other than the debtor, the latter can be forced to perform it and pay a civil fine. The court notified by the creditor can compel the debtor, by irrevocable decision, issued with the summoning of the parties, to pay to the state a civil fine between 20 lei and 50 lei (around 4.5 Euro to 12 Euro), established per day of delay until fulfilment of the obligation provided by the writ of execution.

---

105 The list of the authorised mediators was approved by Decision 94/2008 of the Mediation Council.

As a consequence, the compelling of the debtor who refuses to adhere to such a decision is achieved by means of an obligation to pay to the state a civil fine. At the same time, if the debtor still opposes the enforcement, the bailiff may obtain the support of the police, gendarmerie or other agents of public forces.[106]

It is debatable in the jurisprudence if the refusal of one, or both, of the parents to comply with the measures ordered by the court can constitute a justification for the modification of this measure. In principle, the measures regarding the child can be modified if the circumstances taken into consideration by the court when the respective measures were taken, have changed.

Thus, it has been decided that, if custody of the child was given to the mother, by means of presidential decree or final divorce court decision, the father's opposition and the refusal of the minor to comply with the decision under the father's influence, are not factors requiring the re-establishment of custody of the child, as long as the evidence indicates that maintaining the measure is in the interests of the minor. The fact that, during the social investigation, it was mentioned that custody of the minor could be granted to the father cannot affect this solution, as it is not a decisive criterion, but should be taken into consideration in the context of all of the evidence. In such a case it was held that there was no intervening impediment as regards the raising and care of the minor by the mother nor any change of the circumstances which had been taken into consideration in reaching the decision which was now being challenged.[107]

Also, in the case *Iganccolo – Zenide vs Romania*, by the Decision of 25 January 2000, the European Court of Human Rights noted that the provisions of Article 8 of the Convention were infringed, due to the fact that the Romanian authorities had not adopted adequate measures for the return of minors to the plaintiff, as required by Article 7 of the Hague Convention.

In the case *Pini, Bertani, Manera and Atripaldi vs Romania*, however, by the Decision of 22 June 2004, the European Court of Human Rights noted that the provisions of Article 8 of the Convention were not infringed, considering the fact that, in the absence of any relationship prior to adoption, an absolute obligation of the Romanian authorities to ensure the departure of the minors to Italy against their will could not be imposed.

---

106 Romania is party to the European Convention on the personal relations regarding the children, ratified by Law no. 87/2007, as well as in the European Convention on the recognition and enforcement of the decisions in the domain of the custody of the children to which it adhered by Law no. 216/2003.

107 See Bucharest Tribunal, civil department, decision no. 558/1991, decision no. 1220/1991, in *Lege 4*.

Taking into consideration the very complex problems related to the enforcement of court decisions regarding minors, the New Draft Civil Procedure Code proposes a special regulation applicable to the enforcement of such measures by a writ of execution (e.g., the establishment of the home of the minor, the making of a placement order, the return of the minor from the person holding him without a right, the exercise of the rights to have a personal relationship with the minor) .[108] The proposed articles intend to guarantee the enforcement of the court decision as well as to allow the possible change of the measures regarding the minor, which could not be enforced. The fact that, in this domain, coercive measures towards children are not desirable, must be taken into consideration, but – at the same time – a measure of enforcement is considered adequate if it is rapidly applied.

---

[108] Arts. 879–883 of the New Draft Civil Procedure Code institutes, in essence the following mechanism: the enforcement officer will send to the parent or person where the minor is found, the minute of acceptance of the enforcement with a summons in which it shall communicate to the respective person the date when he should be present with the minor on the officer's premises or in another place established by the enforcement officer, to be taken over by the creditor, or will notify him or her to allow the other parent to exercise the right to have personal relations with the minor, according to the programme established in the enforceable title.
If the debtor does not comply with the summons of the enforcement officer, the latter, at the request of the creditor, will notify the court to apply the civil fine provided in Art. 875.
If within one month from the communication of the minute through which the fine was applied, the debtor does not fulfil his obligation, the enforcement officer will start the forced enforcement. The enforcement will be made in the presence of a representative of the General Direction for Social Assistance and Child Protection and, when necessary, a psychologist appointed by him. The presence of the psychologist is not needed if the delegate of the direction has such a qualification. At the request of the enforcement officer, the agents of public security are compelled to help the enforcement, under the provisions of the law. It is not permitted to any person to harass the minor or to exercise pressure on him in order to carry out the enforcement.
If the debtor does not fulfil his obligation, the fine established by the court according to Art. 875 will run until the moment of the enforcement, but not longer then 3 months from the communication of the minute through which the fine was applied.
If the debtor does not fulfil the obligation within the mentioned period of time, as well as if the debtor is in bad faith and hides the minor, the enforcement officer will note this fact and shall immediately notify the prosecutor's office along with the court of enforcement to start the criminal investigation, for the offence of non-compliance with the court decision.
If the enforcement officer finds that the minor himself refuses categorically to leave the debtor or manifests aversion towards the creditor, he shall draft a minute where he shall note his ascertainments, which he shall communicate to the parties and the representative of the General Direction for Social Assistance and Child Protection.
The representative of the General Direction will notify the competent court in whose jurisdiction the minor is found, for the latter to order a programme of psychological counselling for the minor, considering his age, and for no longer than three months.
At the termination of the programme of psychological counselling, the psychologist appointed by the court will draft a report which he shall communicate to the court, the enforcement officer and the General Direction for Social Assistance and Child Protection.
After receipt of the psychologist's report, the enforcement officer shall re-start the procedure of the forced enforcement, according to Art. 880.
If during this procedure also, the enforcement can not be carried out due to the minor's refusal, the representative of the General Direction will immediately notify the competent court for the maintenance of the measures regarding the minor which could not be enforced.

Indeed, the procedures related to the enforcement of parental authority, including the enforcement of issued decisions, need promptness, due to the fact that the passing of time can have irreparable consequences on the relationship between the children and the non-custodial parent.

It is acknowledged that the current procedural enforcement regulation does not correspond completely to the CEFL Principle 3:39 ("Enforcement"), but the special procedure for this type of case which is proposed in the New Draft Civil Procedure Code will change things; despite the fact that the proposed procedure seems to be complicated – while the Principle 3:39(1) provides that any measure in this field should be enforced without delay – it will, nevertheless, ensure consistency with paragraph 2 of the same Principle: "Enforcement should not take place if it is manifestly contrary to the best interests of the child."

59. The right of the child to be heard and to have his opinion taken into account considering his age and maturity, constitutes one of the principles in the domain of the protection of children's rights, enshrined by Article 6(h) Law no. 272/2004, being also one of the fundamental rights of the child. By Article 24 of this law, which develops the content of this principle, the following became statutory:

> a) The child capable of discernment has the right to freely express his opinion on any issue regarding him.
> b) In any judicial or administrative procedure which concerns him, the child has the right to be heard. It is compulsory to hear a child older then 10 years. Still, a child under 10 years can be heard, if the competent authority considers this necessary for the settlement of the case.
> c) The right to be heard offers the child the possibility to request and receive any pertinent information, to be consulted, to express his opinion and be informed of the consequences of his opinion, if it is respected, as well as of the consequences of any decision regarding him.
> d) In all cases, the opinions of the child will be taken into consideration and will receive due importance, according to the age and stage of maturity of the child.
> e) Any child can request to be heard. Reasons must be given for refusal.

This provision has general applicability and is not limited to certain types of causes or to children of a certain age.

Besides these general provisions, there are also particular provisions in certain domains, such as:

> – the granting of custody of a minor to one parent (on divorce or annulment, as well as in case of establishment of parenthood outwith marriage) requires the hearing of a child older then 10 years (Article 42(1) Family Code);

– establishment of the child's residence: according to Article 100 Family Code, in case of disagreement between the parents, the court will decide, after hearing a child older then 10 years;
– the request of the parents for the return of the child from any person keeping him without a right is also settled with the mandatory hearing of a child older then 10 years (Article 103 Family Code).

Obviously, a distinction must be made between the child's right to be heard and the extent to which his opinion is taken into consideration. In certain fields, the law provides not only the condition of the child's hearing, but also requests his consent: for instance, for adoption, consent of the child older then 10 years is required, according to Article 11 Law no. 273/2004; also, measures of special protection can be taken only with the consent of the child older then 14 years, as provided by Article 53 Law no. 272/2004.

All these provisions are in line with the CEFL Principles 3:6 ("Child's right to be heard") and 3:37 ("Hearing of the child").

60. According to Article 144(1) Civil Procedure Code, if the court hears a minor child, the hearing takes place in the council chamber. If, according to the circumstances of the case, the court finds it adequate, it shall hear the minor child without the presence of the parties or other persons. As a consequence, the hearing of the child is carried out directly by the competent authority, which does not exclude the possibility to allow the presence of other persons.

61. Normally, the child is not represented in cases regarding the exercise of parental rights: in cases seeking to settle disagreements between the parents regarding the exercise of parental rights, the child is not himself party to the action, but has the right to be heard.

62. As regards the age and maturity of the child, generally Romanian legislation applies the obligation to hear a child over the age of 10, with the possibility of hearing a younger child, taking into consideration his discernment and maturity.

In the jurisprudence it has been decided that the preference of the children to be given in custody to one of the parents is not a deciding factor, but it cannot be overlooked if the children are of an age when they can correctly assess their interests. [109]

---

[109] See the Supreme Court of Justice, civil department, decision no. 1848 of 5 September 1991, in *Jurisprudence Bulletin, data base.*

SCOTS LAW AND THE CEFL PRINCIPLES REGARDING PARENTAL RESPONSIBILITIES: HARMONY IN PRINCIPLE

Jane Mair and Ian Sharpe

1. INTRODUCTION

The CEFL Principles of European Family Law Regarding Parental Responsibilities begin with a clear statement of harmony in that all societies and systems have experienced similar changes in the relationship of parent and child. This is certainly evident in the context of Scots law where the last century has resulted in radical reconceptualisation of the relationship between parent and child and of the balance between the parties. First, there was a gradual shift from an all-powerful father figure to relatively equal rights for mothers and fathers and then, more recently, the focus has moved to the balance of power between adults and children. In these developments, Scots law has responded to a range of influences: most notably, notions of equality, the concept of the welfare of the child and the growing emergence of the child as a distinct person. In the early stages of reform, there were several piecemeal amendments to traditional rules but more recently, in the 1995 Children (Scotland) Act, there was radical restructuring and restatement of the law relating to parents and children.

The Children (Scotland) Act 1995 was based on the detailed proposals of the Scottish Law Commission. In developing this new statutory framework, the Commission undertook considerable comparative research and was strongly influenced by the Convention on the Rights of the Child and, therefore, while there are differences of approach, Scots law is to a large extent in line with these current international principles. Prior to the 1995 Act, the focus of the parent/child relationship was the notion of parental rights in respect of their children; these rights being situated in a range of statutes and in the common law. There were also various obligations imposed on parents in respect of their children, including those relating to care, welfare, support and education. The 1995 Act marked a very significant change in the law for two principal reasons. First, in a radical departure from previous statutes, it provided that instead of parents having rights over their children they have responsibilities, with rights only to the extent necessary in order to enable them to fulfil their responsibilities. Secondly, the Act gave expression to the detailed content of these rights and responsibilities and in so doing sought to define more clearly than in the past the legal relationship between the parties.

2. RESPONSIBILITIES AND RIGHTS

Principle 3:1 Concept of parental responsibilities

While the CEFL notes that "'parental responsibilities'... is not commonly used as a basic concept in all jurisdictions surveyed",[1] it is a concept which is well established in the Scottish legal framework, although here it is presented together with a group of corresponding parental rights. Parental responsibilities and rights are central to the framework established by the Children (Scotland) Act 1995 which sets out definitions of them,[2] the parties to whom they will be automatically attributed[3] and a range of orders which may be granted by the court.[4] Section 1 of the Act provides that a parent has the following responsibilities:

1. to safeguard and promote the child's health, development and welfare;
2. to provide direction and guidance to the child in a manner appropriate to the stage of the child's development;
3. if the child is not living with the parent, to maintain personal relations and direct contact with the child on a regular basis; and
4. to act as the child's legal representative.

It is further provided that in order to fulfil these responsibilities, a parent has the following rights:

1. to have the child living with the parent or otherwise to regulate the child's residence;
2. to control, direct or guide the child's upbringing in a manner appropriate to the child's stage of development;
3. if the child does not live with the parent, to maintain personal relations and direct contact with the child on a regular basis; and
4. to act as the child's legal representative.[5]

---

1 BOELE-WOELKI, K., FERRAND, F., BEILFUSS, C.G., JÄNTERA-JAREBORG, M., LOWE, N., MARTINY, D. and PINTENS, W., *Principles of European Family Law Regarding Parental Responsibilities*, European Family Law Series No. 16 (Antwerp: Intersentia, 2007), p.26.

2 Children (Scotland) Act 1995, ss.1–3.

3 *Ibid*, s.3.

4 *Ibid*, s.11.

5 *Ibid*, s.2.

The specific elements of the CEFL Principle 3:1 can be seen to fall within the detail of section 1. The principal difference in structure is that Scots law makes a clear distinction between rights and responsibilities and places rights firmly below responsibilities; to be exercised only to the extent that is necessary to enable the parent to fulfil his or her responsibilities. Although the CEFL Principle is entitled "parental responsibilities" in fact it it is explained that these are a collection of "rights and duties". As part of a broader trend in the development of the parent/child relationship, the Scottish model is initially more attractive as it tries to make a clear distinction between these different concepts and to signal a break from traditional notions of parents as having rights over their children. In defining and distinguishing between rights and responsibilities, the Scottish approach attempts to give legal expression to the relationship of parent and child.

Principle 3:2 Holder of parental responsibilities

In terms of fit with Scots law, Principle 3:2 poses no difficulty as it is already provided that parental responsibilities and rights are held by the parents of a child[6] and may be sought by other parties who have an interest.[7] Only parents can acquire parental responsibilities and rights automatically, whereas other parties must apply to the court to be granted them by means of order in terms of section 11 of the Children (Scotland) Act 1995. In exceptional circumstances, parental responsibilities and rights may be transferred to a local authority by means of a Parental Responsibilities Order.[8]

3. RIGHTS OF THE CHILD

Principle 3:3 Best interests of the child

In keeping with other international documents, and in particular the UN Convention on the Rights of the Child 1989, according to the CEFL Principle 3:3 the child's best interests are to be the "primary consideration" in all matters concerning parental responsibilities. This is a principle which is easily met by Scots law, which places the "welfare of the child" as one of the guiding principles governing the operation of the Children (Scotland) Act 1995. Sections 1 and 2 of the Act set out the parental responsibilities and rights and where family life proceeds smoothly then it can be hoped that these can be read as a code of practice for parents in respect of their children. In practice, parental responsibilities and rights are most often considered in the context of family breakdown where

6 *Ibid*, s.1.
7 *Ibid*, s.11(3)(a)(i).
8 *Ibid*, s.86.

application is made to the court for regulation of the parent/child relationship. Section 11 provides for a range of orders which may be sought from the court imposing, removing or regulating parental responsibilities and rights and, in considering making any such order, the court is instructed that it "shall regard the welfare of the child concerned as its paramount consideration and shall not make any such order unless it considers that it would be better for the child that the order be made than that none should be made at all."[9]

That parental responsibilities and rights should be exercised in the best interests of the child is a well established and uncontroversial principle in Scots law which would therefore fit well with the CEFL Principle 3:3. The fact that it is easy to accept this Principle, however, does not acknowledge the substantial difficulty of ensuring that it is put into practice. In Scots law, as with the CEFL Principle, the concept of the best interests, or as in Scots law the "welfare" of the child, is not defined by statute but has developed through the decisions of the court. In deciding what is in the best interests of a child the court engages in:

> a process whereby, when all the relevant facts, relationships, claims and wishes of parents, risks, choices and other circumstances are taken into account and weighed, the course to be followed will be that which is most in the interests of the child's welfare as that term now has to be understood.[10]

In deciding in any particular case, the judge is also likely to be influenced "almost inevitably, by his or her own conception of how a child should be brought up".[11]

In making decisions about parental responsibilities and rights under section 11 of the Children (Scotland) Act 1995, the court is also guided by the principle of minimum intervention; that an order should not be made unless to make one would be better than not making one. In most situations where the issue comes to court,[12] the court will simply approve the arrangements currently in place for the children, since continuing the status quo is generally thought to be best for the child. The preference of the courts for maintaining the status quo can be seen very clearly in the case of *Breingan v Jamieson*.[13] In this case, a child went to live with her aunt, following the death of her mother. The child's parents had separated some time before the mother died and both parents had remarried. When subequently the father sought custody of his daughter, the court upheld the

9 *Ibid*, s.11(7)(a).
10 *J v C* [1970] AC 668 *per* Lord MacDermott at 710 – 711.
11 THOMSON, J., *Family Law in Scotland* (Edinburgh: Tottel, 2006), para 12.6.
12 MAIDMENT, S. has found that "about 94 per cent of divorcing parents agree between themselves the arrangements for the care of their children after divorce": *Child Custody and Divorce: The Law in Social Context* (London: Croom Helm,1984), p.68.
13 1993 SLT 186.

status quo, allowing her to remain with the aunt which is in clear support of the general proposition that:

> If the child is well and happy in the current situation the court should be slow to expose the child to change. The practice of the courts has long been to endorse a satisfactory status quo. The claims of persons caring for the child in a satisfactory manner may override even the claims of a parent.[14]

Thus in many cases, the best interests of the child are substantially assessed by the parents themselves and the court will conclude that it is in the welfare of the child to continue whatever arrangements have been put in place by the parents. In the Commentary on the CEFL Principle 3:3 it is clarified that it is intended to apply to "not only measures taken by competent authorities but also agreements between the holders of parental responsibilities as well as daily decisions by the parents or other holders of parental responsibilities relating to the child's care." While this is a worthy aspiration, and one with which Scots law would concur, it is difficult to put into practice without judicial intervention.

The court has power under section 11 of the 1995 Act to restrict, remove or otherwise regulate parental responsibilities and rights which it could do in the situation where a parent was not adequately caring for and promoting the welfare of the child. In practice, however, except in cases of children in need being raised by a local authority or in the context of divorce or dissolution of a civil partnership, there is unlikely to be judicial scrutiny of whether a parent is acting in the best interests of a child on a daily basis.

Principle 3:4 Autonomy of the child

Scots law seeks to recognise the developing capacity of a child through both the Children (Scotland) Act 1995 and the Age of Legal Capacity (Scotland) Act 1991 and so it complies with the requirement of this Principle to the effect that "the child's autonomy should be respected in accordance with the developing ability and need of the child to act independently". In various statutory provisions, it is recognised that children are autonomous persons who should have capacity to act independently commensurate with their developing understanding and ability. Even where they may still benefit from adult guidance, they should be consulted and encouraged to participate in the decision making process as it affects them. Despite the existence of clear principles and provisions in this area, it remains a difficult aspect of child law in terms of the practical balancing of welfare and autonomy.

---

14 *Butterworths Scottish Family Law Service* (Edinburgh: LexisNexis Butterworths), p.C-320, para C589.

A child's capacity to act independently is primarily governed in Scots law by the Age of Legal Capacity (Scotland) Act 1991. A distinction is drawn in Scots law between a "child" who is under the age of 16 and a "young person" who is between the ages of 16 and 18.[15] In principle, a child under the age of 16 has no legal capacity to enter into any transaction[16] whereas, on reaching the age of 16, he or she acquires full legal capacity.[17] Therefore, while a child of any age has capacity to own property, he or she will not be able to take any action in respect of it until the age of 16 and will require instead to be represented by an adult representative. In order to take account of a child's developing capacity, however, the 1991 Act makes certain albeit limited exceptions to this clear distinction. A child has capacity to enter into transactions "of a kind commonly entered into by persons of his age and circumstances" subject to the proviso that the terms of any such transaction are "not unreasonable".[18] A child who is over the age of 12 also has the capacity to make a will[19] and to consent to any adoption order made in respect of him or her. Not only does such a child have the capacity to consent but his or her consent is a requirement of any adoption order.[20] Although, in respect of a child under the age of 16, the parent as the child's legal representative is entitled to give consent to medical treatment on behalf of the child, where the child is regarded in the opinion of a medical practitioner as having the capacity to understand the nature of the treatment, then he or she may consent.[21]

Principle 3:5 Non-discrimination of the child

The principle of non-discrimination is a widely recognised and broadly applied principle in Scots law as in other European jurisdictions and therefore there should be relatively little difficulty in complying with this Principle. Two particular issues which are highlighted in the CEFL commentary on this Principle are, however, of particular relevance in Scots family law: the marital status of the parents and their sexual orientation.

Historically, a child's legal position was firmly related to whether or not the parents were married, with the status of illegitimacy bringing significant legal as well as social disadvantages.[22] The status of illegitimacy was abolished by means of the Law Reform (Parent and Child) (Scotland) Act 1986, although the treatment of

15 The age of majority is 18: Age of Majority (Scotland) Act 1969, s.1(1).
16 Age of Legal Capacity (Scotland) Act 1991, s.1(1)(a).
17 *Ibid*, s.1(1)(b).
18 *Ibid*, s.2(1).
19 *Ibid*, s.2(2).
20 Adoption and Children (Scotland) Act 2007, s.32(1). Where a child of 12 or over is incapable of giving consent, s.32(2) applies .
21 Age of Legal Capacity (Scotland) Act 1991, s.2(4).
22 In order to be legitimate it was required that the parents of the child be married at the time of conception or birth or at any time in between.

unmarried fathers continues to differ from that of those who are married.[23] Scots law currently provides automatic parental responsibilities and rights to mothers, married fathers and unmarried fathers who have jointly registered the birth of the child. Those unmarried fathers who have not been included on the child's birth certificate can seek to obtain parental responsibilities and rights either by means of a section 4 agreement[24] with the mother or by application to the court in terms of section 11. While this undoubtedly is an example of different treatment of married and unmarried fathers and therefore may be seen as in breach of the principle of non-discrimination, the dominance of the principle of non-discrimination may itself be open to challenge. What Scots law seeks to do is to provide for automatic responsibilities and rights for all those who are in practice involved in a child's life and there may be an argument to the effect that it is that which is in the best interests of the child rather than strict compliance with a principle of formal equality.

The marital status of the adults who care for a child has also been of relevance within the context of adoption. Until recently, although adoption was open to unmarried persons, where a couple wished to adopt jointly they could only do so where they were married. This has now been changed by the Adoption and Children (Scotland) Act 2007[25] which provides for adoption by "a relevant couple" which is defined as being persons who are married, civil partners or cohabitants. The test in respect of cohabitants is that the persons must be living together either as if husband and wife or as if civil partners "in an enduring family relationship".[26] In the Comparative Overview in respect of Principle 3:5, there is specific reference to the position of same sex couples. With the new adoption legislation, it is clear that same sex couples may seek to adopt a child on the same legal basis as opposite sex couples and in theory they should also be able to seek parental responsibilities and rights in a similar way. Section 11 of the Children (Scotland) Act 1985 enables a person to apply to the court for an order granting parental responsibilities and rights in the situation where they "claim an interest".[27] The sheriff court decision in *X v Y* [28] involved a woman in a stable lesbian relationship who gave birth as a result of donor insemination, with the donor being a male friend who was in a stable homosexual relationship. The understanding between the two women and the male donor appeared to be that all would be involved in the child's life although the child would live with and be cared for by the mother and her partner. Following the birth, both the donor and the mother's female partner sought parental responsibilities and rights in respect of the child but while the

23 Discussed further, *infra* under Principle 3:8.
24 Children (Scotland) Act 1995, s.4.
25 s.29.
26 Adoption and Children (Scotland) Act 2007, s.29(3)(c) and (d).
27 1995 Act, s.11(3)(a)(i).
28 2002 SLT (Sh Ct) 161.

sheriff granted them to the man, recognising that he had an interest, they were denied to the mother's partner. It is submitted that this decision was wrong in that the female partner could also establish an interest.

While Scots law can broadly demonstrate compliance with the principle of non-discrimination in terms of sex and sexual orientation, the other grounds to which reference is made in the Commentary are more problematic. In this respect, Scots law is not unusual in that it has become increasingly common to extend the list of prohibited grounds of discrimination without, it seems, full commitment to the practicalities of tackling discrimination in these areas. This is particularly so in respect of the inclusion of "social origin". It is uncontroversial to say that all children should be protected against discrimination on this basis but the reality is in stark contrast to the aspiration. The Child Poverty Action Group in Scotland, for example, reports that one in four children in Scotland are officially recognised as living in poverty[29] and the recent report of the Children's Commissioners highlights the continuing unequal treatment of children in certain communities, with particular mention of gypsy and traveller families, asylum seeker and refugee children.[30] Therefore, while Scots law is in theory in compliance with the CEFL Principle 3:5, much remains to be done in practice to tackle the inequalities in life experienced by many children particularly on the basis of economic and social position.

Principle 3:6 Child's right to be heard

Within the context of the Convention on the Rights of the Child and the developing law of children's rights, Principle 3:6 is a familiar and well established concept in Scots law. The right of a child to be informed and consulted, to be given the opportunity to express his or her views and to have them taken into account is an approach which is inherent in Scots law and its dealings with children. The right of the child to be heard is always placed against the background of the individual child's age and maturity. This principle lies at the heart of a modern legal and social approach to children, their developing capacity and their place within familial and social relationships. In theory, at least, it is a principle with which Scots law fully complies although significant difficulties remain in terms of how to facilitate the hearing of children within the judicial process and how to balance their views with those who assess their best interests.

The principal legislation in Scotland which deals with parental responsibilities and rights is the Children (Scotland) Act 1995 and within its framework there

29 See www.cpag.org.uk/scotland.
30 UK Children's Commissioners Report to the UN Committee on the Rights of the Child at http://www.sccyp.org.uk/UK_Childrens_Commissioners_UN_Report.pdf.

are a number of provisions which give effect to Principle 3:6. The views of a child should be considered not only in the judicial forum of any action concerning parental responsibilities and rights but also within the broader context of decision-making which concerns the child. Section 6 of the 1995 Act provides that the views of a child should be taken into account in "reaching any major decision" which involves the fulfilment or exercise of parental responsibilities and rights.[31] Therefore, even within the context of private, familial life, a child's views should be heard and taken into account in respect of any major decision. This requirement is subject as ever to the child wishing to express an opinion and to the age and maturity of the child although there is a presumption that a child of 12 or more will have sufficient capacity to form and express a view.[32]

While it may be hoped that those with responsibility for and care of children, will consult and listen to them within the context of decision making which affects them, it is primarily within the context of judicial consideration of parental responsibilities and rights that the operation of the requirement to listen to the child can be seen. Section 11 of the 1995 Act sets out the powers of the court to consider applications and make orders in respect of parental responsibilities and rights and in so doing it must act in accordance with three guiding principles. The first is that the welfare of the child must be the paramount consideration (the welfare principle),[33] the second that they should not make an order unless it would be better to do so than not (the principle of non-intervention)[34] and the third is the child's right to be heard.[35] It is provided that in considering whether or not to make an order under section 11, the court should, "so far as practicable" and taking into account the age and maturity of the child, ask the child if he or she wishes to express a view, provide the opportunity to do so and "have regard to such views as he or she may express".[36] Although the court may decide in fact that a child under the age of 12 has sufficient maturity to be heard, there is also a presumption to the effect that a child of 12 and above will have sufficient maturity.[37] The challenge of how best to enable a child to participate in the court process in order to express a view will be considered further in terms of Principle 3:37, but it should be noted that a child does not require to be legally represented in order to exercise the right to be heard.[38]

31 1995 Act, s.6(1).
32 *Ibid*, s.6(1)(b).
33 *Ibid*, s.11(7)(a).
34 *Ibid*.
35 *Ibid*, s.11(7)(b).
36 *Ibid*.
37 *Ibid*, s.11(10).
38 *Ibid*, s.11(9).

Attempts have been made in Scotland, since the introduction of the Children (Scotland) Act 1995, to facilitate the child in expressing his or her views but there is significant criticism of the adequacy and appropriateness of these measures.[39] Within the context of any application in respect of parental responsibilities and rights, there must be intimation to the child concerned of his or her right to express a view.[40] This is subject to the child's age and maturity and with regard to the nature of the order sought and, where appropriate, the sheriff may dispense with intimation.[41] If there is intimation, the child will be sent a letter outlining the nature of the action and informing him or her of the right to express a view. It is then for the child to respond if he or she wishes to do so and thereafter the child's views may be expressed orally, in writing or by means of a solicitor or other representative. Even taking account of the various informal ways in which the child can be assisted to express a view, serious doubts remain about the appropriateness of informing a child by letter of the process and placing the onus on the child of responding to this communication.[42] In addition, concern continues with regards to the confidentiality of any communication which the child may submit and the potential conflict between a child's desire for confidentiality and the right of parents to a fair hearing. [43]

Principle 3:7 Conflict of interests

With the trend away from a more authoritarian relationship between parents and children towards an increasing recognition of the child as an independent legal person with developing capacity, the potential for conflict between the rights and interests of the child and those of the holder of parental responsibilities and rights has grown. In any action in respect of parental responsibilities and rights, the court is obliged to regard the welfare of the child as the paramount consideration[44] and in any major decision concerning the child, the child should be consulted and his or her views taken into account.[45] In any action concerning parental responsibilities and rights, the child concerned may apply to the court on his or her own behalf.[46]

---

39 See for example, SUTHERLAND, E., *Child and Family Law* (Edinburgh: W. Green, 2008), paras. 3-058 – 3-064.

40 OCR 33.7(1)(h).

41 OCR 33.15. See eg *Shields v Shields* 2002 SLT 579.

42 For discussion, see RAITT, F., "Judicial Discretion and Methods of Ascertaining the Views of a Child" (2004) 16 *CFLQ* 151.

43 See *Dosoo v Dosoo* 1999 SLT (Sh Ct) 86; *McGrath v McGrath* 1999 SLT 90; *Grant v Grant* 2000 GWD 5-177.

44 1995 Act, s.11(7)(a).

45 *Ibid*, s.6(1).

46 *Ibid*, s.11(5).

Parental responsibilities and rights include acting as a child's representative and under section 11 of the 1985 Act a third party may apply to the court to be given this responsibility and right. It is also possible for the court to appoint a curator *ad litem* to represent the interests of a child in the course of any action. Specific protection for the interests of the child is also made in respect of the administration of the child's property.[47]

4. PARENTAL RESPONSIBILITIES OF PARENTS AND THIRD PARTIES

Principle 3:8 Parents

Principle 3:8 provides that persons whose legal parentage has been established, should have parental responsibilities for the child. For many reasons; social change, relationship breakdown, assisted reproduction and state intervention in family relations, the question of who has parental responsibilities in respect of a child is not always straightforward. The starting point for the CEFL, as in Scots law, is that the natural parents of the child are the obvious holders of these responsibilities but it is also recognised that in a variety of situations, parental responsibilities may rest with third parties either together with or instead of the birth parents.

In Scots law, a distinction is made between mothers and fathers in the way that parental responsibilities and rights are acquired. According to section 3(1)(a) of the Children (Scotland) Act 1995, a child's mother has automatic responsibilities and rights in respect of her child regardless of whether or not she is married, or has been married, to the child's father. For fathers, their entitlement is affected by marriage to the mother. The father will have automatic responsibilities and rights where he is married to the mother of the child at the time of conception or subsequently.[48] Where the couple is not married, the father will have responsibilities and rights where he is registered as the father[49] or where he has acquired them by means of an agreement with the mother under section 4 of the 1995 Act. This remains an area of debate in Scots law and it has recently been amended by the Family Law (Scotland) Act 2006. The Children (Scotland) Act 1995 provided originally that a father would have parental responsibilities and rights only where he was either married to the mother or where she had entered into an agreement under section 4 of the Act. By such an agreement, the mother could consent to the acquisition by the father of parental responsibilities and rights but only where she herself was in

47 See further discussion of Principle 3:22, *infra*.
48 1995 Act, s.3(1)(b)(i).
49 *Ibid*, s.3(1)(b)(ii).

full possession of her responsibilities and rights.[50] Any such agreement required to be registered in the Books of Council and Session.[51]

The operation of these section 4 agreements was disappointing in that they were relatively rarely used and they were thought to contribute to the public confusion in this area. According to Scots law, there is a distinction between the establishment of parentage and the acquisition of parental responsibilities and rights. Although establishing who is the mother of a child remains in most cases straightforward, issues do arise particularly in respect of assisted reproduction and here it is provided that the woman who carries the child, and no other woman, is to be treated as the mother.[52] Having established parentage, however, the attribution of parental responsibilities and rights to the mother is simple and focuses solely on the relationship between mother and child. For fathers, the position is more complex: first it must be established who is the father and secondly the question of whether or not he has responsibilities and rights is ultimately dependent on the mother. Paternity is established on the basis of a series of presumptions set out in section 5(1) of the Law Reform (Parent and Child) (Scotland) Act 1986. A man is presumed to be the father of a child if he was married to the mother at any point between conception and birth.[53] The second presumption of paternity applies where both he and the mother have acknowledged that he is the father of the child and he has been registered as such in the Register of Births, Marriages and Deaths.[54] Although a married father may register the birth of a child on his own, where the parents are unmarried, the birth must be registered jointly and therefore for a man to benefit from this presumption he requires the consent and co-operation of the mother. Confusion was to some extent created by the Children (Scotland) Act 1995 which introduced a second type of agreement between the mother and an unmarried father. By means of section 4, the mother could enter into an agreement with the father by means of which he would acquire parental responsibilities and rights. Relatively little use was made of this process and one criticism of it was that couples who had acknowledged and registered the unmarried father may have mistakenly assumed that this process of registration also gave responsibilities and rights to the man. The Family Law (Scotland) Act 2006 has amended the 1995 Act to bring it into line with these expectations and now, where an unmarried father is registered on the birth certificate as the father of the child, he will automatically acquire parental responsibilities and rights.[55] It remains a possibility that the couple may make a section 4 agreement. Even with

50 *Ibid*, s.4(1).
51 *Ibid*, s.4(2)(b).
52 Human Fertilisation and Embryology Act 1990, s.27(1).
53 Law Reform (Parent and Child) (Scotland) Act 1986 Act, s.5(1)(a).
54 *Ibid*, s.5(1)(b).
55 Children (Scotland) Act 1995, s.3(1)(b)(ii).

the amendment in 2006, some criticism of Scots law continues on the basis that mothers and fathers, and in particular unmarried fathers, are not treated equally.

One particular issue which is emerging in practice relates to the possibility that a man may be presumed to be the father and obtain parental responsibilities and rights on the basis of registration,[56] but subsequently the mother may deny that he is in fact the biological father. Even if there is DNA evidence which shows that he is not in fact the child's father, it is anticipated that the Registrar of Births would not agree to change the birth certificate as this would then have the result of depriving the man of his parental responsibilities and rights, but without the court having any opportunity to consider the position. Where the mother wished to pursue this approach, she could seek a declarator of non-parentage in the sheriff court or Court of Session, or alternatively might apply to the court under section 11(2)(a) of the Children (Scotland) Act 1995 to have the man deprived of some or all of his parental responsibilities and rights.

Principle 3:9 Third parties

In addition to the parents of a child, any person who has not previously held parental responsibilities and rights but who claims an interest may apply to the court for parental responsibilities and rights in terms of section 11(3)(a)(i) of the Children (Scotland) Act 1995. This provision has been considered, for example, in the context of grandparents,[57] step parents and same sex partners of a parent of the child.[58]

Principle 3:9 is very broad, providing only that parental responsibilities may be attributed to a third party but saying nothing about how or when this should occur, leaving this detail instead to the national legal systems. It might be suggested that there is little that is controversial in the basic principle but that in fact the difficulty is in the detail. In practice, issues may arise as to whether parental responsibilities and rights should be granted to a third party in certain circumstances. It is not uncommon, for example, for other family members to seek an order in respect of a child where for some reason the parents are not able to care for the child. This may occur, for example where the parents have drug or alcohol dependency problems or where there is history of abuse within the family. The court here may be faced with a difficult balancing act between the benefits of maintaining contact between the child and its extended family and the danger that the wider family will allow continued contact between the child and

56 Law Reform (Parent and Child) (Scotland) Act, s.5(1)(b); Children (Scotland) Act 1995, s.3(1)(b)(ii).

57 *F. v F.* 1991 S.L.T. 357.

58 See *X. v Y.*, 2002 Fam. L.R. 58.

its parents. Applications by third parties, usually grandparents, are frequently made within the context of adoption proceedings where it might be questioned to what extent the person is really acting in the interests of the child or in an attempt to hinder the adoption process.[59]

The distinction between "parents" and "third parties" can also in some situations be difficult to draw. Are the parents only those parties who are genetically linked to the child or should the term "parent" be interpreted more broadly to focus on the persons who care for or "parent" the child? Scots law has tended to adopt a broad definition of a "child of the family" in various statutes but has been slower to develop the scope of the notion of parent.[60] Although parental responsibilities and rights in terms of the Children (Scotland) Act 1985 may be held by both parents and third parties, this distinction may itself merit some reconsideration and the use of the term "parental" may be misleading. In *F. v F.* , it was stated by Lord President Hope that the term was "merely a convenient way of describing those rights"[61] but two sheriff court decisions highlighted the question of whether it was appropriate for a child to seek a contact order in respect of a sibling and here it might be argued that the terminology of parental responsibilities and rights may to some extent have clouded the issue of what was being sought, that is some legal assurance for a child that he or she would be able to maintain contact with siblings following the break up of the family.[62]

Principle 3:10 Effect of dissolution and separation

It is provided in this Principle that:

> "Parental responsibilities should neither be affected by the dissolution or annulment of the marriage or other formal relationship nor by the legal or factual separation between the parents".

Scots law complies with this Principle to the extent that divorce, dissolution and separation have no automatic effect on parental responsibilities and rights. This principle, however, highlights the challenge for family law which is to match the theory of the legal rule with the reality of family life. In practice, for many children, it is the breakdown of their parents' relationship which has most effect on parental responsibilities in operation.

---

59 See eg *AB and CD, Petrs* 1992 SLT 1064; *McCreight v City of Edinburgh Council* 2003 Fam LR 2.

60 For further discussion of this issue see MAIR, J., "Parents and Parenting: *McGibbon v McAllister*" 2008 *Edinburgh Law Review* 442.

61 1991 S.L.T. 357 at 361.

62 *D. v H.* 2004 S.L.T (Sh. Ct.) 73; *E. v E.* 2004 Fam. L.R. 115.

One of the guiding principles which the court must follow in applying section 11 of the Children (Scotland) Act is that it should not make an order unless it is satisfied that it would be better to do so than to make no order at all.[63] A change in the nature of the relationship between a child's parents should not in itself necessitate any order in respect of parental responsibilities and rights and where the parties can continue to cooperate in their relations with their children then the court need take no action.

5. EXERCISE OF PARENTAL RESPONSIBILITIES

5.1. PARENTS

Principle 3:11 Joint exercise

Scots family law in general applies equally to both parents and there is no distinction between them in the exercise of parental responsibilities and rights. The starting point is that where both parents have responsibilities and rights in respect of a child they are expected to exercise them jointly but, according to section 2(2) of the Children (Scotland) Act 1995, they may exercise them individually without the consent of the other. According to section 6(1) of the 1995 Act, in respect of "major decisions", anyone exercising parental rights should take into account the opinions of any other person who holds rights and responsibilities, together with the views of the child.

Principle 3:12 Daily matters, important and urgent decisions

As explained above, where both parents are entitled to exercise rights, they may do so independently without the need for consent of the other and, therefore, Scots law allows parents to exercise their rights independently in respect of all decisions. In the case of major decisions, where practicable, one person exercising parental rights must take into account the opinions of the other.[64] The CEFL Principles do not include a detailed definition of what are considered to be important decisions, although Principle 3:12 does give examples including decisions relating to education or medical treatment. In a similar way, Scots law gives no definition of what is meant by "major decisions".[65]

63 1995 Act, s.11(7)(a).
64 *Ibid*, s.6(1)(b).
65 *Ibid*, s.6(1).

Principle 3:13 Agreement on exercise

As discussed, parents may exercise their rights independently and in practice that is what is likely to happen in most families where there is a reasonable level of co-operation between the parents.

Principle 3:14 Disagreement on exercise

Although either parent may act independently, it is also open to the other to apply to the court where there is disagreement as to the exercise of responsibilities and rights. This can be done by the party seeking a "specific issue order" under section 11(2)(e) of the Children (Scotland) Act 1995.

Principle 3:15 Sole exercise upon agreement or decision

In many families, as a matter of practice, parental rights and responsibilities may be exercised by one or other parent acting independently, but express provision for agreement as to exercise is also made by means of section 3(5) of the 1995 Act. This provision makes it clear that no person may abdicate their responsibilities and rights but they may nonetheless enter into an agreement whereby the responsibilities and rights will be exercised or fulfilled by another person. It is thus open to parents to agree that the responsibilities and rights will be exercised by only one parent.

Principle 3:16 Exercise by one parent

In the case of a child born to a married couple, then the starting point will be that both parents will have responsibilities and rights but in the case of a child born to an unmarried mother, she alone will have automatic responsibilities and rights. In that situation, the father may acquire responsibilities and rights by application to the court, by means of a section 4 agreement with the mother or, since the Family Law (Scotland) Act 2006, where he is jointly registered as the father of the child on the birth certificate.

5.2. THIRD PERSONS

Principle 3:17 Exercise in addition to or instead of the parents

In Scots law, only parents will automatically have parental responsibilities and rights[66] but any person with "an interest" may apply to the court to be granted

[66] *Ibid*, s.3.

responsibilities and rights under section 11(3) of the Children (Scotland) Act 1995. This could include other relatives of the child, for example grandparents, or any other person, for example a teacher or doctor, who has an interest in the welfare of the child. Section 11(1) enables the court to make an order in respect of parental responsibilities and rights and subsection (2) further clarifies that the order can be general or specific, with reference to contact, residence or a specific issue. While section 11 may be used to deprive a person of their parental responsibilities and rights, it is clearly expressed that an order: "shall have the effect of depriving a person of parental responsibility or parental right only in so far as the order expressly so provides and only to the extent necessary to give effect to the order".[67] In other words, where parental responsibilities and rights are given to a third person, any existing responsibilities and rights of a parent will continue except where expressly restricted.

Principle 3:18 Decisions in daily matters

Despite its broad title, Principle 3:18 is in fact directed towards the specific situation of the partner of a parent with whom a child is living. Scots law does not deal expressly with this particular situation although some provision is made for a person in this position. Where a child is living with one parent and his or her spouse, civil partner or cohabitant, the latter could apply for parental responsibilities and rights in terms of section 11(3)(a)(i) as a person who claims an interest. Even without such formal application there is provision in section 5(1) of the 1995 Act for a person over the age of 16 who has de facto care or control of a child but does not have parental responsibilities and rights. Such a person has the responsibility "to do what is reasonable in all the circumstances to safeguard the child's health, development and welfare"[68] and this includes the giving of consent in respect of any medical or dental treatment where the child himself does not have capacity to consent and subject to the proviso that the carer does not know that a parent of the child would refuse to consent. The possibility was considered prior to the recent Family Law (Scotland) Act 2006 of introducing an agreement whereby a parent could confer parental responsibilities and rights on their partner in a way similar to that provided unmarried fathers in terms of section 4 of the 1995 Act, but this proposal was rejected.

---

67 *Ibid*, s.11(11).

68 *Ibid.*

6. CONTENT OF PARENTAL RESPONSIBILITIES

As previously outlined, Scots law makes a clear distinction between parental responsibilities[69] and parental rights[70] and provides that the rights are only available to the extent that they facilitate the fulfilment of the responsibilities. Although this is not a distinction which is so clearly expressed in the CEFL Principles, the substance of both systems is broadly similar.

6.1. THE CHILD'S PERSON AND PROPERTY

Principle 3:19 Care, protection and education

Principle 3:19 sets out a general provision to the effect that those with parental responsibilities should provide care, protection and education which is appropriate to the "child's distinctive character and developmental needs". This is broadly similar to the provision of Scots law in terms of section 1 of the 1995 Act which sets out the responsibility to "safeguard and promote the child's health, development and welfare"[71] and to provide direction and guidance "in a manner appropriate to the stage of development of the child".[72] In order to fulfil these responsibilities the parent has a corresponding right to "control, direct and guide … the child's upbringing".[73] The responsibility in respect of health, development and welfare and to provide direction applies in respect of children up to the age of 16,[74] whereas the responsibility to provide guidance continues until the child is 18.[75]

The responsibility to care for a child is clearly central to parental responsibilities and in making any order under section 11 of the Act, the court must regard the welfare of the child as the paramount consideration.[76] The responsibility of a parent to care for their child is further strengthened by the existence of criminal sanctions against a parent who abandons or neglects their child.[77] A child may also be considered as in need of compulsory measures of supervision and be referred to a children's panel where he or she is suffering as a result of a lack of parental care.[78]

69 *Ibid*, s.1.
70 *Ibid*, s.2.
71 *Ibid*, s.1(1)(a).
72 *Ibid*, s.1(1)(b).
73 *Ibid*, s.2(1)(b).
74 *Ibid*, s.1(2)(a).
75 *Ibid*, s.1(2)(b).
76 *Ibid*, s11(7)(a)
77 Children and Young Persons (Scotland) Act 1937, s.12(1).
78 Children (Scotland) Act 1995, s.52(2)

Within the general context of care and development, specific reference is made to education, religious upbringing and medical treatment. In addition to the parental responsibility in terms of section 1 of the 1995 Act, parents are also under a specific duty to ensure that their children receive suitable education until the age of 16.[79] This duty is placed within a broader statutory framework for ensuring that a child attends school[80] and which makes provision for parental choice of local authority school.[81]

While providing religious education to a child falls within the scope of the parental responsibility under section 1 of the 1995 Act, the welfare of the child continues to be the primary consideration. Therefore in the situation where a Jehovah's Witness refuses to consent to a blood transfusion for their child, their refusal may be overruled.[82] The issue of religious upbringing has been considered by the Scottish courts on occasion and in the past it has been evident that it was considered to be in the child's interests to be given a religious upbringing,[83] although the courts have not been prepared to decide between the merits of different religions.[84]

Caring for a child's health falls within the scope of the parental responsibility to provide care and protection[85] and by means of the responsibility[86] and right[87] parents may consent to medical treatment on behalf of a child. This will continue until the child reaches the age of 16 at which point he or she may consent.[88] A child under the age of 16 may also have capacity to consent to medical treatment if in the opinion of the medical practitioner "he is capable of understanding the nature and possible consequences of the procedure or treatment."[89] Although there are arguments as to why this enabling provision should also be interpreted as including the right to refuse consent,[90] it is not expressly included by section 2(4) and to date there have been no Scottish cases on this point.

According to Scots law, a person who holds parental responsibilities and rights has the responsibility to provide direction and guidance[91] and the right to control

79 Education (Scotland) Act 1980, ss.30 – 31.
80 *Ibid*, s.35.
81 *Ibid*, ss.28 and 28A – H.
82 Children (Scotland) Act 1995, s.11(2)(e) – specific issue order.
83 *McClements v McClements* 1958 SC 286.
84 *McNaught v McNaught* 1955 SLT (Sh Ct) 9.
85 Children (Scotland) Act 1995, s.1(1)(a).
86 *Ibid*, s.1(1)(d).
87 *Ibid*, s.2(1)(d).
88 Age of Legal Capacity (Scotland) Act 1991, s.1(1)(b).
89 *Ibid*, s.2(4).
90 For an outline of these arguments see THOMSON, *supra* note 11, para. 10.2.
91 Children (Scotland) Act 1995, s.1(1)(b).

the child[92] and within the scope of these provisions, the issue of discipline or punishment of a child may arise. The CEFL Principle 3:19(2) provides that a "child should not be subjected to corporal punishment or any other humiliating treatment" and this is one of the few Principles with which Scots law may not fully comply.[93] The starting point is that physical punishment of a child will constitute assault but provision is made for a parent to justify their conduct on the basis of section 51 of the Criminal Justice (Scotland) Act 2003. In considering the question of justification, the court must consider the following factors:

> (a) the nature of what was done, the reason for it and the circumstances in which it took place;
> (b) its duration and frequency;
> (c) any effect (whether physical or mental) which it has been shown to have had on the child;
> (d) the child's age; and
> (e) the child's personal characteristics (including, without prejudice to the generality of this paragraph, sex and state of health) at the time the thing was done.[94]

It is further provided that the assault will not be justifiable where it included a blow to the head, shaking or the use of an implement.[95] This provision seeks to introduce clearer guidance and control in respect of the traditional right of a parent, or a person who has care of a child,[96] to use reasonable physical chastisement but by leaving open the possibility of physical punishment it does not fully comply with the CEFL Principle.

Principle 3:20 Residence

Principle 3:20 can be interpreted as applying to both the question of domicile of a child and the day-to-day issue of where and with whom a child should live. In Scots law, where a child's parents are both domiciled in the same country, then the child shall have the domicile of the parents provided that he or she has a home with one or both of them.[97] In any other case, the child's domicile will be that of the country with which he or she "has for the time being the closest connection".[98]

---

92 *Ibid*, s.1(2)(b).
93 Issues of non-compliance of the UK with the ECHR have previously been considered in this area in *A v United Kingdom* (1999) 27 EHRR 611.
94 Criminal Justice (Scotland) Act 2003, s.51(1).
95 *Ibid*, s.51(3).
96 *Ibid*, s.51(1).
97 Family Law (Scotland) Act 2006, s.22(1) and (2).
98 Children (Scotland) Act 1995, s.22(3).

Providing a suitable home for a child clearly falls within the parental responsibility to safeguard and promote a child's health, welfare and development.[99] Section 2(1)(a) of the Children (Scotland) Act 1995 sets out that a person with parental responsibilities and rights has the right to have a child living with him, although as with all rights in the Act this exists only "in order to enable him to fulfil his parental responsibilities". Alternatively there is a right to "regulate the child's residence".[100]

Where the holders of parental responsibilities are living together, then issues as to residence are unlikely to arise but, on breakdown of the adult relationship, residence of the children is likely to be a key issue. Scots law has a preference for parental agreement and although application to the court may be made in respect of residence in terms of section 11 of the Children (Scotland) Act 1995, the court will not make an order "unless it considers that it would be better for the child that the order be made than that none should be made at all".[101] There is, therefore, a clear preference for private parental regulation of residence with the court interfering with the status quo only where it is clearly in the interests of the child.

No specific provision is made with regards to the nature of any agreement between the parents as to residence and it is therefore open to them to agree on shared or alternative residence. Principle 3:20(2) provides that where alternate residence is agreed between the holders of parental responsibilities, such agreement should be "approved by a competent authority". Such approval is not required as a matter of course by Scots law but there is provision for the court to consider arrangements for the care of children within the context of other related actions, eg divorce or judicial separation.[102] In the course of any such action, the court must consider whether a section 11 order, including a residence order, should be made in respect of the arrangements or proposed arrangements for bringing up any children, it can request further information on these arrangements and, if necessary, postpone granting decree in the principal action.[103]

Where the parents cannot reach agreement as to residence, or where the court considers that their arrangements are not suitable,[104] then a court order as to residence can be made in terms of section 11 of the 1995 Act. A residence order may be made under section 11(2)(c) regulating the arrangements as to with

99 *Ibid*, s.1(1)(a).
100 *Ibid*, s.2(1)(a).
101 *Ibid*, s.11(7)(a).
102 *Ibid*, s.12(1). This power applies equally in the context of an action for declarator of nullity in respect of either marriage or civil partnership or dissolution of civil partnership.
103 *Ibid*, s.12(2).
104 *Ibid*, s.12.

whom the child should live or where there is to be shared residence, setting out the arrangements for alternate or periodic residence with different persons. In making any such order, and with regard to the child's age and maturity, he or she will be given the opportunity to express any views and these shall be taken into account by the court.[105] It is presumed that a child of 12 or more will have sufficient age and maturity to express a view.[106]

Principle 3:20 makes express reference to the ability and willingness of parents to co-operate, their personal situation and the distance between the residences of the holders of parental responsibilities and the child's school and requires that these be taken into account in making a decision as to alternate residence agreements. While Scots law does not make express reference to these circumstances, any residence order in terms of section 11 must be made in accordance with the principle that the child's welfare is "the paramount consideration" and such circumstances would fall within the scope of that consideration. Where the court is considering making an order under section 11(1) in relation to parental responsibilities and rights, in terms of which two or more persons would have to co-operate with one another as respects matters affecting the child",[107] the court shall take that into account.

Principle 3:21 Relocation

Where parental responsibilities and rights are held by more than one person, then they can each exercise these responsibilities and rights independently.[108] Where there is a dispute between the holders and they cannot reach agreement on the exercise of their rights, then application can be made to the court in terms of section 11. It is specifically provided that, no person may remove a child who is habitually resident in Scotland from the United Kingdom[109] without the consent of any person[110] who has the right to regulate the residence of the child or to maintain contact with the child.[111] In the situation where one parent wishes to move with the child outwith the UK, and cannot obtain the agreement of any other relevant person, he or she could apply to the court for a specific issue order in terms of section 11(2)(e). As ever, the court will decide the issue based on the best interests of the child and, as can be seen in *M. v M.*, the prospect of a better

105 *Ibid*, s.11(7)(b).
106 *Ibid*, s.11(10).
107 *Ibid*, s.11(7D).
108 *Ibid*, s.2(3).
109 *Ibid*, s.2(3).
110 As defined in *ibid*, s.2(6).
111 In terms of *ibid*, s.2(1)(a) or (c).

standard of living following relocation may take precedence over maintenance of regular contact with the non-resident parent.[112]

Principle 3:22 Administration of the child's property

The responsibility of administering a child's property falls within the parental responsibilities set out in section 1 of the Children (Scotland) Act 1995 and this, together with the right and responsibility of the parent or holder to act as the child's representative, gives parents control of their children's property. Any person who claims an interest[113] may apply to the court for an order in this respect. In general, children acquire legal capacity at the age of 16[114] but below that age they may enter into transactions of a kind commonly entered into by persons of his or her age and circumstances and which are not unreasonable.[115]

Under section 10(1)(b) of the 1995 Act, the holder of parental responsibilities and rights is entitled to do anything in respect of the property which the child could do if he or she had full legal capacity. According to section 10, the person administering the child's property is obliged to act as a reasonable and prudent person would act on his or her own behalf[116] and when the person ceases to act as the child's representative, which will usually be when the child reaches the age of 16, he or she is obliged to account for intromissions with the child's property.[117] In accounting, a person shall not incur any liability where the child's property or assets have been used in the "proper discharge of the person's responsibility to safeguard and promote the child's health, development and welfare."[118]

Section 9 of the Children (Scotland) Act sets out particular provisions for dealing with situations where a child receives substantial sums of property, most often by means of trust or inheritance payment. The legislation focuses on the point prior to transfer of the property from, in most cases, a trustee or executor, to the parents. Where the property exceeds £20,000, the person holding it must seek direction from the Accountant of Court as to administration of the property[119] and where the value is between £5,000 and £20,000, such direction may be sought.[120] Where such direction is sought, the Accountant of Court may direct that a judicial factor

112 *M. v M.* 2000 Fam. L.R. 84.
113 Children (Scotland) Act 1995, s.11(3)(a)(i).
114 Age of Legal Capacity (Scotland) Act 1991, s.1(1).
115 *Ibid*, s.2(1).
116 Children (Scotland) Act 1995, s.10(1)(b).
117 *Ibid*, s.10(1).
118 *Ibid*, s.10(2).
119 *Ibid*, s.9(2)(a).
120 *Ibid*, s.9(2)(b).

should be appointed, that part or all of the property be transferred to him or that it be transferred direct to the parent or guardian.[121]

Principle 3:23 Restrictions

Principle 3:23 focuses on specific transactions which may be of particular significance in respect of a child's property. Scots law in the current framework takes the approach that the holder of parental responsibilities and rights should in general be left to administer the child's property[122] but with special provisions being in place for the most common situations where significant assets are likely to be transferred to a child; by means of inheritance or payments for a trust. In these situations, the legal framework in sections 9 and 10 of the 1995 Act, which allows for supervision by the Accountant of Court, will apply.[123]

Principle 3:24 Legal representation

To act as a child's legal representative is both a responsibility and a right of the holder of parental responsibilities and rights in terms of sections 1 and 2 of the Children (Scotland) Act 1995. This applies always bearing in mind the developing capacity of a child to act on his or her own behalf. As a general rule, a child acquires legal capacity at the age of 16[124] but below that age a child may enter into transactions of a kind common to his or her age and circumstance.[125] It is specifically provided in the Age of Legal Capacity Act 1991, that a child under the age of 16 may instruct a solicitor in connection with any civil matter,[126] and may sue or defend in any civil proceedings.[127] In either case, the child's capacity to do so will depend on "a general understanding of what it means to do so" and such understanding is presumed in a child of 12 or above.[128] In order to address some of the problems in practice which may be encountered by a child who seeks to appoint a solicitor, the Law Society for Scotland in 2004 issued specific guidance for Children's Lawyers.[129] In any judicial action, the court may also appoint a curator *ad litem* to protect the interests of a child.[130]

121 *Ibid*, s.9(5).
122 *Ibid*, s.10(1)(b).
123 Discussed, *supra* under Principle 3:22.
124 Age of Legal Capacity (Scotland) Act 1991, s.1(1).
125 *Ibid*, s.2(1).
126 *Ibid*, s.2(4).
127 *Ibid*, s.2(4A).
128 *Ibid*, s.2(4A).
129 *Child Protection and Representation Principles for Children's Lawyers*, Law Society for Scotland, 2004.
130 It is possible, although very unusual in practice, for a child to be represented by a solicitor and also to have a curator.

6.2. MAINTENANCE OF PERSONAL RELATIONSHIPS

Principle 3:25 Contact with parents and other persons

Principle 3:25 makes provision for contact to be maintained or established between a child and his parents, close relatives and possibly also persons with whom the child has close personal relations. In terms of Scots law, a person falling into each of these categories might be entitled to parental responsibilities and rights which include both the responsibility[131] and the right[132] "to maintain personal relations and direct contact with the child on a regular basis". It is made clear in both sections 1 and 2 of the 1995 Act that the responsibility and the right to maintain contact relates to the parent or other relevant person with whom the child is not regularly living. One of the orders which the court may make in terms of section 11 is an order to regulate arrangements for contact (a "contact order")[133] and, as with all section 11 orders, the court's paramount consideration must be the welfare of the child.

Principle 3:26 Content of contact

Although Scots law does not expressly define the nature of "contact", in practice it conforms with the provision in Principle 3:26. Where the court makes a contact order[134] it will usually focus on the regularity or timing of the contact arrangements rather than on the nature of the contact itself although it may in certain circumstances make provision for supervised contact which could involve another family member or independent third party. Scotland now also has a network of Child Contact Centres where supervised contact may take place.[135]

Principle 3:27 Agreement

Principle 3:27 provides that the holders of parental responsibilities may make an agreement with respect to contact and this is a principle with which Scots law has no difficulty as the starting point is always to favour the agreement of the parties, with the courts only intervening where the making of an order is regarded as better than no order.[136] In reaching any major decision with regards to parental responsibilities or rights, the parties should always, where practicable, take

131 Chidren (Scotland) Act 1995, s.1(1)(c).
132 *Ibid*, s.2(1)(c).
133 *Ibid*, s.11(1)(d).
134 *Ibid.*
135 For discussion see Scottish Executive, *Scottish Child Contact Centres* at https:.www.scotland.gov.uk/Resource/Doc/47171/0025532.pdf.
136 Children (Scotland) Act 1995, s11(7)

account of any wishes of the child, bearing in mind his or her age and maturity.[137] While there is no requirement that such an agreement be scrutinised or approved by the court, it will consider the appropriateness of any arrangements in relation to children within the context of an action relating to the breakdown of the adult relationship.[138]

Principle 3:28 Restrictions

Whereas a parent or other holder of parental responsibilities and rights has a prima facie responsibility and right to maintain contact and personal relations with a child, their exercise is always subject to the paramount consideration of the welfare of the child. In making an order in respect of contact, that must be the court's primary concern and therefore Scots law conforms with Principle 3:28. The views of the child, as discussed above, are of particular importance in contact arrangements. Although the starting point is that the maintenance of contact with both parents is in the interests of the child, particular concerns are sometimes raised in the context of situations where the parents have had an abusive relationship. Section 11(7A) to (7E) now expressly requires the court to consider the dangers and risks associated with abuse when deciding whether to make an order in respect of parental responsibilities and rights. This can include the situation where the abuse is not directed at the child but it could be relevant in particular where the parent seeking to establish contact with the child has previously abused the primary carer of the child.

Principle 3:29 Information to parents

While the provision of information to parents could fall within the general responsibilities and rights set out in sections 1 and 2 of the 1995 Act and in particular the provisions relating to contact and personal relations, Scots law does not currently make express provision in respect of the communication of personal information to the parent with whom the child is not living. In practice, where parents enter into an agreement relating to the children within the context of separation or divorce, a provision requiring the exchange of information is often included.[139]

---

137 *Ibid*, s.6.

138 ie divorce, judicial separation, declarator of nullity (marriage or civil partnership) and dissolution (civil partnership): Children (Scotland) Act 1995, s.12.

139 Often, as a matter of practice, when parents separate, school information and reports on the child will only be provided to the parent with whom the child has his or her principal home. There is no requirement that they be provided to both parents.

7. TERMINATION OF PARENTAL RESPONSIBILITIES

Principle 3:30 Termination

Scots law is broadly in compliance with Principle 3:30 relating to the termination of parental responsibilities. With the exception of the responsibility to provide guidance to a child, which continues to operate until the child reaches 18,[140] the other responsibilities and rights will terminate when the child reaches 16.[141] The responsibility to provide guidance is subject to the proviso that it is appropriate to the child's stage of development and it is argued that this flexibility brings it broadly within the aim of the Principle. According to Scots law, a person may marry at the age of 16 and so the requirement that parental responsibilities end on marriage is also met, again subject to the exception in respect of the provision of guidance.

The requirement that parental responsibilities should be terminated when a child is adopted is also met by Scots law which provides, according to section 12(1) of the Adoption (Scotland) Act 1978, that the effect of an adoption order is to vest parental responsibilities and rights in the adoptive parents. This will apply also in the case of a step-parent adoption. Protection for the existing holders of parental responsibilities and rights is, however, made in that they must consent to an adoption order.[142] A significant modification of this approach results from the new Adoption and Children (Scotland) Act 2007 which will permit a person whose parental responsibilities and rights were extinguished by means of an adoption order to apply subsequently for a contact order, with leave of the court.[143] While this new provision is well intentioned and will allow persons, not just parents, who have previously had parental responsibilities and rights to maintain or re-establish contact with a child subsequent to adoption, it is likely to prove difficult to implement in practice and may deter potential adoptive parents.

Principle 3:31 Death of the parents

The parental responsibilities and rights of a parent will terminate on their death but as either holder can exercise their responsibilities and rights independently, then, if there is a surviving parent, he or she can continue to act alone. Whereas a parent cannot delegate or transfer their responsibilities and rights to another person, a parent may appoint a guardian to act on his or her death.[144] The appointment,

---

140 Children (Scotland) Act 1995, s.1(2)(b).
141 *Ibid*, s.1(2)(a) and s2(7).
142 Or the need for consent must be dispensed with by the court: Adoption (Scotland) Act 1978, s.16(2)(b).
143 Adoption and Children (Scotland) Act 2007, s.107.
144 Children (Scotland) Act 1995, s.7(1).

which will often be in the parent's will, must be in writing and signed[145] and the appointment must be accepted by the guardian.[146] Where a guardian is appointed in this way, then he or she shall have parental responsibilities and rights under sections 1 and 2 of the 1995 Act, subject to any orders under section 11.[147] The rights of any surviving parent will subsist and both the parent and guardian will continue to be able to exercise their responsibilities and rights independently, subject to any section 11 orders.[148]

8. DISCHARGE AND RESTORATION OF PARENTAL RESPONSIBILITIES

Principle 3:32 Discharge of parental responsibilities

In Scots law, the key provision with respect to attribution, exercise and discharge of parental responsibilities and rights is section 11 of the Children (Scotland) Act 1995. The powers of the court under this provision make it clear that Scots law complies with the CEFL Principle 3:32. Section 11(2)(a) enables the court to "deprive a person of some or all of his parental responsibilities and parental rights in respect of a child". In making an order under section 11 to deprive a person of parental responsibilities and rights, the court is required to act according to the three guiding principles: that the child's welfare is the paramount consideration, that it should not make an order unless it would be better to do so than not to act and that the child should be given the opportunity to express his wishes and that they should be taken into account, always subject to the age and maturity of the child.[149]

Principle 3:33 Request for discharge of parental responsibilities

The court may make such an order where an application is made by a person who does not have parental responsibilities and rights but who "claims an interest",[150] a current holder[151] or past holder[152] of parental responsibilities and rights or where no such application has been made but the court on its own initiative considers that it should make such an order.[153] Such a request may be made to the court

145 *Ibid*, s.7(1)(a)(ii).
146 *Ibid*, s.7(3).
147 *Ibid*, s.7(5).
148 *Ibid*, s.7(1)(b).
149 *Ibid*, s.11(7)(a) and (b).
150 *Ibid*, s.11(3)(a)(i).
151 *Ibid*, s.11(3)(a)(ii).
152 *Ibid*, s.11(3)(a)(iii).
153 *Ibid*, s.11(3)(b).

either independently or as part of any other action[154] and in practice will most often be made in the context of divorce proceedings.

Principle 3:34 Restoration of parental responsibilities

Section 11 gives the court very broad scope to regulate the exercise of parental responsibilities and rights and, as seen above, it can include the attribution of responsibilities and rights. An application for a section 11 order can be made by a person who has had parental responsibilities and rights in the past and it is therefore clear that the court may decide to confer responsibilities and rights on a person who had previously been deprived of them.[155] As ever, the court must act with the welfare of the child as the paramount consideration, with regard to the principle that they should only act where it would be better to do so than to take no action and having regard to the views of the child where he or she wishes to express them and taking account of the age and maturity of the child.[156]

9. PROCEDURE

Principle 3:35 Competent authority

In Scots law, decisions concerning parental responsibilities and rights in terms of the Children (Scotland) Act 1995 are made by the sheriff court or Court of Session and so Scots law complies with this Principle.

Principle 3:36 Alternative dispute resolution

Scots law provides that parties may at any time reach agreement in the form of a Minute of Agreement and it is estimated that such agreements are used in approximately one third of divorces in Scotland.[157] Minutes of Agreement may be registered in the Books of Council and Session or the Sheriff Court Books. Where an agreement is reached within the context of a divorce action, it is referred to as a Joint Minute of Agreement and the court may be asked to grant decree in terms of the agreement. Although parties are encouraged to settle matters for themselves, and there is much discussion about the potential benefits where arrangements

154 *Ibid*, s.11(1).
155 This does not apply where a person has lost his or her parental responsibilities and rights as a result of an adoption order although this will be subject to section 107 of the new Adoption and Children (Scotland) Act 2007. See *supra* note 143. For further comment, see *West Lothian Council v M* 2002 SLT 1155 at p. 1160.
156 Children (Scotland) Act 1995, s.11(7).
157 WASOFF, F., MCGUCKIN, A. AND EDWARDS, L., *Mutual Consent: Written Agreements in Family Law* (Edinburgh: Scottish Central Research Unit, 1997).

have been agreed rather than imposed, in respect of children the court does retain power to intervene. In the course of any action, the court must consider whether a section 11 order should be made in respect of parental responsibilities and rights.[158] Any person who is entitled in terms of section 11(3) may also at any time seek an order under section 11, regardless of the existence of an agreement and in considering the application the court must follow the principle that the paramount consideration is the welfare of the child.[159]

In seeking to regulate matters by agreement rather than by means of judicial action, the parties may act on their own initiative or they may make use of an alternative means of dispute resolution. The most established method is mediation which is provided in Scotland by way of Family Mediation Scotland which was set up in 1987 and which replaced the earlier and more restricted Scottish Family Conciliation Service. Parties may themselves seek mediation, they may be referred by their solicitor or by the court in the context of judicial action. Increasingly, family lawyers are themselves becoming qualified as Comprehensive Accredited Lawyer Mediators (CALM) which may help to address one of the concerns raised about mediation which is that parties may agree to solutions which are not in their best interests in terms of their legal rights.

Another, more recent, approach to settlement of family disputes which is becoming increasingly used in Scotland, is that of collaborative law. This is a method which is based around meetings between parties together with their solicitors. The solicitors will collaborate to set up a joint meeting with both parties and this process will continue until agreement is reached. Following the initial client solicitor consultation, instead of the solicitors engaging in the traditional adversarial approach, they collaborate in order to establish a framework of meetings at which both parties will work towards establishing agreement. This approach again can be seen to address the concerns that alternative dispute resolution may not always be in line with the legal rights of each party. In collaborative law, although the objective is to work together towards agreement, each party has his or her own legal adviser present at all stages in the process. The initial agreement on which the process is based involves all parties committing themselves to trying to reach agreement without recourse to the courts. If in fact agreement cannot be reached, the lawyers must withdraw from the proceedings and any legal action could only be initiated by new lawyers. "By removing this threat it gives both the clients and their solicitors a vested interest in looking for constructive ways in which to resolve issues."[160]

---

158 Children (Scotland) Act 1995, s.12.

159 *Ibid*, s. 11(7).

160 EDWARDS, L. AND GRIFFITHS, A., *Family Law* (2nd ed.) (Edinburgh: W.Green/Thomson, 2006), para. 15–46.

Principle 3:37 Hearing of the child

Scots family law strongly endorses the child's right to be heard in any process concerning the child, but the practicalities of how to hear the child and to facilitate the child in expressing his or her views remain a significant challenge. While the legal provisions seek to promote the best interests of the child as the paramount consideration, the very involvement of the child and the potential pressure to express a view and to be involved in proceedings which are adult by their nature may cause significant harm to the child's welfare. The Scottish courts may appoint a curator *ad litem*[161] to obtain the views of the child, or provision may be made for a child to speak to the sheriff in chambers. Concerns have been raised about the appropriateness of relying on such short interviews with a child in any subsequent decision.[162] A very practical concern which a child may have about expressing his or her views in private is the extent to which they will remain confidential. Although the sheriff in *McGrath v McGrath* sought to protect the wishes of the child for confidentiality, this approach was overturned by the Sheriff Principal on appeal who held that there was no right of confidentiality and that the parties were entitled to a fair hearing.[163] Particularly in the context of an acrimonious dispute between parents, it is understandable that a child may be reluctant to express his or her views without reassurance that these will not be disclosed to the parents.

Principle 3:38 Appointment of a special representative for the child

In the course of any action concerning parental responsibilities and rights, the child who is the subject of the action may himself or herself apply to the court in terms of section 11 of the Children (Scotland) Act 1995.[164] In any case, a child who has sufficient understanding may instruct his or her own solicitor and the court may choose to appoint a curator *ad litem* to protect the interests of the child in the course of any action. This has been discussed further in terms of Principle 3:24.

Principle 3:39 Enforcement

The issue of enforcement of responsibilities and rights within the context of family relationships is of course a difficult one. Section 11 of the Children (Scotland) Act 1995 gives the court considerable power and discretion to restrict, grant and otherwise regulate parental responsibilities and rights and in practice the main

---

161 See discussion, *supra* under Principle 3:24.

162 See eg *W v W* 2003 Fam LR 85 which is discussed in *Butterworths Scottish Family Law Service*, *supra* note 14, p.C-1141 at para. C1841.16B.

163 *McGrath v McGrath* 1999 SLT (Sh Ct) 90.

164 Children (Scotland) Act 1995, s.11(5).

sanction for a parent who does not fulfil his or her responsibilities is that they may be removed in the interests of the child.

10. CONCLUDING REMARKS

In general, Scots law is broadly in compliance with the CEFL Principles and although the basic framework is different in that Scots law draws a clearer distinction between responsibilities and rights, the substance is largely in harmony. Scots law too makes less of a distinction between parents and third parties, focusing instead on the automatic attribution of responsibilities and rights to (most) parents and the need for third parties to apply to the court to be granted parental responsibilities and rights. It is not surprising that there should be this level of compliance as both Scots law and the CEFL are building on the already established principles set out in particular in the UN Convention on the Rights of the Child. Where Scots law struggles to apply the principles in practice is where the theory of legal rules comes into contact with the practice of family life, and here, it seems that the CEFL Principles offer little assistance.

PART TWO
RE-TESTING THE TESTED: THE SAME AND THE DIFFERENT

THE CEFL PRINCIPLES OF EUROPEAN FAMILY LAW REGARDING PARENTAL RESPONSIBILITIES AND DANISH LAW

Annette Kronborg and Christina G. Jeppesen de Boer

1. INTRODUCTION

The purpose of this contribution is to assess if, and to what extent, Danish law on parental responsibilities is in accordance with the CEFL Principles. This assessment will be made in relation to each Principle and in a general assessment at the end.

Danish law on parental responsibilities may be found in a singular Act: *Lov om Forældreansvar* (Act on Parental Responsibility) which entered into force on 1 October 2007.[1] This Act only regulates matters with respect to the child's person. The regulation concerning the administration of the child's property and legal representation may be found in *Værgemålsloven* (Act on Guardianship).[2] The parent(s) who has parental authority is also the guardian by operation of the law.

The conceptual development in Danish law on parental authority is dominated by legislative reform. Case law is therefore rarely relevant with respect to this development.[3] During the last three decades in particular three reforms entering into force in 1986, 1996 and 2007 have revised this area of law.[4] The major purpose of the reform in 1986 was to provide for the possibility of joint parental authority after divorce and for unmarried parents upon joint request of the parents. In 1996 joint parental authority after divorce and for unmarried parents was strengthened in the sense that it no longer was required that parents should

1 Act No. 499 of 06.06.2007. Before this Act it was regulated in the singular Act on Parental Authority and Contact (*Lov om Forældremyndighed og Samvær*).

2 Compilated Act No. 1015 of 20.08.2007.

3 There is also, as yet, a limited influence of human rights in Danish case law, see JEPPESEN DE BOER, C.G., *Joint Parental Authority* (Antwerp: Intersentia, 2008), Chapter II and III.

4 See for a more extensive historical overview: JEPPESEN DE BOER, *Ibid*, Chapter II.

agree upon a contact arrangement for the continuation or allocation of joint parental authority.[5]

In March 2005 a Commission was established to consider the need for reform concerning, amongst others, a stronger child centered perspective in decisions on parental authority and contact, the possibility of enforcing joint parental authority against the wishes of one parent and the possibility of establishing shared residence against the wishes of one parent.

The Commission published its report in May 2006[6] containing a draft proposal for a revised act on parental authority and contact. The majority of the Commission proposed a limited possibility to establish joint parental authority against the wishes of one parent. The proposal did not contain the possibility to establish shared residence against one parent's wishes.

In December 2006, however, the Danish Minister of Family and Consumer Affairs released a press statement stating that political agreement had been reached on the drafting of a new proposal, which would go further than the Commission's proposal. This proposal should contain the principle that joint parental authority is the general rule and that shared residence orders should be possible. The new proposal contained a completely rewritten Act (now the Act on Parental Responsibility) and a new Explanatory report.[7] The proposal was published in December 2006, adopted on 10 May 2007 and entered into force on 1 October 2007. The new Act and the explanatory report incorporates many of the suggestions and deliberations of the 2006 Commission but also goes further.

The main changes concerning parental authority are that joint parental authority becomes the main rule in all cases. The court can only allocate sole parental authority to one parent (in all cases where there is joint parental authority) in cases where there are weighty grounds for such an allocation. An alternative to the allocation of sole parental authority is the establishment of primary residence with one parent. This legal concept is new in Danish law. The Explanatory report considers that most disputes concerning parental authority in reality are disputes concerning the child's primary residence. A general duty to notify the other parent in case of relocation is placed upon both parents (whether they have parental authority, primary residence or not) in order to reconsider contact

5 In connection with a reform on the law on parentage, the law was changed with effect from 01.01.2002 providing for the automatic continuation of joint parental authority after divorce. In case a parent requested sole parental authority such was always allocated, in other words it was not possible to enforce joint parental authority against one parents' wishes.

6 Commission report No. 1475/2006. *Betænkning om Barnets perspektiv, Forældremyndighed, Barnets bopæl, Samvær og tvangsfuldbyrdelse.*

7 L 133, *Forslag til lov om forældreansvar*, 2006/2007.

arrangements and ultimately the allocation of parental authority and primary residence. The Act makes it possible for the court or administrative authorities to establish a contact arrangement which amounts to shared residence against the wishes of one parent. Such an enforced establishment does, however, require the establishment of primary residence with one parent. Shared equal parenting in relation to time allocation as well as equal legal rights remains open only to parents who agree.

2. PARENTAL RESPONSIBILITIES

2.1. DEFINITIONS

Principle 3.1. Concept of parental responsibilities

The Danish concept of parental responsibilities continues to be *forældremyndighed* which is best translated as parental authority. It has been considered to change this concept into a concept which would reflect the responsibility[8] of the holder(s) rather than the authority. It has, however, been rejected on the grounds, amongst others, that such a concept would be misleading with respect to the authority which the holder(s) have and secondly that a mere change of wording without de facto change to the concept itself would be inappropriate. Further it has been viewed to be an incorrect signal to divest a parent of "responsibility" in a procedure concerning the allocation of sole parental authority.[9] The responsibility of the holder(s) has nonetheless been stressed in the last reform, amongst others, in the title of the Act which since 2007 is *Lov om Forældreansvar* (Act on Parental Responsibility).

The purpose of the Act on Parental Responsibility and the reason for the change in title of the Act is reasoned in the Explanatory report as follows:

> The title of the Act "Act on parental authority and contact" is no longer adequate when separate decisions concerning residence are introduced. At the same time the proposal contains substantial changes to the law on parental authority and implements an important principle, which is; that a child has the right to two parents. This fundamental principle means that the parents, regardless of the fact that they do not live together anymore, must take responsibility for the child, for one thing by caring for the child, for another thing by co-operating on important issues concerning the child. It is also the responsibility of both parents that there is contact with the parent with whom the child does not live. The title of the Act is consequently an

8 In the Danish language the term would be responsibility in the singular.
9 Commission report No. 1279/1994, p. 185 and Commission report No. 1475/2006, p. 270.

illustration of its purpose – that the parents have and take responsibility for the child by co-operating on parental authority and contact.[10]

Parental authority in Danish law is defined to cover the care for the child and the authority to make decisions concerning the child's person from the perspective of the child's interests and needs. The child must be treated with respect and must not be subjected to physical abuse or other degrading treatment.[11] This definition is in line with the CEFL Principle concerning the content of parental responsibilities (Principle 3:19). The Danish Act does not further define the concept such as the CEFL Principle does, but it may be inferred from legal literature that it also covers education, maintenance of personal relationships and the determination of residence.[12] The administration of property and legal representation falls under the concept of guardianship. The holder(s) of parental authority are also the holder(s) of guardianship by operation of the law. Consequently Danish law accords with the CEFL definition.

Principle 3:2 Holder of parental responsibilities

The Danish Act on Parental Responsibility has no separate definition of the holder(s) of parental authority. It may be inferred from the Act that no more than two persons can have parental authority. Further, parental authority cannot be held partly such as provided for by the CEFL Principle. It is possible for third persons to have parental authority through transfer. Transfer of parental authority to two persons is only possible when these two persons are married; the CEFL Principle concerning holders is thus broader than Danish law.[13]

2.2. RIGHTS OF THE CHILD

Principle 3:3 Best interests of the child

The Danish Act on Parental Responsibility only contains one general principle concerning the best interests of the child. According to the Act all decisions made pursuant to the Act must be made in accordance with the best interests of the child.[14] The fact that it is now a general principle does not prevent further qualification in specific provisions, for example, that joint parental authority may

10 L 133, Comments to Art. 11.
11 Art. 2, Act on Parental Responsibility.
12 DANIELSEN, S., *Lov om forældremyndighed og samvær* (Copenhagen: Danmarks Jurist- og Økonomforbund, 1997), p. 58.
13 Art. 13(2), Act on Parental Responsibility.
14 Art. 4. Before the 2007 Act various provisions in the Act contained qualifications of the "best interests".

only be terminated upon request of one parent if there are "weighty grounds".[15] This is, however, also the case for the CEFL Principles.

The CEFL Principle is also applicable to agreements between the parents and decisions of the parents concerning care.[16] This is not the case for Danish law where the application concerns "decisions taken by the authorities according to the Act".[17]

Principle 3:4 Autonomy of the child

The Danish Act on Parental Responsibility does not contain a general rule concerning the child's increasing autonomy such as contained in the CEFL Principle. It is, however, recognised that the powers inherent in the concept of parental authority decreases as the child approaches the age of 18.[18] In relation to guardianship there is specific regulation. Here the parent/guardian must consult the minor aged 15. Further the minor can dispose of his or her own labour income.[19]

Specific regulation concerning the child's autonomy in relation to medical treatment and in relation to child protection measures exists. A child aged 15 has an autonomous position in relation to medical treatment.[20] A child aged 15, and for some decisions aged 12, has independent legal standing to appeal against decisions on child protection measures.[21]

The Danish approach to child autonomy is specific for certain areas of law rather than general as stipulated by the CEFL Principles and may be viewed to be narrower, yet also more specific, than the CEFL approach.

---

15 Art. 11. See further *infra* 2.3.

16 BOELE-WOELKI, K., FERRAND, F., BEILFUSS, C.G., JÄNTERA-JAREBORG, M., LOWE, N., MARTINY, D. and PINTENS, W. (eds) *Principles of European Family Law Regarding Parental Responsibilities*, European Family Law Series No. 16 (Antwerp: Intersentia, 2007), principle 3:3, Comment 3, p. 38.

17 L 133, p. 11–12 and comments to § 4. The 2006 Commission had suggested that the principle also apply to decisions of the parents, this suggestion was not adopted.

18 DANIELSEN considers the legal position of children in relation to their parents to be a neglected area of law, DANIELSEN, S., *"Børns rolle under forældremyndighedstvister"*, *TFA* 2004, p. 280. A child aged 10 may, since 2007, informally approach the Regional State Administration in matters concerning parental authority, residence and contact. The regional State Administration can then summon the parents to a meeting and may appoint a child expert. The parents are, however, not obligated to participate and the Administration cannot make a decision *ex officio*, Art. 35, Act on Parental Responsibility.

19 Art. 26(1) and 42, *Værgemålsloven* (Guardianship Act), Act No. 1015 of 20.08.2007.

20 *Sundhedsloven* (Health Act), Act No. 546 of 24.06.2005.

21 Art. 32(3), 48 and 167, *Serviceloven* (Act on Social Services), Compilated Act No. 979 of 01.10.2008.

Principle 3:5 Non-discrimination of the child

There is no explicit principle of non-discrimination against children (or their parents) in Danish law as provided in the CEFL Principle.[22] It may, however, be deduced from case law that a principle of non-discrimination applies and Danish law must be viewed to be in accordance with the CEFL Principle.[23]

Principle 3:6 The child's right to be heard

According to Article 5 of the Danish Act on Parental Responsibility the child's point of view must be considered in all matters concerning the child depending upon age and maturity. This article covers more than a mere hearing of the child. As with the CEFL Principle it is aimed at ensuring that the child participates in the decision making process. Nonetheless it does not stretch out to encompass decisions or agreements between the parents such as the CEFL Principle.[24]

Principle 3:7 Conflict of interests

There is no general conflict of interests rule in Danish law corresponding to the rule laid down in Principle 3:7. It is not entirely excluded that a temporary holder of parental authority may be appointed when there is a conflict of interests.[25] In matters pertaining to guardianship the Regional State Administration may appoint a temporary holder of guardianship.[26] Further it is possible, though not common, that in a legal procedure concerning parental authority and contact a special representative for the child is appointed.[27]

2.3. PARENTAL RESPONSIBILITIES OF PARENTS AND THIRD PERSONS

Principle 3:8 Parents

Principle 3:8 provides for parental responsibilities to be a consequence of legal affiliation. This is not the case in Danish law. Danish law does, however, provide

22 The Danish constitution does not provide a general non-discrimination principle. The principle of non-discrimination is contained in the implemented ECHR and in various Acts. These various acts are generally only applicable in relation to the labour market.

23 The principle of non-discrimination in relation to the parents' different religions was addressed extensively by the Supreme Court in relation to the allocation of parental authority, Højesteret, UfR 2001.2518H.

24 L133, Comments to § 5. Principles, *supra,* note 16 , principle 3:6, Comment 1, p. 54.

25 DANIELSEN, *supra* note 12, p. 449 and TFA 2006.356CS.

26 Art. 47, Guardianship Act.

27 Art. 450d, *Retsplejeloven* (Procedural Act), Compilated Act No. 1069 of 06.11.2008.

for this result in most cases. Pursuant to Article 6 of the Danish Act married (legal) parents have parental authority,[28] and pursuant to Article 7 unmarried co-habiting (legal) parents have parental authority by operation of the law.[29] Furthermore in cases where the most common paternity procedure has been utilised (the care and responsibility statement) the father automatically obtains parental authority. In a minority of cases, for example, where parental authority has been established judicially or the care and responsibility statement has not been utilised, the mother has parental authority alone.[30] The father may, however, at any time apply for an allocation of joint parental authority.[31]

Principle 3:9 Third persons

Third persons may have parental authority over a minor child if such has been transferred to them in accordance with Article 13(2) of the Danish Act on Parental Responsibility. The term is transfer (*overførsel*) although an actual transfer does not necessarily take place in situations where, for example, the parent's partner obtains parental authority together with the parent. Parental authority may only be transferred to two persons together if they are married. This means that transfer is not possible to a parent's partner if they only co-habit or to two persons of the same sex whether they have entered into a registered partnership or not.[32] Two same-sex partners may have joint parental authority over a child in situations where the one partner has adopted the other partner's child. In Danish law, the possibility to transfer parental authority to third persons may be viewed to be limited in comparison with the CEFL Principle considering that only a complete transfer is possible and considering the further limitation concerning persons.

Principle 3:10 Effect of dissolution and separation

According to the CEFL Principle parental authority is unaffected by separation or divorce. This is also true in Danish law as joint parental authority continues automatically after divorce, legal separation and factual separation.[33] Nonetheless the possibility exists that sole parental authority is allocated to one parent in this situation where there are "weighty grounds" for such an allocation.[34] Weighty grounds may be present, for example, if there is a substantial conflict level,

28 This also applies when the parents are legally separated or have been married within 10 months before the child's birth.

29 This also applies when the parents co-habited within 10 months before the child's birth.

30 Only approximately 4% of children are born to single mothers, HEIDE OTTOSEN, M., *Samboskab, Ægteskab og Forældrebrud*, (Copenhagen: Socialforskningsinstitutet, 2000), p.43.

31 Art. 14(1), Act on Parental Responsibility.

32 Marriage is only open to two persons of opposite sex. Two persons of the same sex may enter into a registered partnership.

33 Art. 8, Act on Parental Responsibility.

34 Art. 11, Act on Parental Responsibility.

violence, sexual abuse or unsuitability to have joint parental authority due to alcohol or drug abuse or a serious mental disease.[35] Danish law thus comes close to the CEFL Principle concerning discharge.[36]

2.4. EXERCISE OF PARENTAL RESPONSIBILITIES

The CEFL Principles distinguish the holding of parental responsibilities from the exercise hereof. The Principles hereby provide a two layered concept of parental responsibilities with the distinct possibility of regulation at two levels. Danish law does not provide such a two layered concept. Exercise is not a legal term in Danish law. Rather, Danish law provides for the types of decisions which can be made in respect of children whose parents do not live together. These decisions are: the allocation of parental authority (only in whole), the determination of residence and relocation (when parents' have joint parental authority and do not live together), and a decision concerning contact.

Paramount for the understanding of this distinction in the CEFL Principles is three notions.[37] The first notion is that once parental responsibilities belong to a person, this person "cannot divest him or herself of the whole package of rights and duties".[38] This notion is not equally relevant for Danish law where a parent may agree with the other parent to allocate sole parental authority to this parent. Such an agreement becomes valid upon notification to the State Administration and is not subject to scrutiny.[39]

Secondly, it is possible to have parental authority without (legally) exercising it.[40] Danish law does not provide for a regulation of the exercise.

Finally, the termination of joint parental responsibilities is to be viewed in the context of *discharge* (to be understood in the context of child protection measures) rather than as a means of solving disputes between the holders.[41] Discharge of parental authority is not possible in Danish law and does not take place when child protection measures are taken.

35 L133, Comments to § 11.
36 Principle 3:32.
37 JEPPESEN DE BOER, *supra* note 3 (2008), p. 150.
38 Principles, *supra*, note 16, Introduction, p. 14.
39 Only in cases where the parents do not live together, Art. 10, Act on Parental Responsibility.
40 Principles 3:15, 3:13 and 3:14.
41 Principles 3:14 and 3:32.

Principle 3:11 Joint exercise

Parents who hold joint parental authority in Danish law have equal rights with respect hereto as a starting point, corresponding to the Principle laid down by the CEFL. This starting point is modified when a decision or agreement establishing residence with one parent is made.

Principle 3:12 Daily matters, important and urgent decisions

Danish law provides for the parent with whom the child primarily resides to act alone in daily matters and for the contact parent to do so in relation to contact in accordance with the schedule listed below.[42] If the child resides with both parents on an equal basis both parents may act in daily matters. In important matters both parents (having parental authority) must agree. The Danish regulation is more specific than that provided for in the CEFL Principles. Danish law does not explicitly provide for a specific rule in case of urgency as does the CEFL Principle.

Holders jointly	The resident parent	The contact parent
Guardianship Important medical treatment and important surgery Choice of school Relocation outside the jurisdiction incl. Greenland and the Faeroe Islands Choice of names Religious matters Marriage Passport	Direct daily care Day care After-school care Leisure activities Relocation within the jurisdiction	Decisions related to contact - direct care Leisure activities

Principle 3:13 Agreement on exercise

Parents are free to agree upon matters of parental authority in Danish law. Nonetheless, to be legally binding, only agreements concerning contact and residence can be reviewed. Agreements concerning, for example, choice of school and medical treatment may be reviewed to have a quasi-legal nature. They are not subject to review on the basis of the "best interests" principle and are also unenforceable. Agreement between parents plays a prominent role in Danish law and parents are free to agree also upon the allocation of parental authority (joint/sole/transfer between the parents), the establishment of residence and contact. Such agreements are not subject to review and may be directly enforceable.

42 L133, Comments to § 3. The list is non-exhaustive.

Principle 3:14 Disagreement on exercise

The CEFL Principles provide for general access to the settlement of disputes between the parents concerning "important matters". From the comments it may be derived, however, that the competent authority's competence should not be limited to certain issues.[43] Danish law does not provide such general access. Rather it provides for a decision concerning only the allocation of parental authority, contact and for the establishment of residence and relocation.[44] It has been a conscious choice of the Danish legislature not to provide for such general access although arguably, the access has been increased in the legislative reforms of 1996 (contact) and 2007 (residence and relocation).[45]

The fact that parents cannot bring a dispute concerning, for example, medical treatment or the choice of a school before a competent authority does not mean that the State Administration and the ordinary courts are not faced with these types of disputes. In the first place parents may apply for counseling or mediation and receive such. In the second place such disputes may be the reason for an application for the termination of joint parental authority and/or the establishment of residence. It is possible that such disputes may be solved through a temporary decision (pending the proceedings) concerning parental authority or residence thereby empowering one parent to make the decision.

Principle 3:15 Sole exercise upon agreement or decision

Danish law does not provide for a legal regulation of *sole exercise* of parental authority (as opposed to sole parental authority which is provided for) as does the CEFL Principle.

Principle 3:16 Exercise by one parent

In Danish law as in the CEFL Principle the parent who has sole parental authority also "exercises" all rights inherent to this concept.

---

43 Principles, *supra*, note 16, Principle 3:14, Comment 1, p. 98.

44 In relation to guardianship it is possible to bring a dispute before a competent authority.

45 In case a general access was created, this was seen as involving "public parenting", Commission report 1279/1994, p. 14.

2.5. THIRD PERSONS

Principle 3:17 Exercise in addition to or instead of the parents

Danish law does not provide for an allocation of exercise of parental authority. An allocation of parental authority to a third person is possible in addition to the parent (when this parent has sole parental authority). This is only possible to the parent's partner of the opposite sex who is married to this parent. Further when there is no parent with parental authority, an allocation to a third party or to a married couple is possible. It is not possible for more than two persons to have parental authority.[46]

Principle 3:18 Decisions in daily matters

There is no provision in Danish law granting the parent's partner authority to act in daily matters such as provided for by the CEFL Principle. The CEFL Principle does not, however, provide this partner with more competence than what may follow from a delegation from the competent parent, something which although unregulated, is also possible in Danish law.

2.6. CONTENT OF PARENTAL RESPONSIBILITIES

Principle 3:19 Care, protection and education

As stated above care, protection and education are also core elements of the Danish concept of parental authority. Danish law also contains a ban on the use of physical punishment and other degrading treatment.[47]

Principle 3:20 Residence

It has been possible to establish the child's residence (*bopæl*) in Danish law since the 2007 revision.[48] Article 17(1) of the Act on Parental Responsibility provides that the court will decide with whom the child should reside in cases where the parents hold joint parental authority and disagree on the child's residence.

Parents are free to agree that the child should have an alternate/shared residence with both parents. Such agreement is not subject to scrutiny as provided for by

46 Art. 13(2), Act on Parental Responsibility.
47 Art. 2, Act on Parental Responsibility and above Section 2.1.
48 Before 2007 it was necessary to terminate joint parental authority when parents could not agree on the child's residence.

the CEFL Principle. A decision on shared residence against the will of one of the parents is possible only in the sense of time allocation, which means that the child will have an established residence with one of the parents and a contact arrangement amounting to half of the time with the other parent (de facto a 50/50 share arrangement).[49] This distinction is relevant in Danish law since the resident parent has the right to relocate within the jurisdiction and the right to decide on day care arrangements.[50] There is no list of relevant considerations for the establishment of an alternate/shared residence. The considerations mentioned in the CEFL Principle are, however, also relevant in Danish law.

Principle 3:21 Relocation

The present regulation of relocation enacted in 2007 makes a distinction between relocation within the jurisdiction (the geographical part of Denmark excluding Greenland and the Faeroe Islands) and relocation outside this jurisdiction applying in situations where the parents have joint parental authority. The resident parent (by agreement or decision of the court) has the right to relocate inside the jurisdiction. Relocation outside the jurisdiction requires parental agreement or a decision of the court.[51] The relocation may nonetheless provide a reason for the court to change the child's residence to the other parent depending upon the individual circumstances of the case.[52] The Danish regulation is not wholly in accordance with the CEFL Principle where any relocation requires agreement between the parents or a decision of the court.

Danish law, as the CEFL Principle, provides a duty to notify in case of relocation. Danish law does, however, provide a duty for both parents, whether they have parental authority or not and whether the child resides with this parent or not, to notify the other with respect to intended relocation, whereas the CEFL Principle only requires the resident parent to notify the other.[53]

Principle 3:22 Administration of the child's property

The holder(s) of parental authority is also the child's guardian and administers the child's property according to the Guardianship Act.[54] As provided for by the CEFL Principle such must be done with due care and diligence.[55] Danish law does

---

49 Art. 17, Act on Parental Responsibility.
50 See further; *supra* 2.4. and *infra* 2.6.
51 Art. 17, Act on Parental Responsibility. Such a decision must relate to a specific residence abroad.
52 L133, Comments to Art. 17.
53 Art. 3a, Act on Parental Responsibility.
54 Art. 2, Guardianship Act.
55 Art. 24 and 25, Guardianship Act.

not provide the guardian with a limited right to make gifts or to use the income for the needs of the family such as provided for by the CEFL Principle since the income only may be used to support the child.[56]

Principle 3:23 Restrictions

Danish law also contains restrictions concerning property acquired through a testamentary disposition and gifts such as provided for by the CEFL Principle. Furthermore, minors who have reached the age of 15 may dispose of their own income.[57] Finally, authorisation is necessary for certain transactions.[58]

Principle 3:24 Legal representation

A minor under the age of 18 is legally represented by the holder(s) of parental authority in Danish law in accordance with the CEFL Principle.[59] A minor does not have a general right to self-representation depending upon age and maturity as provided for by the CEFL Principle.[60]

2.7. MAINTENANCE OF PERSONAL RELATIONSHIPS

Principle 3:25 Contact with parents and other persons

Pursuant to Article 18(1) of the Act on Parental Responsibility, the child's connection with both parents is maintained through the right to contact with the parent with whom the child does not reside. The possibility to obtain a decision on contact is reserved for legal parents who do not reside with the child and is thus not dependent upon the holding of parental authority. The child's right to contact does not establish a duty for the unwilling parent in Danish law. On this point Danish law is not in accordance with the CEFL Principle.[61]

Close relatives do not have a right to contact in Danish law but contact may be established in situations where one or both parents are deceased or where there

56 Art. 25(2), Guardianship Act.
57 Art. 42(1), 1st sentence, Guardianship Act.
58 Art. 39, Guardianship Act.
59 Art. 2, Act on Parental Responsibility. For matters pertaining to guardianship, the guardian(s) (who in most cases is also the holder of parental authority) represents the minor, Art. 1, Guardianship Act.
60 In child protection procedures the minor has a more explicit independent legal standing, see further; Act on Social Services.
61 Principles, *supra* note 16, Principle 3:25, Comment 2 and 3, p. 173.

is limited contact with a parent.[62] Further, there is no provision providing for contact with persons who have a close personal relationship with the child.[63] On these points Danish law is more restricted than the CEFL Principle.

Principle 3:26 Content of contact

Danish law on the content of contact is in accordance with the CEFL Principle although it should be mentioned that other forms of contact such as through telephone or e-mail is stipulated as an exception.[64]

Principle 3:27 Agreement

Parents are, as provided for by the CEFL Principle, free to make agreements on contact in Danish law and such agreements are not subject to scrutiny.

Principle 3:28 Restrictions

Danish law provides for the possibility of placing restrictions or conditions upon contact and for the possibility of stopping or denying contact similar to the CEFL Principle. While the general criterion is the best interests principle, administrative case law has contained a strong presumption in favour of contact. This strong presumption has been critised in a socio-legal evaluation of Danish contact practices.[65] It has been stipulated in the last revision that the determining factor for the decision is the child's interests in the contact arrangement.[66]

Principle 3:29 Information to parents

A parent who does not have parental authority has the right to receive information from third parties, for example, from the school and medical institutions.[67] The other parent has no duty to provide information. The right of a parent who has parental authority is derived from the possession of parental authority. The Danish provision differs from the CEFL Principle by laying this duty upon third

62 Art. 20, Act on Parental Responsibility. The possibility to establish contact with close relatives was enacted in 2007.

63 If the child has been placed in care, such may be possible pursuant to the Act on Social Services. This Act regulates all contact (also of legal parents) with children placed in care.

64 Art. 22, Act on Parental Responsibility.

65 HEIDE OTTOSEN, M., *Samvær til barnets bedste*, (Copenhagen: Socialforskningsinstitutet, 2004).

66 Art. 21 and 4, Act on Parental Responsibility.

67 Art. 23, Act on Parental Responsibility.

parties only, whereas the CEFL Principle is mainly directed towards the other parent.[68]

2.8. TERMINATION OF PARENTAL RESPONSIBILITIES

Principle 3:30 Termination of parental responsibilities

Danish law is in accordance with the CEFL Principle on termination. Consequently parental authority is terminated when the child reaches majority at the age of 18, if the child enters into marriage before this age,[69] if the child is adopted or dies.

Principle 3:31 Death of the parents

Danish law draws an additional distinction concerning the allocation of parental authority after a parent's death than the CEFL Principle. It is hence not only relevant whether the surviving parent had parental authority but also relevant whether the surviving parent resided with the child. If the surviving parent had parental authority and resided with the child this parent would automatically continue to have parental authority. If the parent had parental authority but did not reside with the child, parental authority would also continue automatically, yet a third person may apply for parental authority to the exclusion of the surviving parent. This is only granted if it is considered necessary for the child.[70] If the surviving parent did not have parental authority, parental authority may be allocated to this parent or a third person. The surviving parent has a preferential position.[71]

Furthermore, Danish law has special regulation for the situation where the surviving parent has caused the other parents' death.[72]

2.9. DISCHARGE AND RESTORATION OF PARENTAL RESPONSIBILITIES

Danish law does not provide for the possibility of discharge of parental authority. In case child protection measures are taken this is done in accordance with the Act on Social Services. Such may limit the competence of the parent to decide on

68 Principles, *supra* note 16, Principle 3:29, Comment 3, p. 196. The CEFL does, however, leave the matter of third parties to national law.

69 Unless a condition concerning minority is placed upon the approval of a minor entering into marriage.

70 Art. 15, Section 1, Act on Parental Responsibility.

71 Art. 15, Section 2, Act on Parental Responsibility.

72 Art. 15, Section 1 and 3, Act on Parental Responsibility.

the child's residence etc. but does not formally affect parental authority in a way similar to that provided for by the CEFL Principles.[73]

2.10. PROCEDURE

Principle 3:35 Competent authority

The competence to make decisions on parental authority and contact are split between an administrative authority, the Regional State Administration, and the ordinary courts. The general principle is that all cases must begin with the State Administration. Only if the parents do not reach agreement can the case be submitted to the court by the State Administration.[74] In cases concerning contact, the courts are only competent to make a decision if a case concerning parental authority or residence is pending before the court.[75]

Principle 3:36 Alternative dispute resolution

The use of alternative dispute resolution is part and parcel of the administrative approach in Danish law. The Regional State Administration has child experts and mediators in house and their services are free of charge for the parents. These services may also be requested in situations where formally there is no legal case. Further, the use of alternative dispute resolution in courts has been strengthened in the last revision of the Act on Parental Responsibility.

Principle 3:37 Hearing of the child

The child must be involved in a case concerning parental authority, residence or contact so that the child's perspective and views may come to light.[76] This is possible through a formal hearing of the child or through the use of child experts. The child need not be involved if this will be harmful to the child or if it is considered to be unnecessary.

A conversation will generally take place with a child from the age of seven while the perspective of younger children will be brought to light through the use of child experts.

73 Principles 3:32, 3:33 and 3:34.
74 Art. 31, Act on Parental Responsibility.
75 Art. 38, Act on Parental Responsibility.
76 Art. 34, Act on Parental Responsibility.

Principle 3:38 Appointment of a special representative for the child

The appointment of a special representative for the child in legal proceedings is possible in Danish law. Such is not, however, common and not required in cases where there may be a conflict of interests.[77] Danish law places more emphasis upon the use of child experts who may fulfil this function.

Principle 3:39 Enforcement

Danish law provides an efficient system of enforcement which must be considered to be in accordance with the CEFL Principle. A special division of the court (*fogedretten*) is charged with enforcement. Direct enforcement is possible with respect to both court decisions and private agreements explicitly stating that they may serve as a foundation for enforcement concerning parental authority, residence and contact.[78] Enforcement is not possible if the physical or mental health of the child is seriously endangered.

3. FINAL ASSESSMENT

Danish law is, to a large extent, in accordance with the CEFL Principles. The differences may be categorised into three different groups.

Some of the differences between the CEFL Principles and Danish law may be explained by the difference between law and values. The Principles are partly based on a desire to contribute to common European *values* while national *legislation* is a legal notion. Even though the Principles also aim at harmonisation of family law, the Principles are the expression of values to a greater extent than national law. This means that - apart from the definitions of concepts – they are of an idealistic nature. Danish national law may be viewed to be closer to the implementation of the values and thus more closely related to making the values operate in the realities of the families. We may understand two of the differences between the Principles and Danish law on this background. In the first case, the Principles also cover matters within the private realm of the family while Danish law covers cases only. Secondly, the Principles hold that the parents have a duty to have contact with the child.

Another type of difference between the Principles and Danish law follows from the Principles' definition of parental responsibilities. The former traditional

---

77 Art. 450d, Procedural Act and above Section 2.2.

78 Art. 537(1) and 478(1), Procedural Act. Agreements concerning parental authority must be notified in order to be directly enforceable.

distinction of status between children born in or outside marriage has been replaced by a broad definition of holders of parental responsibilities reflecting the persons with whom the child has a close family tie. This is supplemented with access to decisions of disputes between the holders and division of competence at the level of exercise. On the contrary, Danish law continues to rule some persons out through the concept of parental authority as described above concerning Principles 3:8 and 3:9. Danish law may hereby be understood to challenge Principle 3:5 on non-discrimination because parental authority may be understood as a replacement of the traditional distinction based on status. The advantage of the Danish regulation is that it limits the access to start a procedure which may be beneficial to the child.

A last type of difference is where Danish law actually differs irrespective of the two types of differences mentioned above. An example is the lack of general access to dispute settlement in Danish law. This could be understood to reflect upon an engagement in alternative dispute resolution. This approach may simultaneously explain why parental agreements are not subject to review in Danish law. The authority of the courts/administrative authorities has been replaced by the parents' joint authority.

A MORE PRINCIPLED APPROACH TO PARENTAL RESPONSIBILITY IN ENGLAND AND WALES?

Rebecca Probert, Stephen Gilmore and Jonathan Herring

1. INTRODUCTION

The concept of "parental responsibility" was introduced to England and Wales by the Children Act 1989, being broadly defined as "all the rights, duties, powers, responsibilities and authority which by law a parent of a child has in relation to the child and his property".[1] The very breadth of this definition is likely to facilitate the incorporation of the Principles into domestic law, in terms of the two sharing a common core; moreover, the greater detail to be found in the Principles would meet one of the criticisms that has been levelled at the concept of parental responsibility. This said, incorporation of certain of the Principles would inevitably meet with some challenges.

2. THE CONCEPT OF PARENTAL RESPONSIBILITY

It has often been noted that the broad definition of parental responsibility set out in the Children Act 1989 is in fact no definition at all. It not only fails to identify the types of rights and responsibilities that are encompassed by the term, but also does not indicate what parental responsibility is *for*. The explicit statement in Principle 3:1 that parental responsibilities are those rights and duties "aimed at promoting and safeguarding the welfare of the child" does, however, resonate with judicial pronouncements on the issue. As Lord Fraser put it in *Gillick v West Norfolk and Wisbech Area Health Authority and Department of Health and Social Security*:[2]

1 Children Act 1989, s. 3(1).
2 [1986] 1 A.C. 112.

> parental rights to control a child do not exist for the benefit of the parent. They exist for the benefit of the child and they are justified only in so far as they enable the parent to perform his duties towards the child, and towards other children in the family.[3]

While there has been some debate as to whether certain types of parental responsibilities should be described as "parent-centred" rather than "child-centred",[4] none of the rights encompassed within the concept of parental responsibility is *entirely* parent-centred, even if the degree of discretion accorded to parents does allow for parents to give expression to their own preferences and values in deciding how best to meet their responsibilities. Thus the focus on promoting and safeguarding the child's welfare in Principle 3:1 seems to capture the current approach of English law rather better than the current statutory formulation of parental responsibility.

The non-exhaustive list set out in Principle 3:1 would also be a useful addition to the English statute book. The lack of any statutory list of parental responsibilities has been criticised by a number of commentators. Despite such lack, there have been a number of attempts to distil such a list from the existing rights and duties of parents that are scattered through different pieces of legislation or rooted in the common law.[5] These different rights and responsibilities could be easily allocated to the categories set out in Principle 3:1.[6]

However, Principle 3:1, read together with Principles 3:2 and 3:9, appears to be considerably wider than the English definition of parental responsibility, in that English law, unlike the Principles, defines parental responsibility by reference to the various rights, duties, powers, authority and responsibilities which by law *a parent has*. By contrast, the Principles appear to do so by reference to the function of the rights and duties, namely to safeguard and promote children's welfare. On this view it is possible that anyone who is acting in any way to care for or protect a child (for example a teacher or babysitter) would be exercising parental responsibilities. The width of this definition may encounter some resistance given the narrower definition in English law.

In this jurisdiction parental responsibility is ostensibly a single concept: an individual either possesses it or not. Yet the idea of holding parental responsibilities

3 *Ibid*, at p. 170 D - E.

4 I.e., whether the responsibilities exist to be exercised for the benefit of the parent or for the child: see McCALL SMITH, A., "Is Anything left of Parental Rights?" in SUTHERLAND, E. and McCALL SMITH, A., *Family Rights, Family Law and Medical Ethics* (Edinburgh: Edinburgh University Press, 1990).

5 See e.g. LOWE, N. and DOUGLAS, G., *Bromley's Family Law* (Oxford: Oxford University Press, 2007), p. 377; PROBERT, R., *Cretney's Family Law* (London: Sweet & Maxwell, 2006), p. 221.

6 Whether this is equally true of the more directional and aspirational elements set out in subsequent Principles will be considered later.

"in whole or in part", as set out in Principle 3:2, does in fact more accurately represent the current law. Upon examining the rights and responsibilities that are comprised within "parental responsibility", it is clear that there are a number of distinctions between different holders of parental responsibility. For example, a local authority with parental responsibility cannot appoint a guardian for the child, or consent or refuse consent to the child's adoption,[7] or cause a child to be brought up in any religious persuasion other than that in which he would have been brought up had a care order not been made.[8] A non-parent who has acquired parental responsibility as a result of a residence order is similarly prevented from appointing a guardian or consenting or refusing consent to the child's adoption, while the latter limitation also applies to a special guardian.[9] It would be more accurate to say that such persons possess parental responsibilities "in part" rather than attributing "all" rights and duties to them and then explaining which they do not, in fact, enjoy.

Even in the context of parents with parental responsibility, it is slightly misleading to describe parental responsibility as encompassing "all" the rights and duties they possess. Parents have a number of rights and duties that flow simply from the status of being a parent: the parent in question will enjoy or incur them regardless of whether he has parental responsibility, while non-parents with parental responsibility will not. Examples include the parents' duties to ensure that their child receives "efficient full-time education"[10] and to make child support payments under the Child Support Act 1991 in relation to a child under 18,[11] and their rights of intestate succession under the Administration of Estates Act 1925. Since *a parent's responsibilities*, and *parental responsibility* as defined by section 3 of the Children Act 1989, are not necessarily the same,[12] the more modest formulation of parental responsibilities in the Principles as simply "a collection" of rights and duties is a more accurate description of English law than is our current statutory definition.

3. PARENTAL RESPONSIBILITY AND THE RIGHTS OF THE CHILD

The issue of parental responsibility is inevitably intertwined with that of the rights of the child, whether the child's right to have his or her best interests

7 Children Act 1989, s. 33(6)(a) and (b); and s. 12 (3).

8 Children Act 1989, s. 33(6)(c).

9 Children Act 1989, s. 14C(2)(b).

10 Education Act 1996, s. 7.

11 Child Support Act, 1991, s. 1.

12 See HERRING, J., *Family Law* (Harlow: Pearson, 2007), pp. 385–6 for a list of the differences between rights given to a parent and those given to a parent with parental responsibility.

respected when the parent is deciding how to exercise parental responsibility, or the right to self-determination that may limit the parent's ability to exercise parental responsibility. Principle 3:3 provides that the best interests of the child should be the "primary" consideration "[i]n *all* matters concerning parental responsibilities".[13] This is similar to the approach in article 3 of the United Nations Convention on the Rights of the Child, to which the UK is a signatory. To an extent Principle 3:3 simply reinforces the fact that parental responsibilities as envisaged by the Principles are child-centred: parental wishes may play a role but can only be secondary to the best interests of the child. Presumably this does not mean that parents are required to put their children first in all matters, since there will be scope to characterise some issues which parents must address as not (or not primarily or directly) an aspect of parental responsibility, even where the issue may have a profound effect upon the child. An example might be the parents' decision to separate. And, realistically, it will only be if the parents' exercise of parental responsibility is challenged by another, that parents may be required to adopt or accept a certain course of action.

Whether or not the approach in Principle 3:3 coincides with English law is, however, a matter of some debate and interpretation. The principal difficulty that English law might encounter with Principle 3:3 is section 1(1) of the Children Act 1989. This provides that whenever a court is considering a matter with respect to a child's upbringing or the administration of the child's property, the child's welfare shall be the court's "paramount" consideration. While section 1(1) is of limited scope, applying only in the circumstances set out in the subsection, with no real application outside the context of litigation (and thus Principle 3:3 is both weaker and broader), the difficulty lies with the House of Lords' interpretation of "paramount". Paramount has been interpreted to mean that the welfare of the child is the sole consideration.[14] So, while the Principles, with the use of the word "primary", suggest that there could be cases where the interests of others will mean that the course which best promotes the interests of the child will not be followed, that could never happen under the paramountcy principle as currently interpreted. On that interpretation, the Principles appear to offer considerably weaker protection to the child's interests than English law. However, there is a convincing argument that, in the light of the introduction into English law of articles of the European Convention on Human Rights, as scheduled to the Human Rights Act 1998, the paramountcy principle cannot continue to focus exclusively on the child's interests: it must be reformulated to take account of individuals' Convention rights, principally in this context the right to respect for

13 Emphasis added.
14 See *J v C* [1970] AC 668, at 710–711.

family life within article 8 of the Convention.[15] It may be added that, even as currently interpreted by the House of Lords, the English courts have found ways to accommodate parents' interests when applying the paramountcy principle.[16]

The better view, therefore, may be that English law is not inconsistent with Principle 3:3. Even if it is, the fear that the Principles may not offer sufficient protection to children's interests is mitigated by Principle 3:7, which makes it clear that the interests of the child "should be protected whenever they may be in conflict with the interests of the holders of parental responsibilities." Arguably this formulation succeeds in reconciling the demands of the European Convention on Human Rights with the approach of current domestic law: substituting "primary" for "paramount" acknowledges that there are other interests at stake and, while stipulating that the interests of children are to be protected, ensures that children will not suffer as a result of the balancing exercise required by the Convention.[17]

Turning to the autonomy rights of the child, while there is increasing recognition of children's autonomy in English law, it is unclear whether Principle 3:4 – respecting the child's autonomy "in accordance with the developing ability and need of the child to act independently" – has been fully embraced. There is a popular view that the House of Lords decision in *Gillick v West Norfolk and Wisbech Area Health Authority*[18] (*Gillick*) recognised the child's autonomy interest in the manner described in Principle 3:4, particularly in Lord Scarman's opinion which stated that "parental right yields to the child's right to make his or her own decisions when he reaches a sufficient understanding and intelligence to be capable of making up his own mind on the matter requiring decision."[19] However, this interpretation of *Gillick* is not universally admired,[20] and in subsequent decisions the English courts have been willing to override the decisions of competent

15 As required by s. 3 of the Human Rights Act 1998, and see, eg, HERRING, J., "The Human Rights Act and the welfare principle in family law: conflicting or complementary?" [1999] 11 *Child and Family Law Quarterly* 223; BONNER, D., FENWICK, H., and HARRIS-SHORT, S., "Judicial approaches to the Human Rights Act" (2003) 52(3) *International and Comparative Law Quarterly* 549. CHOUDHRY, S. and FENWICK, H., "Taking the rights of parents and children seriously: confronting the welfare principle under the Human Rights Act" (2005) 25(3) *Oxford Journal of Legal Studies* 453. FORTIN, J., "Accommodating children's rights in a post Human Rights Act era" (2006) 69 *Modern Law Review* 299.

16 HERRING, J., "The Welfare Principle and the Rights of Parents", ch. 5 in BAINHAM, A., DAY SCLATER, S. and RICHARDS, M., (Eds), *What is a Parent? A Socio-Legal Analysis* (Oxford: Hart Publishing, 1999).

17 This is not to say, of course, that their interests will always take precedence.

18 [1986] 1 AC 112.

19 *Ibid*, at p. 186D. See EEKELAAR, J., "The Emergence of Children's Rights" (1986) 6 *Oxford Journal of Legal Studies* 161; EEKELAAR, J., "The Eclipse of Parental Rights" (1986) 102 *Law Quarterly Review* 4.

20 See e.g., GILMORE, S., "The Limits of Parental Responsibility", ch. 4 in PROBERT, R., GILMORE, S., and HERRING, J. (eds), *Responsible Parents and Parental Responsibility* (Oxford: Hart, 2009) (challenging John Eekelaar's interpretation of *Gillick*).

adolescents where the teenager's decision would lead to irreparable harm or death.[21] They have also indicated that medical treatment can lawfully be carried out in the face of a child's refusal to consent, provided a medical practitioner has the consent of a person with parental responsibility.[22]

The more specific "right to be informed, consulted and to express his or her opinion" (Principle 3:6) is also problematic. A distinction must be drawn between the extent to which children are involved in court proceedings and the extent to which they are informed of issues within the private family sphere. The state has been reluctant to impose a requirement on parents to provide their children with certain basic information. One area in which some children may lack basic information is that of their own origins: while a child conceived as a result of donated eggs or sperm after 1 April 2005 has the right to access information about the donor on attaining the age of 18, this is of little use to those who are not informed about the circumstances of their conception.[23] The same applies to children who have been adopted, although the increasing prevalence of later and open adoptions makes it less likely that the circumstances can be concealed in such a case.

The principle that a child should not be discriminated against on any of the grounds set out in Principle 3:5 is now well established within English law. More difficult, however, is the principle that such discrimination should not extend to a child's parents; this is an area where English law does continue to draw certain distinctions, as the next section will demonstrate.

4. THE POSSESSION OF PARENTAL RESPONSIBILITY

There has been much debate as to whether the law should confer parental responsibility on all legal parents automatically,[24] with the possibility of

---

21 See e.g., *Re W (A Minor) (Medical Treatment: Court's Jurisdiction)* [1993] Fam 64, CA. See HERRING, *supra* note 12 at pp. 423–444 for further discussion.

22 *Ibid.*

23 The Human Fertilisation and Embryology Authority (Disclosure of Donor Information) Regulations 2004.

24 See, for example, BAINHAM, A., "When is a parent not a parent? Reflections on the unmarried father and his child in English law" (1989) 3 *International Journal of Law and the Family* 208; *Report on Family Law*, Scottish Law Commission, Law Com No. 135 (1992), at paras 2.36–2.50; BAINHAM, A., "Reforming Scottish children law – sense from north of the border" (1993) 5(1) *Journal of Child Law* 3, at pp. 5–7; CONWAY, H., "Parental responsibility and the unmarried father" (1996) 146 *New Law Journal* 782; LOWE, N. V., "The Meaning and Allocation of Parental Responsibility – A Common Lawyer's Perspective" (1997) 11 *International Journal of Law, Policy and the Family* 192; BARTON, C., "Equal responsibility for all fathers?" (1998) 142(17) *Solicitor's Journal* 401; GILMORE, S., "Parental responsibility and the unmarried father – a new dimension to the debate" [2003] *Child and Family Law Quarterly* 21.

withdrawing it from those deemed unsuitable to possess it, or whether it should restrict eligibility.
The principle that all parents whose legal parentage[25] has been established "should have parental responsibilities for the child" (Principle 3;8) is one towards which this jurisdiction has been gradually moving. Under the Children Act 1989 the legal mother of a child invariably acquires parental responsibility, as does the legal father who is married to the mother.[26] Adoptive parents also acquire parental responsibility automatically upon the making of the adoption order[27] (which may now be made in favour of married couples or civil partners or those in an enduring family relationship); and a similar mechanism exists for conferring the legal status of a parent, and parental responsibility, upon the commissioning parents in surrogacy cases.[28]

However, under the Children Act as it initially passed into law, a father who did not marry the mother could only acquire parental responsibility by formal agreement with the mother[29] or by order of the court.[30] A relatively small number of men obtained parental responsibility by one or other of these means. In 2002, however, the 1989 Act was amended to provide that a father would automatically acquire parental responsibility if he jointly registered the child's birth with the mother on or after 1 December 2003,[31] thereby bringing the law into line with the common misperception that joint registration already had this effect.[32] Since that date, this provision has enabled far more fathers to acquire parental responsibility, and it is now only a small minority of new fathers who will not acquire parental responsibility in this way.[33]

Moreover, current proposals to make joint birth registration the norm have the potential to reduce the proportion of fathers without parental responsibility still further. At present the unilateral registering of both parents' names is not possible if the parents are not married to each other, unless a court order has been

25 "Legal parentage" is more usually referred to as parenthood in this jurisdiction, with parentage being reserved for the genetic link between parent and child: see BAINHAM, A., "Parentage, Parenthood and Parental Responsibility: Subtle, Elusive Yet Important Distinctions" in BAINHAM ET AL, *supra* note 16.

26 Children Act 1989, s. 2(1).

27 Adoption and Children Act 2002, ss. 46–51 and s. 67.

28 Human Fertilisation and Embryology Act 1990, s. 30.

29 Children Act 1989, s. 4(1)(b).

30 Either a parental responsibility order (Children Act 1989 s. 4(1)(c)) or a residence order, the granting of which requires the court in addition to grant him a parental responsibility order, which is not lost if the residence order is subsequently revoked (ss. 8, 10 and 12(1)).

31 Children Act 1989, s. 4(1)(a), as amended by Adoption and Children Act 2002, s. 111.

32 See e.g. PICKFORD, R., *Fathers, Marriage and the Law* (London: Family Policy Studies Centre for the Joseph Rowntree Foundation, 1999); SMART, C. and STEVENS, P., *Cohabitation Breakdown* (London: Family Policy Studies Centre for the Joseph Rowntree Foundation, 2000).

33 Even before this provision was introduced, a challenge brought under the ECHR to the UK"s treatment of such fathers failed to make any progress: *B v. UK* [2000] 1 F.L.R. 1.

obtained confirming paternity.[34] The government is now proposing that mothers will be able to identify the father of their child without him being present, although he will not be recorded until he has been contacted and his paternity either acknowledged or established.[35] Similarly, fathers will be able to declare their paternity and, once established, have it recorded.[36] Joint birth registration will be a legal requirement unless it is "impossible, impracticable or unreasonable."[37] The first two categories are ones that are implicitly acknowledged by the Principles: joint registration is deemed to be impossible where the father is unknown and impracticable where his whereabouts are unknown;[38] in both of these cases legal parentage would not have been established. The gap between the universality of Principle 3:8 and English law is thus narrowed to the circumstances in which it is regarded as unreasonable to require joint registration. Three examples of what would be "unreasonable" are given by the government. Those cases where "it would be unreasonable to expect registrars to take excessive steps to trace a father who has not come forward" could again simply be categorised as a case in which legal parentage has not been established. The second relates to the case of the "young and vulnerable mother" where a social worker or medical practitioner has advised that "it would not be in the mother's or the child's interest to register the father."[39] Given that the Principles envisage that parental responsibility may be discharged where the person's "behaviour or neglect causes a serious risk to the person or property of the child" (Principle 3:32), this exemption could be seen as a means of short-circuiting the process of awarding and then removing parental responsibility where the father poses a danger to the child. The final example of unreasonableness is that of "the rare and extreme cases of men who have received a conviction for rape."[40] In both this and the second exemption, the welfare of the mother assumes a greater importance than it does in the context of the Principles: however, given the concerns that were expressed in the course of consultation, any further move towards universal parental responsibility might well prove difficult.

The Principle that parental responsibilities "may in whole or in part also be attributed to a person other than a parent" (Principle 3:9) can be dealt with more briefly, since it is sufficiently broad to cover current English law on this point. At present parental responsibility may be conferred on non-parents by

---

34 See Births and Deaths Registration Act 1953, s. 10, as amended by Children Act 1989, Sch. 12, para. 6.

35 Department for Work and Pensions, *Joint birth registration: recording responsibility* (June 2008), Cm 7293, para. 28. For discussion, see BAINHAM, A., "What is the point of birth registration?" [2008] *Child and Family Law Quarterly*, 449.

36 At para. 29.

37 At para. 25.

38 It is, however, suggested that re-registration should be encouraged if the father's whereabouts become known.

39 At para. 27(3).

40 *Ibid.*

various different means: in the case of a step-parent,[41] by a parental responsibility agreement or order; in the case of a person with whom the child is to reside, by a residence order[42] (whether sole or shared);[43] in the case of certain defined applicants,[44] by a special guardianship order; and by being appointed as the guardian of the child.[45] It may even vest in an institution such as a local authority by way of a care order[46] or an emergency protection order.[47]

Similarly, Principle 3:10 – that "[p]arental responsibilities should neither be affected by the dissolution or annulment of the marriage or other formal relationship nor by the legal or factual separation between the parents" – is in accordance with English law.[48] Indeed, it was fundamental to the very conception of parental responsibility as set out by the Law Commission that it should be capable of surviving parental separation.[49] In practice, of course, there may be differences of opinion between the now-separated parents as to how parental responsibility should be exercised, which leads on to the question of how the court regulates the exercise of parental responsibility in cases of disagreement.

5. THE EXERCISE OF PARENTAL RESPONSIBILITY

Once the law has made provision for more than one person to possess parental responsibility, it must necessarily provide for the consequences of this. The ideals that parental responsibilities should be exercised jointly and that parents should have "an equal right and duty to exercise such responsibilities" (Principle 3:11) are ones to which English law subscribes, whether the parents are living together or separated. Similarly, the Principle that each parent with parental responsibility should have "the right to act alone with respect to daily matters" finds a parallel in section 2(7) of the Children Act 1989. This, although not confined to "daily matters", has been interpreted as if it were,[50] the courts having held that parental

41 This term includes the civil partner of the child's parent (Children Act 1989, s. 4A as amended by Civil Partnership Act 2004, s. 75(2)), but not, at present, the parent's cohabitant.

42 Children Act 1989, ss. 8 and 12(2).

43 Children Act 1989, s. 11(4). See GILMORE, S., "Court decision-making in shared residence order cases: a critical examination" [2006] 18 *Child and Family Law Quarterly* 478, 491–492.

44 See Children Act 1989, s. 14A(5). This includes a local authority foster parent with whom the child has lived for a period of at least one year immediately preceding the application.

45 Children Act 1989, ss. 5 and 6.

46 Children Act 1989, s. 33(3)(a).

47 Children Act 1989, s. 44(4)(c).

48 Although note that a marriage that both parties know to be void at the time of the child's conception will not confer parental responsibility on the child's father: Legitimacy Act 1976, s. 1(1) and Children Act 1989, s. 2(1).

49 Law Commission, *Family Law: Review of Child Law: Guardianship and Custody*, Law Com No. 171 (1988), para. 2.11.

50 For criticism, see EEKELAAR, J., "Do Parents have a Duty to Consult?" (1998) 114 *Law Quarterly Review* 337; EEKELAAR, J., "Rethinking Parental Responsibility" [2001] *Family Law*

responsibility entails a "right to be consulted on schooling, serious medical problems and other important occurrences in the child's life",[51] issues very similar to those listed in Principle 3:12(2). The Children Act also specifies that certain decisions do require the concurrence of all those possessing parental responsibility,[52] and provides that parental responsibility cannot be exercised unilaterally where this would conflict with an existing court order.[53] In practice it is unlikely that there will be a court order in place unless the parents have separated and disagree about the child's upbringing. A court order on one particular issue will not, however, prevent a parent from making decisions on other issues: as the Law Commission noted, "parents should not be regarded as losing their position, and their ability to take decisions about their children, simply because they are separated or in dispute with one another about a particular matter."[54]

Principle 3:12 provides that in urgent cases a parent should have the right to act alone. Perhaps this should also make clear that the urgency is such that it is impossible (or at least not reasonably practicable) for one parent to consult the other, for one can imagine some situations where a matter may be urgent, yet consultation would be very easy (for example, where a child needs urgent surgery and both parents are in the hospital waiting room just outside the operating theatre). It may be noted that both the Principles and the Children Act 1989 fail to provide an effective enforcement mechanism for breaches of the obligation to consult, especially where the decision is over a matter which is irreversible.

The provision for parents to agree on the exercise of parental responsibilities in Principle 3:13 would be uncontroversial, as long as neither purported to surrender their own parental responsibility by such agreement, which would run counter to section 2(9) of the Children Act. Similarly, the law already provides for the judicial resolution of disputes envisaged by Principle 3:14,[55] and all holders of parental responsibility would have standing to bring such disputes before the court.[56]

While the outright surrender of parental responsibility is prohibited, a person who has parental responsibility "may arrange for some or all of it to be met by one

426; and MAIDMENT, S., "Parental Responsibility – Is there a Duty to Consult?" [2001] *Family Law* 518.

51 *Re H (Parental Responsibility)* [1998] 1 F.L.R. 855, at 859A (Butler-Sloss LJ), and see specifically *Re G (Parental Responsibility: Education)* [1994] 2 F.L.R. 964; *Re PC (Change of Surname)* [1997] 2 F.L.R. 730; *Re J (Specific Issue Orders: Child's Religious Upbringing and Circumcision)* [2000] 1 F.L.R. 571.

52 This is implicit in s. 2(7) and explicit in s. 13(1).

53 Children Act 1989, s. 2(8).

54 Law Commission, *supra* note 49.

55 By way of a specific issue order in s. 8 of the Children Act 1989, on which see GILMORE, S., "The nature, scope, and use of the specific issue order" [2004] *Child and Family Law Quarterly* 367.

56 Children Act 1989, s. 10.

or more persons acting on his behalf",[57] which is consistent with Principles 3:15 and 3:17; a court may also grant parental responsibility on certain conditions or otherwise limit its exercise, as envisaged by Principle 3:15(b).

The day-to-day role of the parent's partner is recognised by Principle 3:18; such explicit recognition is lacking in the Children Act, although it has been proposed that a parent's cohabitant should be able to acquire parental responsibility in the same way that a parent's spouse or civil partner can under the current law.[58] However, section 3(5) of the Children Act 1989 does recognise the realities of day-to-day life, providing more broadly that a person who has care of the child but does not have parental responsibility may "do what is reasonable in all the circumstances of the case for the purpose of safeguarding or promoting the child's welfare." And in practice, the adults living with the child will be able to be involved in making decisions about the child unless there is a specific challenge to that decision by a non-resident parent.

6. THE CONTENT OF PARENTAL RESPONSIBILITY

The actual content of parental responsibility is a topic that has until recently[59] received relatively little academic attention in this jurisdiction. Much of the content has to be inferred from the sanctions for non-performance. Thus, for example, there is no positive statutory provision that parents must care for their children, but a lack of care may lead to the child being removed from the parents and even to prosecution for neglect. Education, by contrast, is one area in which there is a positive statutory provision, with parents being advised of their duty to cause their children to receive efficient full-time education suitable to their age, ability and aptitude, and any special educational needs. There is thus no inherent obstacle to incorporating the statement of positive duties as set out in Principle 3:19(1).

More difficult is the statement that "the child should not be subjected to corporal punishment or any other humiliating treatment". While this view is one to which many in this jurisdiction would subscribe, English law continues to allow parents and those *in loco parentis* to administer "reasonable punishment" provided that this does not amount to a battery causing actual bodily harm or a more serious offence.[60] Even this modification of the earlier defence of "reasonable chastisement" – which was a defence to a wider range of offences – only occurred as late as

57 Children Act 1989, s. 2(9).

58 Resolution, *Reforming the law for people who live together: A consultation paper* (September 2008), p. 20.

59 For a recent attempt to redress this see PROBERT ET AL, *supra* note 20.

60 Children Act 2004, s. 58.

2004, and was the result of an amendment promoted by private members rather than the government. The promised review of the operation of this modified defence[61] dismissed the responses stating that legal protection for children had not improved, and concluded that the UK had met its international obligations.[62] The likelihood of the government adopting Principle 3:19(2) is therefore remote.

Similarly, while the factors set out in Principle 3:20(2) are those that the courts already look at when deciding whether or not to make a shared residence order,[63] there is at present no requirement that court authorisation be sought for such an arrangement, and such a requirement would run counter to the core principle of the Children Act 1989 that an order of the court should not be made unless doing so would be better for the child than making no order at all.[64]

So far as relocation is concerned, assuming that the factors listed in Principle 3:21(3) are in no order of priority, there would be no difficulty in incorporating them into domestic law, since they largely reflect the current approach of the courts. At present there is no positive duty on the parent wishing to relocate to inform the other parent of this – unless there is a residence order in force, in which case the written consent of every person with parental responsibility, or the consent of the court, is required[65] – but the other parent would in any case be able to apply for an order with the aim of preventing such relocation. Such disputes between parents are to be resolved by the courts in accordance with the best interests of the child, but it is noticeable in the case-law that the welfare of the child is perceived to be closely linked to the wishes of the primary carer who wishes to relocate.[66] If English law were to rank the factors listed in Principle 3:21(3) in order of relevance to the outcome of such disputes, arguably "the free movement of persons" would rise from last to first place in the list.

The task of administering the child's property does not necessarily fall to a person with parental responsibility: land or other property may be held for the benefit of the child under a trust, in which case it is the trustee who is responsible for its administration.[67] All persons who administer property on behalf of another

61 Department for Children, Schools and Families, *Review of Section 58 of the Children Act 2004* (2007), Cm 7232, available at http://www.dfes.gov.uk/publications/section58review/.

62 See CHOUDHRY, S., "Parental responsibility and corporal punishment" in PROBERT ET AL, *supra* note 20.

63 For a detailed account of the case law, see GILMORE, S., "Court decision-making in shared residence order cases: a critical examination" [2006] 18 *Child and Family Law Quarterly* 478.

64 Children Act 1989, s. 1(5).

65 Children Act 1989, s. 13(1)(b).

66 HAYES, M., "Relocation cases: is the Court of Appeal applying the correct principles?" [2006] 18 *Child and Family Law Quarterly* 351; and see also HERRING, J. and TAYLOR, R., "Relocating Relocation" [2006] 18 *Child and Family Law Quarterly* 517.

67 See COOKE, E., "'Don't spend it all at once!' Parental responsibility, and parents" responsibilities, in respect of children's contracts and property" in PROBERT ET AL, *supra* note 20.

– whether parents or unrelated persons – owe fiduciary duties to that person, and these duties do not vary according to his or her age. Moreover, children who own property outright can deal with it as they wish: there is no requirement that someone with parental responsibility should oversee their expenditure.

Legal representation is another area in which the supposed responsibilities of a parent become more difficult to discern on closer inspection. Representing a child in legal proceedings is listed as an aspect of parental responsibility in all standard legal texts, but, as Sawyer has pointed out, while parents may do so, they "have no *responsibility* to act as their child's representatives; nor, indeed is it always clear how the responsible parent exercises the right to do so."[68] The rules of court in civil proceedings do not give precedence to the parent, simply permitting any adult without a conflict of interest to take on the role of "litigation friend";[69] in family proceedings, by contrast, the interests of the child are often identified with the interests of a particular parent, thereby obviating the need for separate representation.

The provisions that contact should be in the best interests of the child (Principle 3:26(2)) and may be "restricted, terminated or made subject to conditions by the competent authority if the best interests of the child so require" (Principle 3:28) are in accordance with the current approach of English law. As noted above, in deciding such matters a court in England and Wales must apply the child's welfare as its paramount consideration under section 1(1) of the Children Act 1989. In the light of section 1(1), however, English judges have found jurisprudential difficulty with the language of rights in this context,[70] and therefore the characterisation of contact as a right in Principle 3:25 may present some difficulty for English law. Even where a court order has been made, the definition of a contact order in English law means that the correlative obligation attaching to any court order of contact[71] is upon the child's resident parent to allow contact; it is "not directed at the child to submit to, still less to be forced into, visits or staying with the absent parent".[72] The law places no enforceable duty upon a non-resident parent who does not wish to maintain contact[73] and any enforceable duty against the

68 SAWYER, C., "Children's representation by their parents in legal proceedings", in PROBERT ET AL, *supra* note 20, p. 216.

69 See further SAWYER, *supra* note 68, at p. 217.

70 See the discussion by Thorpe LJ in *Re L (A Child) (Contact: Domestic Violence); In Re V (A Child); In Re M (A Child); In Re H (Children)* [2001] Fam 260, at pp. 290–295.

71 S. 8 defines a "contact order" as "an order requiring the person with whom a child lives, or is to live, to allow the child to visit or stay with the person named in the order, or for that person and the child otherwise to have contact with each other".

72 *Re M (Minors) (unreported)* 26 January 2000.

73 See *Re L (A Child) (Contact: Domestic Violence); In Re V (A Child); In Re M (A Child); In Re H (Children)* [2001] Fam 260, at 294: "The errant or selfish parent cannot be ordered to spend time with his child against his will however much the child may yearn for his company and the mother desire respite. The court's power is restricted to those cases in which the absent parent

resident parent arises only upon the making of a contact order. Decisions from the European Court of Human Rights to the effect that the refusal of contact may infringe a parent's article 8 rights suggest that contact is not entirely a rights-free zone,[74] but whether the protection afforded by article 8 is properly regarded as a "right of *contact*" is a matter of some debate.[75] On one view, article 8 protects a right to *respect for family life*, *one* fundamental *element* of which is the mutual enjoyment by parent and child of each other's company. To say that there is a right of contact may be characterising the protection too strongly, since in a particular case there may be another aspect of family life, such as peaceful enjoyment free from domestic violence, which may also command respect.

Given the current emphasis on agreement rather than adjudication, the suggestion that parents and other persons may agree on contact without the need for court approval is also in line with English law. Whether it offers sufficient protection to the children in question is another matter: it is worth recalling that a number of children have died or been seriously injured in the course of contact arrangements pursuant to a consent order that had received the imprimatur of the courts.[76]

The amount and quality of contact between a parent and child may provide evidence of a parent's commitment, and of attachment between the parent and child, both of which are material factors when an English court considers whether to confer parental responsibility. However, contact and parental responsibility are viewed by the English courts as separate issues, requiring independent consideration. An example is provided by *Re D (Lesbian Mothers and Known Father: Contact and Parental Responsibility)*.[77] In that case a man donated sperm so that a lesbian couple could produce and raise a child together. The couple's view was that the donor would be acknowledged as the child's father but would play only a minimal role in the upbringing, with contact perhaps once every three weeks. Following the birth of the child, however, it became apparent that the father envisaged a greater role in the child's life, and the couple became concerned when he sought to "interfere" in matters concerning the child's medical treatment and education. On the father's application for parental responsibility and contact,

seeks and the parent with care opposes either the principle or the detail of contact. Furthermore it must be recognised that contact is no more than a mechanism for the maintenance and development of relationships and the court's powers are restricted to regulating the mechanism and do not extend to the underlying relationships."

74 See e.g., BAINHAM, A., "Contact as a Right and Obligation" in BAINHAM, A., LINDLEY, B., RICHARDS, M. and TRINDER, L., (eds), *Children and Their Families – Contact, Rights and Welfare* (Oxford: Hart, 2003).

75 GILMORE, S., "Disputing contact: challenging some assumptions" [2008] 20 *Child and Family Law Quarterly* 285, especially at pp. 299–300.

76 SAUNDERS, H., *Twenty-nine Child Homicides: Lessons still to be learnt on domestic violence and child protection* (Bristol: Women's Aid, 2004).

77 [2006] EWHC 2 (Fam), Black J. See also *Re B (Role of Biological Father)* [2008] 1 FLR 1015, FD (Hedley J).

parental responsibility was granted on condition that he did not seek to exercise it in matters of the child's health and education. He was also granted limited contact, for fear that that would undermine the couple's care of the child.

Beyond the immediate nuclear family, the law has done little to intervene in issues of contact. A number of groups – in particular those representing grandparents – would no doubt welcome the suggestion that contact "should be established between the child and his or her close relatives" (Principle 3:25(2)). At present English law does nothing to prevent such contact, but equally it does very little to facilitate it. The relatives of a child have no special status when seeking a contact order from the court: unless they fall into certain categories by virtue of having cared for the child, they must seek the leave of the court even to apply for such an order.[78]

The suggestion that a parent has "the right to be informed about matters concerning the personal situation of the child" (Principle 3:29) may be more controversial. If it is intended to convey that each parent is entitled to the same information about the child, then its incorporation would pose no problem; there have, of course, been cases in which a court has decided that a particular parent should not receive information about the child, but these explicit exceptions confirm the general rule. However, if it means that a parent has the right to require any and all information about a child from a third party, then problems do arise because it fails to pay adequate regard to children's rights to confidentiality. One of the most significant cases in English child law arose out of a mother's demand that her daughters should not be provided with contraceptive advice without her knowledge and approval; it was resolved by the House of Lords that the decision whether to provide such advice lay with the child's doctor, rather than the parent, and that although consultation would be encouraged, medical confidentiality could not be breached.[79]

---

78 FERGUSON, N. et al, *Grandparenting in Divorced Families* (Bristol: Policy Press, 2004).

79 *Gillick v W. Norfolk and Wisbech AHA* [1986] AC 112. *Gillick* was applied and developed in: *R (Axon) v Secretary of State for Health (Family Planning Association intervening)* [2006] EWHC 37 (Admin), in which Silber J declined to accept a mother's argument that her right to respect for family life in Article 8 of the European Convention on Human Rights (in Schedule 1 to the Human Rights Act 1998) required that she be informed should her daughter seek abortion advice or treatment. His Lordship held that once a child was of sufficient understanding to consent to such treatment, the parent's Article 8 right was extinguished. On the issue of confidentiality, see, LOUGHREY, J., "Can you keep a secret? Children, human rights, and the law of medical confidentiality" [2008] 20 *Child and Family Law Quarterly* 312.

7. ENDING PARENTAL RESPONSIBILITIES

In English law, as in Principle 3:30, parental responsibility comes to an end where the child reaches the age of 18, marries or enters into a civil partnership, or dies; upon adoption, it is transferred to the adoptive parents, although a recent reform allows a parent's partner to adopt the child without terminating the parental status and responsibility of that parent (although it would have the effect of terminating the parental responsibility of the other parent).[80]

However, parents with parental responsibility may extend their care for their child after their own deaths by appointing the person whom they wish to act as a guardian for their child.[81] *When* such appointment actually takes effect will depend in any given case on whether there is another surviving parent with parental responsibility and whether there was a residence order in favour of the deceased parent,[82] but *whether* such appointment takes effect does not depend upon the approval of the court. The court does, however, have the power to revoke such appointment,[83] or to appoint another person as the child's guardian,[84] and the relevant local authority will be under a duty to take steps to protect a child for whom no person has parental responsibility.[85]

Whether parental responsibility may be discharged during the parent's lifetime, as envisaged by Principle 3:32, is a more controversial matter. It is clear that the local authority may take steps to protect a child who is at risk of harm, and that a court may make a care order if the child is suffering, or likely to suffer, significant harm as a result of the parents' actions.[86] But while the making of a care order confers parental responsibility on the local authority,[87] it does not extinguish the parental responsibility of the parents. This reflects the "partnership" principle that was core to the Children Act 1989, the idea being that the parents and the local authority would work in partnership to foster the best interests of the child. It has always, it should be acknowledged, been an unequal partnership, both legally – the local authority has the right to determine how the parents may meet their parental responsibility for the child in case[88] – and practically. But it would be a significant step to hold that the parent in question was deprived of parental responsibility altogether, especially since the aim in most cases is rehabilitation

80 Adoption and Children Act 2002, ss 51(2) and 67(2).
81 Children Act 1989. s. 5(3).
82 Children Act 1989. s. 5(7) and (8).
83 Children Act 1989, s. 6(7).
84 Although only if an application is made to the court, or if there are family proceedings before the court: Children Act 1989, s. 5(1) and (2).
85 Children Act 1989. s. 20(1)(a).
86 Children Act 1989. s. 31(2).
87 Children Act 1989. s. 33(3)(a).
88 Children Act 1989. s. 33(3)(b).

rather than the permanent removal of the child.[89] Under the Children Act 1989, local authorities cannot (inter alia) change the child's religion or consent to adoption or change the child's name, without the consent of the parents.[90] These rights that a parent of a child in care currently has would be lost if the Principles were adopted in English law.

Indeed, it is only in very rare cases that parental responsibility will be removed from a parent. There is no means – short of adoption – whereby parental responsibility can be removed from those on whom it is automatically conferred. Parental responsibility may, however, be removed from a father who was not married to the mother,[91] or from a step-parent,[92] and there have been cases in which the courts have made an order to this effect.[93]

8. PROCEDURE

Decisions on parental responsibility are the role of the court (see Principle 3:35); this court may be the family proceedings court, the county court or the High Court. Should the court take the view that it needs further information about the circumstances of the child, as envisaged by Principle 3:35(2), it may request a report from the Children and Family Court Advisory and Support Service.[94]

The emphasis on alternative dispute resolution in Principle 3:36 is very much in line with the current approach of English law. The provision of such alternatives is key to the Private Law Programme, implemented in 2004, although the extent to which mechanisms such as in-court conciliation are successful in providing a long-term solution to more difficult cases has been questioned.

Practical problems also arise in the context of Principle 3:37. There is certainly growing agreement that children should be heard in proceedings that affect them.[95] But how this is achieved, and the extent to which it is appropriate to involve children in family proceedings, remains a matter of debate. While the "ascertainable wishes and feelings of the child" assume first place in the welfare

89 *Johansen v Norway* (1986) 23 EHRR 33.

90 See HERRING, *supra* note *12* at 610–11 for a fuller discussion.

91 Children Act 1989. s. 4(2A).

92 Children Act 1989. s. 4A(3).

93 See e.g. *Re P (Terminating Parental Responsibility)* [1995] 1 F.L.R. 1048.

94 Children Act 1989, s. 7(1).

95 See e.g. Family Justice Council, *Enhancing the Participation of Children and Young People in Family Proceedings* (2008), para. 1, available at http://www.family-justice-council.org.uk/docs/Participation_of_young_people.pdf.

"checklist" that must be taken into account in contested applications for certain orders,[96] such wishes and feelings may be ascertained by indirect means.

Children are not automatically heard in family proceedings: they do not necessarily have someone who is appointed for the specific purpose of representing their interests. There is specific provision for children to be made parties to the proceedings, and to have separate representation by a guardian ad litem;[97] in addition, competent children may, with the leave of the court, have party status and participate without such a guardian.[98] There is an as yet unresolved debate as to the circumstances in which separate representation should be provided, but even the narrow formulation proposed by the government – that it should be restricted to cases in which there is a "legal need"[99] – could potentially cover the circumstances set out in Principle 3:38, and the response to this proposal suggests that a wider formulation might be appropriate.[100]

Moreover, even those children who are party to the proceedings in their own right may be excluded from the court. The Family Justice Council has, however, called for judges to ensure that children who are party to the proceedings are able to attend court.[101]

Finally, the enforcement of orders relating to parental responsibility – in particular orders requiring one parent to make the child available for contact with the other – has attracted much attention in recent years, and new measures have been introduced to achieve this.

9. CONCLUSION

In conclusion, there are many areas in which the law of this jurisdiction could benefit from the incorporation of the Principles: in providing a more accurate description of the concept of parental responsibility; in making explicit those responsibilities of parents that are currently only implicit and in sending a message as to what is expected of a responsible parent; and in encouraging a more child-focused approach. There are, however, points on which English law

96 Children Act 1989, s. 1(3)(a) and (4).
97 Family Proceedings Rules, r. 9.5.
98 Family Proceedings Rules, r. 9(2A).
99 Department for Constitutional Affairs, *Separate Representation of Children* (2006), CP/20/06, p. 21.
100 It was acknowledged by the Department for Constitutional Affairs in *Separate Representation of Children: Summary of Responses to a Consultation Paper* (2007), CP(R) 20/06, at p. 7, that "[m]any respondents did not agree that the definition of "legal need" was sufficient" and that others sought clarification of the boundary between "legal" and "welfare" needs.
101 Family Justice Council, *supra* note 95, para. 20.

might prove resistant, either because the Principles as formulated run counter to the key principles underpinning the Children Act or where change might prove politically difficult. But, taken as a whole, they have the potential to provide a more principled approach to parental responsibility.

PART THREE
AN ASPIRANT CANDIDATE: DO VALUES CLASH?

HOW DOES TURKISH FAMILY LAW FARE COMPARED TO THE PRINCIPLES OF EUROPEAN FAMILY LAW REGARDING PARENTAL RESPONSIBILITIES?

Esin Örücü and Canan Arin

1. INTRODUCTORY OVERVIEW

Since Turkish Family Law was not one of those considered when the "Principles of European Family Law Regarding Parental Responsibilities" were being drawn up,[1] and there was therefore no Turkish report accompanying the research prior to producing the Principles, it is helpful to give a general picture of Family Law in Turkey as far as is relevant to our inquiry,[2] as was done in an earlier publication juxtaposing Turkish Family Law and the "Principles of European Family Law regarding Divorce and Maintenance between Former Spouses".[3] Thus this first section deals with a brief overview. Section two sets the general scene in Turkey. Section three considers Turkish law juxtaposed to each Principle, first presenting the situation in Turkish law and then assessing this in the light of the relevant Principle. To achieve these ends both the Questionnaire containing 62 questions drafted by the Organising Committee of the Commission on European Family Law and the ensuing Principles have been considered.

The "family unit" has always been regarded as the essence of Turkish society, both during the Ottoman Empire and the Republic of Turkey. Within this family, which traditionally was the extended family, children are considered to be the

---

1 BOELE-WOELKI, K., FERRAND, F., BEILFUSS, C. G., JANTERE-JAREBORG, M., LOWE, N., MARTINY, D. and PINTENS, W., (eds) *Principles of European Family Law Regarding Parental Responsibilities*, European Family Law Series, No. 16 (Antwerp: Intersentia, 2007).

2 Some areas such as contesting and establishing parentage, adoption, child abduction, the name of the child and child maintenance, all being covered by international conventions, will not be covered here since the Principles have not dealt with these.

3 See ÖRÜCÜ, E, "Turkish Family Law Facing the Principles of European Family Law" in ÖRÜCÜ, E. and MAIR, J., (eds) *Juxtaposing Legal Systems and the Principles of European Family Law on Divorce and Maintenance*, European Family Law Series, No. 17 (Antwerp: Intersentia, 2007), pp. 183–209.

most important elements. In fact the reason for getting married can be said to be to reproduce.[4] However, the general attitude towards children is that they are needed to look after the family business, the agricultural land and, to care for parents in their old age. This has been the case in the Ottoman Empire and still is the case today. In fact there are age-old sayings indicating the absolute relationship between child and parent. For instance, when a child is first taken to school, the parents used to say to the teacher: "His flesh is yours, his bones are mine".[5] In relation to moulding and shaping a child, it is often said: "One who can't beat his daughter, will one day beat his own knee (in desperation)".[6] In addition, according to tradition, a child should be seen but not heard. Though things may have changed to a certain extent in urban cities, the old values live on in the rural areas and in families with rural roots, who have now migrated to major cities and foreign countries in Europe.

In rural communities, families have a large number of children in an attempt to combat the adverse effects of early child deaths by producing a pool of offspring. Again traditionally, the most important link between the parents and the child is the blood link and there was a distinction between legitimate and illegitimate children in law until 1988, depending on the criterion of whether the parents were married to each other or not at the time of conception: the blood-line for men being of utmost importance. Adoption was prohibited to those who had children of their own until 2002.

Until the signing and ratification in 1995 of the Convention on the Rights of the Child 1989, in 2002 of the European Conventions on the Exercise of Children's Rights 1996, and the changes to the 1926 Civil Code in 2002 and to the 1982 Constitution, the law may have to some extent reflected this tradition. However since these events there is little lacking, at least in law, and Turkish Family Law would not clash with the Principles in any major way, as will be seen below.

Today, families, mothers and children are protected first in the framework of the 1982 Constitution and the relationships in the family are regulated in the Turkish Civil Code (TCC) of 2002.[7]

---

4 That is why, for instance, men try to divorce their wives if they are barren. This they cannot do, since this is not a ground for divorce. The General Assembly of Civil Law of the Court of Cassation (*Yargıtay*) states that infertility of women by itself cannot be a ground for divorce. See HGK; 1992/626; 1992/648; 11/11/1992.

5 "Eti senin, kemiği benim".

6 "Kızını dövemeyen, dizini döver".

7 The Turkish Civil Code of 1926 was a reception of the Swiss Civil Code and the new Civil Code of 2002, which is an amended version of the 1926 Code, follows closely the Swiss amendments over the years.

2. SETTING THE TURKISH SCENE TODAY

Under Chapter Three of the present 1982 Constitution on "Social and Economic Rights and Duties", Article 41, entitled "Protection of the Family", first states that "the family is the foundation of Turkish society and is based on the equality of the spouses", and then says that the State shall take the necessary measures and establish the relevant organisation to ensure the peace and welfare of the family, especially where the protection of the mother and children is involved. The next article on the right and duty of training and education, to be seen below, is also related to the bringing up of the young, though not related directly to the parents.

Family Law forms the second book of the TCC. The first part of this book is on the law of marriage. The second part is on kinship, and it is here that we see most of the sections related to custody (parental responsibility) and the rights of the child. There are extensive sections in the TCC covering the law of persons, family law, law of succession, and the relationship between the child and the parents or the guardian, under the concepts of *velayet* "custody" and *vesayet* "guardianship". The rights of the child and parental responsibilities are dispersed throughout these chapters.

Personality starts at the moment of birth when a child is completely separated from the mother's body and is then alive (section 28). The child becomes the subject of rights after it is conceived, if it is subsequently born alive (section 28/2), and in the law of inheritance, a child conceived but not yet born, may be a legal heir, if it is born alive.

Kinship between a mother and a child is established through birth; between the child and the father through filiation, that is, the presumption that a child born to a married woman is that of her husband's, or acknowledgement or by a court decision on paternity. This relationship can also come into existence through adoption (section 282).

As part of the law of persons, between sections 11 and 16 TCC, we see that majority (*rüşt*) is at 18 years of age, that minors having reached the age of 15 could be deemed by a court to be a major upon their own request and the consent of their parents (*veli*) or guardian (*vasi*), that marriage (the legal age for which is 17 for both sexes) confers majority, that minors are considered as a rule not to have the capacity to make fair judgments (*temyiz kudreti*) and act reasonably,[8] that

8 At what age can a child "discern" the consequences of his/her actions is not determined in law. Since at what age a child starts to act reasonably is a question of fact, this will be determined in each case by the judge. In addition, a child may be able to make fair judgments with regard to certain matters in which he/she may have had some experience.

minors do not have full capacity to act, that minors who do not have the capacity to make fair judgments cannot undertake obligations without the consent of their statutory representatives, and that minors who have the capacity to make fair judgments, that is, those who are mature, have limited capacity (*mahdut ehliyet*), and are liable for their delictual acts.

There are then disparate sections of the Code related to the rights of the child. For instance, section 166 dealing with divorce by mutual consent and divorce for irretrievable breakdown, states that in order to grant divorce, the judge has to be satisfied with the arrangements made regarding financial matters and the children. He can modify the arrangements in the interests of the spouses and the children. While considering the rights of the parents from the point of view of children, section 182 states that when the court decides on divorce or separation, where possible, it listens to the parents, to the guardian if the child is under guardianship, and then determines the rights of the parents and their relationship with the child. Custody is given to one of the parents. In regulating the personal relations between the parent who is not given custody and the child, the health, education and moral well-being of the child is given special consideration. This parent must contribute to the expenses of raising the child according to his/her financial means. The court has continuing jurisdiction to enter new orders for the welfare of the child, based on changed circumstances (sections 182, 183).

3. TURKISH FAMILY LAW JUXTAPOSED TO THE PRINCIPLES OF EUROPEAN FAMILY LAW

3.1. DEFINITIONS

Principle 3:1 Concept of parental responsibility

The provisions of custody are codified in the Turkish Civil Code (TCC) of 2002 and previously of 1926. In the 2002 Civil Code, the general aspects of custody are covered between sections 335 –351.

Principle 3:1 defines the concept of parental responsibilities as "a collection of rights and duties aimed at promoting and safeguarding the welfare of the child" with five heads to consider: care, protection, education; maintenance of personal relationships; determination of residence; administration of property; and legal representation. These heads become subjects of later Principles.

The concept used in Turkish Family Law to cover parental responsibilities is *velayet*, that is, custody. In fact, *velayet* is seen more as a power given to the parents by law, that is, parental authority encompassing all parental duties, rights and competences over the person and property of the child (section 335). Today, as a rule, children who have not attained majority (below the age of 18) are under *velayet*, that is, the custody of their parents, custody being jointly used by them during the existence of marriage and bestowed upon only one upon the break up of marriage. Custody cannot be taken away from the parents unless there are just causes. Children who are majors, but are impaired, are also under *velayet*, unless the judge decides to appoint a *vasi* (guardian) for them (section 335). For children in full-time education, *velayet* is extended. In certain circumstances to support the child is a lifelong duty as a matter of principle, and so is the duty of a child to support his or her parents.

Married persons living together share *velayet* equally and have a duty to exercise joint custody over minor children and maintain them. Maintenance is understood to mean giving children sufficient physical and moral care, choosing how they should be educated and preparing them for life. Financial duties of the parents continue even if *velayet* is taken away from them. The rights and powers derived from and attached to *velayet* can be viewed as powers and duties over the person of the child, and powers and duties over the property of the child.

The content of *velayet* corresponds with the definition of parental responsibilities established by the Council of Europe White Paper Principle 18. As will be seen below, the term *velayet* in Turkish law covers care and protection, personal relationships, education, legal representation, residence and administration of property.

Though the interests of the child is paramount, it can be assumed that the rights of the child are subservient to those of the parents since the child is under an obligation to obey the decisions of the parents (section 339/2). Commensurate with the maturity of the child, the parents must allow the child to regulate his/her own life, and take into consideration his/her views when making important decisions about the child, as far as possible (section 339/3). The child cannot leave the home permanently without the consent of the parents and cannot be taken away from them without a just cause (section 339/4). The parents give the child's name (section 339/5). If parents are married, the child carries the family surname, that is, the father's, and if they are not, the surname of the mother (section 321).[9]

Turkish law does not tally fully with the CEFL Principle 3:1, which uses the concept of "parental responsibilities" rather than "parental power" or "parental

9 When a father, who had custody, sued to change the surname of the child, the *Yargıtay* said that the surname is a personality right that cannot be changed by another; that even upon divorce, the child carries the father's surname. So unless the father changes his own surname by a court decision, or the child, reaching majority, decides to take another surname by a court decision, the child's surname cannot be changed. The right to *velayet* does not bestow such a right upon the father. 2007/1509; 2007/3520; 17/04/2007, (2007) 33 *Yargıtay Kararları Dergisi*, 2265–2266.

authority". Though Turkish law does not define *velayet* any further, the trend of Turkish law seems to be best represented in a power relationship.[10] However, as stated earlier, the content of this power is to be used for the care, protection and education of the child in keeping with the Principle, and the power does encompass care and protection, personal relationships, education, determination of residence, administration of property and legal representation. As already stated, this is also in keeping with the definition provided by Principle 18 of the White Paper of the Council of Europe. The parents take and implement necessary decisions related to the care and education of the child, keeping the interests and welfare of the child in mind (section 339/1).

Section 340 TCC deals with the duty of the parents for the education of the child according to their means. They must secure and protect the physical, mental, spiritual, moral and societal development of the child. Parents must provide adequate general and vocational education and training in keeping with the child's ability and inclination: this is especially so for children who are physically or mentally impaired (section 340/2). Section 341 deals with religious upbringing and education, the determination of which is the right of the parents. All agreements limiting this right are void. A major is free to choose his/her own religion (section 341/3). Parents are also legal representatives of children in their custody (section 342), and third parties in good faith may assume that one parent is acting with the consent of the other (section 342/2).

Additionally, in the section on the general principles of marriage, among the rights and obligations of the spouses, section 185 cites the obligation of the spouses to contribute to the happiness of the marriage union together and to secure the care, education and protection of their children. It is noteworthy that section 322 dealing with reciprocal duties of the members of the family, states that, "the mother, father and the child have the duty to help each other, show respect and understanding to each other and protect the honour of the family as necessitated to maintain the peace and unity of the family". This section gives voice to the culture and traditions of Turkish society.[11]

---

10 The *Yargıtay* defines *velayet* as encompassing the maintenance, education, training, protection and representation of the child. There can be no interference with the duty of *velayet* of the parents unless conditions exist for the removal or change of the *velayet* holder. In the instant case, the father had the *velayet*. The *Yargıtay* said that the fact that he was not actually exercising this right and duty, did not justify the decision of the lower local court that the children could continue their education placed with their maternal grandmother. See 2007/16702; 2007/17570; 17/12/2007, (2008)34 *Yargıtay Kararları Dergisi*, 627–628.

11 It may be interesting to note that according to the *Yargıtay*, since everyone is under the duty to support his/her ascendants, descendants and siblings who otherwise would be destitute (sec. 364) and since fault plays no role here, though it is a fact that when family ties are broken, the duty to pay alimony comes to an end, in the instant case, the son who is affluent must pay for the minimum living expenses (sec. 395) of his 70 years old father whose fault indeed led to the breaking of family ties, but who is now destitute (sec.366). The Court said that: "Alimony for

The child under *velayet* has limited capacity. The child is responsible for his/her own obligations with his/her own patrimony (section 343). If the child under *velayet* can discern, he/she can act for the family with the parents' consent and the parents enter an obligation as a result of such action (section 344). For a child to enter into obligations towards his/her parents, a *kayyım* (curator), appointed by the judge, must participate in the transaction and the judge must approve of it, since there might be a conflict of interests here (section 345).

Thus it can be said that Turkish law can live with this Principle, although it might mean a further change in the mind-set and a need to go beyond the changes introduced in 2002. The concept of "parental responsibilities" does not entirely agree with the concept of *velayet*, which weighs the scale towards the parents rather than the child, and therefore, "duties and powers" still seem to represent the predominant approach. Turkish legal terminology rests on a different view, but part of the common core as to content is the same. The nuances reflect the predominant traditional culture even today.

Principle 3:2 Holder of parental responsibilities

According to Principle 3:2, a holder of parental responsibilities is any person having the rights and duties listed in the previous Principle. Such persons could be the parents as well as others, in addition to or instead of the parents.

The fundamental rule in Turkish Family Law is that, while married, the spouses use parental rights together, thus parents together are the primary holders of parental responsibilities (section 336).[12]

When life in common comes to an end, the judge can give custody to one of the parents (section 336/2). The 1926 TCC did not consider the position of the child where the parents were living separately while married. This was a gap which was filled by the *Yargıtay* (the Court of Cassation) to the effect that the judge will ex officio fill the gap by letting the child stay with one of the parents and regulate the

help (*yardım nafakası*) is a social duty necessitated by moral maxims and tradition, which the law maker has not left to the conscience of individuals or society but regulated as a legal duty, the limits of which are to be found in section 365 TCC". 2007/19271; 2008/860; 22/01/2008, (2008) 34 *Yargıtay Kararları Dergisi*, pp. 1076–1079.

12 When during married life one parent, without the knowledge of the other, filed a law suit to correct the entry of a child in the Registry of Birth, Death and Marriage, and the lower court did not ask for the consent of that other, the *Yargıtay* opined that during marriage, sec. 336 TCC does not give priority to one of the parents over the other, that sec. 342 gives parents equal status in representing the child and therefore to be valid, either both parents must file the law suit, or if one does, the other must acquiesce in writing or by being present in the court during the trial. 2007/8860; 2007/9468; 08/11/2007.

personal relationship with the other.[13] The new section 336/2 TCC considers cases of legal separation, so the *Yargıtay* position still pertains.

Upon the death of one of the parents, custody will be normally conferred upon the surviving parent.[14] Upon divorce, custody will be held by the parent given the child (section 336/3).[15]

For children with limited capacity, the judge can, if he deems necessary, appoint a *vasi* (guardian), who then holds responsibilities similar to parental responsibilities by analogy (section 335/2).

If the parents are not married, the mother has custody of the child (section 337). However, if the mother is a minor, impaired, dead, or if custody is taken away from her for just cause, then the judge either appoints a *vasi* or gives the custody to the father, in accordance with the interests of the child (section 337/2).

As for step-children, the spouse who is not the parent must show care for, and interest in, such children and support the parent spouse, and in keeping with the circumstances, if necessary, represent him/her for the needs of the child (section 338). However, he or she does not become the holder of parental responsibilities.

There is no other reference to the holders of parental responsibilities in the TCC as to parent's partner, the child's grandparents, foster parents, or other persons with family ties, though they can request the establishment of "personal relationship" in exceptional circumstances and if in keeping with the interests of the child (section 323). However, if the child is placed with one of these and the parents are dead, then they would acquire rights and duties as a *vasi*, which by analogy would be similar to the rights and duties bestowed upon the parents.

---

13 First decided in 1967 and thereafter referred to by later decisions such as 1657/1869; 03/03/1980, (1980) 8 *Yargıtay Kararları Dergisi*, p. 1075.

14 However, this is not an automatic transfer. The decisions of the *Yargıtay* on this point are not consistent. See 1981/6261; 1081/279; 20/01/1981, (1981 *Yargıtay Kararları Dergisi*, pp 471–473 supporting automatic transfer, and 1979/1090; 1979/1348; 20/02/1979, (1979) *Ankara Baro Dergisi*, p. 78, supporting the view that a court decision, viewing the "changed circumstances" is necessary.

15 Although as a rule, the court practice is that a minor child is given to the mother, since the essence of *velayet* is the interests of the child, the court weighs the circumstances before making such a decision. For instance, in a case in 1978, the *Yargıtay* opined that, though there might be good reasons to give a minor child to the mother, in the instant case, she was in financial difficulties and was looked after by her sister, while the father was very well off; thus the *velayet* should be given to him. 1978/2–179; 1978/677; 16/06/1978, (1978) 9 *Yargıtay Kararları Dergisi*, p. 1438. However, this is an exceptional decision. As many decisions of the Second Division of the *Yargıtay* show, "Unless there is any persuasive evidence showing that it is harmful for the child's body, morality or mental development to stay with the mother, it is wrong to give the custody to the father". See Y2HD: 1997/13071; 1997/14311; 26/12/1997.

Thus Turkish law is much more restrictive than the Principles as to holders of parental responsibilities.

3.2. RIGHTS OF THE CHILD

Principle 3:3 Best interests of the child

The "interests of the child" is at the heart of parental responsibilities also in Turkish Family Law. This is always the primary consideration. It is sometimes referred to as "for the well-being of the child", sometimes, "in the interests of the child", sometimes "for the welfare of the child". However there is no specific provision or such strong wording in the TCC similar to Principle 3:3. While amending the TCC in 2002, it might have been regarded more appropriate to leave "the best interests of the child" rather vague, to be concretised by judges using discretion.

Principle 3:4 Autonomy of the child

In Principle 3:4, there is a call for respect for the autonomy of the child in accordance with the developing ability, and need of the child to act independently. In Turkish law, the child does become the subject of rights after it is conceived, if it is subsequently born alive (section 28/2), and in the law of inheritance, a child conceived but not yet born, may be a legal heir, if it is born alive. Yet, Turkish society on the whole would not regard a minor as being an autonomous individual with rights of his/her own. However, the law does so regard, though it is stated that a child under custody has limited capacity.

In fact, according to section 339/3, the parents should allow the child to regulate his/her own life commensurate with his/her maturity, and as far as possible, take into consideration his/her views when making important decisions about the child. Though the child's preferences are to be considered, whether this happens in fact is doubtful. Thus, the autonomy of the child is a theoretical concept in Turkish law.

The acceptance of this Principle would mean for the majority of Turks quite a change in the approach to children.

Principle 3:5 Non-discrimination of the child

As far as the legal status of children is concerned, the Turkish system has been simplified and the concepts of legitimate and illegitimate children have been abandoned in 1988. Instead, the Code talks of children born into wedlock and out of wedlock; though they are treated equally. The word "*nesep*" (filiation or lineage) has been replaced by the word "*soybağı*" (family tie), a neutral concept.

Children are not discriminated against in law on any of the grounds the Principle lays down. Neither are adults, since according to the Constitution all are equal before the law (article 10); discrimination on any ground is prohibited. An amendment to article 10 of the Constitution in 2004 has given additional support to equality stipulating that the State is under an obligation to ensure that equality between women and men is implemented in actuality. However, societal discrimination exists undoubtedly between children born within and outwith marriage, on grounds of sex, and most possibly on grounds of ethnicity and language.

Thus, this Principle would reiterate and strengthen the existing legal stance once more and may help to swing around old established traditions.

Principle 3:6 Child's right to be heard

Principle 3:6 lays down that within the boundaries of age and maturity, the child should have the right to be informed and consulted, and to express his/her opinion in all matters concerning him/her. His/her views should be given due weight.

In keeping with article 12 of the Convention on the Rights of the Child 1989, the 2002 TCC has indeed taken this obligation on board. Prior to 2002, there was no such provision in the Civil Code. As seen above, the parents must allow the child, commensurate with his/her maturity, to regulate his/her own life, and take into consideration, as far as possible, his/her views when making important decisions about the child (section 339/3). Whether this happens in fact in individual cases is questionable. In any case, this is not an absolute right and the child's age and maturity influence the assessment related to whether or not the child could be heard. In addition, the weight to be attributed to the child's opinion is indeterminate. There is also no distinction made in Turkish law between the right to be informed, to be consulted and to express opinions.

Following divorce, custody is decided upon after both parents have been heard (section 182). While considering the rights of the parents from the point of view of children, section 182 states that when the court decides on divorce or separation, where possible, it listens to the parents, or to the guardian if the child is under guardianship, and then determines the rights of the parents and their relationship with the child. Though there is no overt requirement in the TCC that the children should also be heard, the *Yargıtay*'s constant view is that according to the European Convention on the Exercise of Children's Rights 1996, article 3 and 6, ratified by and put into effect in Turkey in 2002, a court can decide on custody only after a child, regarded by domestic law as having developed a sense of comprehension, is given the opportunity to receive all relevant information, to be consulted and to express his/her preference, and the opinion of an expert is taken.[16] Since many of the lower courts do not seem to adhere to this development, the situation can only be corrected on appeal. In addition, the court has continuing jurisdiction to enter new orders for the welfare of the child, based on changed circumstances (sections 182, 183).

Although, especially since 2004,[17] the Convention on the Rights of the Child 1989 and the European Convention on the Exercise of Children's Rights 1996 have been the leading lights for the changes in Turkish law and the adoption of the Principle will again bring further strength to the right of the child, practice may not reflect this change of mentality fully.

Principle 3:7 Conflict of interests

This Principle gives priority to the interests of the child by stating that wherever there is a conflict between his/her interests and the interests of the holders of parental responsibilities, the child's interests should be protected. This is not in keeping with Turkish law and social reality in essence, since it is assumed that "parents know best". The present law does not overtly state this Principle. The assumption is that parents protect the interests of the child. Prior to 2002 it was even the case that when there was a clash of opinions between the parents, the father's opinions carried greater weight as against the mother's (TCC 1926 section 263). Today there is total equality between the parents, but not between the parents and the child.

However, conflict of interests is considered in a number of sections of TCC 2002 in relation to certain issues, and the *Yargıtay* has always taken this matter seriously.[18] The first issue appears in the section on the limits of personal relations

16 See for instance, Y2HD. 2005/12496; 2005/15273; 8.11.2005, (2006) 32 *Yargıtay Kararlar Dergisi*, 376.

17 Article 90/5 of the Constitution states that: "International agreements duly put into effect carry the force of law. No appeal to rhe Constitutional Court can be made with regard to these agreements, on the ground that they are unconstitutional. In conflicts arising between different provisions of a domestic law and an international agreement related to the fundamental rights and freedoms, the provisions of the international agreement will be taken as the basis." This last sentence entered the Constitution in 2004.

18 Legal representation of the child may become a problem when there is conflict of interests between the parents and the child. Thus, in a case in 1965, where the father was a film producer and signed a contract with a film company to involve his minor child in the making of a film, this contract was deemed to be valid. However, as the dissenting opinion rightly pointed out, this contract, entering the small girl under an obligation, was solely in the interests of the father and so there was a need for the appointment of a *kayyım* (curator). 1965/975; 1965/3137; 06/11/1965, (1966) *İl. Ve Kaz. İç. Der.*, p. 4724.

between the child and the parent who has not been given custody. Section 324/1 states that the mother and the father are under a duty to refrain from harming the child's relationship with the other parent, and hindering his/her education and development. If as a result of such personal relationship the child's peace is endangered, the mother or the father uses this right contrary to their duties enumerated in section 324/1, does not take a serious interest in the child, or if there are other important reasons, the right to establish personal relationships can be refused or taken away from them (section 324/2). This is a new and useful rule. Under the old TCC, personal contact with the parent not given custody, was an absolute rule. This caused harm to the child and the ex-wife, especially in cases where the fathers and the husbands were violent. Such a husband had the opportunity to know the whereabouts of his ex-family, and under the pretext of seeing the children, he raided the house and harmed both the children and his ex-wife, physically or otherwise.

These limitations also apply to third parties (especially relatives such as grandparents) who may have been conferred with the right to personal relationships with the child (section 325).

More specifically, section 346 on the protection of the child, states that if the interests and the development of the child are endangered, and the parents cannot take the appropriate measures, or do not have the means to do so, then, the judge would take appropriate steps for the protection of the child.

It may be interesting to note that though the holder of custody of a child born outwith marriage is the mother (section 337 TCC), the *Yargıtay* is of the opinion that in a law suit related to paternity, there might be a conflict of interests between the mother and the child, the mother may not always act in the interests of the child, and therefore, it is appropriate to appoint immediately a *kayyım* (curator) for the representation of the child (section 426/1), and for his/her protection (sec. 301/3).[19]

As to the child's property rights, the parents, who have the right to manage, use, and spend the income of the child's property, may not show the necessary care in their actions in which case the judge can take a number of decisions to secure the property (section 360) and finally, may transfer the management of such property to a *kayyım* (section 361).

The most important consequence of a conflict of interests would be the taking away of the *velayet* from the parents, the conditions for which will be seen below. This

[19] See 2001/17671; 2002/781; 29/01/2002, (2002) 28 *Yargıtay Kararları Dergisi*, pp. 851–852.

would occur if no results can be obtained from the measures taken to protect the child, or if the court decides that such measures would be inadequate (section 348).

In conflict of interests, normally, a *kayyım* is appointed.

3.3. PARENTAL RESPONSIBILITIES OF PARENTS AND THIRD PERSONS

Principle 3:8 Parents

Persons, whose legal parentage has been established, should have parental responsibilities for the child. These persons are the mother and the father of the child. Kinship between a mother and a child is established through birth, between the child and the father through the presumption that a child born to a married woman is that of her husband's. A father can be a parent also through acknowledgement or by a court decision on paternity. These cases are based on the principle of filiation. Such a relationship can also come into existence through adoption (section 282).

Thus, as pointed out above, the fundamental rule in Turkish Family Law is that while married, the spouses use parental rights together, thus parents together are the primary holders of parental responsibilities (section 336). If the parents are not married, the mother has custody of the child (section 337). However, if the mother is a minor, impaired, dead, or if custody is taken away from her for just cause, then the judge either appoints a *vasi* or gives the custody to the father, in accordance with the interests of the child (section 337/2). Also, when life in common comes to an end, the judge can give custody to one of the parents (section 336/2). Custody will then be held by the parent given the child (section 336/3), with the other parent having only the right to personal relationship.[20] Turkish law does not regard joint custody at this stage to be in the best interests of the child. This is not in keeping with the Principles.

A subsequent marriage of the parent given custody does not bring custody to an end, unless the interests of the child are adversely affected, in which case the custody holder can be changed, or the judge would appoint a *vasi* (section 349).

---

20 For instance in a case, where the father who was a Christian claimed that the mother was bringing up the child according to the Jewish faith and this was an abuse of her rights, the *Yargıtay* stated that upon divorce, the parent who is given the *velayet* has an absolute say in the religious upbringing of the child. The Court opined that the father had no say since the child was given to the mother, and what she was doing did not amount to an abuse of her powers. 1978/8661; 1978/9031; 27/12/1978, (1979) 2 *Ankara Barosu Dergisi*, pp. 80–81.

This does not alter the obligation of the parents to contribute to the expenses of the caring and the educating of the child (section 350).

As a rule, upon the death of one of the parents, custody will be conferred upon the surviving parent who will then be the sole holder of parental responsibilities.

Principle 3:9 Third persons

In Turkish law parental responsibilities cannot be attributed in whole or in part to a person other than a parent. Therefore, this Principle would be alien to Turkish law.

When a *vasi* has to be appointed to a child by a court, and the *velayet* has been removed from the parents, the *vasi* can exercise some of the rights of custody but does not become a holder of parental responsibilities. The same applies to other persons responsible for the child such as a family or an institution with which the child may be placed (section 347/1). This may happen if the physical and mental development of the child is endangered by staying with the parents, or if the child is morally abandoned and is removed from his/her parents' home by a court decision. This could also happen upon the request of the parents or of the child, if the remaining of the child within the family disrupts family peace beyond what the family could be expected to endure, or if nothing else can be done.

If, for whatever reason, the parents cannot take due care of the management of the property of the child, the judge takes appropriate measures (section 360/1). If the property is in danger and there is no other way of preventing this situation, the judge may transfer the management to a *kayyım* (section 361/1). This does not involve the transfer of parental responsibilities. The parents themselves cannot transfer *velayet* to any other person either. They cannot renounce their rights and duties in the interest of third parties.

A step-parent does not become the holder of parental responsibilities though he/she may exercise some rights with the consent of the parent of the child (section 338/2). Neither registered partnership nor informal partnership is accepted in Turkish law. Married couples can only adopt together and acquire joint parental responsibilities (section 306). There is one exception to this rule in section 307, which states that a married person can adopt alone if the other spouse has diminished mental capacity, his/her whereabouts is not known for at least two years, or the spouse wanting to adopt can prove that there is no possibility of adopting jointly since the spouses have been separated by a court decision for at least two years.

Principle 3:10 Effect of dissolution and separation

Upon divorce, only one spouse is given custody and personal relationship with the other is determined in the best interests of the child, with health, education and moral welfare being considered, parallel with the Convention on the Rights of the Child, which Turkey signed and ratified in 1995 (section 324). The TCC does not specifically provide a criterion to direct the choice between the mother and the father. This means that the judge is expected to decide in the best interests of the child. The fault of the spouse in the divorce case should have no impact on the choice in granting custody. The *Yargıtay* decisions show that a very young child is usually given to the mother, that siblings are not normally separated, and that the age and personality of the child, and the environment in which the parents live play a decisive role. Any agreement reached by the parents does not bind the judge, though he listens to their views.

The spouse who is not granted *velayet* has the right to ask for the establishment of appropriate personal relations with the child (section 323). He/she has to contribute to the expenses of raising the child in proportion to his/ her means. If a child, having reached majority, is still in full-time education, the parents have to support him/her. This is called "alimony for help" (*yardım nafakası*) and is distinct from the "participatory alimony" (*iştirak nafakası*), which ends when a child reaches majority (sections 328, 364).

The major difference with the Principles here is that there is no joint custody after divorce, and since custody is given to one of the parents, from the point of view of the other, some of the parental responsibilities disappear. In Turkey, joint custody after divorce or separation is not regarded in the best interests of the child, possibly because most divorces end in acrimony.

3.4. EXERCISE OF PARENTAL RESPONSIBILITIES

3.4.1. Parents

Principle 3:11 Joint Exercise

Parents exercise parental responsibilities together and they have an equal say in all matters. This Principle accords with Turkish law but not necessarily with societal facts. Turkey is a male dominated society and the father's wishes would hold sway, especially when there is disagreement. The 1926 Civil Code reflected this mentality closely, as the father had the last say in case of disagreement, especially since he was the head of the family (section 263 TCC 1926). Today, married persons living together share *velayet* equally and have a duty to exercise joint custody over minor children and maintain them. Maintenance is understood to mean giving children sufficient physical and moral care, choosing how they should be educated and preparing them for life.

The exceptions to joint exercise have already been discussed above.

Turkish law is part of the common core and this Principle reiterates and strengthens the present law.

Principle 3:12 Daily matters, important and urgent decisions

With respect to daily matters parents can act alone, the presumption being that the other consents. The Principle states that the other parent should be informed without undue delay, if this action involves important decisions related to education, medical treatment, residence of the child or the administration of his/her property. Here the Principle is referring to urgent cases.

The TCC has only one reference to this matter in section 342 in relation to third parties in good faith who can benefit from such a presumption when dealing with only one of the parents – that the parent acting alone has the consent of the other.

Principle 3:13 Agreement on exercise

There is no reference in the TCC to "agreement on exercise" of parental responsibilities. It is assumed that the parents agree on the exercise of their responsibilities.

However, in case of divorce by mutual consent the spouses have to submit to the court a written agreement as to financial arrangements and the arrangements for the children. The judge may or may not accept this agreement. If the judge does not agree with the arrangements and does not think it is in the interests of the children, he/she can propose an amendment and the spouses have to accept this, otherwise, divorce would not be granted (section 166). This is the only occasion when the TCC refers to an agreement.

Principle 3:14 Disagreement on Exercise

Prior to 2002, if there was disagreement on the exercise, the father's views had precedence (section 263 TCC 1926). The mother's position within marriage has been enhanced by the abolition of a father's right to make final decisions in disputes. Now the parents have to reach consent. If they cannot, then, the Family Court judge may have to play an active role. These courts were established in 2003,[21] to deal mostly with protective, educational and social aspects of family life, to be seen below under 3:35.[22]

This far Turkish law is in keeping with Principle 3:14. However, the Principle seems to give instructions to the judge on what to do under 3:14(3): either divide the exercise between the parents or decide the dispute. Such an instruction would not be accepted in Turkish law since the judge has unfettered discretion here. This may in fact be what he/she may do, but not under instruction. The criterion to be applied in taking decisions would be the interests of the child.

Principle 3:15 Sole exercise upon agreement or decision

This seems to be a repetition of Principle 3:14, put a different way. There is nothing more to add here. All that should be reiterated is that private agreements do not bind the judge's discretion, since family law is considered to be a matter of public order.

Principle 3:16 Exercise by one parent

This Principle is a logical consequence of the situation for a lone parent. There is nothing more to add here. The position of unmarried parents was seen above (see under 3:8).

3.4.2. Third Persons

Principle 3:17 Exercise in addition to or instead of the parents

According to this Principle, a person other than the parents can exercise parental powers in part or in whole. In Turkish law, as a rule, step-parents, relatives, a family or institution under whose care the child is placed, and the guardian all acquire some such rights as additions to, rather than substitution for, the parents. These issues have been dealt with above (see under 3:9).

Principle 3:18 Decisions in daily matters

This Principle only deals with the daily decisions taken by the partner of the parent of the child. In Turkish law, the partner would not acquire any rights. If the term

---

21 See Law No: 4787 of 9 January 2003 on the Establishment, Functions and Procedures of Family Courts (*Aile Mahkemelerinin Kuruluş, Görev ve Yargılama Usullerine Dair Kanun*) published on 18/1/2003 in *Resmi Gazete*: 24997.

22 *Id.*, sec. 7. " [...] considering the protection of mutual love, respect and tolerance within the family, determining the problems spouses and children face with a view to resolving these by peaceful means and encouraging such resolution whenever necessary by expert advice".

"step-parent" is substituted for the "partner", then this has been already discussed above (see under 3:9). Section 338 TCC deals with this issue.

3.5. CONTENT OF PARENTAL RESPONSIBILITIES

3.5.1. The child's person and property

Principle 3:19 Care, protection and education

The parents meet the cost of the care, education and protection of the child (section 327). This obligation continues until the child reaches majority (section 328). If, having reached majority the child is still in full-time education, the parents are under the obligation to support the child according to the conditions and in keeping with what could be expected of them (section 328/2).[23] Parents must secure and protect the physical, mental, spiritual, moral and societal development of the child.

Section 340 of the TCC deals specifically with the obligation of the parents to educate the child according to their means. Parents must provide general and vocational education and training in keeping with the child's ability and inclination. This is especially so for children who are physically or mentally impaired (section 340/2).

In fact, the right to education is also established by the Constitution (article 42). Primary education for eight years is compulsory for all citizens and is free of charge in State schools. The State also provides scholarships and other means of assistance to enable students of merit who lack financial means, to continue their education. Freedom of training and education is cited as a social right and duty with stringent conditions attached. For instance, no one can be deprived of the right to learning and education, however the scope and this right is to be defined and regulated by law. Training and education should be conducted along the lines of the principles and reforms of Atatürk (the founder of the Republic), on the basis of contemporary science and educational methods, and under the supervision

[23] See for instance 2005/12338; 2005/16008; 18/07/2005, (2005) 31 *Yargıtay Kararları Dergisi*, pp. 1760–1762, where the *Yargıtay* opined that, since in the instant case, the major child is in full-time education, the lower court should not have decided by way of constructive interpretation, that the father should continue to pay "contributory alimony" (*iştirak nafakası*) which ends upon majority (sec. 328), but, being under the duty to care for the child until the end of his education, the father should continue to support the child until the end of this education. Also see 2008/2228; 2008/4572; 17/03/2008 where the *Yargıtay* stated that since in the instant case, the major child was studying at a university, had no job or patrimony, the mother's claim that the father should pay an appropriate alimony (*nafaka*) (sec. 364) should have been accepted by the lower court, as parents should continue to support a child who is in full-time education after majority (sec. 328).

and control of the State. In addition, the freedom of training and education does not relieve the individual from loyalty to the Constitution. Another restriction is that no language other than Turkish can be taught as a mother tongue to Turkish citizens at any institution of training or education,[24] though foreign languages can be taught in schools and by schools offering education in a foreign language, by following the rules determined by law.[25] It is also stated in this article 42/9 that the provisions of international treaties are reserved.

Section 341 TCC deals with religious instruction and education, the determination of which is the absolute right of the parents.[26] All agreements limiting this right are void. However, religious and moral education and learning is under the supervision of the State according to article 24/4 of the Constitution.

The Principle can be regarded as being in accordance with Turkish law thus far, however, the second paragraph related to the child not being subjected to corporal punishment is not included in the TCC. This could be added and in any case would accord with the position in the European Convention of Human Rights and the Convention on the Rights of the Child, both of which are binding on Turkey. The question is, should it have a place in a Civil Code? In fact, prior to 2002 amendments, the 1926 Civil Code did include a section specifically related to the "right of chastisement" of the parents (section 267), which has been left out of the 2002 TCC.[27] This omission could be interpreted to mean that this second paragraph of the CEFL Principle could be presumed to exist.

Principle 3:20 Residence

The habitual residence and domicile of a child under custody is deemed to be the place of residence of his/her parents, or if they do not have a common residence, the residence of the parent who has custody (section 21). The child

24 However, recently, Kurdish can be taught as a mother tongue in higher education institutions.

25 To appreciate these restrictions one has to understand the history of the Ottoman Empire and the Turkish Republic, as well as the importance of laicism (a Constitutional principle), and cultural pluralism. For this, see ÖRÜCÜ, E., "Judicial navigation as official law meets culture in Turkey" (2008) 4:1 *International Journal of Law in Context*, pp. 35–61.

26 The fact that custody is an absolute right of the parents has some negative consequences in Turkish society. The parents decide on the religious education of the child. Recently children as young as five are being sent to Qu'ran courses by their parents, where they are told for instance, that not to cover the head is a sin. Such children lose their capacity to think freely and will not be in a position to make an independent choice when they reach majority. The rights of the child to develop his/her potential to the full should trump the parents' unfettered right to give religious instruction to the child; and rights can be limited by constitutional principles, one of which is "laicism" (article 2).

27 However, the 2005 Turkish Penal Code (TPC) in sec. 232 talks of the: "One who abuses the power to discipline arising out of the duty to teach manners and train (*terbiye*) a child who is under his/her care to educate, [...], may receive a prison sentences for up to one year". There is no mention of the limits set to the activities to be undertaken "to discipline" here.

cannot permanently leave this residence without the consent of the parents (section 339/4).

This Principle states that where holders of parental responsibilities who are jointly exercising these responsibilities, are living apart, they should agree with whom the child resides. This situation is not covered by the TCC, would be against the fundamental provisions for *velayet*, and such agreement would therefore remain a private matter. If the parents are divorced, then, according to TCC they would not be using joint custody and the court would have decided on matters related to allocation of custody and to "personal relationship", and the conditions under which the child spends his/her time. The judge has discretion in these matters. Therefore this Principle can only be regarded as laying down guidelines for judges such as the age and opinion of the discerning child, the distance of the residence of the parent to be allocated custody to the child's school and so on.

Principle 3:21 Relocation

Relocation of the parent who is the holder of parental responsibilities (and this would mean after divorce or separation) and the ensuing change of the residence of the child is not covered by the TCC, and the parent who has custody would not have to consult the other parent. However, upon a complaint by the other parent who has the right to personal relationship, the judge may intervene and consider the situation as falling under "changed circumstances" and there may even be a change in who has custody. Section 183, which is among the provisions related to divorce, refers tangentially to this issue: where new situations necessitate, the judge would take measures either ex officio or upon the request of one of the parents, in cases where one of the parents marries someone else, is relocated, or dies.

This Principle would be a welcome addition to the TCC, but the factors laid down to be considered by the competent authority, could only act as guidelines. We must also keep in mind that at present there is no joint custody upon divorce in Turkish Family Law.

Principle 3:22 Administration of the child's property

Administration of the child's property is extensively covered in the TCC between sections 352 and 363, with an additional reference in section 327.

Principle 3:22 states that in administrating the property, the holders of parental responsibilities should show due care to preserve and, where possible, increase the value of the property; not make gifts from it unless under a moral obligation; and the income not needed for the administration of the property or the maintenance and education of the child, may, where necessary, be used for the needs of the family.

Turkish law is even more protective of the property of the child. Section 327 for instance, states that the expenses of the care, education and the protection of the child is to be met by the parents, and it is only if they are very poor, or the child's special circumstances require extraordinary expenses, or in the presence of a reason out of the ordinary, can they spend an appropriate amount from the property of the child to meet the expenses of his/her maintenance and education, and this only with the permission of a judge.

Section 352 states that the parents have the right and duty to manage the child's property as long as the child is under their custody. If they do not fulfil this duty the judge will intervene. The parents can use the property of the child (section 354). The parents can spend the income from the property of the child primarily for the care and education of the child; and only then to meet the family needs in proportion to fairness. The excess income is to be added to the property of the child (section 355). Payments in the form of capital, compensation for damages and the like can be partially used for the care of the child. It is up to the judge to allow further use of the property of the child for his/her care and education, where need be (section 356). Upon the termination of marriage, the parent who is given custody must submit an inventory of the child's property showing the accounts of the income from the property to the judge and inform him of major changes in the holding or the investments (section 353).[28]

28 In 2005, the İskenderun Family Court regarded as serious a claim of unconstitutionality of section 353 of the TCC and referred the matter to the *Anayasa Mahkemesi* (the Constitutional Court). The claim was that since parents using custody jointly while married do not have to seek the approval of the judge in administering the property of the child (section 352), section 353 violated the principle of equality (art. 10) by obliging the parent to whom custody is given after the marriage comes to an end, to submit an inventory of the patrimony of the child and report to the judge important changes in the property and investments made. The concern was that section 353 does not introduce objective criteria as to why the single parent in this context is treated differently to the parents acting together, or to a single parent in other circumstances, such as the mother of an illegitimate child, who is not under this obligation. The fact that the marriage has come to an end, either by divorce or death, seems to be the only reason. This is a questioning of the relationship between that parent and the child and can have a detrimental impact on their tie. According to section 352, the judge would only intervene if the parents administering the property of the child do not perform their duties, whereas according to section 353, the single parent has an obligation to report to the judge in any event. The *Anayasa Mahkemesi* unanimously rejected the claim saying that the various parents referred to, do not share equal status and therefore, there is no violation of the principle of equality before the law. The Court opined that the logic of section 353 is to protect the child and take appropriate measures in cases where parental responsibilities are not jointly used: the property of the child may be harmed as a result of lack of knowledge, of negligence or intent of the single parent; the aim is to guarantee the protection of the child's property by placing it under judicial security. This does not remove the right to custody or damage the core of the right, both of which are prohibited by the Constitution. (2005/60; 2008/162; 13.11.2008; *Resmi*

Principle 3:23 Restrictions

Parents cannot spend for their own benefit the interest from accounts gifted to the child by third parties, or set up by third parties with explicit stipulation that the income is solely for the child to use. Unless otherwise stipulated by the third party, the parents can manage these accounts and investments (section 357).

The child's statutory portion in a testamentary disposition may exclude the parents from administration (section 358). The testator can leave the administration to a third party, and with the proviso that this person reports to the justice of the peace at certain times.

The child has the right to administer and use property given to him/her by the parents for the furtherance of a profession or vocation, and his/her own earnings (section 359). However, if such a child is sharing accommodation with the parents, they can ask him/her to contribute an appropriate amount for his/her maintenance (section 359/2).

If the parents do not show diligence in the management of the child's property, the judge may take appropriate measures for the protection of the property (section 360). He can give instructions as to how to manage the property, and if he is not satisfied with the information and accounts submitted to him, he can decide that a *vasi* be appointed (section 360/2).

If the property is in danger, the judge may decide to transfer the administration to a *kayyım*. This measure applies equally to the child's property not administered by the parents. The same measure can be taken, if the judge suspects that the income from the child's property is not being used in keeping with the law (section 361).

When custody or rights to administration comes to an end, the parents transfer the property of the child, with an inventory, to the now major child, to the *vasi* or the *kayyım* (section 362). The parents are responsible in returning the property in the same manner as a legal agent. They are under an obligation to return only what they have received from others in lieu of the property they transferred in good faith. They do not pay compensation for the amount they have spent for the child or the family in keeping with the law (section 363).

Gazete 27090; 24/12/2008). This decision does not explain why a single parent, acting alone, is less trustworthy than two parents acting together. They should either all act under judicial scrutiny or not, irrespective of whether there is one parent or two. There is discrimination here against single parents and support for staying married, that is, the status quo.

The above indicates that Turkish law is very much in keeping with Principle 3:23 and is even more demanding, and that accommodating this Principle would not be a problem in any way.

Principle 3:24 Legal representation

The Principle talks more generally of "holders of parental responsibilities". In Turkish law, parents are the legal representatives of children in their custody (section 342). This representation is as to the person, property, and as to litigation. Third parties in good faith may presume that each parent is acting with the consent of the other (section 342/2). The *vasi* or the *kayyım*, where there is one, acts by analogy in the same manner as the parents.

The child under custody has limited capacity. However, the child is responsible for his/her own obligations with his/her own patrimony (section 343). If the child under custody can discern, he/she can act for the family with the parents' consent and the parents enter an obligation as a result of such action (section 344).

For a child to enter into obligations towards his/her parents, or obligations towards third parties for the benefit of the parents, a *kayyım* appointed by the judge must participate in the transaction, and the judge must approve of it (section 345). However, there is no further overt provision covering conflict of interest between the child and the parents. In such a case, the provisions discussed above under Principle 3:23 can also be relevant.

3.5.2. Maintenance of personal relationships

Principle 3:25 Contact with parents and other persons

The child and the parents should be in contact at all times. This is a given and is not cited specifically in Turkish law. This becomes an issue when one parent is given custody after divorce or separation. In such cases, the relationship with the other parent must be maintained. In Turkish law the parent who is not given custody of the child, has the right to ask for the establishment of appropriate personal relationship (section 323). This parent also has the obligation to pay "participatory alimony" for the maintenance of the child until the child reaches majority. Here what is to be taken into account are the needs of the child, the financial means of the parent to pay the "participatory alimony" and the financial means of the parent who has been given the *velayet*.

Third parties, and especially close relatives,[29] have the right to ask for the establishment of contact with the child in exceptional circumstances and for the benefit of the child (section 325). Who these persons are is not cited by the TCC. As to persons with whom the child has developed close relations, in practice, contact would be established only in exceptional circumstances. From the wording of the TCC, it can be assumed that the right to personal relationships is viewed from the point of view of the parents, close relatives and others, rather than of the child.

Principle 3:26 Content of contact

The content of the contact, that is, what it entails, is to be determined by the judge through whom the personal relationship is established. There is no overt provision on this matter in Turkish law. What constitutes adequate contact is assessed according to the circumstances of the specific case. Factors relevant to visiting rights could be the child's age and personality, his/her own wishes if the judge considers appropriate, the distance from the home of the parent who has custody and so on.[30]

In a recent case, where divorce was based on mutual consent and the *velayet* was given to the mother, the *Yargıtay* decided that arranging the father's contact with the child once a week in the mother's home was a restriction on the *velayet* of the mother.[31]

Principle 3:27 Agreement

The only time when an agreement as to the child's position is mentioned in the TCC is in section 166 related to divorce by mutual consent and divorce for irretrievable breakdown, which states that in order to grant divorce, the judge has to be satisfied with the agreement of the spouses regarding financial matters and the children. He/she can modify the agreement in the interests of the spouses and

29 Cases indicate that a special status has been accepted especially for grandparents. In a Unification of Decisions, the *Yargıtay* established in 1959 that as an alimentary relationship could develop between the grandparents and the child in the future, it is in the interests of the child, and especially for his/her moral and emotional development, to form personal relationships with the grandparents. Thus, if the parent who has custody hinders this relationship, it would be regarded as misuse of the *velayet* duty and the judge could then take necessary measures.

30 For instance, in a case where the father had the *velayet*, the *Yargıtay* opined that, "Since the two parents live a long distance apart, it should have been decided that the mother could keep the child for a certain period every so often. Instead, it was decided that she should travel every other week to where the father is and see the child in a public place for two hours. This is not an acceptable arrangement and does not satisfy the needs of the mother." 976/1976; 624–837/1976; 03/02/1976, (1976) 11 *Yargıtay Kararları Dergisi*, p. 1547.

31 2006/17160; 2007/6186; 12/04/2007, (2007) 33 *Yargıtay Kararları Dergisi*, pp. 1657–1658. The Court was of the opinion that custody could be changed or personal relationships could be reconsidered if it was regarded that circumstances had changed.

the children. Otherwise, how the parents agree on contact with themselves and with others remains a private matter and would not be legally binding. Any private agreement reached by the parents on the exercise of parental responsibilities does not bind the judge either. It is for the judge, who assesses the situation and the best interests of the child, to decide this matter. Judicial discretion cannot be limited by an agreement of the parents.

Principle 3:28 Restrictions

Contact and personal relationships may be restricted or terminated by a judge if the best interests of the child so requires. If the interests of the child or his/her development are endangered, and the parents cannot find a solution to the problems, or cannot manage to do so, the judge would take appropriate measures to protect the child (section 346).[32] If the physical and mental development of the child is detrimentally affected, the child is not taken care of properly, or the child is morally abandoned, the judge can remove the child from the parents and settle him/her with another family or an institution (section 347). This could also happen if leaving the child with his/her parents may cause disruption to the peace of the family to an unacceptable degree. The request to the judge for removal of the child could come from the parents or the child (section 347/2). These events and circumstances are to be weighed by the judge using his discretion.

In addition, according to section 324, if either of the parents harms the personal relationship of the child with the other parent, or obstructs the education and development of the child, or if the peace of the child is detrimentally affected because of personal relationship with a parent, or the parents do not take a serious interest in the child, or there are other just causes, the right to contact can be restricted or refused altogether (section 324).[33]

---

32 In a recent case, the *Yargıtay* opined that in Turkish law the judge decides *ex officio* according to the Code of Civil Procedure section 76. When the parents do not fulfil their duties, he can take necessary measures to protect the child (sec. 346 TCC). Thereupon, he (as justice of the peace) appoints a *vasi* for the child (sec. 348). In such a case, the interests of the parents and the child are in conflict, and therefore, the child should be represented by a *kayyım*. The court can also take interim measures (sec. 349 and 429 TCC). In the instant case, the father was in jail, the mother had abandoned the child, the child was in a protective institution and there was no consent of the father to give the child for adoption. 2002/6834; 2002/7495; 4.6.2002; (2003) 29 *Yargıtay Kararları Dergisi*, pp. 17–18.

33 The *Yargıtay* altered the arrangements for custody when it was understood from the file that the parent with custody obstructed and hampered the personal relationship of the child with the other parent by not letting the child know of the new address of that parent and not allowing the child to attend a meeting with that parent, thus adversely affecting the child's family ties and mental development. See Y2HD. 2002/3930; 2002/4731; 4/4/2002, (2003) 29 *Yargıtay Kararlar Dergisi*, p. 356.

Principle 3:29 Information to parents

There is no overt provision covering this Principle in Turkish law. It is to be expected that teachers or the medical professionals would inform the parents of issues concerning the child. In cases where the custody has been given to one of the parents in case of divorce or separation, the parent to be informed would normally be the one who has custody.

3.6. TERMINATION OF PARENTAL RESPONSIBILITIES

Principle 3:30 Termination

Under normal circumstances, in keeping with the Principles, parental responsibilities terminate on the child's reaching majority, entering into marriage, being adopted and dying. This can be gleaned from several sections of the TCC, rather than under the rubric of termination.

However there are other circumstances covered by the TCC, with four relevant sections dealing with this subject. Personal relationship can be terminated if the child's well-being is under threat, if the parents abuse this right, do not take an interest in the child, or there are other just causes (section 348).[34] The mere existence of a blood tie does not give the right to abuse the rights of the child.[35]

If other measures for the protection of the child cannot ensure the child's welfare or if they appear a priori to be insufficient, the judge can decide, as the last resort,

---

34 Here mention must be made of the 2005 Penal Code sec. 233/1: "Upon complaint, a person who does not perform his/her duties arising from Family Law, of care, education and support, may be imprisoned for up to one year." This should also be viewed under Enforcement Principle 3:39.

35 One aspect of the absolute right of the parents to educate and bring up the child is that it leads to the abuse of the child, especially in eastern and south-eastern regions of Turkey. Families living in these regions have many children – sometimes up to 8 or 10. Some female children at the ages of 13 or 14 are given as brides by illegal marriages (solely religious marriages) to much older men. Though this practice is a violation of section 103 "offences against sexual immunity" of the Penal Code by constituting "sexual abuse of the child", and carries a prison sentence, this is only possible when the facts come to the knowledge of the authorities. Both the Convention on the Rights of the Child and the Turkish Constitution article 17: "everyone has the right to life, and the protection and development of his material and moral being", are violated. The child-bride is totally unprotected by law. No restraining or protection orders can be issued, since, though Law 4320 is meant to protect persons subjected to violence, as its title "Law on the Protection of the Family" indicates, only a legally formed family is covered. Neither can the minor girl inherit upon the death of her "husband". Though the Penal Code section 103 foresees a prison sentence for from eight to 15 years for the man who "marries" such a minor, this is again only possible if the facts come to the knowledge of the authorities. The best way forward is to develop further the means of protecting of the child from the parents. Otherwise the prohibition against early and forced marriages will not work.

on withdrawing of parental responsibilities. The two conditions under which this route can be followed are enumerated in section 348. The first is the inadequacy of the parents to perform the duties of *velayet* because of inexperience, illness, impairment, being somewhere else or similar circumstances; the second is the parents not showing sufficient interest in the child, or seriously neglecting the obligations towards the child.[36] This is not a sanction against the parents, but a protective measure to secure the welfare of the child. Any interested party can alert the court.

If custody is removed from both parents, a *vasi* will be appointed.[37] Unless otherwise stipulated in the court decision, the removal of *velayet* will cover all present and future offspring.

The remarriage of the parent holding custody is not a cause for the removal of custody. However, if the interests of the child so requires, the holder of custody can be changed, or custody can be removed and a *vasi* appointed (section 349). This would be the case not only upon remarriage, but also for other changed circumstances such as moving to a new place, or death, whereupon the judge can take necessary measures either ex officio or upon the request of the parents (section 183).[38]

When custody is removed, the obligations of the parents to contribute to the upbringing and education of the child continue (section 350). If the parents or the child do not have the financial means, the State will cover these expenses.

Section 351 stipulates that if circumstances change, the measures for the protection of the child should be reconsidered in view of these new circumstances. If the reasons that led to the removal of custody no longer exist, the judge will re-establish custody ex officio or upon the request of the parents.

---

36 In a case where the father of the children was dead, and the mother, who had custody, had killed her husband and was in prison with no possibility of being discharged soon, the *Yargıtay* decided that she could not perform her *velayet* duties. Basing its decision on sections 336/3 and 348 TCC, the *Yargıtay* opined that her *velayet* should be terminated, and a *vasi* should be appointed by the *vesayet* authorities. 2006/10576; 2007/220; 23/01/2007, (2007) 33 *Yargıtay Kararları Dergisi*, pp. 451–452.

37 As a rule, only one *vasi* is to be appointed (sec. 413). However, if more than one is necessary, because the property is in more places than one, or the affairs are complicated, then their consent is required regardless of whether they are going to work together or separately. See 2007/17126; 2007/17601; 17/12/2007, (2008) 34 *Yargıtay Kararları Dergisi*, p. 211.

38 The *Yargıtay* often changes the holder of custody. See cases *supra*.

Principle 3:31 Death of the parents

Upon the death of one of the parents, *velayet* will be given as a rule, to the surviving parent (section 336/3). If the parents are not married and therefore the holder of parental responsibilities is the mother, then upon her death, the judge will, in keeping with the interests of the child, either appoint a *vasi* or give the custody to the father (section 337). The death of both parents is not mentioned in the TCC. However, in such a case, by analogy, the judge will appoint a *vasi* or place the child in an institution and decide on measures to protect the person and property of the child.

3.7. DISCHARGE AND RESTORATION OF PARENTAL RESPONSIBILITIES

Principle 3:32 Discharge of parental responsibilities

This Principle has been dealt with under termination above (Principle 3:30). In Turkish law termination, removal and discharge seem to overlap. Behaviour and serious neglect would fall under section 348 discussed above.

Principle 3:33 Request for discharge of parental responsibilities

Again this matter has been discussed above under Principle 3:30.

Principle 3:34 Restoration of parental responsibilities

This issue has been covered under Principle 3:30 above.

3.8. PROCEDURE

Principle 3:35 Competent authority

In Turkish law the competent authority to take decisions in Family Law matters is a court. Since February 2003, the judges of the specially established Family Courts are the competent authority.[39] Family Courts (*Aile Mahkemeleri*) deal mostly with protective, educational and social aspects of family life, above all considering "the protection of mutual love, respect and tolerance within the family, determining

[39] See Law No: 4787 *supra* note 21.

the problems spouses and children face with a view to resolving these by peaceful means and encouraging such resolution whenever necessary by expert advice".[40]

Where Family Courts have not yet been set up, *Asliye Hukuk Mahkemeleri* (Civil Courts of First Instance) will act as Family Courts. Law No: 4787 section 4 stipulated that issues arising out of sections 118–395 TCC, that is, the second book of the TCC on Family Law, except the third part on *vesayet* (guardianship), will be dealt with henceforth by the Family Courts.[41]

No administrative bodies are involved in such matters.

Principle 3:36 Alternative dispute resolution

There is no alternative dispute resolution (ADR) per se in Family Law matters. The only innovation is the involvement of the new Family Courts established in 2003. These courts are still being set up. This area of law needs to be further developed in Turkey and could be achieved via the Family Court structure. In fact, as seen under 3:35, these courts determine the problems spouses and children face with a view to resolving these by peaceful means and encouraging such resolution whenever necessary by expert advice. This means they are also to act as mediators.[42]

Principle 3:37 Hearing of the child

In Turkish Family Law, the child is not heard in all proceedings concerning parental responsibilities by the competent authority. When a child should be heard, is decided upon by the judge in charge of the proceedings. Under Principle 3:6 above, the child's right to be heard is fully discussed. Here again note that the *Yargıtay* takes this right more seriously now. For example, as noted above, though in divorce proceedings, there is no requirement in the TCC that the children should be heard, since 2004, the *Yargıtay* reiterates that according to the European Convention on the Exercise of Children's Rights 1996, article 3, a court can only decide on custody after a child, regarded by domestic law as having developed a sense of comprehension, is given the opportunity to receive all relevant information, to be consulted and to express his/her preference, and

40 *Ibid*, sec. 7.

41 See as examples, 226/13771; 2007/5285; 02/04/2007, (2007) 33 *Yargıtay Kararları Dergisi*, pp. 1257–1258, dealing with a case related to change of *velayet*; 2006/14243; 2006/15231; 08/11/2006, (2007) 33 *Yargıtay Kararları Dergisi*, pp. 874–875, dealing with an objection to the establishment of filiation, and 2007/20848; 2008/3187; 28/02/2008, dealing with the non-payment of expenses of the education of minor children by the father, contrary to the agreement in the protocol drawn up during the divorce case.

42 See Law No: 4787 sec. 7.

the opinion of an expert is taken.[43] However, there are no specific guidelines as to how and where the child should be heard or what weight should be given to the views of the child and when.

The TCC mentions the child's right to be heard in section 339 in that the parents should allow the child, in a manner commensurate with the child's maturity, to manage his/her life, and, as far as possible, consider his/her views in decisions concerning the child.

Principle 3:37 overlaps with Principle 3:6 (see above).

Principle 3:38 Appointment of a special representative for the child

Serious conflict of interests between the parents and the child is not specifically considered by the TCC. Only in matters related to the property of the child is this touched upon. The welfare of the child being at risk is regarded as more serious. However, as the rule is that parents are the only legal representatives of the child, the matter can be dealt with by two possibilities: to appoint a *vasi* or a *kayyım* for the child. The competent judge would deal with this matter using discretion.

Principle 3:39 Enforcement

As all court decisions are to be adhered to, in principle, enforcement is not a specific issue in this context. Residence and contact may prove to be the main areas of concern. The Code on Enforcement can be applied, threat of penalties (imprisonment or fine) may be used, force can be used to elicit pecuniary support (maintenance support contributions), and the 2005 Turkish Penal Code (TPC)[44] can be activated if, for instance, the parent with visiting rights absconds with

---

43 Y2HD. 2005/12496; 2005/15273; 8.11.2005, (2006) 32 *Yargıtay Kararlar Dergisi*, p. 376. In this case the father was an alcoholic and the mother was living with a married man. The child was 15 and was staying with her father and grandmother. The *Yargıtay* decided that she was mature enough to have her views taken and therefore should have been asked for her views, and expert evidence should have been used when deciding custody. The legal basis was the Convention article 3.

44 Offences against the family are covered between sections 230 and 234 in this Code. In addition, sections 103 and 104 deal with sexual abuse of a child

the child,[45] a parent seriously neglects the child,[46] or sexually abuses the child.[47] However coercive measures of enforcement are used with constraint.

Principle 3:39(2) can be problematic however, as we do not know who will decide that enforcement is not in the best interests of the child, let alone what is the best interests of the child.

4. CONCLUDING REMARKS

The ultimate message of the Principles is convergence of Family laws in Europe, inspired by certain facts and values. Free movement of persons in the European Union and the human rights framework underpin the activity of the CEFL. Most of the underlying values are already pre-determined by a number of conventions and international and European instruments.

The major considerations are to clarify, reinforce and improve the legal position of the child, to achieve fairness and justice for the child caught up in cross-border relationships, to protect the child's rights, welfare, and best interests regardless of the circumstances of birth, to enable the child to participate in decision-making, and to secure the autonomy of the holders of parental responsibilities to agree on parental responsibility matters, subject to scrutiny.

In the essence of the Principles are the joint exercise of parental responsibilities to continue after divorce or separation and also joint exercise of parental

45 Section 234 TPC deals with the abduction and detention of a child. If the parent whose right to custody has been removed, or a blood relation, abducts or detains a minor not yet 16, without using force or threats, the sentence is imprisonment for from three months to a year. If force or threats are used, or if the child is below 12 years of age, the sentence is doubled.

46 TPC section 233/1 has already been mentioned under Principle 3:30 *supra*. Another paragraph of this section (sec. 233/3 TPC) deals with prosecution for neglect. It says that even though their custody rights may have been removed, the parents, who cannot show material and moral care and seriously endanger the morality, security and health of their children by habitually drinking, or using drugs and other substances, or as a consequence of insulting and belittling behaviour, will be imprisoned for from three months to one year.

47 Section 103 lays down a general principle that sexual abuse of a child carries a sentence of imprisonment for from three to eight years. Any sexual activity against minors below the age of 15 or who lack the capacity to comprehend the action or its consequences, or any sexual act against any minor using force, threat or deception, or if the act involves penetration, the sentence is imprisonment for from eight to 15 years; and if sexual abuse is perpetrated by ascendants, step-father, guardian [...] the sentence is increased by half. Section 104 TPC states that sexual relations with a minor of 15 will be sentenced for from six months to two years imprisonment upon complaint. If the perpetrator is more than five years older than the victim, the sentence is doubled. If such a sexual relationship takes place within the family, abusing the powers arising from it, the sentence is increased by half. If as a consequence, a minor has to leave the family home, the sentence cannot be for less than one year's imprisonment. However, consider here, comments in footnote 35 *supra*.

responsibilities for unmarried parents. "Parental responsibilities" is the preferred terminology, reflecting parental duties and parental care, rather than parental power or parental authority, and custody or guardianship. In addition, the autonomy and the interests of the child are central to the mentality of the Principles.

Turkish Family Law would encounter a number of problems facing the Principles of European Family Law regarding Parental Responsibilities. The most important problem would be a change in the mentality as to the autonomy and rights of the child as opposed to the rights of the parents. The Principles demand the strengthening of the position of the child by stressing the autonomy of the child and his/her right to be heard all through, reducing the power and rights of the parents to duties and responsibilities, and expanding the circle of persons who can use parental responsibilities. One consequence could be that the concept "*velayet*" might have to be redefined or replaced. This would prove to be a serious problem.

The Principles also reflect an ideal situation with parents amicably divorced, holding joint custody. In Turkey most divorces are acrimonious. The ex-spouses do not see each other. In cases where they remain amicable, society regards this as bizarre, especially if there are subsequent marriages. So, joint custody after divorce would only be acceptable if the decision is left to the agreement of the spouses combined with hearing the views of the child. If this was no more just an option but the rule, again, this would create problems.

On many of the issues arising under the provisions of Family Law, Family Courts[48] set up in 2003 have competence.[49] These Courts need to be further developed and their competences widened.

As discussed above under various of the Principles, Turkish societal realities will not improve under these Principles. Many of these Principles correspond with the existing Turkish law. The problems faced in Turkey are in social realities, traditional values, lack of education and implementation. The Principles, in the same manner as the Turkish Civil Code and the Constitution, will reflect the rhetoric and further strengthen it – which is a good thing in itself – but will not address the inherent problems. The Principles are not a panacea to real issues of family relationships.

---

48 See Law No: 4787 *supra* note 21.

49 *See Yargıtay* decisions on competence discussed *supra*.

PART FOUR
COMPARATIVE ASSESSMENT

HARMONISED NORMS OF PARENTAL RESPONSIBILITIES FACING REALITY

Jane Mair and Esin Örücü

1. INTRODUCTION

The current Principles Regarding Parental Responsibilities,[1] as with the previous CEFL Principles Regarding Divorce and Maintenance Between Former Spouses,[2] are intended for those legislators considering "modernising the law" within national, European and international contexts and for whom they "may serve as a frame of reference and inspiration".[3] Unlike the Principles on Divorce, however, these Principles have emerged from a background of pre-existing harmonisation measures in the form of a number of conventions and international and European instruments. In drafting the Principles, the CEFL acknowledged the influence of a range of existing measures, in particular the UN *Convention on the Rights of the Child 1989*, the *Hague Child Protection Convention 1996* and the *European Convention on Human Rights 1950.* In addition, reference was made to several recent Council of Europe Conventions relating to children,[4] to the White Paper on *Principles Concerning the Establishment and Legal Consequences of Parentage 2002*[5] and to the developing influence of the European Union in this field through the *Brussels II bis Regulation*, the *European Charter of Fundamental Rights 2000* and the European Commission's Communication *Towards an EU Strategy on the Rights of the Child.* The CEFL, in drafting the Principles Regarding Parental Responsibilities, was therefore working in an environment of existing attempts at harmonisation[6] and so the initial question to be considered is the extent to which

1 BOELE-WOELKI, K., FERRAND, F., BEILFUSS, C. G., JÄNTERA-JAREBORG, M., LOWE, N., MARTINY, D. and PINTENS, W., (eds) *Principles of European Family Law Regarding Parental Responsibilities*, European Family Law Series No. 16 (Antwerp: Intersentia, 2007).

2 BOELE-WOELKI, K., FERRAND, F., BEILFUSS, C. G., JÄNTERA-JAREBORG, M., LOWE, N., MARTINY, D. and PINTENS, W., (eds), *Principles of European Law Regarding Divorce and Maintenance Between Former* Spouses, European Family Law Series No. 7 (Antwerp: Intersentia, 2004); considered in ÖRÜCÜ, E. and MAIR, J. (eds) *Juxtaposing Legal Systems and the Principles of European Family Law on Divorce and Maintenance*, European Family Law Series No.17 (Antwerp: Intersentia, 2007).

3 BOELE-WOELKI ET AL, *supra* note 1, p.5.

4 *Ibid*, at p.16.

5 See http://www.oeu.int.

6 Some of the measures bring in unified rules.

the Principles add value to the measures already in place. Do they represent a further modernisation and rationalisation of what already exists in this field?

The existence of this wide range of previous conventions and other instruments in the field of children's rights and the relationship between parents and children, gives rise to an expectation that a reasonable level of harmony might be evident in the domestic systems themselves. When one considers the national reports, as presented in the volume *European Family Law in Action Volume: III,*[7] many of the answers to the CEFL questionnaire reveal that there is a common core on which some of the Principles are based. The general approach is similar in many systems, to a large extent as a result of their moves towards compliance with the existing international and European conventions in this area. There is also evidence of the influence of shared developing theories and concepts of childhood, children's rights and the relationship between parents and children in many of the national jurisdictions. In other words, this is a field of family law where it appears that harmonisation should be relatively easy for the reason that much of the background work has already been done.

Convergence of family laws in Europe is the ultimate message of the Principles, inspired by certain facts and values. The first fact is the free movement of persons in the European Union and the necessity of having, as far as possible, uniform regulations throughout the area pertaining to parent and child relationships. The human rights framework is the other, though covert, fact. The main aim is to clarify, reinforce and improve the legal position of the child with the added concern to achieve fairness and justice for the child caught up in cross-border relationships. The major considerations are the child's rights and welfare, the protection of the best interests of the child born within or outwith marriage, participation of the child in decision-making and the autonomy of the holders of parental responsibilities to agree on parental responsibility matters, subject to scrutiny.

2. DOMESTIC STATE OF HARMONY?

Despite the level of shared concepts and developments, however, a number of the family law systems surveyed here would encounter some problems facing the Principles of European Family Law regarding Parental Responsibilities. The most important problem would be a change in the mentality as to the autonomy

---

7 BOELE-WOELKI, K., BRAAT, B. and CURRY-SUMNER, I., (eds) *European Family Law in Action Volume III: Parental Responsibilities*, European Family Law Series No.9 (Antwerpen: Intersentia: 2005). The integral reports can also be found on the CEFL website: www.law.uu.nl/priv.cefl.

and rights of the child as opposed to the rights of the parents. The Principles demand the strengthening of the position of the child by stressing the autonomy of the child and his/her right to be heard, reducing the power and rights of the parents to duties and responsibilities, and expanding the circle of persons who can exercise parental responsibilities.

In assessing the extent to which the Principles fit with the legal systems considered, we have chosen to concentrate on three aspects: parental responsibilities, which is an area where there is significant divergence; the content of parental responsibilities, where despite broad convergence there is some non-compliance, and parents and third parties, where there is considerable diversity.

2.1. PARENTAL RESPONSIBILITIES

Changes in the social form of the family and in the parent/child relationship are widespread and in many jurisdictions they have been reflected in changing legal rules and terminology, in particular in a shift away from the notion of parental rights or authority over children towards parental responsibilities in respect of children. The traditional legal model, which guaranteed to protect the rights of parents over their children, has, in many domestic systems, moved towards a model which is centred on the child as the focus of protection. This trend is reflected in the language of the CEFL Principles. Despite acknowledging that it is not a term widely used throughout Europe,[8] the CEFL opted to describe the concept which underlies the legal relationship between parent and child in the Principles, as that of "parental responsibilities".[9]

As the CEFL foresaw, some systems in our survey do not conform strictly with this Principle in respect of terminology. Estonia currently has no general concept of parental responsibilities but instead lists the specific rights and duties of a parent,[10] which are broadly similar in content to those listed under Principle 3:1. The detailed nature of the rights and duties makes it clear that they are accorded to a parent "in order that he or she may ensure and protect the well-being of his or her child"[11] and this focus of Estonian law on the child rather than the parent fits well with the tone of the CEFL concept of parental responsibilities even if the terminology does not match precisely. This too is likely to change if the Estonian Draft Family Law Act, which includes a concept of parental responsibilities, comes into force.

8 BOELE-WOELKI ET AL, *supra* note 1, pp. 26 – 27.
9 Principle 3:1.
10 See Estonia, *supra* at p.??.
11 See Estonia, *supra* at p.??.

Malta continues to use "the Roman law concept of parental authority"[12] and, although the detailed obligations of care and protection which fall within the scope of parental authority are broadly similar to those listed in Principle 3:1, the terminology does not match. The move towards equality, which is widespread, has shifted the notion from one of paternal authority to gender neutral parental authority although this development is relatively recent[13] and as the CEFL recognised, "[e]ssentially the same social, economic and political changes"[14] have taken place, although "not always [...] within the same time periods."[15] The relatively restricted provision for a child to express his or her opinion in the context of the exercise of parental authority, which applies only in respect of a child over the age of 14, raises an issue as to the extent to which the approach in Malta has moved away from a firmly hierarchical relationship between parent and child towards one which is more evenly balanced. Other aspects of the Maltese concept of parental authority, for example, the fact that "parents are given the right to expect the child to obey them"[16] offer interesting insight into the Maltese approach beyond the outward aspect of terminology. Without judging the question of whether the existence of such an expectation is a good or bad thing, it is noteworthy that the CEFL Principles, together with many other domestic European systems, have moved towards concepts of parental responsibilities which focus to a much greater extent on the actions of the parents rather than those of the children. Broadly, there is considerable ground in common between the parental authority of family law in Malta and the CEFL concept of parental responsibilities although it is evident that "the notion of responsibility is still to replace authority vis-à-vis children."[17]

England uses the concept of parental responsibility, as set out in the Children Act 1989, but it lacks a detailed list of rights and responsibilities which fall within this concept, as set out in Principle 3:1. The English position might be criticised on two counts: on the basis that "it not only fails to identify the types of rights and responsibilities that are encompassed by the term, but it also does not indicate what parental responsibility is *for*."[18] Although the statutory framework is less detailed and clearly defined than that envisaged by Principle 3:1, jurisprudence suggests a close correspondence with the CEFL model and in particular in view of the words of Lord Fraser in *Gillick* to the effect that "parental rights to control a child do not exist for the benefit of the parent. They exist for the benefit of the

12 See Malta, *supra* at p.61.
13 Since 1 December 1993. See further, Malta, *supra* at p.61.
14 BOELE-WOELKI ET AL, *supra* note 1, p.13.
15 *Ibid.*
16 See Malta, *supra*, discussion of Principle 3:2 at p.67.
17 See Malta, *supra* at p. 99.
18 See England, *supra* at p.213.

child".[19] This approach appears to fit well with that which informs the CEFL Principles, to the effect that the parent and child relationship is to a substantial extent child-focused, with parents exercising rights and duties for the benefit of their children rather than as a consequence and confirmation of their superior legal authority.

Danish law has been substantially reformed in the recent past with the coming into force of the Act on Parental Responsibility in 2007. While this legislation represents a significant reform of the existing legal framework, it is interesting to note that the Act itself is entitled the Act on Parental Responsibility but the concept "is best translated as parental authority".[20] It is commented that, although a change of name to parental responsibility was considered prior to the statutory reform, it was "rejected on the grounds, amongst others, that such a concept would be misleading with respect to the authority which the holder(s) have and secondly that a mere change of wording without de facto change to the concept itself would be inappropriate."[21] Although the definition of parental authority in Danish law is neither as detailed nor extensive as that provided in Principle 3:1, it appears that there is considerable consistency between the Principle of parental responsibilities and the Danish concept of parental authority.

While Scots law uses the concept of parental responsibilities it also uses a corresponding concept of parental rights. Whereas the CEFL Principle is presented under the heading of parental responsibilities but goes on to provide that this involves a collection of rights and duties, the Scottish approach is to distinguish more clearly between the nature of parental responsibilities and parental rights; the latter exist only to the extent that is necessary to enable a parent to fulfil his or her responsibilities. Although Scots law involves a more precise delineation between these different concepts, it is in substance broadly in line with the CEFL Principle concerning parental responsibilities.

For Romanian family law, the collection of rights, duties and obligations which correspond to the CEFL concept of parental responsibilities is described as parental protection. As with Scots law, it is provided that the parental rights are recognised only to the extent that they are necessary to enable parents to fulfil their obligations in respect of protection. This concept has emerged from a series of reforms shifting the focus of family law from the traditional concept of parental power, more specifically paternal power, towards the more child-centred notion of parental protection.

---

19 *Gillick v West Norfolk and Wisbech Area Health Authority and Department of Health and Social Security* [1986] 1 A.C. 112 at 170 D – E, discussed *supra* at England, p.213.

20 See Denmark, *supra* at p.197.

21 *Ibid.* This is an interesting insight which will be considered further, *infra*, in assessment of the Principles themselves.

Though Turkish society gives prominence to the importance of children within the family, their legal position remains more clearly subordinate to that of their parents than the CEFL model seems to require. The Turkish concept of *velayet* or custody "can be viewed as powers and duties over the person of the child, and powers and duties over the property of the child."[22] In a similar way to the law in Malta, "[t]hough the interests of the child is paramount, it can be assumed that the rights of the child are subservient to those of the parents since the child is under an obligation to obey the decisions of the parents".[23] While this power based relationship is closer to a traditional model of parent / child relations and not fully compliant with the CEFL values, it fits well with the dominant domestic Turkish framework of family life.

2.2. CONTENT OF PARENTAL RESPONSIBILITIES

It is in the context of Chapter V of the CEFL Principles, dealing with the content of parental responsibilities, that there is most evidence of convergence in the common understanding of what being a parent involves. Despite some variation in the detail of parental responsibilities, there is considerable harmony in terms of the content of parental responsibilities as involving caring for, protecting and educating the child, maintaining contact with the child and caring for his or her property.

Danish law is broadly consistent with the CEFL Principles to the extent that "care, protection and education are […] core elements of the Danish concept of parental authority"[24] and in terms of the management of a child's property, the protective framework is similar to that provided by the Principles. Noticeable differences lie in the preference in Danish law for parental agreement and the exercise of parental authority which is not always subject to judicial scrutiny and therefore in respect of some Principles there is not strict conformity.[25] Scots law, in a similar way, is largely in conformity with the content as set out in the Principles but, because of its preference for non-intervention, provision is not always made for judicial scrutiny. Any person with an interest may apply to the court for an order regulating parental responsibilities and rights but the court will not make such an order unless it is satisfied that it would be better to do so than to make no order at all.[26] For that reason, there is a clear preference for parental agreement and the parents are to a large extent trusted to act in the interests of the child.

22 See Turkey, *supra* at p.239.
23 *Ibid.*
24 See Denmark, *supra* at p.205.
25 See BOELE-WOELKI ET AL, *supra* note 1: Principle 3:21 discussed at p.12 and Principle 3:27, discussed at p.14.
26 Children (Scotland) Act 1995, s.11(7)(a), discussed further at Scotland, *supra* p.164.

Although Scots law complies with much of the content of parental responsibilities as detailed in the Principles, the structure of the provisions is different because of the clear distinction between parental responsibilities and parental rights.

Of the systems considered, only two could be argued to meet the CEFL requirement in respect of protecting the child from physical punishment: Principle 3:19(2) provides that "the child should not be subjected to corporal punishment or any other humiliating treatment". Denmark fully complies with the Principles in respect of chastisement of the child. Romania similarly outlaws the use of corporal punishment or other humiliating treatment in respect of a child. A child is entitled to respect for his or her dignity as a fundamental principle of chidren's rights within Romanian law[27] and a child may only be disciplined in a manner which is consistent with this principle: it being specifically prohibited to use corporal punishment.

In this respect, Scots law does not measure up to Principle 3:19(2). A parent has the responsibility to provide direction and guidance to the child[28] and the complementary right to control, direct and guide the child's upbringing.[29] In the provision of such guidance, the possibility of physical chastisement is not ruled out and, although corporal punishment would prima facie constitute an assault, the actions of the parent may be justified in terms of section 51 of the Criminal Justice (Scotland) Act 2003. This provision sets out a list of factors to be considered by the court including the nature of the punishment, the reason for it and the circumstances. It is also expressly provided that the conduct will not be justifiable where it included a blow to the head, shaking or the use of an implement.[30] The issue of corporal punishment has similarly been reviewed in England in recent years and the decision to ban it was not taken, with parents and those *in loco parentis* continuing to be able to exercise "reasonable chastisement".[31] Physical punishment also remains a possibility for parents according to the family law in Malta, with discipline being regarded as "an essential element of the exercise of parental authority".[32] As with Scotland and England, the appropriate concept is that of "reasonable chastisement", and although no definition of this is provided it is clear that a distinction must be made between this and excessive or grievous conduct. In Estonia, there is no express general prohibition of corporal punishment by parents or other carers of the child, although there are specific provisions outlawing corporal punishment in institutions including schools

27 Art.6(g) Law no. 272/2004 discussed *supra* at Romania, 8(d).
28 Children (Scotland) Act 1995, s.1(1)(a).
29 *Ibid*, s.2(1)(b).
30 Criminal Justice (Scotland) Act 2003, s.51(3). For further discussion, see Scotland, *supra* at p.180.
31 See England, *supra* at p.223.
32 For further discussion, see Malta, *supra* at p.82.

and care homes and prohibiting against "humiliating, frightening or punishing the child in any way that abuses the child, causes bodily harm to the child, or otherwise endangers his or her mental or physical health."[33] Not only is there no express legal prohibition, but public attitudes in Estonia continue to view corporal punishment as "an acceptable part of raising a child."[34] In the Civil Code, Turkish law makes no specific reference to physical chastisement of the child although it is argued that Turkey's acceptance of both the European Convention of Human Rights and the Convention on the Rights of the Child, together with the fact that a provision relating to the parental right of chastisement was included in the previous Civil Code of 1926, but not in the 2002 one, might together be taken as evidence of compliance with the CEFL Principle.[35] As with Estonia, however, some doubt remains as to how well this approach fits with public opinion.[36]

It is evident, therefore, that while all of the systems are broadly in agreement as to the content of parental responsibilities, their attitudes as to how these responsibilities should be fulfilled and in particular the way in which they reflect the nature of the relationship between parents and children demonstrate greater diversity. The tension between parental authority and parental responsibility continues and this is perhaps most evident in the context of chastisement. Only Denmark and Romania are fully in compliance with the CEFL prohibition against corporal punishment whereas, for all of the other systems, the right to use physical chastisement is viewed as one element of the parental responsibility – and right – to direct, guide and discipline a child. For these countries, compliance with the CEFL Principle seems unlikely, particularly as in several of them there has been recent reconsideration of this area of law.

2.3. PARENTS AND THIRD PARTIES

In Chapter III of the Principles, the CEFL sets out the basic framework by means of which parental responsibilities may be held by both parents and third parties. These Principles are further developed in Chapter IV where the exercise of parental responsibilities by both groups is set out in greater detail. Although the domestic legal systems generally recognise the possibility that parental responsibilities may be held by persons who are not legally defined as parents, there is considerable diversity in terms of the specific national provisions. The CEFL Principles draw a distinction between the attribution and the exercise of parental responsibilities [37] and, in terms of the attribution, only require, in the broadest terms, that parental

33 Discussed at Estonia, *supra* at p.25.
34 *Ibid.*
35 See Turkey, *supra* at p.253.
36 See discussion of societal attitudes to children in Turkey, *supra* at p.236.
37 See BOELE-WOELKI ET AL, *supra* note 1, Comment (2) at p.77.

responsibilities may be attributed either wholly or partly to a third party. Although most of the systems may be argued to be in compliance with the Principles, that is perhaps a reflection of the fact that the Principles in this respect are extremely broad, as it is clear from the national systems that there is considerable diversity among their provisions.

In assessing the extent to which the national systems comply with the CEFL Principles in this context, there are two distinct issues to consider. The first is in respect of Priciple 3:8 which provides that all persons, whose legal parentage has been established, should have parental responsibilities. In other words, there should be an automatic link between parentage and parental responsibilities. The second issue relates to Principle 3:9 and the requirement that parental responsibilities may be attributed to third parties together with or in substitution of parents. Although both of these Principles are clear and straightforward, it is evident from consideration of the national systems under review here that compliance in practice is much more complex.

In respect of the first issue, it is the position of the unmarried father that gives rise to difficulty. In both Scotland and England, the provisions, although different in their legal source, are very similar in effect. For both jurisdictions, mothers will automatically have parental responsibilities as a consequence of their maternity. A legal father who is married to the mother will also automatically acquire parental responsibilities and, in the case of an unmarried father, the parental responsibilities will be obtained on the basis that the parents have jointly registered the birth. Both systems have relatively recently reviewed this area of law and decided positively against automatic attribution of responsibilities to all fathers preferring instead to focus on birth registration as an indication of acknowledgement of the father's role. In England there are further proposals under consideration which would involve moving towards making joint birth registration "a legal requirement unless it is 'impossible, impracticable or unreasonable'".[38] In these systems the approach is to focus on factual relationships and registration rather than on the legal status of parentage and although there is therefore no strict compliance with the CEFL Principle, the outcome appears similar. Estonian law is broadly similar in that, although there is no discrimination between married and unmarried parents to the extent that in respect of each, parental responsibilities "arise from the filiation of the child", the ways in which that filiation are established are different depending on the marital status of the parties. Where the couple is married then the husband is presumed to be the father but in respect of unmarried persons, "the filiation of the child is established on the basis of a joint written application of the father and mother".[39] Here, as

38 Discussed at England, *supra* p.220.
39 Discussed *supra* at Estonia, p.30.

with the position in England and Scotland, the parentage of the unmarried father and the subsequent attribution to him of parental responsibilities, depends on joint acknowledgement of his paternity.

According to Danish law, although it does not comply with Principle 3:8 to the effect that parental responsibilities should be a consequence of legal affiliation, it does "provide for this result in most cases".[40] As with the other systems discussed, through a variety of different provisions depending on whether the parents are married or unmarried and when unmarried, depending on how the paternity of the father has been established, both parents will acquire parental authority. As with Scots law, in the case of an unmarried father who does not automatically obtain parental responsibilities, he may nonetheless apply for them.

The Turkish system is the one least able to comply with the Principles relating both to parents and third parties. Where the parents of a child are married then both will have and be able to exercise parental responsibilities but in the case of a child born outwith marriage, the mother alone will have custody with no provision being made for the unmarried father. In respect of parents and third parties, parental responsibilities can only be attributed to parents. Where the parents are not able to provide adequate care for the child then a *vasi* or guardian may be appointed by a court and the custodial rights of the parent will be removed but, while the guardian may exercise similar rights in some respects to those of a parent, he or she does not acquire parental responsibilities. Similarly, where it is the property of the child which is not adequately protected by the parents, it can be placed in the administrative control of a *kayyim* by the court but again there is no attribution of parental responsibilities.

The position in Estonia is to some extent similar in that parental responsibilities are granted principally only to the parents of a child although extensive provision is made for the appointment of a guardian who will then operate within a legal framework which is broadly similar to that of parental responsibilities.[41] Whereas the Child Protection Act provides a child with the right to maintain contact with close relatives, no similar statutory right exists in respect of the relatives. Although the operation of guardianship allows for third parties to have care of and control of a child, it is clear from the Estonian legal provisions that a distinction is made between parents and third parties. In both this system and that of Turkey, there is provision for protection and care of the child's person and property by a third party where the parents are not able to do so adequately but in both systems there is a clear distinction between this system of protection and that of parental responsibilities.

40 See Denmark, *supra* p.201.
41 See discussion at Estonia, *supra* p.34.

In Malta, parental responsibilities are predominantly attributed to the parents of a child but in certain circumstances, for example on adoption or where a child is subject to a care order, they may be vested in some other person. In such a case, parental responsibility is removed from the parent and granted to the third party as a substitute. This would seem to be in compliance with Principle 3:9 because of its very broad and undefined terms and similarly may comply with Principle 3:17 which requires that the responsibilities may be exercised in addition to or instead of the parents.

In England, while it is legal parents who acquire parental responsibilities automatically as a consequence of their status, parental responsibilities may also be granted to third parties in a range of situations: step-parents may acquire them by means of a parental responsibility order or agreement, a person with whom the child is to have his or her residence by means of a residence order or in other situations they may be acquired by a special guardianship order.[42]

3. IDEAL PRINCIPLES?

It is the aim of this part not only to assess how well each of the domestic legal systems considered would comply with the CEFL Principles, but also to analyse the Principles themselves. As previously discussed, this second set of Principles applies in an area of family law where there have already been several other international and European standard setting measures and so it is appropriate to consider what value they have added. The Commission has explained that the Principles, "are primarily directed towards national, European and international legislators who are considering modernising the law in this field. They may serve as a frame of reference and inspiration."[43] It is therefore appropriate to assess the Principles against that stated aim and to consider to what extent they represent an ideal framework to which individual legal systems should aspire. In other words, do the CEFL Principles in fact provide a suitable framework for modern family law in this area? The Principles shall be assessed against two criteria: first, are the CEFL Principles better than the measures which currently exist and secondly, how well do they satisfy the aim stated by the CEFL that they should act as an inspiration and as a tool for modernisation? Are the different policy aims compatible?

---

42 Discussed *supra* at England, p.220.

43 BOELE-WOELKI ET AL, *supra* note 1, at p.5.

3.1. BETTER PRINCIPLES?

To some extent the challenge faced by the Commission in developing these Principles is made more difficult by the relative level of harmony which has already been achieved by means of, in particular, the UN Convention on the Rights of the Child. To choose an area where there already exist a number of related and relevant international measures may seem an obvious option in that the starting point should be one of greater pre-existing harmony but the expectation then is that these Principles should represent an improvement on the current provisions. What value do the Principles add to the list of European conventions and agreements? It is true that in order to appreciate the value of the CEFL Principles, they must be considered together with the comments and comparative overviews following each Principle. One would therefore think that the CEFL Principles, considered together with comments and comparative overviews, should present a more complete picture, but in essence they do not. A thorough and extensive comparative research has been carried out, yet the leading principles are largely based on the international and European instruments. Thus the Principles are not innovative enough.

An initial criticism of the CEFL Principles might be made on the basis that they are relatively long and in places appear repetitive. Compared to the *Model Family Code*,[44] where Parental Responsibility, together with Child Support and Parental Protection, are dealt with in a total of 21 short Principles, the CEFL Principles bear more resemblance to a detailed statutory code. While the CEFL has used a sensible and coherent structure, defining the basic concepts, outlining the distinct aspects of attribution and exercise of parental responsibilities, the roles of parents and third parties, the effect of termination of the parents' relationship and the relevant procedures, it has the effect of making the substance appear rather repetitious. This is particularly evident in terms of the separate treatment of "Parents" and "Third parties" within the context of the "Exercise of parental responsibilities". These could have been treated together under one heading.

The level of detail provided in some places may be argued to be at the expense of the impact of the "Principles". As a source of inspiration and as a starting point for debate in this area, a shorter and clearer set of Principles might have been of greater value. As with the earlier Principles on Divorce, it is often in the detail that there is national divergence. Reduced to a bare set of Principles, there is much greater harmony among the individual legal systems, with relatively little disagreement about the fundamental obligations of the relationship of parent

44 SCHWENZER, I. in collaboration with DIMSEY, M., *Model Family Code: From a Global Perspective*, European Family Law Series No.12 (Antwerp: Intersentia, 2006), Title 4: Parental Responsibility.

and child, the focus on the welfare of the child, the preference for both parents to take responsibility for their child and to maintain personal relations with the child. In most systems there is a high degree of commonality in terms of goals and objectives and the diversity exists primarily in the detail of how they seek to achieve these ends.

In the Introduction to the Principles, it is explained that they are restricted largely to the area of private law and that they will not include certain other aspects of child law. They distinguish between parentage and parenting, they do not include child support and, by looking only at private law, they exclude "public welfare, intervention by the state, [and] measures taken as a result of criminal offences committed by children"[45] and in so doing the Principles follow a traditional framework. One explanation for choosing this approach is that it is used in other similar documents but it might be argued that this again was an opportunity for the Commission to take a more radical approach and to question some of these traditional distinctions. With rapidly changing and diversifying family forms, the development of assisted reproduction and the growing number of re-constituted or "blended" families where children live with and are cared for by step-parents, cohabitants and other adults, does it remain appropriate to distinguish between parentage and parenting? It is a well known and widespread problem that parents who have financial obligations of support are often recalcitrant payers where they have no or very little personal relationship with the child. Many children are in practice supported by adults with whom they live in a family setting, but who have no legal obligation to maintain them, and again it might be asked if the Commission could have taken this opportunity to seek to integrate aspects of personal parental responsibilities with obligations of financial support. As it becomes more difficult to maintain a strict separation between public and private law within the domain of the family, as the family is regarded as an important point of regulation and intervention for a range of policies, does it continue to make sense to treat aspects of child law separately according to whether they are classified as public or private? Aside from the difficulty of drawing a line between public and private in terms of legal regulation, for many children and families the line in practice is far from clear between private family life and public protection and intervention. Concerns about inadequate parenting, children at risk and children in need, highlight the intersections and often difficult relations between public and private and it is questionable whether the Principles should continue to treat these aspects as distinct and segregated elements of the legal regulatory framework. That the CEFL has chosen to follow a well established approach is not surprising but if the Principles are truly to provide inspiration for forward looking legislation and modernising debate then it seems that some of these traditional divisions may need to be further challenged.

---

45 BOELE-WOELKI ET AL, *supra* note 1, pp. 21–22.

3.2. MODERN PRINCIPLES?

An important aspect of the work of the CEFL in producing Principles, is to provide inspiration for reform and to assist in the development at national or European level of modern legislative frameworks. There is, and will continue to be, much debate as to the function of family law; should it reflect social change or should it contribute to such change? In practice the relationship between law and society and the interaction of family law and the way we live our family lives is complex and multi-directional. These are issues that attract a great deal of academic attention and the role of families, family law and family policy is at the forefront of much governmental and state concern. Although on one level, the CEFL Principles fit within an apparent progression from a traditional patriarchal, marriage-centred model of parent/child relations to a more modern model which seeks to promote equality, individuality and to acknowledge greater diversity in relationships, on another it is not clear that they have fully engaged with some of the current debates surrounding parents and children.

Several aspects of the Principles might be regarded as "modern" in that they represent a shift from a widely accepted and traditional regulatory model of parent/child relations. The use of the concept of "parental responsibilities", the shift away from parental responsibilities being attributed to and exercised by only the parents of a child to include also third parties, and the presumption in favour of continuing joint parental responsibilities regardless of the breakdown of the relationship between the parents, might all be described as modern developments in the Principles. In each of these areas, however, it might be argued that the progression from traditional to modern is not clear and, in each, more detailed consideration of a range of issues and arguments would be of benefit. There are also significant dangers in promoting what is perceived to be the "modern" solution to a particular family law issue. There can be considerable disagreement as to what is the "modern" solution, and it should be recognised that "[t]here are a variety of approaches, many of which can claim to be modern and progressive."[46] While there is little in the Principles which does not, at first reading, appear modern, the value of the provisions must always be assessed in the context of their practical implementation. The politically correct and apparently progressive provision will not necessarily benefit the child as intended when it is put into practice in individual legal systems or within the context of personal family lives.

46 MCGLYNN, C., *Families and the European Union: Law, Politics and Pluralism* (Cambridge: Cambridge University Press, 2006) at p.196.

3.2.1. Parental responsibilities and responsible parents

It has become increasingly common to speak of responsibilities instead of rights and duties within the context of family relationships and their legal regulation. The shift in language reflects a move away from more authoritarian models of family relationships and also fits well with theories of citizen and state which focus on the "relationship between rights, responsibility and citizenship at the heart of a new social contract between citizens and the state."[47] What, however, is the significance of the choice of the term "parental responsibilities" in the CEFL Principles: does it represent a break with more traditional concepts of rights and duties or is it a mere change of terminology?

The CEFL in the Introduction to the Principles highlights the common trends in parent and child relations from strict paternal authority, through equal parental rights of both mothers and fathers, towards a more balanced and less hierarchical relationship between adults and children, which may be represented by a change in terminology from parental rights to parental responsibilities. There is a suggestion that the choice of terminology in the Principles is part of this gradual progression rather than representing a sharp change in approach in that, having used the concept of parental responsibilities, the Principles go on to explain that the concept incorporates a collection of rights and duties. If the term "responsibilities" is to be used, it should be adopted after consideration of the possible implications of using the word. To use the term "responsibilities" and then to include within it both rights and duties gives mixed messages. Traditionally, family law operated to identify situations in which parents had rights over children and to identify those children for whom certain adults were responsible, in that they owed them legal obligations. The distinction between "legitimate" and "illegitimate" issue was primarily related to identifying those children in respect of whom adults had obligations of support and also those who might inherit from their parents. Parental rights have also been seen as legal rights to control children. The focus of parental responsibilities is quite different and reflects the move towards a more child-centred framework. This is to be embraced. But is it an appropriate concept to describe the CEFL approach? When the concept of parental responsibilities is to be used, the component elements of these responsibilities should be analysed and classified more carefully. To what extent are the parents exercising rights and to what extent are they fulfilling obligations? If we look at what is covered by parental responsibilities in the Principles and parental rights in the legal systems, they seem to be the same. So what has changed?

---

[47] JAMES, A., "Responsibility, Children and Childhood" in BRIDGEMAN, J., KEATING, H. AND LIND, C., *Responsibility, Law and the Family* (Aldershot: Ashgate, 2008) at p.145.

In several of the jurisdictions considered in this book, the concept of parental authority remains more dominant than that of parental responsibilities and it may be that we should consider more carefully the change in terminology and ensure that it fits with the underlying legal provisions. While it may be fashionable and politically correct to move away from authority to responsibility, is it in accordance with social practices and expectations? Should the Principles take account of these problems or, better still, should the legal systems move forward?

We agree that the use of the word "responsibilities" fits with a child-centred approach that emphasises the welfare of the child in that the term has implications of responsible parenting. It can be used as a means of encouraging the adults with the care of a child to provide such care to an acceptable standard. With growing social concern about children and young people, and the role of families in helping to reduce youth crime and delinquency, it becomes increasingly important to emphasise the responsibility of parents to care for and control the development of their children. With the development too of children's rights there is some movement towards the idea that a child should have a right to have responsible parents. These ideas are not developed in the CEFL Principles which, by adhering to a traditional private law context, overlook broader public implications of family regulation. Neither does the content of parental responsibilities bring anything new to aid the problems of our times: for example, criminal justice policies, responsibility for children's anti-social and offending behaviour and the related parenting orders.

It is common when speaking of responsibilities to counterpose them to rights:

> The mantra of "no rights without responsibilities" has come to symbolise the approach of the government to the relationship between the individual, the state and the community. Whilst its meaning is fairly well understood in relation to adults, what, precisely, it means in relation to children and young people remains far from clear.[48]

It has become an increasingly accepted model of childhood that a child has developing capacity and this approach is reflected in a legal framework which attributes increasing rights and legal capacity to a child to match his or her developing maturity. As a child acquires capacity and responsibility, how does this affect the rights and responsibilities of the parents? It is common for the responsibilities of the parents to diminish as the capacity of the child grows: such a progression is offered by the "developmental paradigm" and the "standard child". The CEFL Principles might be criticised for their failure to consider the relationship between the responsibilities of the parents as compared to the responsibilities of the child. An emerging issue in some domestic systems is

48 *Ibid* at p.163.

the extent to which the responsibilities of the parents do diminish as the child acquires capacity. This can be seen, for example, in the English so-called "*Gillick* capacity test" where a child, under the age of consent of 16, is treated as having the right to consent where he or she is considered by the relevant medical practitioner to have the necessary capacity to understand the nature of the medical procedure concerned.[49] There has been some debate over whether a child who is assessed as being "*Gillick* competent", alone has the capacity to consent or whether the parents retain the right to consent on the child's behalf. Similar issues arise in respect of the criminal responsibility of a child. Where a child is treated as having sufficient maturity to be held responsible for his or her actions in terms of criminal law, do the parents of that child continue also to have responsibility? Current policy may take the view that both may be held responsible:

> In an attempt to address the "me first" culture ... children must be made to accept responsibilities for the harm they have caused. The parents of anti-social or offending children are also held to account. This has been described as the strategy of "responsibilisation".[50]

As commented in respect of the recent Danish reforms, there is no value in using the word "responsibilities" instead of authority if it is simply a change of terminology. Indeed the identification of authority and power and parental rights with a traditional system which was largely focused on the rights of the father and later of the parents, need not automatically lead us to conceive of progress only in terms of the rejection of these terms and their replacement with the concept of responsibilities. It is clear both from the Introduction to the Principles and from the domestic systems considered in this book, that the term "parental responsibilities" is not in widespread use in European countries. To ensure that the choice of the terminology "parental responsibilities" is not merely rhetorical, the infill must also be modernised.

3.2.2. Parents, third parties and de facto parenting

It is a fundamental element of the Principles, that parental responsibilities are not the sole domain of a child's parents. They will primarily be attributed to and exercised by the parents of a child but they may also be held and fulfilled by third parties, either together with, or instead of, the parents. A modern system of family law requires that it should be recognised that family relationships are increasingly diverse and it cannot be assumed that all children will live in traditional, dual

---

49 Discussed at England, *supra* at p.217.

50 KEATING, H., "Being Responsible, Becoming Responsible and Having Responsibility Thrust upon Them: Constructing the 'Responsibility' of Children and Parents" in BRIDGEMAN ET AL, *supra* note 47, p.126.

parent, marriage based families. It might be questioned, however, whether the Principles go far enough in this respect or whether they remain too much of a compromise between the traditional family and the modern social acceptance of varied relations. In a modern legal framework, is it sufficient to include both parents and third parties or has the Commission missed an important opportunity to consider more radically the nature of parents, parenting and childcare?

In considering who should hold and exercise parental responsibilities, there are many separate and interrelated issues to consider. Who is a parent and how is parentage defined by law? Modern legal systems, in devising rules for the identification of parents, need to ensure that they adapt to fit changing social patterns and also developing methods of reproduction. Some legal systems may provide for different categories of parent: genetic parents and social parents. Separate from, but related to, the question of parentage, is the important issue of identifying those adults who have parenting rights and responsibilities in respect of children. Should all genetic parents automatically have parental responsibilities in respect of their children? Should the partner of a genetic parent, whether married or not, have a legally recognised relationship, involving rights and responsibilities, in respect of the child? Is it sufficient for a modern legal system to recognise the possibility of granting parental responsibilities to a range of adults beyond a child's genetic parents or should there be a more widespread rethinking of the provision of parenting towards children?

The CEFL Principles make it clear that the issue of how to establish parentage is to be left to the domestic law of the individual states. While this may be understandable and fits with a system where a distinction persists between parents and parenting, it may be that there should be deeper consideration of this issue. Why does family law regulate the issue of parentage? Clearly there are important social and psychological issues of identity and emotional well-being associated with the establishment and disclosure of parentage but what are the principal legal concerns? Identifying the parents of a child by law has traditionally been related to kinship, lineage and questions of property:

> Sometimes the identification of a child's parents is contested. In some circumstances, claiming the entitlements of parenthood is of paramount importance and hence, parenthood is a status eagerly sought. Individuals compete, either legally or socially, for the status of 'parent'. In other circumstances, the obligations imposed upon a parent may be more salient and so individuals seek to avoid being identified as the parent of a child.[51]

---

[51] SHAPIRO, J., "Changing Ways, New Technologies and the Devaluation of the Genetic Connection to Children" in MACLEAN, M., (ed) *Family Law and Family Values*, (Oxford: Hart Publishing, 2005) p. 81.

The parental responsibilities dealt with in the Principles are closely related to the personal development of a child and to his or her lack of legal capacity. The CEFL framework is based on the principle that, having established legal affiliation, then parental responsibilities should automatically follow. Third parties, although they may obtain parental responsibilities, are a secondary category and it is provided that "parental responsibilities of third parties remain an exception".[52] In particular, three groups of third parties are identified as having a good claim to parental rights: a child's grandparents, foster parents and other parties who have close family or other ties to a child.[53]

Although in many cases, a child will live with and be cared for by at least one of his or her natural parents, developments in assisted reproduction together with changing social conditions make it much more common for children to live in family situations together with a range of adults to whom they have no genetic connection. Either the traditional model of parentage based on marriage may be modernised by extending the legal consequences of marriage and genetic parenting to an expanding range of analogous relationships or alternatively a more radical restructuring of the approach to parenting may be adopted. To move away from a framework based on the traditional model of two natural, heterosexual parents may also assist with the practical dilemma of what to call the persons who hold parental responsibilities and indeed how to describe the responsibilities themselves. Assisted reproduction and adoption by same sex couples raises the very practical legal issue of how to describe the two same sex adults who care for a child. To move away from the two parent model also clarifies the issue of whether more than two persons may simultaneously hold and exercise parental responsibilities in respect of a child.

Whereas the CEFL Principles are progressive to some extent in that they recognise the possibility of parental responsibilities being attributed to and exercised by third parties in some, undefined, circumstances, they remain relatively restricted by reliance on the traditional model of establishing parentage and of clearly distinguishing between parents and third parties. Their commitment to a principle that grants automatic parental responsibilities on the basis of established parentage, although progressive to the extent that it moves away from reliance on marriage as a determining factor, appears out of step with national systems which have decided to concentrate on the de facto acknowledgement of parentage, in respect of fathers, rather than the simple establishment of the genetic relationship. Other approaches have atttempted to move further away from a traditional model by focusing on a "'child-centric' lens that seeks to give pre-eminent weight to relationships that nurture children by contributing to

52 BOELE-WOELKI ET AL, *supra* note 1, p. 77.
53 *Ibid*, p. 72.

their health, happiness and self-awareness."[54] A more radical reconsideration of parentage and parenting may also assist in the development of a more inclusive framework which recognises that, even with amendments and extensions, "the nuclear family model is a powerful ideal and is used as a template to exclude those who do not fit within its pattern,"[55] and moves beyond it.

4. IDEALS IN PRACTICE?

It could be asked whether it is legitimate for the legislature to interfere and try to change tradition and social reality? How far can concessions be given to tradition? How can a balance be struck? What kind of problems may be caused for society by slavishly adhering to a standard model? Should the ensuing dilemmas be acknowledged, accepted or ignored? What are the consequences of each of these stances? Individuals do not order their family practices with primary reference to political boundaries or the state legal tradition. Indeed, there are even conflicting ideas and concerns within a single legal tradition's regulation of families. This internal complexity of the tradition cannot be overlooked.[56]

Moreover, how are the sociological realities to be taken into consideration? While the national discussions highlight the diversity and difference between societies and legal frameworks, they also create a strong sense that there is much in common. The accommodation of diverse interests within families and the difficulty of regulating personal life is a challenge which is shared in all legal systems and it is essential that principles, no matter how ideal in theory, must also work in practice. The CEFL Principles reflect the values of an ideal world, one towards which the legal systems are expected to strive. Many of the Principles do not describe reality and therefore may remain as legal constructs. They represent aspirations and do not necessarily reflect actuality. It is true that these Principles are geared towards law reform. However, can we say that the aspirations are realistic?

Two of the strongest themes which inform the Principles are that the child should be the focus of the legal framework and that the parent/child relationship should not be affected by changes in the relationship between the parents. In a European context these are familiar provisions which are well known and established in

54 CAMPBELL, A., "Conceiving Parents through Law" (2007) 21 *International Journal of Law, Policy and the Family* 242.

55 RAMSEY, S.H., "Constructing Parenthood for Stepparents: Parents By Estoppel and De Facto Parents Under the American Law Institute's Principles of the Law of Family Dissolution" (2001) 8 *Duke Journal of Gender American Law and Policy* 285.

56 See LECKEY, R., "Cohabitation and Comparative Method" (2009) 72:1 *Modern Law Review*, pp. 48–72.

some domestic systems but nonetheless they are in many cases less than ideal in terms of their practical implementation. If they are to benefit children in the way that is intended, then it is not enough for them to be adopted and championed by the CEFL as Principles, they need to be supported and made to work in practice. Obviously this cannot be a criticism of the Principles themselves but of national reform procedures.

4.1. A CHILD-CENTRIC MODEL

In many legal systems, and certainly since the adoption of the UN Convention on the Rights of the Child, it has become commonplace to give the child a central role in any decisions affecting him or her. This is seen in two particular principles: the welfare or best interests provision and the right of the child to be heard. While it would have been surprising for the CEFL Principles not to be based around these two principles, it is important to highlight the ongoing challenges which they present in practice. It is easy to repeat the mantra of the best interests of the child but the difficulties should not be overlooked of how to assess and protect these interests. It is similarly straightforward to state the right of the child to be heard in decisions which concern him or her but practically difficult to facilitate the child's participation in the otherwise adult process of decision making.

The Principles are firmly grounded in a model of parent and child relations which increasingly aspires towards individual equality. This move was first seen in the "emancipation of women, which led to the replacement of the more or less absolute power of the married father as the head of the family by the equal responsibility of both the mother and the father".[57] This transformation of the legal relations between parents has more recently been reflected in the increasingly egalitarian nature of the relationship between parents and children. The declining authority of parents combined with the growing emergence, particularly through the development of children's rights, of the child as a distinct legal person, have contributed towards a significant shift in the way that the relationships between parents, and between parents and children, are conceived. This legal shift reflects widespread developments within social theory which conceive of the child as a developing adult: "From the developmental perspective we view the child's progress as an approach towards a terminus which is the state of adulthood,"[58] as "becoming" rather than "being". While this approach may be preferred to one which draws a clear distinction between parents, who have full legal capacity and power, and children who have none, it involves difficult questions as to how to assess the child's maturity and stage of development and how to balance this

57 BOELE-WOELKI ET AL, *supra* note 1, p. 13.
58 ARCHARD, D., *Children: Rights and Childhood* (London: Routledge, 1993) at p. 33.

with the corresponding diminution in parental control. The Principles are to be commended for disentangling and non-intertwining of age and competence though many of the systems under survey seem to adhere to age as a determining factor to being "en route".

Principle 3:3 provides that "in all matters concerning parental responsibilities the best interests of the child should be the primary consideration" and, while individual national systems and different international measures may differ in their choice of terminology, it is a well established and supported approach. In its Commentary, the CEFL notes that it is a concept which is generally not further defined either in other international instruments or in national legal provisions.[59] On that basis, the CEFL Principle leaves it as a concept to be applied by national systems without any further guidance. While this has many benefits in terms of enabling it to be applied appropriately within specific national and family circumstances, the practical application of the best interests concept is not without criticism. It should be remembered that,

> [w]hile it is relatively uncontentious to accept that the child's welfare should be paramount [...] it is quite another matter to attempt to formulate what it is that promotes or detracts from a child's welfare. [60]

How should the welfare of a child be assessed? In an ideal world it might be thought that the persons best suited to protect and promote the welfare of a child are the child's parents but issues may arise where the values of the parents do not match those of the majority in society, those who have a particular but specific interest in the child's development, for example, doctors, or those who have a supervisory and adjudicatory role – the judges. While the Commentary in Principle 3:19 indicates that a parent should have the freedom to educate and guide their child in a religious context as part of their parental responsibilities, religion and particular religious beliefs are an example of a situation in which the assessment of a child's welfare may be very different depending on the belief system and religious philosophy of those making the assessment. A doctor may assess a child's welfare in narrower clinical terms than a parent who is concerned for the child's holistic welfare. The CEFL Principles offer no guidance as to how these different assessments should be balanced and while it is acknowledged that "the welfare of the child is not a technical legal concept"[61] and that it will remain to some extent a subjective test, informed by the beliefs, values and experiences of

59 See discussion of Principle 3:3 at BOELE-WOELKI ET AL, *supra* note 1, pp.34–38.

60 SUTHERLAND, E. E., *Child and Family Law* (2nd ed) (Edinburgh: W.Green/Thomson, 2008), para.6–147.

61 CLIVE, E.M., *The Law of Husband and Wife in Scotland* (4th ed) (Edinburgh: W.Green, 2007), p.505.

the assessor, consideration should be given to how the best interests test is applied in practice.

It is provided by Principle 3:25 that both the child and the parents should have the right to maintain regular contact with each other. There is discussion in the Commentary of questions as to whether the right of parents to contact should be accompanied by a duty on the parents to maintain regular contact and of the extent to which similar provisions should apply in respect of other categories of persons with whom the child has close ties. In all of this discussion, there is an underlying assumption that contact with both parents is in the best interests of the child and that the problem lies in negligent parents who do not comply with their obligation to maintain contact. There is, however, no reference to the question of whether or not a child wishes to maintain contact. To what extent can this Principle be said to focus on the child or does it still reflect, to a greater extent, the needs and wishes of the non-resident parent?

Similar questions can be asked in respect of the right of the child to be heard. As provided for in Principle 3:6, the right of the child to be consulted, informed and heard should apply in all matters concerning him but, in practice, the child most often is formally heard in the context of disputes – usually in court – between the parents. Here care is needed to ensure that the hearing of the child operates for the benefit of the child and is not used as a tool by either parent to assist in achieving the goals identified by the parents. The difficulties of facilitating the child in giving his or her opinion in a court setting are well known but it would be inappropriate to concentrate on the child's right to be heard only within the context of judicial proceedings. The CEFL Principles express a strong preference for agreement rather than adjudication and this is to a large extent reflected in the national systems which have been considered. Research, and experience, would tend to support the view that where the parties can reach agreement as to aspects of family relations then that is likely to work in practice to a greater degree than where a solution is imposed upon them. It is difficult, however, to integrate this preference for agreement with the emphasis on the child's right to be heard. Concern is already expressed about the extent to which the weaker adult party, may not benefit from a negotiated agreement and it is therefore essential that practical consideration be given as to how children may participate in and influence mediation, negotiation and other informal decision making procedures. Indeed, children's right to participate, for example in mediation work, may be more important than the right to be heard. A major shift of emphasis is needed which the Principles do not actively encourage.

4.2. PARENTAL SEPARATION AND CONTINUING RELATIONSHIPS

Increasing relationship breakdown, separation and divorce are factors of modern life throughout Europe and therefore the need to provide for parenting, when adult relationships terminate, is common to all modern legal systems. The Principles have strongly endorsed the approach that both parents should have equal parental responsibilities and that these should be unaffected by status of the relationship between the parents. While this is an approach which appears to protect the child from circumstances over which he or she has no control, that is the relationship between his or her parents, it is in many cases very difficult to apply in practice.

All of the national systems considered in this book have legal provisions to the effect that where both parents have parental responsibilities, they are equal. This applies in all of the systems during the existence of marriage or other relationship between the parents. In some systems it is explicitly said that there may not always be equality in practice: in Turkey, for example, commenting on the CEFL Principle 3:11, it is stated that:

> Parents exercise parental responsibilities together and they have an equal say in everything. This principle accords with Turkish law but not necessarily with societal facts. Turkey is a male dominated society and the father's wishes would hold sway, especially when there is disagreement.[62]

In other systems, it is suggested that while the law provides for equal parental responsibilities, in practice, primary child care is often provided by one parent, most often the mother.[63]

While compliance, at least in theory, with the Principle of equal parental responsibilities is possible for all of the systems considered, and it appears a relatively well established provision which fits with wider principles of gender equality, a more difficult Principle to accommodate and to implement is that which provides that the divorce or separation of the parents should have no effect on their parental responsibilities. In many legal systems, it has become increasingly accepted that the breakdown of the relationship between the parents should not affect their continued joint exercise of parental responsibilities. This approach, which is adopted by the CEFL Principles, has as a starting point the continuation of parental responsibilities regardless of what happens to the

---

62 See *supra* Turkey at p.249.
63 See *supra* Estonia at p.35.

relationship between the adults. This is a modern approach in that it appears to favour the child, to focus on the continuing relations of the adults with their child rather than concentrating on the needs and wishes of the adults and allowing their relationship to dictate what happens to the children. The CEFL Principles have embraced this approach by providing that parental responsibilities should not be affected by the separation or divorce of the persons who hold and exercise these responsibilities.

Even in legal systems where this fits with the domestic provisions of family law, there remain significant challenges. While it may be a theoretical ideal, it remains extremely difficult for many couples, in practice, to co-operate to the required level with their ex-partner. In many legal systems, for those going through the process of splitting from their spouse or partner, the primary legal objective will be to achieve a clean break and yet at the same time they are being required to maintain their relationship with their child and to combine in terms of providing joint parenting. Even for couples whose separation is fairly friendly this combination of objectives is likely to prove difficult. In most of the national systems considered, divorce or separation has no effect on parental responsibilities and joint exercise of them is at least an option for parents. In Turkey, custody must be given to one parent only following divorce: "joint custody after divorce or separation is not regarded in the best interests of the child, possibly because most divorces end in acrimony."[64]

Other challenges may also be raised in respect of the preference for ongoing joint parenting. While considerable research indicates that it is best for children to maintain relations with both parents following divorce or separation, the evidence is not conclusive and as ever the quality of the relationships between the adults themselves and with their children is central to the success of the continuing contact.[65] The importance of effectiveness of post-divorce contact on the adjustment of a child may also be affected by the quality of the child's relationship with the non-residential parent prior to the divorce. The situation is often highlighted of the father being in the unusual position of spending more time alone with his child after divorce than during the relationship. It is not to say that such a situation may not produce beneficial relationships in the longer term but it needs to be recognised that introducing a legal presumption in favour of ongoing contact with both parents is not in itself a panacea to the potential impact of divorce or separation on children. It may also be perceived as a threat to the parent who has had primary responsibility for childcare – in many cases the mother: "while equal parenting post-divorce remains an ideal, where it is

64 See *supra* Turkey at p.249.
65 For discussion of a range of research into post-divorce contact see MUELLER-JOHNSON, K., "Supporting Conflicted Post-Divorce Parenting" in MACLEAN, *supra* note 51.

not supported by equal parenting pre-divorce, considerable hardship results, predominantly for women who were primary carers".[66]

To make joint parenting post-separation or divorce work requires a good level of co-operation between the parents and may require considerable support to help all parties to adjust. The introduction of a bare legal provision is unlikely to be enough. This is particularly relevant in the situation where the relationship between the adults has been hostile and possibly abusive. In that situation, considerable concerns have been raised about the benefits of maintaining contact with the non-resident parent, assuming that person was also the perpetrator of the abuse. Even with the provision of supervised contact and the possibility of contact taking place within a supervised contact centre, the emotional impact on the parent who has residence and in turn on the child may question the benefits of maintaining contact. Increasingly it is suggested that it may not always be in the interests of a child to maintain relations with both parents.

So although to have the option of joint parenting and even to consider arrangements such as alternate residence may be described as progressive measures, to insist on such arrangements in all cases or even to begin from a presumption in their favour may not be of benefit. A modern system is surely above all else a system which allows for diversity and which recognises and accommodates individuals. While joint parenting and continued contact may be a good thing for many children and families it may not always work or be appropriate. It has also been argued that far from being modern and progressive it can be viewed as an attempt to salvage the traditional family in a society which is increasingly concerned about family breakdown:

> [s]ociety requires that there is a strong counterpart to increased freedom for the couple: the accompanying obligation for both parents to maintain their responsibility towards their child and to respect and encourage the other parent's responsibility.[67]

Principles should aid in the establishment of parenting as culture rather than as practice.

5. CONCLUDING REMARKS

An argument can be made against harmonised norms superseding cultural diversity. The rhetoric of such norms suggests supremacy and finality, as it is the

---

66 MCGLYNN, *supra* note 46 at p.89.

67 VONECHE, L.C. AND BASTARD, B., "Can Co-Parenting Be Enforced? Family Law Reform and Family Life in France" in MACLEAN, *supra* note 51, at p.98.

ultimate expression of generality and homogeneity; yet, cultural context indicates open-endedness, at times incommensurable co-existence of cultures, values and viewpoints, and diversity.[68] If legal frameworks are to function satisfactorily, cultural context must be taken into account.

There is a commonly held assertion that the EU is a union of common values. The CEFL Principles rely on this assertion. However, it is also acknowledged that Europe is a space of immense cultural diversity. When the existence of diversity both in socio-culture and legal culture within the boundaries of the EU is recognised, then, it must be admitted that there is no actual unity, and there is no uniform entity brought about by the EU: there is heterogeneity within its borders.[69] This acknowledgement does not have to go so far as to claim that a plurality of parallel legalities should operate simultaneously. What are the limits of the diversity of values within the EU? Can these limits be drawn both theoretically and empirically? How can the differences be accommodated within an overarching legal framework? Do the CEFL Principles regarding Parental Responsibilities provide for such a framework? There is also a form of unity created by the EU however. Do the CEFL Principles help us in enhancing this unity? So, though it may be awkward, can we conclude that there is both unity and diversity within the boundaries of the EU.[70] Where do the Principles stand in this context?

With these in mind, a claim can be made that the actors best suited to the task are judges performing a balancing act considering "actuality" and using the bottom-up model to alleviate the harshness of the top-down model,[71] which more often than not, reflects the "rhetoric" of inclusiveness, seen as a sine quo non of our times.[72] However, in an effort to meet the demands of unity for example, the realities of social relationships have been ignored and brushed aside, in the hope that things would conform to the new ideal.[73] This is most striking in the area of

---

68 See for a discussion of issues central to the concept of diversity FREDMAN, S., "Double Trouble: Multiple Discrimination and EU Law" (2005) 2 *European Anti-discrimination Law Review*, 13.

69 See for a discussion of the paradox of "unity in diversity", HENDRY, J., "'Unity in Diversity': Questions of (Legal) Culture in the European Union", (2008) 3:1 *Journal of Comparative Law*, pp. 289–294.

70 *Ibid.*

71 See ÖRÜCÜ, E., "Judicial navigation as official law meets culture in Turkey" (2008) 4.1 *International Journal of Law in Context*, 35.

72 Consider the notion of "mainstreaming" gender, which also amounts to "sidelining", in the second half of the 1990s at the EU level. See KOK, W. and High Level Group *Facing the Challenge: The Lisbon Strategy for Growth and Employment* (Luxembourg: European Communities, 2004). However also consider the idea of "intersectionality" used in the diversity discourse and in understanding inequalities. See YUVAL-DAVIS, N., "Intersectionality and Feminist Politics" (2006) 13:3 *European Journal of Women's Studies*, 193.

73 See WALBY, S., "The European Union and Gender Equality: Emergent Varieties of Gender Regime" (2004) 11:1 *Social Policy*, 4.

family law, in the relevant conventions and now in the CEFL Principles. Though the Principles themselves are non-binding, harmonised rules for inspiration, still they address themselves to legislatures, hence to the top-down law making process. Judges, as navigators between rhetoric and actuality, must be fully prepared and equipped to act creatively to fill the gaps and give direction to the legal rules in order to satisfy the needs of the society, which they serve.[74] The courts must be allowed to mitigate the standardising impact of the Principles. The Principles on the whole do not seem to cater for this, addressing themselves to the national legislatures alone.

It can be claimed that there is now developing a universal tendency towards a private law, especially family law, which is more society-oriented.[75] The CEFL Principles regarding Parental Responsibilities do not seem to support such a stance either. For instance, it is true that rights discourse can strengthen the politics of gender justice; but in the process "family realities" must be protected.[76] Therefore what is most needed, is judges equipped with more discretion. The CEFL Principles do not provide judges with much discretion and contribute to the creation of a standardised normative system to deal with culturally diverse societies, which is still a fact in the European Union.

The CEFL Principles on Parental Responsibilities do, however, represent a considerable achievement in terms of the bringing together of a range of national systems on child law and they aim to promote and further develop the importance of placing the child at the centre of the the legal framework of regulation. While there is much convergence and little disagreement with many of the Principles, there are also many difficult issues and practical challenges which the Principles do not tackle. Although individual legal systems may diverge in their detailed approach to the implementation of similar principles and social and cultural perspectives may develop at different speeds and with diverse influences and concerns, the practical challenges which face all of the systems are more notable for their commonality than for what distinguishes them. No matter how ideal the provisions and principles may appear in theory, they require to be implemented in practice in a way which is consistent with their underlying objective.

74 See ÖRÜCÜ *supra* note 71.

75 CHEREDNYCHENKO, O., "The Constitutionalization of Contract law: Something New under the Sun?" (2004) 8(1) *Electronic Journal of Comparative Law*, 1 at 4.

76 See OKIN, S.M. ET AL, (eds) *Is Multiculturalism Bad for Women?* (Princeton University Press, 1999).

ANNEXES: THE QUESTIONNAIRE AND THE PRINCIPLES

QUESTIONNAIRE

INTRODUCTION

The following definitions of parental responsibilities are used in international instruments:

1. **Hague Convention of 19 October 1996 on jurisdiction, applicable law, recognition, enforcement and co-operation in respect of parental responsibility and measures for the protection of children**

   Article 1 sub 2: For the purposes of this Convention, the term ' parental responsibility' includes parental authority, or any analogues relationship of authority determining the rights, powers and responsibilities of parents, guardians or other legal representatives in relation of the person or the property of the child.

2. **Council Regulation (EC) No 2201/2003 of 27 November 2003 concerning jurisdiction and the recognition and enforcement of judgments in matrimonial matters and the matters of parental responsibility, repealing Regulation (EC) no 1347/2000**

   Article 2 sub 7: The term 'parental responsibility' shall mean all rights and duties relating to the person or the property of a child which are given to a natural of legal person by judgment by operation of law or by agreement having legal effect. The term shall include rights of custody and rights of access.

3. **Council of Europe: 'White Paper' of 15 January 2002 on principles concerning the establishment and legal consequences of parentage**

   Principle 18: Parental responsibilities are a collection of duties and powers, which aim at ensuring the moral and material welfare of children, in particular:
   - Care and protection
   - Maintenance of personal relationships
   - Provision of education
   - Legal representation
   - Determination of residence and
   - Administration of property.

This questionnaire uses the definition of the Council of Europe (White Paper) as a working definition.

A. GENERAL

1. Having regard to the concept of parental responsibilities as defined by the council of europe (see above), explain the concept or concepts used in your national legal system.
2. Explain whether your national concept or concepts encompass:
   (a) care and protection;
   (b) maintenance of personal relationships;
   (c) provision of education;
   (d) legal representation;
   (e) determination of residence;
   (f) administration of property.
   (please answer (a), (b), (c), (d), (e) and (f) separately).
3. In what circumstances (e.g. Child reaching majority or marrying) do parental responsibilities automatically come to an end?
4. What is the current source of law for parental responsibilities?
5. Give a brief history of the main developments of the law concerning parental responsibilities.
6. Are there any recent proposals for reform in this area?

B. THE CONTENTS OF PARENTAL RESPONSIBILITIES

7. Describe what the contents of parental responsibilities are according to your national law including case law.
8. What is the position taken in your national law with respect to:
   (a) Care;
   (b) Education;
   (c) Religious upbringing;
   (d) Disciplinary measures and corporal punishment;
   (e) Medical treatment;
   (f) and legal representation.
   (Please answer (a), (b), (c), (d), (e) and (f) separately).
9. What is the position taken in respect of the child's right to be heard with regard to the issues mentioned under Q 8 ((a)-(f)). What relevance is given to the age and maturity of the child?
10. Do(es) the holder(s) of parental responsibilities has(have) the right to administer the child's property?
11. If yes, explain the content of this right.
12. Are there restrictions with respect to:
    (a) Certain goods and/or values (inherited property, gift…);

(b) Salary of the child; or
(c) Certain transactions?
(Please answer (a), (b) and (c) separately).

13. Are there special rules protecting children from indebtedness caused by the holder(s) of parental responsibilities?
14. Do the contents of parental responsibilities differ according to the holder(s) of parental responsibilities (e.g. married, unmarried, parents not living together, stepparents, foster parents or other persons). If so, describe in some detail how it differs.

C. ATTRIBUTION OF PARENTAL RESPONSIBILITIES

I. *Married parents*

15. Who has parental responsibilities when the parents are:
    (a) Married at the time of the child's birth;
    (b) Not married at that time but marry later?
    (Please answer (a) and (b) separately).
16. How, if at all, is the attribution of parental responsibilities affected by:
    (a) Divorce;
    (b) Legal separation;
    (c) Annulment of the marriage;
    (d) Factual separation.
    (Please answer (a), (b), (c) and (d) separately).
17. To what extent, if at all, are the parents free to agree upon the attribution of parental responsibilities after divorce, legal separation or annulment of the marriage? If they are, are these agreements subject to scrutiny by a competent authority.
18. May the competent authority attribute joint parental responsibilities to the parents of the child even against the wish of both parents/one of the parents? To what extent, if at all, should the competent authority take account of a parent's violent behaviour towards the other parent?
19. Provide statistical information on the attribution of parental responsibilities after divorce, legal separation or annulment of the marriage.

II. *Unmarried parents*

20. Who has parental responsibilities when the parents are not married?
21. Does it make a difference if the parents have formalised their mutual relationship in some way (registered partnership, civil union, pacte civil de solidarité…).
22. Under what condition, if at all, can
    (a) The unmarried mother;

(b) The unmarried father, obtain parental responsibilities.
(Please answer (a) and (b) separately).

23. How, if at all, is the attribution of parental responsibilities affected by the ending of the unmarried parents' relationship?
24. May the competent authority attribute joint parental responsibilities to the parents also against the wish of both parents/one of the parents? To what extent, if at all, may the competent authority take into account a parent's violent behaviour towards the other parent?
25. To what extent, if at all, are unmarried parents free to agree upon the attribution of parental responsibilities after the ending of their relationship?
26. Provide statistical information available regarding the attribution of parental responsibilities for unmarried parents.

III. Other persons

27. Under what conditions, if at all, can the partner of a parent holding parental responsibilities obtain parental responsibilities, when, he/she is:
    (a) Married to that parent;
    (b) Living with that parent in a formalised relationship (registered partnership, civil union, *pacte civil de solidarité*...);
    (c) or living with that parent in a non formalised relationship?
    (Please answer (a), (b) and (c) separately).
28. Does it make any difference if the partner of the parent holding parental responsibilities is of the same sex?
29. How, if at all, is the attribution of parental responsibilities in the partner affected by the ending of his/her relationship with the parent? Distinguish according to the different relationships referred to in Q 27 and Q 28.
30. To what extent, if at all, is the parent holding parental responsibilities and his/her partner free to agree upon the attribution of parental responsibilities after the ending of his/her relationship with the parent? Distinguish according to the different relationships referred to in Q 27 and Q 28.
31. Under what conditions, if at all, can other persons not being a parent or a partner of a parent holding parental responsibilities, obtain parental responsibilities (e.g. members of the child's family, close friends, foster parent...)? Specify, where such other persons may obtain parental responsibilities, if it is in addition to or in substitution of existing holder(s) of parental responsibilities.
32. Under what conditions, if at all, can a public body obtain parental responsibilities? Specify, where it is so obtained, if it is in addition to or in substitution of existing holder(s) of parental responsibilities.
33. To whom are the parental responsibilities attributed in the case of:
    (a) The death of a parent holding parental responsibilities;

(b) The death of both parents of whom at least one was holding parental responsibilities at the time of the death?
(Please answer (a) and (b) separately).

34. To what extent, if at all, may the holder(s) of parental responsibilities appoint a new holder(s) upon his/her/their death? If such an appointment is permitted, must it take place in a special form, e.g. will?

D. THE EXERCISE OF PARENTAL RESPONSIBILITIES

I. *Interests of the child*

35. In exercising parental responsibilities, how are the interests of the child defined in your national legal system?

II. *Joint parental responsibilities*

36. If parental responsibilities are held jointly by two or more persons, are they held equally?
37. If parental responsibilities holders cannot agree on an issue, how is the dispute resolved? For example does the holder of parental responsibilities have the authority to act alone? In this respect is a distinction made between important decisions and decisions of a daily nature? Does it make any difference if the child is only living with one of the holders of the parental responsibilities?
38. If holders of parental responsibilities cannot agree on an issue, can they apply to a competent authority to resolve their dispute? If applicable, specify whether this authority's competence is limited to certain issues e.g. residence or contact.
39. **To what extent, if at all, may a holder of parental responsibilties act alone if there is more than one holder of parental responsibilities?**
40. **Under what circumstances, if at all, may the competent authority permit the residence of the child to be changed within the same country and/or abroad (so called relocation) without the consent of one of the holders of parental responsibilities?**
41. Under what conditions, if at all, may the competent authority decree that the child should, on an alternating basis, reside with both holders of parental responsibilities (e.g. every other month with mother/father)?

III. Sole parental responsibilities

42. Does a parent with sole parental responsibilities have full authority to act alone, or does he/she have a duty to consult:
(a) The other parent;
(b) Other persons, bodies or competent authorities?
(Please answer (a) and (b) separately).

E. CONTACT

43. Having regard to the definition by the Council of Europe (see above), explain the concepts of contact used in your national legal system.
44. To what extent, if at all, does the child have a right of contact with:
    (a) A parent holding parental responsibilities but not living with the child;
    (b) A parent not holding parental responsibilities;
    (c) Persons other than parents (e.g. grandparents, stepparents, siblings etc...)?
    (Please answer (a), (b) and (c) separately).
45. Is the right to have contact referred to in Q 43 also a right and/or a duty of the parent or the other persons concerned?
46. To what extent, if at all, are the parents free to make contact arrangements? If they can, are these arrangements subject to scrutiny by a competent authority?
47. Can a competent authority exclude, limit or subject to conditions, the exercise of contact? If so, which criteria are decisive?
48. What if any, are the consequences on parental responsibilities, if a holder of parental responsibilities with whom the child is living, disregards the child's right to contact with:
    (a) A parent;
    (b) Other persons?
    (Please answer (a) and (b) separately).

F. DELEGATION OF PARENTAL RESPONSIBILITIES

49. To what extent, if at all, may the holder(s) of parental responsibilities delegate its exercise?
50. To what extent, if at all, may a person not holding parental responsibilities apply to a competent authority for a delegation of parental responsibilities?

G. DISCHARGE OF PARENTAL RESPONSIBILITIES

51. Under what circumstances, if at all, should the competent authorities in you legal system discharge the holder(s) of his/her/their parental responsibilities for reasons such as maltreatment, negligence or abuse of the child, mental illness of the holder of parental responsibilities, etc.? To what extent, if at all, should the competent authority take into account a parent's violent behaviour towards the other parent?
52. Who, in the circumstances referred to in Q 51, has the right or the duty to request the discharge of parental responsibilities?
53. To what extent, if at all, are rights of contact permitted between the child and the previous holder of parental responsibilities after the latter has been discharged of his/her parental responsibilities?

54. To what extent, if at all, can the previous holder(s) of parental responsibilities, who has been discharged of his/her parental responsibilities, regain them?

H. PROCEDURAL ISSUES

55. Who is the competent authority to decide disputes concerning parental responsibilities, questions of residence of the child or contact? Who is the competent authority to carry out an investigation relating to the circumstances of the child in a dispute on parental responsibility, residence or contact?
56. Under what conditions, if any, may a legally effective decision or agreement on parental responsibilities, the child's residence or contact, be reviewed by a competent auythority? Is it, e.g., required that the circumstances have changed after the decision or agreement was made and/or that a certain period of time has time has passed since the decision or agreement?
57. What alternative disputes solving mechanisms, if any, e.g. mediation or counselling, are offered in your legal system? Are such mechanisms also available at the stage of enforcement of a decision/agreement concerning parental responsibilities, the child's residence or contact?
58. To what extent, if at all, is an order or an agreement on parental responsibilities, the child's residence or contact enforceable and in practice enforced? Describe the system of enforcement followed in your national legal system. Under what conditions, if at all, may enforcement be refused?
59. To what extent, if at all, are children heard when a competent authority decides upon parental responsibilities, the child's residence or contact, e.g., upon a dispute, when scrutinizing an agreement, when appointing or discharging holder(s) of parental responsibilities, upon enforcement of a decision or agreement?
60. How will the child be heard (e.g. directly by the competent authority, a specially appointed expert or social worker)?
61. How, if at all, is the child legally represented in disputes concerning:
    (a) Parental responsibilities;
    (b) The child's residence; or
    (c) Contact?
    (Please answer (a), (b) and (c) separately).
62. What relevance is given in your national legal system to the age and maturity of the child in respect of Q 59–61?

PRINCIPLES OF EUROPEAN FAMILY LAW REGARDING PARENTAL RESPONSIBILITIES

PREAMBLE

Recognising that, notwithstanding the existing diversities of national family law systems, there is nevertheless a growing convergence of laws;

Recognising that the free movement of persons within Europe is hindered by the remaining differences;

Desiring to contribute to common European values regarding the child's rights and welfare;

Desiring to contribute to the harmonisation of family law in Europe and to further facilitate the free movement of persons within Europe;

The Commission on European Family Law recommends the following Principles:

CHAPTER I: DEFINITIONS

Principle 3:1 Concept of parental responsibilities

Parental responsibilities are a collection of rights and duties aimed at promoting and safeguarding the welfare of the child. They encompass in particular:

(a) care, protection and education;
(b) maintenance of personal relationships;
(c) determination of residence;
(d) administration of property, and
(e) legal representation.

Principle 3:2 Holder of parental responsibilities

(1) A holder of parental responsibilities is any person having the rights and duties listed in Principle 3:1 either in whole or in part.
(2) Subject to the following Principles, holders of parental responsibilities are:
    (a) the child's parents, as well as
    (b) persons other than the child's parents having parental responsibilities in addition to or instead of the parents.

CHAPTER II: RIGHTS OF THE CHILD

Principle 3:3 Best interests of the child
In all matters concerning parental responsibilities the best interests of the child should be the primary consideration.

Principle 3:4 Autonomy of the child
The child's autonomy should be respected in accordance with the developing ability and need of the child to act independently.

Principle 3:5 Non-discrimination of the child
Children should not be discriminated on grounds such as sex, race, colour, language, religion, political or other opinion, national, ethnic or social origin, sexual orientation, disability, property, birth or other status, irrespective of whether these grounds refer to the child or to the holders of parental responsibilities.

Principle 3:6 Child's right to be heard

Having regard to the child's age and maturity, the child should have the right to be informed, consulted and to express his or her opinion in all matters concerning the child, with due weight given to the views expressed by him or her.

Principle 3:7 Conflict of interests
The interests of the child should be protected whenever they may be in conflict with the interests of the holders of parental responsibilities.

CHAPTER III: PARENTAL RESPONSIBILITIES OF PARENTS AND THIRD PERSONS

Principle 3:8 Parents
Parents, whose legal parentage has been established, should have parental responsibilities for the child.

Principle 3:9 Third persons
Parental responsibilities may in whole or in part also be attributed to a person other than a parent.

Principle 3:10 Effect of dissolution and separation
Parental responsibilities should neither be affected by the dissolution or annulment of the marriage or other formal relationship nor by the legal or factual separation between the parents.

CHAPTER IV: EXERCISE OF PARENTAL RESPONSIBILITIES

SECTION A: PARENTS

Principle 3:11 Joint exercise

Parents having parental responsibilities should have an equal right and duty to exercise such responsibilities and whenever possible they should exercise them jointly.

Principle 3:12 Daily matters, important and urgent decisions

(1) Parents having joint parental responsibilities should have the right to act alone with respect to daily matters.

(2) Important decisions concerning matters such as education, medical treatment, the child's residence, or the administration of his or her property should be taken jointly. In urgent cases a parent should have the right to act alone. The other parent should be informed without undue delay.

Principle 3:13 Agreement on exercise

(1) Subject to the best interests of the child, parents having joint parental responsibilities may agree on the exercise of parental responsibilities.

(2) The competent authority may scrutinize the agreement.

Principle 3:14 Disagreement on exercise

(1) Where parents having joint parental responsibilities cannot agree on an important matter they may apply to the competent authority.

(2) The competent authority should promote agreement between the parents.

(3) Where agreement cannot be reached the competent authority should divide the exercise of parental responsibilities between the parents or decide the dispute. Nigel: do we have to insert a comma after reached?

Principle 3:15 Sole exercise upon agreement or decision

Subject to the best interests of the child a parent may exercise parental responsibilities alone

(a) upon agreement between the parents according to Principle 3:13, or

(b) upon a decision of the competent authority.

Principle 3:16 Sole exercise by one parent

If only one parent has parental responsibilities he or she should exercise them alone.

SECTION B: THIRD PERSONS

Principle 3:17 Exercise in addition to or instead of the parents
A person other than a parent may exercise some or all parental responsibilities in addition to or instead of the parents.

Principle 3:18 Decisions in daily matters
The parent's partner living with the child may take part in decisions with respect to daily matters unless the other parent having parental responsibilities objects.

CHAPTER V: CONTENT OF PARENTAL RESPONSIBILITIES

SECTION A: THE CHILD'S PERSON AND PROPERTY

Principle 3:19 Care, protection and education
(1) The holders of parental responsibilities should provide the child with care, protection and education in accordance with the child's distinctive character and developmental needs.
(2) The child should not be subjected to corporal punishment or any other humiliating treatment.

Principle 3:20 Residence
(1) If parental responsibilities are exercised jointly the holders of parental responsibilities who are living apart should agree upon with whom the child resides.
(2) The child may reside on an alternate basis with the holders of parental responsibilities upon either an agreement approved by a competent authority or a decision by a competent authority. The competent authority should take into consideration factors such as:
   (a) the age and opinion of the child;
   (b) the ability and willingness of the holders of parental responsibilities to cooperate with each other in matters concerning the child, as well as their personal situation;
   (c) the distance between the residences of the holders of the parental responsibilities and to the child's school.

Principle 3:21 Relocation
(1) If parental responsibilities are exercised jointly and one of the holders of parental responsibilities wishes to change the child's residence within or outside the jurisdiction, he or she should inform the other holder of parental responsibilities thereof in advance.

(2) If the other holder of parental responsibilities objects to the change of the child's residence, each of them may apply to the competent authority for a decision.
(3) The competent authority should take into consideration factors such as:
   (a) the age and opinion of the child;
   (b) the right of the child to maintain personal relationships with the other holders of parental responsibilities;
   (c) the ability and willingness of the holders of parental responsibilities to cooperate with each other;
   (d) the personal situation of the holders of personal responsibilities;
   (e) the geographical distance and accessibility;
   (f) the free movement of persons.

Principle 3:22 Administration of the child's property

(1) The holders of parental responsibilities should administer the child's property with due care and diligence in order to preserve and where possible increase the value of the property.
(2) In administering the child's property the holders of parental responsibilities should not make gifts unless the gifts are deemed to be made under a moral obligation.
(3) The income derived from the child's property which is not needed for the proper management of the property or for the maintenance and education of the child may, where necessary, be used for the needs of the family.

Principle 3:23 Restrictions

(1) The holders of parental responsibilities should not administer property acquired by a child through a testamentary disposition or a gift, if the testator or the donor so instructed.
(2) Similarly the earnings by the child should not be administered by the holders of parental responsibilities unless the child is not of sufficient age and maturity to decide himself or herself.
(3) Where transactions can have significant financial consequences for the child the authorisation of the competent authority should be necessary.

Principle 3:24 Legal representation

(1) The holders of parental responsibilities should legally represent the child in matters concerning the child's person or property.
(2) Legal representation should not take place where there is a conflict of interest between the child and the holders of parental responsibilities.
(3) Having regard to the child's age and maturity, the child should have the right to self-representation in legal proceedings concerning himself or herself.

SECTION B: MAINTENANCE OF PERSONAL RELATIONSHIPS

Principle 3:25 Contact with parents and other persons

(1) The child and the parents should have the right to obtain and maintain regular contact with each other.

(2) Contact should be established between the child and his or her close relatives.

(3) Contact may be established between the child and persons with whom the child has close personal relations.

Principle 3:26 Content of contact

(1) Contact comprises the child staying for a limited period of time with or meeting a parent or person other than a parent with whom he or she is not usually living; and any form of communication between the child and such person.

(2) Such contact should be in the best interests of the child.

Principle 3:27 Agreement

(1) Subject to the best interests of the child, the parents and the other persons identified under Principle 3:25(2) and (3) may agree on contact.

(2) The competent authority may scrutinize the agreement.

Principle 3:28 Restrictions

Contact may be restricted, terminated or made subject to conditions by the competent authority if the best interests of the child so require.

Principle 3:29 Information to parents

A parent should have the right to be informed about matters concerning the personal situation of the child.

CHAPTER VI: TERMINATION OF PARENTAL RESPONSIBILITIES

Principle 3:30 Termination

(1) Parental responsibilities should be terminated in the case of the child:

(a) reaching majority;

(b) entering into a marriage or registered partnership;

(c) being adopted;

(d) dying.

(2) If a parent's partner adopts the child of the parent the parental responsibilities in relation to the other parent should be terminated.

Principle 3:31 Death of the parents

(1) If parents have joint parental responsibilities and one of them dies the parental responsibilities should belong to the surviving parent.

(2) If a parent having sole parental responsibilities dies, responsibilities should be attributed to the surviving parent or a third person upon a decision by the competent authority.

(3) On the death of both parents, of whom at least one parent had parental responsibilities, the competent authority should take protective measures in respect of the person and the property of the child.

CHAPTER VII: DISCHARGE AND RESTORATION OF PARENTAL RESPONSIBILITIES

Principle 3:32 Discharge of parental responsibilities

The competent authority should discharge the holder of parental responsibilities, wholly or in part, where his or her behaviour or neglect causes a serious risk to the person or the property of the child

Principle 3:33 Request for discharge of parental responsibilities

(1) The discharge of parental responsibilities may be requested by:
   (a) any parent having parental responsibilities;
   (b) the child, and
   (c) any institution protecting the interests of the child.

(2) The competent authority may also order the discharge of parental responsibilities of its own motion.

Principle 3:34 Restoration of parental responsibilities

Having regard to the best interests of the child, the competent authority may restore parental responsibilities if the circumstances that led to the discharge no longer exist.

CHAPTER VIII: PROCEDURE

Principle 3:35 Competent authority

(1) All decisions on parental responsibilities should be taken by the competent authority which can either be a judicial or an administrative body.

(2) Where necessary, the competent authority should appoint any suitable person or body to investigate the child's circumstances.

Principle 3:36 Alternative dispute resolution

In all disputes regarding parental responsibilities alternative dispute resolution mechanisms should be available.

Principle 3:37 Hearing of the child

(1) Subject to Principle 3:6, the competent authority should hear the child in all proceedings concerning parental responsibilities but if it decides not to hear the child it should give specific reasons.

(2) The hearing of the child should take place either directly before the competent authority or indirectly before a person or body appointed by the competent authority.

(3) The child should be heard in a manner appropriate to his or her age and maturity.

Principle 3:38 Appointment of a special representative for the child

In proceedings concerning parental responsibilities in which there could either be a serious conflict of interests between the child and the holders of parental responsibilities or in which the welfare of the child is otherwise at risk, the competent authority should appoint a special representative for the child.

Principle 3:39 Enforcement

(1) Failing voluntary compliance, a decision by the competent authority and an enforceable agreement concerning parental responsibilities should be enforced without delay.

(2) Enforcement should not take place if it is manifestly contrary to the best interests of the child.

European Family Law Series

1. *Legal Recognition of Same-Sex Couples in Europe*, K. Boele-Woelki and A. Fuchs (eds.)
2. *European Family Law in Action Volume I: Grounds for divorce*, K. Boele-Woelki, B. Braat and I. Sumner (eds.)
3. *European Family Law in Action Volume II: Maintenance Between Former Spouses*, K. Boele-Woelki, B. Braat and I. Sumner (eds.)
4. *Perspectives for the Unification and Harmonisation of Family Law in Europe*, K. Boele-Woelki (ed.)
5. *Family Law Legislation of the Netherlands*, I. Sumner and H. Warendorf
6. *Indépendance et interdépendance patrimoniales des époux dans le régime matrimonial légal des droits néerlandais, français et suisse*, B. Braat
7. *Principles of European Family Law Regarding Divorce and Maintenance Between Former Spouses*, K. Boele-Woelki, F. Ferrand, C. González Beilfuss, M. Jänterä-Jareborg, N. Lowe, D. Martiny and W. Pintens
8. *Inheritance Law Legislation of the Netherlands*, I. Sumner and H. Warendorf
9. *European Family Law in Action Volume III: Parental Responsibilities*, K. Boele-Woelki, B. Braat and I. Curry Sumner (eds.)
10. *Common Core and Better Law in European Family Law*, K. Boele-Woelki (ed.)
11. *All's well that ends registered?*, I. Curry-Sumner
12. *Model Family Code – From a global perspective*, I. Schwenzer and M. Dimsey
13. *Harmonisation of Family Law in Europe. A Historical Perspective*, M. Antokolskaia
14. *Brussels II bis: Its Impact and Application in the Member States*, K. Boele-Woelki and C. González Beilfuss (eds.)
15. *Tensions between Legal, Biological and Social Conceptions of Parentage*, I. Schwenzer (ed.)
16. *Principles of European Family Law Regarding Parental Responsibilities*, K. Boele-Woelki, F. Ferrand, C. González Beilfuss, M. Jänterä-Jareborg, N. Lowe, D. Martiny and W. Pintens (eds.)
17. *Juxtaposing Legal Systems and the Principles of European Family Law on Divorce and Maintenance*, E. Örücü and J. Mair (eds.)
18. *Convergence and Divergence of Family Law in Europe*, M. Antokolskaia (ed.)
19. *European Challenges in Contemporary Family Law*, K. Boele-Woelki and K. Sverdrup (eds.)
20. *Children and their parents*, M. Vonk
21. *La capacité de l'enfant dans les droits français, anglais et écossais*, L. Francoz-Terminal
22. *Joint Parental Authority*, C.G. Jeppesen de Boer
23. *Debates in Family Law around the Globe at the Dawn of the 21st Century*, K. Boele-Woelki (ed.)

24. *European Family Law in Action Volume IV: Property Relations between Spouses*, K. Boele-Woelki, B. Braat and I. Curry-Sumner (eds.)
25. *Foundational Facts, Relative Truths. A Comparative Law Study on Children's Right to Know Their Genetic Origins*, J. Blauwhoff
26. *Imperative Inheritance Law in a Late-Modern Society. Five Perspectives*, Christoph Castelein, René Foqué and Alain Verbeke (eds.)